IMPROVING

MENTAL

HEALTH

in the Workplace

Endorsements

This exciting book provides current and compelling evidence on workplace mental health in the South African context. It begins by examining the impact of COVID-19 and other issues unique to the workplace. The second theme reviews several aspects of the mind-body wholistic approach. It concludes with examples of innovations in treatment, including neuroscience, resiliency, mindfulness, purpose, and future trends. Vandayar's chapter on the role of employee assistance programmes (EAP) in supporting both individual workers (via traditional onsite counselling services and newer remote technologies) and the work organization is especially useful as a guide for employers.

Mark Attridge, PhD, MA, President, Attridge Consulting, United States

The onset of the COVID-19 global pandemic occurred against the backdrop of a pre-existing mental health crisis, the symptoms of which were already widespread and escalating amongst workforces globally, with the World Health Organization having just labelled employee burnout a medical condition, identifying chronic workplace stress as its primary cause. The stressors associated with the COVID-19 pandemic have only served to exacerbate this crisis, with the OECD reporting a worldwide deterioration in mental health in 2020. Addressing this "parallel pandemic" has emerged as a collective social responsibility. It will only be via a holistic approach and collaborative effort involving all key stakeholders that we can hope to solve the mental health challenges that will linger in the workplace long after the COVID-19 pandemic is brought under control. This timely publication provides an invaluable selection of insights from a diverse range of recognized subject matter experts, highlighting the complexities and multidimensional nature of workplace mental health, and offering practical suggestions on how organizations can best support and equip their respective workforces to prevail over this pervasive affliction.

David Conradie, Human Capital Trend Analyst,
Future of Work Strategist, Leadership Transformation Advisor

This book provides a fascinating description of the multiple impacts of the global pandemic on the mental health and wellbeing of the workforce. It offers a comprehensive framework of understanding for all those seeking a meaningful grasp of the complexities that the current context has given rise to. It is not only thought-provoking but also practical, sound, and well written. The authors are all experts in their respective fields and their contributions provide the reader with a host of suggestions on how to navigate the many social, emotional and wellbeing challenges emerging from the rapidly evolving world of work. As both an industry leader and a seasoned mental health professional it is my strong recommendation that this book becomes an important reference guide for all those who take seriously the significant social, occupational and psychological upheaval created by recent global events.

Andrew Davies, CEO, ICAS International

The global and local impact of COVID-19, and the knock-on amplification of inequality, poverty, unemployment, gender-based violence, injustice, financial distress, uncertainty, grief, loss, and general impact on society, to call-out a few red flags particularly in South Africa in recent months, has raised the matter of mental wellness to beyond the tick-box approach to Boardroom priority. Mental health is a strategic imperative. Every company is called upon to tackle mental health head-on. The urgency has never been greater to mobilise our collective expertise in support of and impactful response and set of actions to address mental health in the workplace. This book could not have been published at a more pertinent time. This must-read will enable you to improve your understanding of mental health in the current context, develop insights into holistic approaches and frameworks to address it, and provides tips and tools on how to cope with mental health in the context of the future world of work and further unknown complexities that might still lie ahead for us.

Dr Shirley Zinn, Chair and Non-Executive Director on multiple Boards

This well-timed book is a must read for any employer who cares about employee and organisational wellbeing. Navlika and colleagues meticulously offer well-thought through insights on the pervasive challenge of mental health illnesses in the workplace. They carefully unpack the macro and micro level drivers of this phenomenon and aptly place their analysis within the context of the overwhelming COVID-19 pandemic, and it's intersecting multidimensional effects on employees, organisations, economies and accelerated structural changes worldwide. The authors make compelling arguments for employer driven and sponsored mental health strategies and interventions to help employees cope with anxiety, depression, mood disorders and a plethora of psychosocial issues and for these interventions to be integrated into the broader employee and organisational wellness strategy.

Dr Nceba Ndzwayiba, Group Director: Human Resources
and Transformation – Netcare Limited

First published in 2021.

ISBN: 978-1-86922-911-5
eISBN: 978-1-86922-912-2

Published by KR Publishing
P O Box 3954
Randburg
2125

Republic of South Africa

Tel: (011) 706-6009
Fax: (011) 706-1127
E-mail: orders@knowres.co.za
Website: www.kr.co.za

Typesetting, layout and design: Cia Joubert, cia@knowres.co.za
Cover design: Marlene De Lorme, marlene@knowres.co.za
Editing & proofreading: Valda Strauss, valda@global.co.za
Project management: Cia Joubert, cia@knowres.co.za

IMPROVING
MENTAL
HEALTH
in the Workplace

Edited by

Navlika Ratangee

kr
publishing

2021

Table of contents

Foreword by Prof Bonang Mohale

Congratulations to Navlika Ratangee on the culmination of this book on this truly profound subject. After having collectively spent more than 566 days in national lockdown in response to the pandemic, looking after one's mental health has never been more important. About 1 781 people in the country have committed suicide in the four months following the declaration of the lockdown in March 2020.

In May, mental health experts told SABC News that South Africans are increasingly experiencing depression due to financial burdens and stress brought about by the coronavirus pandemic and resultant lockdown. They also highlighted the fact that the COVID-19 virus has consequently sparked anxiety, panic and an increase in substance abuse.

Globally, every year, close to 800 000 people take their own lives and there are many more who attempt suicide. Every suicide is a tragedy that affects families, communities and entire countries, and has long-lasting effects on the people left behind. Suicide is a serious global public health problem; however, suicides are preventable with timely, evidence-based and often low-cost interventions. For national responses to be effective, a comprehensive multisectoral suicide prevention strategy is needed.

The most prevalent mental health issues are centred around finance, relationships, alcohol and substance abuse, etc. The pandemic has also exacerbated inequality as, like poverty, the pandemic has primarily a black and feminine face. These are the two groups that are most exposed, vulnerable, have most co-morbidities, cannot afford good nutrition, have less time for regular exercise, live in over-crowded neighbourhoods, and are most exposed to pollution. They are also totally dependent on the inaccessible and overcrowded public health system and have poor support mechanisms. Even Eskom's rolling black-outs affect the poor disproportionately as they cannot afford alternatives.

South Africa urgently needs to put in place mechanisms not only to deal with the devastating social impact of Covid-19, whether from the trauma caused by the economic fallout from the virus, the mass loss of human lives or the effect of 'cabin fever' from the lockdowns. Record numbers of people are already suffering from post-traumatic stress disorder (PTSD) – the combination of stress, anxiety and depression. It is very likely that the incidents of suicides will jump in a country with already high suicide rates. South Africa has the eighth highest rate of suicide in the world, with around eight thousand people committing suicide every year – the third biggest cause of unnatural death after homicide and unintentional reasons. Violence, whether in families, on the roads, workplaces, educational institutions and in communities are also on the rise. There has been a terrifying rise in domestic violence and abuse against women and children. There is also a rise in marriage breakdowns as well as drug and alcohol abuse. So too is a rise in familicide – murder-suicide or murder in which a person kills multiple close family members, whether spouses, children or relatives.

Especially now that most people are working remotely for organisations, often alone, with very little human interaction, we must reiterate that our people (and their families) look after their mental health and must continue to be safe, comply and respect their neighbours! This will enable companies to continue to receive high performance with high integrity and the employees will also continue to make quality decisions at high speed, with leadership from every seat (not just the C-Suite), thereby increasing employee engagement, agility, sustainability and resilience. The intent is to achieve high levels of inclusiveness where the leadership is constantly respectful, visible, supportive, and understanding which is literally felt by our employees and therefore increases the feeling of connection and caring. Now, more than ever, our colleagues must feel needed, valued, wanted and appreciated because we have succeeded in creating a conducive environment where each and every, single, solitary employee can be very comfortable in showing up and feeling that I can be myself. Where, especially their individual career paths and succession planning is continuously discussed, affirmed and reiterated.

By way of an example, Shell South Africa is absolutely obsessed with Health, Safety, Security and Environment (HSSE) and their aspirations for 'zero harm.' This is the number one item on their agenda in all their meetings. It accounts for 25 percent of every employee's Short-Term Incentives/bonus. People are promoted based on their HSSE leadership. They have succeeded in putting systems and processes in place to support, train, measure, evaluate, monitor, etc. The company's daily HSSE performance is prominently displayed through a very simple traffic-light system. Health is not just the absence of disease and infirmity. It is the state of physical, emotional, social and spiritual wellbeing. They put the wellbeing of their people first, before profits.

This book provides multiple ideas on how one goes about promoting mental health as an individual and an organisation. This is relevant in the context of the pandemic but also beyond the pandemic.

We just have to accept the fact that certain things will never go back to how they used to be. The pandemic plummeted us all into a different space. I have personally come to terms with the fact that I must never in my life again underestimate the power of a spontaneous hug or any physical contact. I have adapted to look with my heart and not my eyes only. Time is very limited and it is necessary that I embrace all those that cross my path in a very different way than I did before. It has never really been 'me, myself and I' in the past, but now, it is even less so, as contact with people is the pillar of my life – my BETTER normal!

Bonang Mohale is the Chancellor of the University of the Free State, Professor of Practice in the Johannesburg Business School (JBS) College of Business and Economics, Chairman of both The Bidvest Group Limited and SBV Services. He was previously the chairperson of Shell South Africa until end of 2017 and past president of the BMF. Bonang was also in leadership roles of several major South African and multinational companies including Otis Elevators, South African Airways, Sanlam Limited and Drake & Scull Integrated Facilities Management. He authored the bestselling book *Lift as You Rise*.

About the editor

Navlika Ratangee is currently the Managing Director of ICAS Southern Africa. A GIBS MBA graduate and Clinical psychologist with diverse experience in human capital management, behavioural risk, change management, managerial consulting, global management consulting, leadership, women in leadership, organisational resilience and organisational strategy. She also has a wealth of experience in dealing with mental health in the workplace and has consulted to many South African corporates in this regard.

Navlika has an abundance of training, customer engagement experience and has been selected by McKinsey & Company for their WomEnpower event, developing future female leadership for the global community. She regularly acts as a guest lecturer at GIBS, is a group mentor for PGDip and MBA programmes, and research examiner for MBA programmes.

Completing her MBA in 2016 with distinction, Navlika was also awarded the prize as top graduate for the programme. She has furthered her executive education at Harvard Business School, Boston. Navlika has presented at many conferences locally and internationally and has also been a contributor of a chapter in 2 books Managing the COVID-19 vortex and Tourism, Travel and COVID-19, called *Promoting personal and workplace mental health in the age of COVID-19*.

About the contributors

Rakhi Beekrum

Rakhi is a professional Counselling Psychologist in private practice for 12 years, working in inpatient and outpatient settings. Focus on individual and couples therapy as well as corporate webinars. Regularly featured in print and electronic media and has been featured on television, including SABC News, eNCA & Carte Blanche. She obtained a Master of Social Sciences (MSocSc), and is an MBA mentor/academic tutor at Henley business school. Rakhi obtained her Master of Social Sciences (MSocSc) in Counselling Psychology at the University of KwaZulu-Natal. Contact information: rakhibeekrum@gmail.com

Dr Graeme Codrington

Graeme is an expert on the future of work. He is a researcher, author, presenter and board advisor working across multiple industries and sectors. Speaking internationally to over 100,000 people in more than 20 different countries every year, his client list includes some of the world's top companies, and CEOs invite him back time after time to share his latest insights and help them and their teams gain a clear understanding of how to successfully prepare for the future.

Graeme is CEO of TomorrowToday, a global firm of futurists and business strategists. He is also a guest lecturer at five top business schools, including the London Business School, Duke Corporate Education and the Gordon Institute of Business Science. He has five degrees, including a Doctorate in Business Administration (DBA), a Masters in Sociology, and other professional degrees in Accounting, Arts and Theology, and Youth Work. He has written five books, including the award winning, *"Mind the Gap"* and *"Leading in a Changing World"*. Contact information: graeme@tomorrowtodayglobal.com

Dr Nikki Connellan

Nikki is the Chief Medical Officer at ICAS South Africa. She obtained her MBBCh (cum lauda); DA (SA) from the University of the Witwatersrand in 1994 and has worked in the fields of Obstetrics and Gynaecology, Psychiatry, Anaesthetics and HIV/AIDS both in South Africa and the UK.

Nikki joined ICAS in 2017 to manage the Absence, Incapacity and Disability, Musculoskeletal, Maternity, and most recently COVID-19 programmes as Chief Medical Officer.

Particular fields of interest are female health, chronic pain and in particular its link to mental health and ensuring a multidisciplinary clinical approach to the management of high-risk employees in the workplace according to a "one healthy employee" rationale.

She has more recently become involved in the Management of COVID-19 in the workplace and has a particular interest in "Long COVID". Contact information: nconnellan@icas.co.za

Dr Jopie de Beer

Jopie is a founder and the current CEO of the JvR Africa Group of Companies, consisting of JvR Psychometrics, JvR Consulting Psychologists and JvR Academy. Established in 1994, the business entities in the JvR Africa Group have grown to include exceptional client solutions with regard to talent assessment and development. With a focus on the constructive use of assessment data and metrics, as well as excellent client service, technology and innovation, the companies have built a recognised and respected brand for highly professional and trustworthy people solutions in Africa.

Jopie is a psychologist with many years of experience. She relies on an outstanding team of professionals who share her passion, drive and vision for every person to be given the opportunity to develop to their full potential.

In 2017 she received a Lifetime Achievement Award from the University of Johannesburg for her contribution to Entrepreneurship in South Africa. Contact information: Jopie@jvrafrica.co.za

Dr Karina de Bruin

Karina has been registered as a Counselling Psychologists since 1995. She has worked in a variety of contexts, including private practice, Student Counselling and Development, and Higher Education Policy Research. She obtained a DPhil (Higher Education) in 2000. Karina was also a senior lecturer in the Department of Psychology (UJ), where her teaching and research focused mostly on career development psychology. For the past nine years, she is the Managing Director of JVR Academy. She has published in numerous peer-reviewed journals and other publications. Contact information: karina@jvrafrica.co.za

Ingra Du Buisson Narsai

Ingra is the co-founder and Director of NeuroCapital Consulting, which consults to some of South Africa's leading and most admired companies. She is an award-winning Organisational Psychologist in private practice.

Ingra has 20 years of executive-level experience in corporate South Africa, including Group HR Director (Famous Brands Ltd), HR executive (Aegis Insurance/RMBH Group), and HR Director (Usko/Bytes Technology). Ingra is also an established leadership and executive coach and is affiliated with the Wits Business School (WBS) in South Africa, where she supervises and examines the work of postgraduate students in Business and Executive Coaching.

Ingra's academic qualifications include an MCom (Organisational Psychology), PGCNL and Masters of Science (MSc) in Neuroscience of Leadership. She is busy with her PhD in Organisational Neuroscience. She is an Executive Committee Member of the Society for Industrial and Organisational Psychology of South Africa (SIOPSA) and the Chair for the Interest group of Applied Organisational Neuroscience (AONS).

She is the bestselling author of the newly published book *"Fight, Flight or Flourish: How neuroscience can unlock human potential"*. Ingra's special skills lie in being a catalyst for change and creating break-through organisational behaviour solutions. She actively pursues the increasing visibility of neuroscientific approaches and diagnostics in the study of organisational behaviour. Contact information: ingra@neurocapital.co

Dr Angela Whitford du Plessis

Angela obtained her PhD in Occupational Social Work, University of the Witwatersrand in 1995. She is an experienced commercial consultant with a demonstrated history of working in the management consulting industry. Strong legal professional skilled in Executive Development, Conflict Resolution, Executive Coaching, Employee Training, and Management Development.

After leaving Investec Bank in October 2008, Angela completed a course in Mediation at the University of Stellenbosch's Business School and is accredited as a Civil and Commercial Mediator by the ADR Group, based in the UK. In March 2009, she underwent training in Family Mediation and is now SAAM accredited. In July 2009 Angela completed the CEDR Commercial Mediation course and is also accredited by this organization, based in London. Angela was a volunteer family mediator at Family Life Centre. Angela has published and presented various journal articles, chapters and conference papers. Contact information: angelawdup@gmail.com

Dr Vanessa Govender

Vanessa's occupational medicine and public health career spans over 25 years, mainly in the mining, engineering and construction sectors, across many geographies. She is passionate about serving workers to restore and build their dignity.

Vanessa has led health and multidisciplinary teams in multinational blue chip companies, developing integrated Occupational Health, HIV/AIDS, TB, Silicosis and Wellness policy frameworks to drive strategy beyond just legislative compliance. Through her company Masakhane Strategic Health Consulting (Pty) Ltd, Vanessa consults widely to diverse clients bringing cutting edge knowledge to inform policy, strategy, leadership behaviours, COVID-19 health risk communications and clinical standards for the prevention, early diagnosis, and compensation of occupational lung diseases.

She currently holds positions as consultant to Anglo American's global COVID-19 response and is a lecturer/academic coordinator for the Post Graduate Diploma in Occupational Health at Wits School of Public Health. She is an Associate Member of the Colleges of Public Health Medicine of South Africa and is appointed as a member of the Medical Advisory Panel to the Tshiamiso Trust.

In 2019, acknowledging her contribution and clinical acumen in the field of Occupational Medicine, Vanessa was appointed as a Specialist: Occupational Medicine by the Health Professionals Council of South Africa. Vanessa completed her undergraduate medical degree (MBBCh, 1993) and postgraduate studies (Diploma in Occupational Health-1999, Masters in Public Health Policy and Management – 2007), at Wits University. In addition she has completed numerous international executive business education courses at Harvard University and London School of Business.

She is an internationally published author, researcher, speaker & presenter. Contact information: vanessa@masakhanehealth.co.za

Joanna Kleovoulou

Joanna is inspired to assist all to live masterfully. She is a professional Clinical Psychologist, workshop facilitator, speaker, supervisor, entrepreneur, wife, mother and friend, and in private practice for 14 years. She is the founder and owner of PsychMatters Centre® in Bedfordview, Johannesburg South Africa, a psychology, healing and wellness space. Frequently featured on television, in print and electronic media and a regular slot on Radio702 and SAfm Radio to address mental health matters. She has contributed to Natasha Sutherland's Book *"Bitter Sweet"*, has written two chapters on *Mental Health in the workplace* with KR Publishing and some of her writing has been featured in journal articles.

With her experience working in child and adult inpatient, outpatient and corporate settings she loves dealing with all age groups addressing motivation, resilience, change, stress, mood, anxiety, OCD, trauma, bereavement/loss, couples/relationship difficulties and self-esteem. Accredited EMDR® practitioner – an evidence-based effective neuro-therapeutic technique to process trauma and other mental conditions. Joanna has developed and presented workshops for adults in private and corporate settings, teachers, parents and children. She believes building children's resilience from young is key to being a successful contributing member of society as an adult: The iMatter Kids Club® – is a workshop and activity book to build resilience for kids that she has developed.

Joanna has a Masters at the University of the Witwatersrand in Clinical Psychology. She holds honours degrees in Business Management (UFS) and Psychology (UJ) and a B.A. Communications (UFS). An affiliate member of the S.A Depression & Anxiety Group, and supervises her local Police Victim Support Counsellors and presents postpartum depression prevention talks at baby clinics on a volunteer basis. Contact information: joanna@psychmatters.co.za

Val Leeming

Val is a Director of Interface and has been providing financial life skills workshops to the corporate market place for the past 18 years.

As a qualified teacher, with 18 years' experience in personal financial matters as a financial coach and trainer, she is passionate about Financial Health and Education in South Africa. Val believes in outcome based education and in planting seeds within a workshop environment that can be nurtured and supported by innovative electronic support programs and financial coaching models.

Val Leeming has a Bachelor degree and a post graduate in Higher Education. She is a passionate about helping people improve their financial lives.

Interface is recognized as a leader in financial wellness in South Africa, and offer services to companies including, PwC, Multichoice, Glencore, Deloitte, Afrocentric Health, and a number of Banks in South Africa. Contact information: val@interfaceinc.co.za

Dr Frank Magwegwe

Frank has a doctorate in personal financial planning from Kansas State University, USA, with a dissertation titled Financial Strain and Worry About Retirement Income Adequacy and is a lecturer at the Gordon Institute of Business Science, University of Pretoria. Frank has extensive corporate experience with a cumulative 22 years in the financial services industry in South Africa. Frank is Founder and Principal Scientist at Thrive Financial Wellness. Organizations that want financial wellness to be a successful business strategy partner Thrive in developing evidence-based employee financial education and wellness solutions based on behaviour change science for their employees. Frank is a financial life planner, educator, and coach with a passion for helping individuals and families to thrive and flourish in life and not just live, through the development of a sense of purpose and good financial habits. Helping people flourish and thrive in life is what drives him every day. Contact information: magwegwef@gibs.co.za

Kim Martin

Kim is a registered dietitian with a post-graduate diploma in clinical sports nutrition, who is passionate about empowering people to achieve nutritional wellness without obsession. She is the founder of Lifestyle Dietetics Registered Dietitians, a private practice that offers virtual nutrition counselling and personalised nutrition programs to help people break free from disordered eating and heal their relationship with food and their bodies. Kim is also co-owner of Lifestyle

Health, an online health shop curated by health experts to provide the very best health products and nutritional supplements to support and restore wellbeing. Her expertise has been featured in numerous publications nationwide, and she has been called on to address both professional audiences and the general public in a number of events. To learn more about Kim's work, please visit www.lifestyledietetics.co.za and connect with her on Instagram at @lifestyledietetics. Contact information: kim@lifestyledietetics.co.za

Zanele Njapha

Zanele, or as her clients call her 'The UnLearning Lady', is an international Transitions Facilitator and Future of Work Speaker, helping companies navigate organisational changes and step confidently into the future of work

If your challenge is navigating an organisational change/transition as a team Zanele is who many such prominent organisations as PwC, Philip Morris International, Vitality Global, Marsh & McLennan, Generali, Saint-Gobain, Volkswagen and others are speaking to.

She is also the host of the highly-rated top 100 in the Entrepreneurship category in: Zambia, SA, Ghana, Nigeria and top 200 in Canada, Portugal and Russia, and entrepreneur-focused podcast 'Future-Fit Fridays', which hosts conversations with global experts on the future of work.

In addition, Zanele is an award-winning speaker, has served as the youngest Exco member of the Professional Speakers Association of Southern Africa, and is an article contributor to Forbes & the Thought Leader section of the Mail & Guardian and was voted #45 on Avance Media's list of Top 100 Most Influential Young South Africans in 2019. Contact information: zanele@tomorrowtodayglobal.com

Dr Ashika Pillay

Ashika is an integrative medical doctor using a holistic approach to wellbeing and optimal performance. She works as an independent leadership and executive coach and also facilitates wellbeing and mindfulness programs for corporates where she provides insight and guidance on resilience, burnout and stress management, and has done many workshops especially in the time of the COVID-19 pandemic and the lockdowns. She brings together the meeting point of understanding the mind and body better to effect personal and professional change and wellbeing. She is also passionate about preventing and managing chronic diseases like diabetes and hypertension better and works one-on-one with clients.

She has a background in pharmaceutical medicine and was the Medical Director at Roche Pharmaceuticals where she has experience in medical marketing, clinical research, leadership, training and mentoring.

She is registered with the HPCSA as a General Practitioner, is also a mentor to coaching students and a board member Institute for Mindfulness of South Africa. She has an MBA from GIBS, is a certified coach and has trained to be a teacher of Mindfulness Based interventions at the University of Witwatersrand.

One of her passions is also writing, and she has a personal blog and also a guest blogger on Lionesses for Africa, a women entrepreneurship platform. She is currently studying towards a Fellowship in Functional Medicine. Her motto is 'True health is the state of alignment of Mind, Body and Purpose.' Contact information: pillay.ashika5@gmail.com

Dr Renate Scherrer

Renate is a registered Clinical Psychologist with the Health Professions Council of South Africa and holds a PhD in Psychology. She is the Managing Director of JvR Consulting Psychologists, a trusted people partner in the area of scientific assessment and development solutions centred on empowering individuals, teams and organisations to thrive in a changing context.

Renate has several years of general consulting experience across numerous industries. She consults mostly in the field of Management and Leadership, focusing on understanding and optimising human potential in the organisational context. She is passionate about the assessment and development of people, i.e. individual coaching; enhancing team synergy through facilitated discussion, awareness and growth; succession planning and executive on-boarding. From a clinical perspective, Renate has a specific interest in the topics of Leadership Derailment, Psychopathy in the Workplace, Toxic Leadership, and Counterproductive Work Behaviour. She is an internationally accredited user and trainer of various psychometric assessments, as well as a regular speaker/presenter at conferences, learning events and tertiary institutions. Contact information: renate@jvrafrica.co.za

Namhla Tambatamba

Namhla has been employed as Head of Wellbeing at Nedbank. Her strategic focus is on guiding the organisation to build and create a culture of care, engagement and high performance. She has an honour's degree in Industrial Psychology, and a Master's in business administration (MBA) plus 4.5 years of general management experience with a focus on overall business performance. She is also registered with the SABPP as Master HR Professional. In addition, Namhla had also been selected for the LEAD Management Programme (at ABSA), the Business Management Programme: Certificate in Practical Management (GIMT) at Sanlam and has also obtained a certificate in financial management. For her love of learning, she is currently doing the Executive Development Programme (EDP) with University of Stellenbosch. Contact information: Namhlagqosha@gmail.com

Dr Rinet van Lill

Rinet has been employed as a clinical psychologist in the public health sector since 2012. She completed her full-time studies at the University of the Free State, where she received a dean's medal, and then obtained a doctoral degree from the University of Pretoria. Rinet has published on topics related to time perspective and unemployment among a young adult population and has a research interest in evidence-based models that can empower psychologists to gain competence in therapeutic work. Contact information: rinetvanlill@gmail.com

Dr Xander van Lill

Xander holds a PhD in Industrial Psychology from the University of Johannesburg and is registered as an industrial psychologist with the Health Professions Council of South Africa. He is currently a senior research associate in the Department of Industrial Psychology and People Management at the University of Johannesburg. He also practises as a research and development specialist at JvR Psychometrics, where he is involved in the sourcing, development, and validation of psychological assessments. He served as an executive member (Chairperson of the Johannesburg Regional Branch) of the Society for Industrial and Organisational Psychology of South Africa (SIOPSA) during which the branch won the best prize for the term 2019/2020. His areas of academic and consulting interests include psychometrics, individual differences, work motivation, social influence, and multivariate statistics. A list of his publications is available on LinkedIn, ResearchGate, or Google Scholar. Contact information: xvanlill@gmail.com.

Radhi Vandayar

Radhi obtained her MBA at Henley Business School-University of Reading. She is currently the People Engagement Director at HLC where she is looking at marrying wellness initiatives with technology platforms to make it more accessible and relevant to the changing work landscape. She is also currently an MBA mentor/academic tutor at Henley business school for their MBA students. As an Alumni of Henley, she wants to be part of their journey in building better business in Africa through our people. Radhi was elected to the post of president elect of the EAPA SA Board. She has served on the board for the last 16 years. She is passionate about people development and therefore works within the Human capital space as a consultant on Employee wellness, for the last 17 years. Her previous position at ICAS is Strategic L&D Manager has exposed her to several industries that has developed her vast experience in people engagement and wellbeing interventions. She has contributed to the EAPA International journal twice over the last 3 years. She has presented at many local and international seminars and conferences on topics related to the Employee wellness field. Contact details: Radhiv@henleysa.ac.za

Our reader

We believe that this book has been written for anyone who is interested in the field of mental health. In fact, it is not just for those interested in mental health, it is also for those who are not interested and need additional insights into why all the fuss about mental health these days. So, whether you are an HR practitioner, a leader, a counsellor or a concerned citizen, this book has been put together with you in mind.

About this book

This book has been put together by experts in the field of mental health, and associated fields, whom have been carefully chosen to share their insights on a specific knowledge area with you. A golden thread that runs through all these chapters is that each and every contributor is passionate about what they do, and in so doing passionate in sharing their knowledge and experience with you in their unique way. We hope that you find this not only useful in its learnings and application but also refreshing and inspirational. There is much to be done in the field of mental health.

The context of this book is mental health and its relation to the workplace. For ease of reference, it has been separated into 3 parts:

Part 1: Mental health in the workplace: Understanding the current context and what has given rise to this increasing concern

Part 2: Mental health is not an island: Wellbeing is holistic and has multiple dimensions

Part 3: Coping mechanisms: Towards a way forward with mental health

The pandemic has changed our lives from what we once knew it to be. The book starts off with a positioning of the current context and why a spotlight has been placed on mental health. Part 1 focuses largely on how the workplace has responded to the mental health pandemic, the trends we are seeing now and what we can expect to see post pandemic, together with some of the major contributors to mental health concerns in the workplace. Included are the common manifestations of mental illnesses which compromises just one component of the broader mental health topic as positioned in this book.

Part 2 recognises that mental health does not exist in a vacuum. We often talk about the dimensions of wellbeing, and that they are all interconnected. This section of the book covers how our physical wellbeing, financial wellbeing and workplaces all link to our mental health and wellbeing. Mental health is not an island and often requires a more holistic approach in taking care of it.

The last section of the book focuses on frameworks and practical suggestions on how to cope given all this information on mental health. This is in the context of individual coping, e.g., mastering the role of neuroscience or mindfulness, to a more macro-approach using the lens of the workplace. We end off with yet another consideration of the importance of mental health and wellbeing, this time in the context of the future world of work. Just in case it didn't hit home as yet that the time is now.

Part 1

Mental health in the workplace: Understanding the current context and unpacking some of the key components and contributors to mental health concerns

---

Chapter 1: Our COVID and Post-COVID context
by: Dr Graeme Codrington and Zanele Njapha

Setting the scene for the current context we are living in and what this means for the post COVID context is an important starting point. This chapter paints the picture of why we need to focus on mental health amongst other things to cope with our current realities but also to prepare for the future and future world of work. It is based on 4 critical premises:

1. As a result of COVID, there are deep structural changes taking place in every part of society and in every industry.

2. COVID is not merely a disruptor in and of itself, it is also a catalyst for accelerated change, especially for digital revolutions and 4IR (Fourth Industrial Revolution) technologies.

3. Uncertainty will be the defining feature of our world for the next few years.

4. The level of structural change and disruption we are experiencing will put severe pressure not only on industries and organisations, but also on all the individuals within them, leading to significant increases in stress and health issues.

Zanele and Graeme, futurists, scenario planners and leadership consultants, share with us why it is imperative to focus on adaption, transition and disruption to thrive. Mental health is a precedent to achieving such objectives and is also the outcome of such capabilities.

Chapter 2: Are we equipped to deal with this? What role does the workplace play in managing mental health?

by: Dr Vanessa Govender

Zoning in on the mental health agenda in the workplace, this chapter takes on the approach of a personal story of a medical doctor responding to the social ills and injustices and the lack of well-managed healthcare in the 1990s. This lays the foundation of how workplaces began to play a vital role in the employee health and wellbeing strategy as a necessity rather than a luxury or 'nice-to-have'. This need continues to weave itself into the current context of the COVID-19 pandemic where mental health support has taken front and centre stage of organisations' responses to navigate through the impact of such a devastating pandemic. This chapter contends that while there are overarching global frameworks for mental health policy and national legislation, some South African workplaces have struggled to position themselves optimally. This chapter provides detailed guidance on workplace mental health policy frameworks and makes the case for the importance of the workplace having the correct support structures to protect and promote employee mental health.

Chapter 3: Trends in mental health in the workplace

by: Navlika Ratangee

With an increase in mental health concerns, organisations have begun to take wellbeing a lot more seriously. The pandemic has enabled wellbeing to be placed front and centre of how organisations are thinking about surviving the current context and building a business for the future. The chapter begins by unpacking the role of stress and mental health, showcasing that we are all susceptible to mental health concerns, and paves the understanding of exactly why it is so prevalent in the current context. This has forced workplaces to recognise that employee wellbeing can no longer be ignored, be a nice to have, or even a tick-box exercise. As a result, companies are committing to invest more in mental health support and programmes for employees. Mental health does not exist in isolation though and it requires a holistic approach to ensure overall employee wellbeing. The impact of remote working is also discussed with a focus on shifting the bar to create a virtual culture of care. Lastly, some consideration for workplace design and strategy is shared to address the mental health concerns of today and tomorrow.

Chapter 4: The post pandemic context: Trauma and fatigue

by: Navlika Ratangee

Infectious disease outbreaks have widespread and pervasive detrimental effects on one's mental health manifesting in fear, distress and anxiety, and may further induce symptoms of depression. This chapter looks into the manifestation of stress, trauma and fatigue as a result of the pandemic and post pandemic. Much of the basis can be understood by gaining insight into the impact of stress on the brain and the realisation that even though we are built to deal with stress, we are unable to deal with sustained levels of stress. The trauma of ongoing stress is evidenced in the experience of invisible losses, secondary trauma, survivor guilt, grief and the experience of loss, acute stress, post-traumatic stress, moral injury and mass trauma. All of these concepts are unpacked in more detail. The chapter concludes with the introduction of the idea of creating post-traumatic growth and some of the protective factors that need to be considered by individuals and workplaces alike.

Chapter 5: Reflections on the relationship between mental health, work, and the workplace

by: Dr Angela Whitford du Plessis

This chapter provides context for how mental health has been neglected in the world of work for the longest time and the importance of increased focus in this area in the workplaces of today. In fact, the workplace is positioned as an important context influencing an individual's mental health in the first place. The interplay of workplace relationships with colleagues and with leadership, workplace culture, the nature of the job, levels of stress at work and job satisfaction are some of the dynamics that can influence the mental health of people in a positive or negative way. This chapter brings to life that when we refer to mental health concerns we are not only referring to a diagnosed depression or anxiety. This is an important concept to understand when thinking about the impact and manifestations of mental health in society at large and the workplace in general. Examples of poor leadership, sexual harassment, racism and poor compatibility in the workplace are provided as case examples for the workplace' dynamics that have a severe impact on one's mental health. The chapter concludes with giving some insights into difficult or courageous conversations to encourage parties in workplace disputes to hold transformative dialogues with the objective to reveal and resolve unintended, hurtful workplace behaviours and dynamics.

Chapter 6: Toxic relationships in the workplace
by: Dr Jopie de Beer; Dr Karina de Bruin and Dr Renate Scherrer

In contrast to the previous chapter, this chapter focuses on the impact that toxic relationships in the workplace have on our mental health and wellbeing. Toxicity in the workplace causes high levels of disengagement, strained relationships leading to high levels of stress, and even resignations. Interestingly this is evident when working together in offices or working virtually online. The authors of this chapter cover the origins of toxicity in the workplace in great detail and then move on to what can be done to manage and mitigate the risk of toxicity in work environments. The final point being made is that employees transition from mentally well and healthy, to being mentally unwell, when the work environment and relationships become toxic.

Chapter 7: Burning the candle on both ends: Dealing with burnout
by Joanna Kleovoulou

The implications of burnout and the associated personal and work-related costs of such conditions is gaining more recognition in the workplace. This chapter covers an explanation of burnout and its link to mental health concerns. The impact of burnout is discussed from worldwide studies with a more thorough understanding of signs, symptoms and outcomes.

One study explains that nearly 70 percent of professionals feel their employers are not doing enough to prevent or alleviate burnout within their organisation. 77 percent of employees say they have experienced burnout at their current job and just under half of all respondents say they have left a job specifically because they felt burned out.

Burnout and its impact on mental health and wellbeing in the workplace can no longer be ignored. This chapter ends with useful insights and strategies on practical things you could do, or that employers could do, to create a healthier environment and to mitigate the risk of burnout.

Chapter 8: Depression and anxiety – A big deal in the workplace

by: Joanna Kleovoulou

Often, when people hear about mental health conditions, depression and anxiety are the first two concerns that came to mind. Even though depression and anxiety are the two most common forms of mental illnesses and certainly the most common in the workplace, it is important to note that mental health is so much broader than just depression and anxiety. In this chapter, clinical psychologist, Joanna, unpacks exactly what depression and anxiety is, the different types of manifestations and the causes of such clinical diagnoses. The impact of depression and anxiety in the workplace cannot be ignored and requires organisations to put in place the necessary support for employees if it is to consider the sustainability of the organisation as a whole. The escalating costs of absenteeism and presenteeism relating to employees who are struggling with feeling stressed and anxious require investment in order to consider the ongoing wellbeing of employees.

Chapter 9: "Dis"traction and "dis"ease

by Dr Ashika Pillay

This chapter unpacks the relationship between technology and our mental health. With the context of COVID-19 and the "always-on" culture, many people rely on technological methods to engage, to work and to do life. It is therefore necessary to take the opportunity to understand the negative and positive effects of technology on your mental health. When we are fully aware of the impact we are less inclined to be controlled and form negative unconscious habits.

The intention of this chapter is to understand distractibility and its impact on our wellbeing so that we can be in control of our attention, time and health in an intentional, deliberate and causative manner. The question around whether we can truly multitask or not is also answered. This chapter provides useful tips to assist you to focus better and to minimise the distraction.

Chapter 1

Our COVID and Post-COVID context

by Graeme Codrington and Zanele Njapha

If COVID had been a short, sharp disruption that was dealt with quickly, we might have been able to just wait it out and then return to whatever constituted a 'normal life' afterwards. Instead, the COVID disruption has been lengthy and will leave a lasting legacy of structural change in many parts of the world. There are four key strategic considerations every business (and individual) must take to heart:

1. We will **not** be "going back to normal" after COVID is history (if it even is ever completely removed from the system rather than becoming an endemic issue we need to learn to live with). There are deep structural changes taking place in every part of society and in every industry.

2. COVID is not merely a disruptor in and of itself, it is also a catalyst for accelerated change, especially for digital revolutions and 4IR (Fourth Industrial Revolution) technologies.

3. The decade ahead will be one of the most disrupted – and disruptive – in history, as a confluence of forces all point towards deep systemic change. Uncertainty will be the defining feature of our world for the next few years.

4. The level of structural change and disruption we are experiencing will put severe pressure not only on industries and organisations, but also on all the individuals within them, leading to significant increases in stress and health issues.

It is impossible to generalise about COVID, and next-to-impossible to predict how the next few years will play out in different industries. A significant segment of the economy has been devastated by COVID. Hospitality, tourism, entertainment, travel, events, exhibitions and related industries have seen their activity drop to almost nothing for an extended period of time. Some of these industries will bounce back after Lockdown restrictions have ended and the virus is no longer a threat to travel or meeting together. In some countries, these industries have received some subsidies from their governments to help protect jobs, but even with this assistance, many businesses will not have survived such an extended period of disruption and will take some time to rebuild, restaff and repair what was broken – if they can at all. But even as these businesses try and recover from COVID, they will be facing a series of other disruptors, from technology and unsettled geopolitics to climate change and shifting social values. As tough as COVID might have been, sadly, the toughest times might still be ahead – if these businesses merely attempt to go "back to normal".

Other industries have faired very well during COVID, even having their best year ever in 2020. These include some suppliers of data, home automation and IT equipment, e-commerce and logistics, many software developers, EdTech suppliers, online gaming and streaming entertainment, many private medical companies, and, interestingly, a lot of veterinarians (apparently many of us bought new pets during Lockdown). Individually this is also true: most people who did not lose their jobs found that they had less expenses and actually ended the year with more money than they had planned for. But these companies and individuals might be lulled into a false sense of security about their success, and fail to realise that surviving COVID is merely the first major disruption of the 2020s, with many more to follow. If they rely on the 'luck' many of them had to just be in the right place at the right time, they might be caught out by a different disruptor in the near future.

COVID as a catalyst for accelerated structural change

Disney+ is a useful specific example of this acceleration of disruption. They're the online streaming platform of Disney, launched in September 2019 to compete with Netflix, Hulu, Showmax, etc. They set themselves the goal of 60 million subscribers by 2024. By February 2021, they had already surpassed 100 million subscribers, and have set a new goal of 250 million by 2025 (we think they're not being anywhere ambitious enough). But more interestingly, in February 2021, Disney announced that not only would they be uploading their entire back catalogue, but all future TV shows, series and movies would be launched *first* into their Disney+ platform. This will have a massive ripple effect across the multi-billionaire dollar entertainment industry, with the movie theatres being impacted most. Why would we pay exorbitant ticket prices to sit in a dirty seat on old popcorn, with someone behind us on their phone and the person next to us giving us COVID? For the same price as one ticket, our family has access for a full month to everything Disney has ever made, in the comfort of our own home. It's a game changer. And instead of taking five years or more, it was done in a few months during COVID lockdown.

Examples like this can be found in every industry and every part of the world. This is not merely a response to a pandemic. These are symbols and symptoms of deep structural change, where entire industry ecosystems are shifting. This is what lies ahead for almost everyone for the rest of the 2020s. It's way too early for anyone to make specific predictions about what will change where and when, but we can be absolutely certain that deep structural change will be the norm for the next decade or two.

Predict or prepare?

In a time of structural change, it is much less important to attempt to predict the future, and a lot more valuable to build adaptability, responsiveness to change and flexibility into our organisational DNA. For the next few months and years, your organisational structure and culture need to be your strategic priority; ahead of all your plans, goals and targets. Whether you had a good year or a horrible one in 2020/21, your success during the rest of the 2020s depends not so much on your ability to anticipate what might happen (although it would be tremendously helpful to develop some form of horizon-scanning capabilities), and much more on your ability to be adaptable and transition quickly from one state to the next. From a workplace perspective, it will also depend on your ability to nurture your best people, not merely assisting them in growing the skills they'll need for a rapidly changing work environment, but also helping them to develop resilience – the attitudes and mental health that will be essential personal foundations for future success.

History, along with the evolutionary past of humanity, has consistently shown us that when deep disruption occurs it is actually a call for us as a species and as an ecosystem to evolve. In other words, the best way for us to deal with disruption in its various forms is to disrupt our very own ways of working and living, our mental models and perceptions.

There is no other adequate response because, as history has taught us, change in our surroundings leaves us with only two options: *adapt or die*. This is as true for individuals and organisations as it is for organisms and species. We don't do this by predicting the future – we do it by developing *the capacity to transition*. This is especially important for two reasons:

1. We can NEVER be prepared for everything: It's impossible to have a scenario set aside to respond to every possible thing that could happen. As a result, when the unexpected happens, we find ourselves ill-equipped to survive, let alone thrive.

2. We may be prepared, but not equipped: The stock crashes, a competitor emerges, a disruption strikes, but if these events are bigger than our scenarios and plans, and require a more systemic or dynamic response than we are built for, our organisations might find themselves at a loss to know what to do. Even worse, in these situations, our most experienced leaders might be the worst people to turn to, as their very experience blinds them to the adaptive nature of the challenge they're currently facing. How do we abandon a business model and policies that have served us faithfully quickly enough to embrace a new way of working before the ship sinks?

We're disrupted, let's disrupt ourselves

We believe that the most successful organisations and individuals of the 2020s will be those that do not try to wait for the end of COVID before looking to the future. Even worse, if your mindset is that after COVID, you'll have time to stabilise, consolidate and rebuild what COVID bruised and broke. Instead, we believe that the progressive approach is to see the COVID disruption as a 'dress rehearsal' for a multitude of disruptions that are rushing towards us. We need to use however much longer COVID disrupts us for as a period of time where we can learn to live *with* disruption – and to do so in a way that makes us stronger at the same time. This isn't about mere survival, it's about building the capabilities required to evolve at pace.

When we think of disruptions, we most often imagine external, uncontrollable forces causing something to happen 'to us'. But what if we decided to get ahead of those external forces and disrupt ourselves? Self-disruption means taking control of the narrative even to the extent that we 'cull' our very own systems, policies, products etc. We are prepared to re-invent and re-imagine. There are many examples of companies that have done this regularly, with the big tech companies being amongst the best at it. New products are allowed to cannibalise the markets of existing ones. Most people know the often-told Kodak story of failure to keep up with change, but not many people know that Kodak actually invented the digital camera – or at least, Steve Sasson, a Kodak employee did, way back in 1975. The company decided to hide his invention, rather than invest in it, because they knew it would destroy their market for camera film. We know how that turned out. Apple, on the other hand, didn't hesitate to allow the iPhone to replace their wildly successful iPod, nor did they worry about the iPad denting iPhone sales. With the aim of opening up wider market opportunities, this self-disruption was well worth it.

Real innovation in the 2020s will not come just from new products or services, new markets or channels to markets, but rather from our ability to change our business models themselves. Although many organisations are committed to 'continuous improvement' and 'innovation hubs', we find that disruptive structural changes are not being made and teams are getting left behind. What's missing for many organisations and individuals is a mindset of adaptability and constant transitioning built into the organisation's DNA. This is what will distinguish the winners from the losers in the rest of this decade.

This is true for organisations as well as individuals. From a personal perspective, mental health becomes the key vehicle in achieving such objectives. From an organisational perspective, taking care of employee mental health becomes critical in achieving such objectives.

Get better at transitioning, don't just change

A transition, as implied by in the Bridges Transition Model (see William Bridges, *'Managing Transitions'*, De Capo Press), is about far more than mere organisational realignment, but about deep structural issues, including how our teams, the embedded systems, on-the-ground-operations and our very business models adapt to new environments.

For example, during a company merger, it's not enough to merely change the reporting structures and start sharing offices. The very cultures need to merge and support the structural change that has been made. This goes as far as shared rituals and cultural practices within the new organisation that cement and echo the change, such as integrating the 'Family Tuesday rituals' of company X and the 'Funky Hat meetings' of company Y. Unless a transition goes hand-in-hand with the psychological changes to be made by each and every team member and the group, we're in for what former General Electric CEO, Jack Welch, was referring to, when he said: *"If the rate of change on the outside exceeds the rate of change on the inside, the end is near."*

From an organisational perspective, we need to develop the skills of transitioning without breaking the business. From an individual perspective, we need to be able to do this without causing so much personal stress that we create physical, emotional, mental or relational harm in the process. Dealing with these issues – at organisational and personal level – is going to be a major theme of the rest of the 2020s. The impact of COVID will cast a long shadow over the next few years.

If only we could predict the future. That would make all of our lives much easier. But that's impossible. The best we can do is to prepare for whatever comes our way, knowing for sure that we are facing ecosystems disruption and deep structural upheaval in the near future, and then build the capability to transition, while ensuring that people feel safe, secure and engaged.

This is going to require that leaders learn new skills in leading their organisations to be in constant transition mode, rather than either seeking certainty and consistency, or moving, year in and year out, from one formal change process to the next. It's going to require leaders to upgrade their emotional intelligence even more than before, and change their approach to be more connected to the people they lead and the lives they live. Leaders who are leading teams in such VUCA (volatile, uncertain, complex and ambiguous) times need to understand that in order to assist their teams to make these ongoing transitions, they must not only understand the intricacy of a transition, but must also apply a different form of leadership that helps people transition better. Many of the skills required to help navigate leaders, individuals and teams through these transitions are detailed in this book. The development and application of these skills will determine your success in the 2020s and beyond.

As author and futurist William Gibson succinctly put it: *"The future is already here – it's just not very evenly distributed."*

Are we equipped to deal with this? What role does the workplace play in managing mental health?

Dr Vanessa Govender

Introduction

In 1989 as young enthusiastic medical students wanting to make a difference in the world, we ventured into the heart of Kwa-Zulu Natal (KZN), into the village of Nkandla to render rural health services to a poverty-stricken community. Day after day we worked at the charming mission hospital, with the Catholic nuns preaching to us the importance of understanding the socio-political context of where people live and work, shaping our young minds about the gross inequalities in health care access and affordability. A few years later, we experienced similar, this time in northern KZN when we visited a leper colony, hidden away in the pristine beaches of Kosi Bay. What torment ravaged my mind to think we could discard humanity like that and leave these outcasts with their tortured bodies and minds, to perish without access to any kind of health care.

A few years later, in 1995, working in a 350-bed hospital just 60 kilometres south of Johannesburg, serving over 20 000 mineworkers, where 90% of our in-patient medical wards testing positivity for HIV, I was alarmed, anxious and totally out of my depth as a fresh medical graduate. In a book chapter in *Sizonqoba! Outliving AIDS in Southern Africa*,[1] we outline how we practised medicine without lifesaving antiretroviral drugs, drawing the curtains and praying for our patients to die peacefully, without their loved ones holding their hands or saying goodbye. The toll this took on us as healthcare workers was devastating. But the toll that it took on those mineworkers far from loved ones and dear families, alone in a distant land, was far more traumatic than we could ever imagine. At that time all that the workplace offered was adhoc social worker services for support.

Fast forward to 2010, and I had just started working at a large multinational infrastructure development company. Despite being caught up in the euphoria of the Soccer World Cup, it was during a Board Committee meeting that the CEO inquired into the spate of suicides over a period of eighteen months.

*Could the workplace have identified the troubled, distracted
workers and prevented these tragedies?*

What were the "red flags" that we missed?

*Could the workplace have better supported the traumatised co-workers
and the bereaved families in the aftermath of these tragedies?*

Totally perturbed and shaken, I had no answers for the CEO, but I certainly hurtled into motion to investigate the situation and submit a business case to establish the Employee Assistance Programme (EAP), as a strategic pillar of the corporate health and wellness framework. The well thought out strategy won the hearts and minds of all employees with the full support of the CEO and the Board.

And here we are in 2021, in the throes of a raging pandemic, where much of my health consulting work pivots upon translating the ever-changing science about COVID-19 into easily understandable educational materials to communicate to all levels of workers, including ensuring that these workers have access to a range of mental health support services at the workplace.

All of this is overwhelming.

And I ponder.

Have we learned anything from our history?

The stark difference between these eras is characterised by the unique demands and responses to mental health in the workplace. Demands are shifting from mental health issues being side-lined to stark attentiveness to the need for mental health services being offered by employers. Likewise, the service delivery models for mental health services have shifted from only social worker support to caring leadership to onsite mental health support and 24/7 anonymous hotlines. All of this has been brought on by our increasingly stressful lives and most recently by the onslaught of the COVID-19 pandemic, resulting in anxiety, depression and mood disorders, along with a rising awareness of the importance of addressing our psychosocial issues as part of our broader health and wellness responses in workplaces and in our communities.

The purpose of this chapter is to elaborate upon why mental health programmes in the workplaces are needed and why many workplaces are not optimally equipped to deal with the challenges. The concern is that despite overwhelming evidence and growing knowledge on the cost-benefits for instituting mental health programmes in the workplace, it has taken three pandemics, HIV, TB and now COVID-19 with devastating mental and psychological consequences, for workplaces to make the paradigm shift to integrate mental health programmes into broader health programmes, into core business risk-management practices, and to ensure that mental health and wellness become part of the culture of the organisation.

Highlighted in this chapter is evidence of how we have evolved in this workplace dynamic by demonstrating how companies in South Africa have navigated this space as part of the workplace response.

This chapter describes the context and chronology of the demand for mental health services. It contends that while there are overarching global frameworks for mental health policy and national legislation, South African workplaces have struggled to position themselves optimally. The role of the workplace, specifically the role of leadership, management, workers, and health professionals, will be explored through case histories, corporate narratives and personal stories over the decades. The conceptual framework to develop workplace policy and the recommendations that are proposed will help build a culture of health and wellness whilst aligning to the global frameworks.

Global mental health workplace policy frameworks

The advent of the Sustainable Development Goals (SDGs) heralded a transformative step from its predecessor, the Millennium Development Goals, with the Health SDG 3 to *"Ensure healthy lives and promote wellbeing for all at all ages"*, incorporating service provision, mental health, substance use and tobacco control targets.[2]

Table 2.1 illustrates that the Health SDG 3 focusses on at least four mental health themes and initiatives. For example, SDG target 3a is on smoking cessation. Studies show that mental health conditions may be associated with higher rates of substance abuse including individuals having higher smoking prevalence than the rest of the population.[3]

Table 2.1: Health SDG 3 "Ensure healthy lives and promote wellbeing for all at all ages" – targets that relate to mental health

SDG Target 3.4 (NCDs)	Countries should *"reduce by one third premature mortality from non-communicable diseases (NCDs) through prevention and treatment and promote mental health and wellbeing"* by 2030
SDG Target 3.5 (Substance abuse)	Countries should *"strengthen the prevention and treatment of substance abuse, including narcotic drug abuse and harmful use of alcohol"*
SDG Target 3.8: (Mental health services)	Countries should *"achieve universal health coverage, including financial risk protection, access to quality essential health-care services and access to safe, effective, quality and affordable essential medicines and vaccines for all"*
SDG Target 3.a (Smoking)	Countries should strengthen the implementation of the WHO Framework Convention on Tobacco Control

According to the World Health Organization (WHO), the socioeconomic costs associated with non-communicable diseases (NCDs) make the prevention and control of these diseases of lifestyle a major development imperative for the 21st century. The rise of NCDs, namely heart disease, stroke, cancer, diabetes and chronic lung disease, are collectively responsible for almost 70% of all deaths worldwide and has been driven primarily by four major risk factors: tobacco use, physical inactivity, the harmful use of alcohol and unhealthy diets.[4] The epidemic of NCDs poses devastating health consequences for individuals, families, communities, and businesses, and threatens to overwhelm health systems that are already overwhelmed with the COVID-19 crisis.

As a risk factor for the NCDs, tobacco use shares significant comorbidity with mental health conditions. It is well documented that people with mental health conditions tend to smoke at two to four times the rate of the general population. Additionally, smokers with a mental health condition tend to smoke more cigarettes than those in the general population and smokers who adopt mental health strategies are more successful at quitting.[3] Thus there is a firm imperative to integrate NCD management programmes with smoking cessation programmes and mental health support.

Goetzel and colleagues offer both a scientific yet pragmatic rationale for better addressing the often-neglected topic of mental health in the workplace.[5] The authors recommend establishing a culture of wellness at workplaces that prevent work-related (occupational) stress that supports the identification and treatment of mental illness. *"Building cultures of health at the workplace should protect and promote health and safety, enhance performance, and reduce socially harmful behaviors."*

It is worth noting and not surprising that in 2007, the *Lancet* in a series of papers, called for the *"global community to scale up services for people affected by mental disorders, including substance use disorders, self-harm, and dementia"*.[6]

A key message from the Lancet Commission on Global Mental Health and Sustainable Development is that *"mental health problems exist along a continuum from mild, time-limited distress to severe mental health conditions"*.[6] The COVID-19 pandemic has created a world where people have found themselves moving along on that continuum in unprecedented ways. More people have succumbed to mental health conditions and some have experienced a worsening of their pre-existing mental health conditions, in ways that have impacted personal and professional lives. Where people had coped well either through pharmacological or non-pharmacological interventions, or a combination of both, they have now found themselves navigating their conditions with difficulty, due to multiple additional stressors brought on by the pandemic, like caring for elderly family members, concerns about catching the virus, having to take care of children's education and caregiving, all while being separated from loved ones.

A conceptual framework for mental health in the workplace

The mental health of workers is an area of increasing concern to many organisations worldwide. Common mental health problems, such as depression, anxiety, substance abuse and stress, affect many individuals, their families, co-workers, and the broader community. Importantly, mental health conditions left unmanaged, can have a direct impact on workplaces through increased absenteeism, reduced productivity (presenteeism), and increased direct and indirect healthcare and business costs.

Conceptual framework for mental health workplace policy

The conceptual framework for mental health workplace policy herewith describes the mental health issues, barriers to access to care and support and proposes a set of recommendations, which are expanded upon later in this chapter. The framework is underpinned by global mental health frameworks, standards, legislation, company risk management frameworks, health and wellness policies and programmes. Companies would do well to develop their own unique conceptual models upon which to build their customised mental health workplace policies.

Global frameworks

The Centers for Disease Control and Prevention (CDC) reports that there is increasing evidence that depression and other mental health problems, relate to systemic organisational dysfunction and is linked with loss of productivity.[7] Several studies of diverse occupations have identified organisational stressors such as high job demands, low job control and lack of social support in the workplace, may be associated with depression. Of course, other contributory factors such as exposure to occupational health and safety hazards (biological, physical, ergonomic, chemical) can trigger occupational stress and/or exacerbate underlying pre-existing mental health conditions.

Recognising this complex interplay, in 1950, in a joint statement, the ILO/WHO defined Occupational Health as *"the promotion and maintenance of the highest degree of physical, mental and social wellbeing of workers in all occupations by preventing departures from health, controlling risks and the adaptation of work to people, and people to their jobs".* This is a direct call to action by employers to institute holistic workplace health and wellness programmes.

ISSUES	**Workplace:** occupational stress, hazardous working conditions, organisational factors – excessive workload, conflict, inequity, poor leadership, lack of communication
	Individual: Anxiety, stress, family, work, financial, health, relationships issues, biological, social, psychological and environmental factos

BARRIERS	Confidentiality and privacy
	Stigma and discrimination
	Fear of job loss
	Threat to career mobility

RECOMMENDATIONS	Situational analysis of issues, barriers, and available data	Develop strategy to implement policy with interventions to meet unmet needs
	Define population at risk	Develop communication and engagement strategy
	Develop steering committee after stakeholder consultaiton	Establish governance structures
	Develop Mental Health workplace policy – 4 step model	Monitor and evaluate

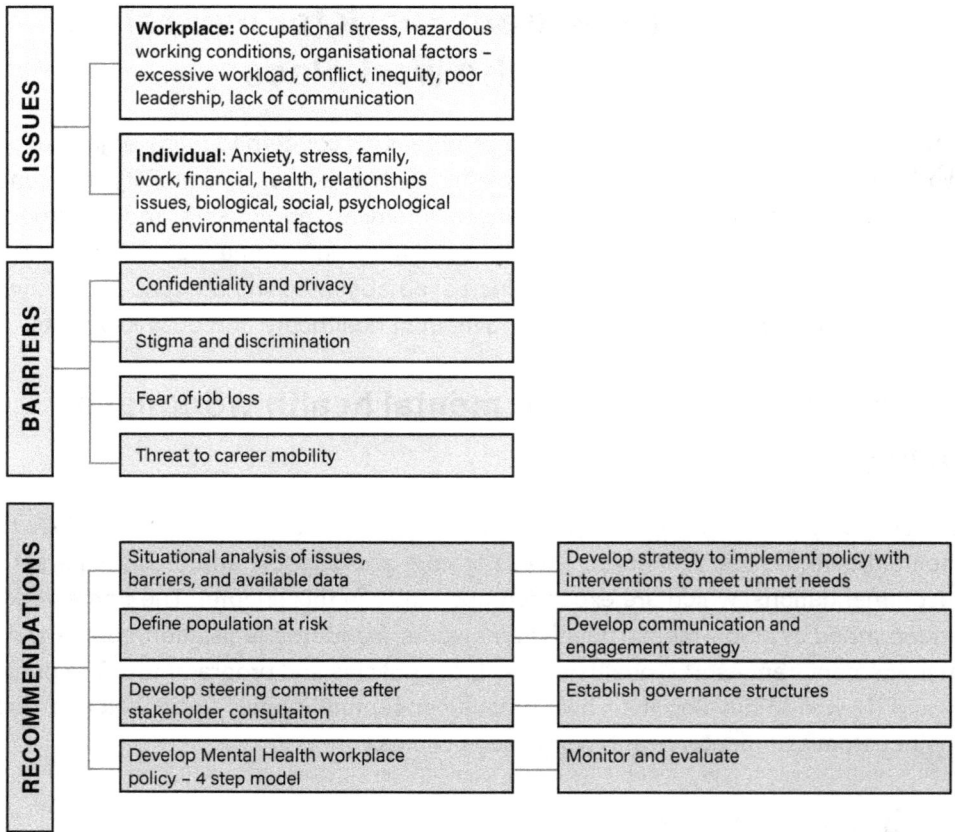

Conceptual Framework for Mental Health Policy – Underpinned by Frameworks, Legislation, Policies, Programmes, Standards

Several decades later, in 2010, the WHO in its Healthy Workplaces report, noted that in addition to its direct medical and workplace costs, mental health conditions (burnout, depression) increased health care costs and lost productivity indirectly by contributing to increased workplace safety incidents, through disengagement, and presenteeism at the workplace. Unaddressed, this could result in business failure, as illustrated in the figure below.[8]

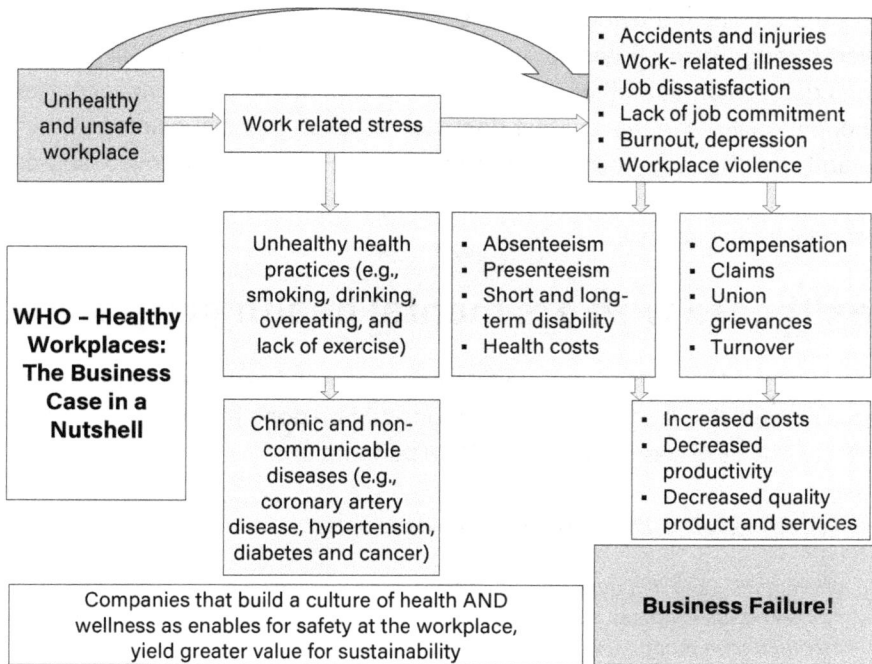

WHO – Healthy Workplaces: The Business Case in a Nutshell

- Unhealthy and unsafe workplace → Work related stress →
  - Accidents and injuries
  - Work- related illnesses
  - Job dissatisfaction
  - Lack of job commitment
  - Burnout, depression
  - Workplace violence

- Unhealthy health practices (e.g., smoking, drinking, overeating, and lack of exercise)
- Absenteeism
- Presenteeism
- Short and long-term disability
- Health costs
- Compensation
- Claims
- Union grievances
- Turnover

- Chronic and non-communicable diseases (e.g., coronary artery disease, hypertension, diabetes and cancer)
- Increased costs
- Decreased productivity
- Decreased quality product and services

Companies that build a culture of health AND wellness as enables for safety at the workplace, yield greater value for sustainability

Business Failure!

Burnout is defined in ICD-11 as follows:

"...a syndrome conceptualized as resulting from chronic workplace stress that has not been successfully managed.

It is characterized by three dimensions:

- *feelings of energy depletion or exhaustion;*
- *increased mental distance from one's job, or feelings of negativism or cynicism related to one's job; and*
- *reduced professional efficacy.*

Much later, in 2019, the WHO published that while it is **not** classified as a medical condition, burnout is included in the 11th Revision of the International Classification of Diseases (ICD-11) as an *"occupational phenomenon".* This brought to the fore the burden of occupational stress and places firm responsibility on employers to respond, both in terms of providing mental health services and in reorganising work systems and structures to build more harmonious working environments.[9] More on burnout in Chapter 8.

Mental health problems are the result of a complex interplay between biological, psychological, social and environmental factors. There is increasing evidence that both the content and context of work can play a role in the development of mental health problems in the workplace. Key factors include: workload (both excessive and insufficient work); lack of participation and control in the workplace; monotonous or unpleasant tasks; role ambiguity or conflict; lack of recognition at work; inequity; poor interpersonal relationships; poor working conditions; poor leadership and communication; conflicting home and work demands.[10]

Despite the convincing evidence of cost effective interventions[11], this has not been followed through with strategies and policies to manage (prevent, diagnose, treat, support) depression and other mental health conditions in the workplace. Note that cost-benefit analysis in this context does not relate to financial gains only, but more importantly to the non-financial, non-tangible gains from improved self-esteem, confidence building in the individual, and eventually to the gains in the company's reputational image as well.

Healthcare workers mental health programmes

Today, unlike back in 1995, there are numerous mental health interventions that can be implemented. Some of these interventions can be done remotely and online, with success, as we have seen during COVID-19 pandemic.

Workplace mental health interventions, some examples:

- *offering 24/7 EAP services and promoting those services*
- *mental health wellness days*
- *mental health recognition screenings*
- *symptom screening questionnaires*
- *placing confidential self-assessments in cafeterias, break rooms, or bulletin boards*
- *training supervisors and leaders in mental health awareness*
- *assisting with access to counselling, psychological and psychiatric services through health insurance benefits.*

Vizheh and colleagues, in 2020 in their study to examine the mental health of healthcare workers, concluded that, the COVID-19 pandemic has aggravated psychological pressure and even mental illness. They recommended that policymakers and managers adopt supportive, encouraging, motivational, protective interventions to include training and education, through effective information and communication platforms.

At the start of the COVID-19 pandemic in SA, in April 2020, a group of concerned colleagues established a weekly online webinar series to address healthcare workers' mental health concerns. We conducted debriefing sessions post shift to offer information and self-help techniques such as mindfulness and breathing.[12] Such was the demand and need, that the idea took flight and spiralled into more established 24/7 counselling services being rendered online to HCWs in SA by various organisations. Likewise, many healthcare organisations and private institutions employing HCWs, went on to develop in-house HCW specific mental health programmes. This swift response from mental health professionals in providing the much-needed mental health support to our HCWs on the frontlines, often on a pro bono basis, was highly commendable at a time of national and global crisis.

Embedding mental health programmes within occupational health

At a pragmatic level in a large organisation, mental health services could be embedded within the occupational health discipline, as purported by the WHO/ILO definition of occupational health. As an example, Putnam and McKibbinn, illustrated that occupational health teams were *"untapped resources"* for the management of depression in the workplace. They maintain that occupational health professionals have the credentials, credibility, training, and experience necessary to build a strong business case, stating that *"Occupational health professionals are the most qualified to design and deliver destigmatized, customer friendly programs and services for employees to access for help with depression, and to integrate their services with other departments such as benefits, health promotion, EAP, and human resources, to create an effective, organization-wide depression initiative."*[13]

An unexpected consequence of the COVID-19 pandemic, is that we know how to do good, if not better at workplace risk assessments. The National Institute for Occupational Safety and Health (NIOSH) provides a conceptual model for prioritising efforts to advance worker safety, health and wellbeing under the Total Worker Health concept[14] incorporating psychosocial hazards at the workplace. As with all hierarchies in the control of workplace hazards (biological, ergonomic, physical, chemical), psychosocial hazards too should be identified and controlled at source. Recognising this gap, in 2020, psychosocial hazard identification and risk management became inaugurated into the new global standard ISO 45003.[15] This international standard outlines practical methodology of best practice for managing psychological health within the workplace, that companies can aspire to:

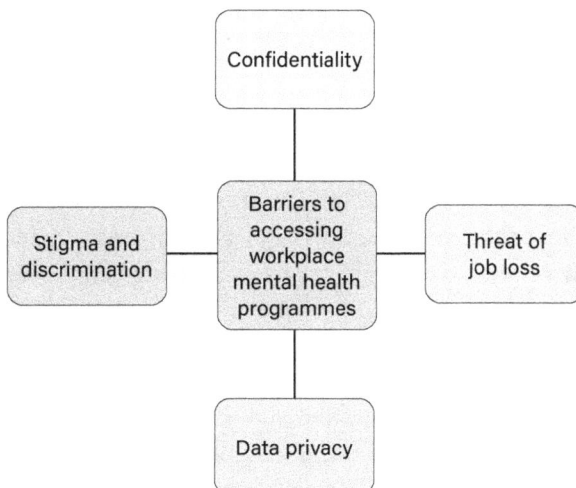

Confidentiality

Barriers to accessing workplace mental health programmes

Stigma and discrimination

Threat of job loss

Data privacy

Economically active adults spend most of their awake hours at work and thus it would make business sense for them to receive supportive services that have the potential to impact productivity and improve performance, at the workplace.

Note I am not under any illusion that this is an easy task. The enormous inequity in distribution and access to mental health services within workplaces and beyond the company gates, coupled with the lack of worker awareness, widespread stigma and discrimination, means that people will not easily disclose their conditions at the workplace.

As a result, the problem that the workplace has in offering assistance through its structures, is that workers have genuine concerns regarding confidentiality, data privacy of personal information, stigma and discrimination and impact on career mobility and fitness for work, should their mental health conditions be disclosed indiscriminately. It is critical to identify and address these barriers to access in developing workplace mental health policy and strategy. In workplaces and in society in general, the vast majority of mental health needs remain unnoticed, unaddressed, undocumented, under-funded and most certainly under-resourced.

In the United Nations (UN) policy brief[16], it is reported that *"countries spend on average only 2% of their health budgets on mental health initiatives"*. Furthermore, international development assistance for mental health is estimated to be less than 1% of all development assistance for health. This is despite the well-documented comorbidity of physical and mental health conditions for diseases such as HIV/AIDS and TB; and now for COVID-19.[17] Thus, both national and workplace responses are hampered by the lack of investment in mental health promotion, prevention and care even before the pandemic, with the UN documenting that there is less than one mental health professional for every 10 000 people, with depression affecting 264 million people globally. The historic underinvestment in mental health needs will be further perpetuated if left unaddressed.

Workplaces would thus do well to institute and fund mental health programmes that would close some of these gaps and strengthen public health systems.

Who are the vulnerable populations at risk in the workplace?

The UN policy brief, identifies vulnerable populations most at risk for mental stress during the COVID-19 pandemic range as those living in closed congregate settings across all ages, with children, adolescents, young adults and women bearing the brunt of social discord. Thus workplaces should take into cognisance the psychosocial circumstances of their workers who might be affected by any of these situations that are external to the workplace, yet impact directly on engagement and productivity at work. The lists below depict the various categories of people who are more prone in this pandemic to be affected by mental health conditions. If economically active, they will be at a workplace and it would be prudent for that workplace to be aware of these population vulnerabilities and respond with the requisite compassion and care.

First responders and frontline workers, particularly workers in health and long-term care	Children	Adolescents and young people
• Play a crucial role in fighting the outbreak and saving lives, under exceptional stress, extreme workloads, difficult decisions, risks of becoming infected and spreading infection to families and communities, witnessing deaths of patients. • Stigmatisation of these workers is common in too many communities. • Reports of suicide attempts and suicide death by healthcare workers	• Emotional state and behaviour has been affected during confinement • At particular risk of abuse during the pandemic. • Children with disabilities, children in crowded settings and those who live and work on the streets are particularly vulnerable. • A UN Policy Brief on the impact of COVID-19 on children has been published	• At risk group in the present crisis, as most mental health conditions develop during this period of life. • Many young people have seen their futures impacted. For example, schools have been closed, examinations have not been held, and economic prospects have diminished.

Woman	People in humanitarian and conflict settings
• A survey on stress levels in the Indian population during the COVID-19 pandemic indicated that 66% of women reported being stressed as compared to 34% of men. • During the current situation of COVID-19, pregnant and new mothers are especially likely to be anxious due to difficulties accessing services and social support and fear about infection. • In some family arrangements there is an increased burden due to additional duties of care-giving such as home-schooling and taking care of older relatives. • As with childhood abuse, the situation of stress and restrictions on movement increases violence towards women.	• Evidence indicates that in conflict settings 1 in 5 people have a mental health condition. The pandemic may exacerbate existing mental health conditions, induce new conditions and limit access to the already scarce mental health services available. • Physical distancing difficult in refugee settings or internally displaced people living in crowded camps or settlements.

Legislative framework and national mental health policy

Under the Constitution of SA, the Occupational Health and Safety Act and the Mine Health and Safety Act, workplaces have a legal obligation to protect the health and safety of all its workers. Companies should ensure that a Health and Wellness strategy includes mental health policy interventions that are well embedded into the culture and relevant structures of the organisation. One way to do that is to gain top leadership support, along with the requisite funding. Another method is to apply risk management principles that are firmly embedded into the risk management frameworks. This means that mental health conditions must be seen as a health risk to the company and, along with other hazards at the workplace, be appropriately addressed.

In SA, the WHO mental health recommendations, are supported by the transformative policy and legislation in the Constitution of the Republic of South Africa (1996); National Mental Health Policy Framework and Strategic Plan of 2014; the Prevention of and Treatment for Substance Abuse Act, No. 70 of 2008; the National Health Policy Guidelines for Improved Mental Health in South Africa of 1997 and the Mental Health Care Act, Act 17 of 2002.

Prior to 2013 there was no overarching national policy guiding these services in SA. The strategic plan of 2014, in particular, is progressive in nature and promotes the notion of good, quality mental health services that are accessible, equitable, comprehensive and integrated at all levels of the health system.[18] Yet, there have been ongoing challenges in accessing mental health services in the country and certainly through our workplaces. Employers have been slow to respond, possibly due to the mental health needs not being realised, workplace interventions not being regulated, hence not monitored and evaluated consistently, and thus not placed on the leadership agenda for due attention and securing of necessary resources to implement such programmes.

Role of the healthcare professionals – a personal testament

A post graduate student in public health once shared with me that the speciality of occupational medicine is possibly the only discipline that is a specialty of context – context of work, life, home, family, social, psychological, within the context of the whole body system and the whole of society. He went on to say that it is really a privilege to be a public health or occupational medicine specialist and suggested that maybe other specialties can adopt some of these models of thinking and caring for patients in order to address the social determinants of health and in so doing address the neglected aspects of mental health.

Context matters!

The specialty of occupational medicine has intrigued me over the last 25 years as it has always been about prevention, with the key tenet being to identify the hazards at the workplace and to control them at source, thereby preventing adverse health effects.

Noting the impact of work on health, and the impact of health on work, a good occupational history can elicit clues to solving the medical puzzle in front of us. As occupational medicine practitioners and healthcare professionals we must remember what we have been taught, since our earliest medical school days about the biopsychosocial model in medicine. The importance of the social determinants of health and how these impact on an individual's health and wellbeing and ultimately productivity, is vital. No medical history, past medical history and occupational history is complete without a robust psychosocial enquiry that starts when the patient walks through the medical practice doors.

As health professionals in corporate settings, we need to recognize that the determinants of health are socioeconomic, environmental, political, and are external and internal to business. Numerous diseases and conditions, both occupational and non-occupational hamper growth, development and prosperity of businesses and of the nation at large. In addition it is recognized that in order to achieve mental wellbeing of the nation, sectors in the socioeconomic, political and health spheres must work together to implement multidimensional and to some extent multidisciplinary interventions. This stance and positioning must be at the front and centre of every country and every employer's response to and recovery from the COVID-19 pandemic. In a workplace setting it is incumbent upon the health professionals, particularly occupational health professionals, who are legal appointees, to be those advocates for your patients and to be the voice of our patients within the business structures. Yes, employee representatives, unions do have a role to play as well, but it is the company doctor or nurse who has the trust and confidence of his/her patients and it is incumbent upon us to maximise on this dynamic.

As a specialist in occupational medicine, it is always both a privilege and an honour to serve workers; most importantly, it is an honour to serve at the frontlines in clinics and hospitals. Why? Because we constantly learn new meanings to the biopsychosocial model from our patients, who till today remain the best teachers. From the bedside years ago, we learnt that our patients were workers. We had to do our best to assist them, usually only physically to recuperate and recover to return to work safely and healthy, so they could continue to be the breadwinners and providers and build the business. Our job was to get them back in shape swiftly, which included subjecting them to a fitness to work test, and if they worked underground it involved doing a heat tolerance test and some physically demanding tasks to test their endurance and physical abilities.

Physical health was our focus!

Most often these young fit men of the mines would pass the "physicals" and return to work. But there was that small proportion who despite our best efforts and with no stigmata of ongoing medical complaints, who could just not pass. Those were the patients who concerned me the most. What was it? They had all the physical strength, yet these "malingerers" as we labelled them just could not pass. It would take years to realise that whilst physically strong, mentally they were crashing after having witnessed co-workers injured in a rock fall, or worse still, witnessed them perish under tons of rock. Post-traumatic stress disorder was probably missed many times in my career.

Mental health was missed!!

As my mining career meandered through various roles as Medical Officer, Occupational Medical Practitioner, Wellness Manager, Head of Health and providing health services mainly for the so called blue-collared workers, migrant within South African borders, across SA borders and across geographies, who are contractually bound on various durations of contracts, I have been constantly learning and teaching. I have treated mainly Black African men, in the pre-antiretroviral era in high HIV positivity times, and I have treated both men and women who feed multiple members of a household back home, usually with low academic and low health literacy levels, and who are vulnerable in terms of what education, health provision or social justice they can access. All of these workers have experienced first-hand the perils of pre-democracy injustices, the trauma of losing loved ones to the HIV epidemic or to a fatal mine accident deep underground. All of these workers at some point in their lives have needed or could have improved their social standing and career paths, and have had a better chance at life, if only they had access to mental health support resources to help them deal with the enormity of the mental health burdens they faced.

Over all these years nothing has impacted me more at a personal and professional level as the lack of adequate mental health services, in public and private healthcare settings and in workplaces, for workers who drive the machinery of those enterprises towards profits, for the corporate office workers and for the healthcare workers who served those large corporations.

"If I was younger and had the wisdom I now possess and was given the opportunity to start my career over again, I would apply myself very differently in how I used the biopsychosocial model to manage my patients."

Throwback to 1996! In those earlier youthful years, my own mental stress propelled me into conducting an enquiry into the perceived stress of nurses working with HIV/AIDS patients, to better understand what were the inner struggles (if any) that they were dealing with.[19] Nurses expressed their experiences with stigma and discrimination, that they were perceived to be "weak" if they exhibited any signs of mental ill-health. They were adamant that the notion that *"stress is for wimps"* and suggestions like *"are you mental?"* must become obsolete and nurses must not be victimised for demonstrating weakness. In addition, they mused that as nurses they should use their strengths within their own collegial circles and verbalise their problems to each other. But not all nurses are able to do this. As one nurse articulated, *"I am fortunate I talk a lot and I'm able to discuss my problems with colleagues at work, but not all of us can do this."*

I too, recall my own perceptions of *"inadequacy and helplessness"* to deal with an incurable disease that was compounded by my patients' own feelings of *"doom and hopelessness"*. Yet, at the same time, my patients were part of the economically active population working in large enterprises, large mining companies, who were part of the global machinations to keep economies not just rolling but thriving.

In a case report written in 1999, Wade and Simon explored an observed phenomenon of pairing among staff members of various disciplines, working with patients with HIV/AIDS patients. The authors called this phenomenon "survival bonding", a mutually supportive environment, which reduced individuals' anxiety, stress and burnout, in the absence of formal mental health services.[20] Given the growing volume of HIV infected patients and the increased workload of healthcare workers, it was important to understand the complex emotional needs of staff, to prevent burnout.

Fast forward to 2021, and many of us are now experiencing a similar toll on a much larger scale, with an increased focus and response to formal organised mental health support services in corporate settings, specifically for healthcare workers who are expected to render mental health support and counselling services when they themselves are in dire need of those services. Despite the noble nature of this profession, health professionals are being attacked. Nurses are being victimised for having COVID-19, and being accused of catching it in taxis and shopping malls and being "careless" and recklessly spreading the disease.[21]

> *Have our health establishments responded appropriately, or have we once again left our healthcare workers to fend for themselves, like we did in the midst of the HIV epidemic?*

These thoughts loomed prominently in my own mental state and inspired some of the COVID-19 work mentioned already: ensuring mental health support for healthcare workers[12] and making sure the right information was being communicated at the right time to the right audience.

If the healthcare workers are being left behind, where work stressors are obvious, what about non-healthcare workplaces, where the triggers for mental health disorders may not be as obvious?

In a study to measure health-related lost productivity and to assess the business implications of a full-cost approach to managing health, 51,648 employee respondents using the Health and Work Performance Questionnaire combined with more than one million medical and pharmacy claims, illustrated that health-related productivity costs are significantly greater than medical and pharmacy costs alone (on average 2.3 to 1). The study examined chronic conditions such as depression/anxiety, obesity, arthritis, and back/neck pain as important causes of productivity loss. Importantly, across different levels of employees, the study found that executives and managers experience as much or more productivity loss from depression and back pain compared to labourers or operators. Participating companies proceeded to use this information to guide their Corporate Health strategies.

In another study, mental health clinicians employed by an insurance company identified workers who might need treatment for mental health conditions.[22] They provided information about how to access it, monitored adherence to treatment, and provided telephone psychotherapy to those workers who did not want to see a therapist in person. The outcomes of 304 workers assigned to the intervention were compared with 300 controls, who were referred to clinicians for treatment but did not receive telephone support. The researchers found that workers assigned to the telephone intervention reported significantly improved mood and were more likely to keep their jobs when compared with those in the control group. They also improved their productivity, equivalent to about 2.6 hours of extra work per week, worth about $1,800 per year (based on average wages) – while the intervention cost the employers an estimated $100 to $400 per treated employee. The researchers are conducting additional research on how to improve access to mental health care in the workplace, and to quantify costs and benefits for employers.

Studies such as these suggest that, in the long term, costs spent on mental health care may represent an investment that will pay off – not only in healthier employees, but also for the company's financial health.

How have workplaces responded?

As history has demonstrated to us with the HIV/AIDS programmes in SA and now with the workplace COVID-19 vaccination programmes, the workplace remains an important entry point into health programmes and policies. Workplaces have a vital role to strengthen and support public health systems, to ensure universal access to prevention, treatment, care and support, for its workers, whilst also reaching out to the communities as part of its corporate social obligations.

What can corporations do to support their workers and their families from the devastating impact of a diagnosis with HIV, AIDS, TB, the NCDs, mental health conditions, and now COVID-19?

In the design and implementation of workplace policies and programmes it is important that these workplace initiatives are integrated into other health and wellness interventions whilst remaining aligned and superseding, where possible, overall national mental health legislation, policies and strategies.

There are many businesses in corporate SA that have developed elaborate and comprehensive occupational health services including mental health programmes, substance abuse programmes and smoking cessation programmes, and where possible, companies have provided for dependants, and family members living in the same household, using various funding mechanisms to do so. Intense information, education and communication programmes have been developed, for employees at all levels, using innovative modalities, to build an environment that is free from the stigma and discrimination of mental health programmes. Over the years, I have witnessed workplace mental health initiatives mature into innovative programmes with novel EAP that provide 24/7 counselling services, advise on a range of life management issues (financial, relationship, childcare), to employees, spouses and sometimes entire families. Sadly, there was no continuity of care beyond employment: psychosocial counselling and support services did not continue upon separation from the employer, to prepare them for life beyond the company gates without employment.

Back in 1995, an innovative partnership with regional recruitment agencies like The Employment Bureau of Africa (TEBA), that made it a tad easier for patients who were being repatriated (usually due to HIV or TB) to be introduced into the referral network for continuous care and support back home. It would be commendable if such partnerships or innovative funding mechanisms for mental health support can be considered during these troubled times by companies.

A company experience – it's all about leadership

When it comes to the lives and livelihoods of its people, there should be no room for complacency or indecision. In 2010, when the CEO of that infrastructure development company categorically stated that he was troubled by a series of suicidal incidents over a few months at one of its companies, and that *"something had to be done"*, I knew at my core that there were deeper psychosocial issues and a dire need for mental health services. In 2010, these services were packaged as EAPs offering a suite of services from 24-hour call centres, to face-to-face counselling services for a range of life issues, such as debt counselling, relationship issues etc. But it was not easy to convince company executives who had not budgeted for this "health and wellness" line item. In fact, safety was all that mattered in those physically demanding work environments. But safety's poor cousin "health" was not getting the attention, and certainly not the investment (both financial and non-financial), it deserved. This was despite growing evidence that supported workplace mental health initiatives that demonstrated good return on investments.

Following some intense lobbying and submitting a good business case along with clear multidisciplinary (health, safety, human resources, unions, Board) commitment, technical specifications, expected outcomes with a monitoring and evaluation framework, and deliverables for the service provider, the EAP was implemented and deeply embedded into the Health and Wellness framework of the organisation.

A few months into the programme, a crane operator at one of the sites presented himself at the company clinic in a distraught state. Through a flood of tears and rage, he pleaded to the nurse in charge to let him go to work because all he wanted to do was to jump off the crane and end his life. His wife had compromised trust and fidelity in their marriage and he was not coping. Swiftly and compassionately the EAP services swung into action, averting what could have been a tragedy. In the words of the CEO:

"If this programme (EAP) has saved even one life, it's a huge gain for all our workers."

Eleven years later, at the time of this writing, that programme is still going strong.

When it comes to decision making, we as Health and Wellness ambassadors must be mindful that we are the voice of the voiceless; we must take cognizance of presenting the full business case, both in financial terms and non-financial terms, to the right people at the right time, i.e. communication is key. Communicate the facts. Communicate the risk. Communicate to the decision makers who can make an impact. These real stories demonstrate how compassionate and caring leadership can fast track sustainable programmes and have impact. Perhaps more importantly, it reflects how partnerships are essential for success, how leadership speaks and behaves and acts out health and wellness; how business, employers, employees, service providers can collaborate for a greater good. It highlights not only what has been done, but how much more needs to be done.

Recommendations: what can companies do to institute mental health programmes?

The COVID-19 pandemic is but one pandemic with many waves. The waves of HIV, TB, obesity, NCDs, mental health, substance use and abuse, tobacco smoking have been with us far too long. As illustrated in the WHO Healthy Workplace model, left unattended, these would lead to business failure. The COVID-19 pandemic has left many health programmes, including already resource-constrained mental health services, re-allocating their resources to the pandemic. For example, the city of Madrid had to repurpose over 60% of its mental health beds to care for people with COVID-19, reducing the number of people attending emergency mental health services by 75%.[16]

Instituting mental health services at the workplace in these COVID-19 times, means leaders can learn from previous and ongoing pandemics and adopt a set of guiding principles aligned to the UN policy brief[16] and the WHO comprehensive mental health action plan.[10] The latter has been extended until 2030 to ensure alignment with the 2030 Agenda for Sustainable Development.

Guiding principles for workplace mental health programmes

- Apply a whole-of-society approach to promote, protect and care for mental health
- Ensure widespread availability of emergency mental health and psychosocial support
- Strengthen effective leadership and governance for mental health
- Provide comprehensive, integrated and responsive mental health services for the future
- Implement strategies for promotion and prevention in mental health
- Compile data, evidence and research for mental health

Policy and strategy development for workplace mental health programmes

The four-step model in planning and budgeting to deliver mental health services, outlined below, has been adapted from the WHO [10, 17] and can be applied to any workplace setting. The details customised to each workplace will assist Human Resources and Occupational Health teams to develop policies and comprehensive strategies for improving the mental health of workers at risk and use existing resources to achieve the greatest possible benefits and provide effective services to those in need. Importantly, as workplaces do with fitness to work assessments, occupational health teams should assist with the reintegration of workers with mental health conditions into all aspects of work, home and community life, to enhance and improve their overall quality of life.

This four-step planning model adopts an approach to analyse data that is available and understand the mental health services that exist, identify the gaps that exist, set priorities, develop and implement the policy. It therefore allows for adaptation according to the structure of the company and available mental health services.

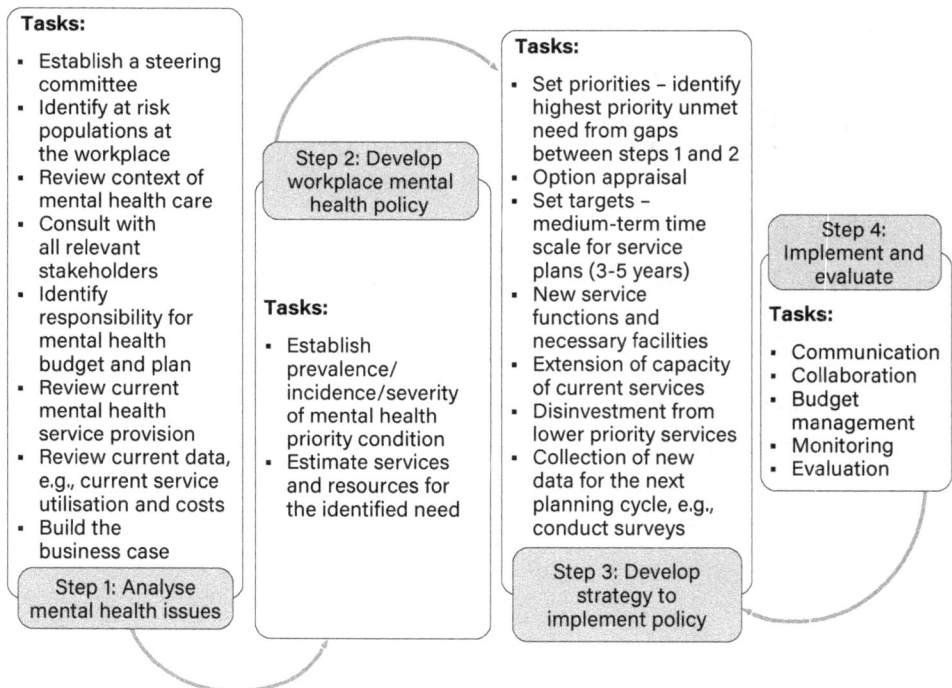

Tasks:
- Establish a steering committee
- Identify at risk populations at the workplace
- Review context of mental health care
- Consult with all relevant stakeholders
- Identify responsibility for mental health budget and plan
- Review current mental health service provision
- Review current data, e.g., current service utilisation and costs
- Build the business case

Step 1: Analyse mental health issues

Step 2: Develop workplace mental health policy

Tasks:
- Establish prevalence/incidence/severity of mental health priority condition
- Estimate services and resources for the identified need

Tasks:
- Set priorities – identify highest priority unmet need from gaps between steps 1 and 2
- Option appraisal
- Set targets – medium-term time scale for service plans (3-5 years)
- New service functions and necessary facilities
- Extension of capacity of current services
- Disinvestment from lower priority services
- Collection of new data for the next planning cycle, e.g., conduct surveys

Step 3: Develop strategy to implement policy

Step 4: Implement and evaluate

Tasks:
- Communication
- Collaboration
- Budget management
- Monitoring
- Evaluation

Figure 2.1: The Four Steps Model in policy and strategy development for mental health services

Step 1: Establish a committee and analyse the mental health issues

Establish a project/steering committee to conduct the tasks required to develop and implement the policy. Conduct a situational analysis as well as the stakeholder mapping and engagement. The population at risk should be clearly defined; the current mental health trends from service providers should be sought, along with the service provision to understand the dynamics of mental health demands and services rendered. Employers are more likely to support a mental health workplace policy if a good business case is developed; one that illustrates a return on investment, i.e. potential costs against potential benefit, if possible. General data showing the link between mental ill-health and reduced productivity and increased costs should be presented. Any existing data should be thoroughly analysed to demonstrate this linkage. Current service providers are ethically and professionally bound to share anonymised, aggregated data of workers for the greater good of the entire workforce. Employers would do well to take the necessary steps to ensure that relevant confidential information is shared timeously, such as crafting well-designed service-level agreements and clear deliverables. Thus, key stakeholder consultations, internally across disciplines, e.g., safety, occupational health, HR, communication specialists, and with external stakeholders such as the EAP and medical benefit providers, and should commence early in the project, and be ongoing throughout the process of developing the policy development, implementation, monitoring and evaluation.

According to the WHO[10], *"all available relevant information should be assembled"*.

Such information might include:

- Human resources data, e.g.,, absenteeism records or number of resignations and reasons thereof;
- Occupational health and safety data, e.g.,, accidents or risk assessments – psychosocial hazards should be documented as part of the workplace risk assessment; in COVID-19 times, many people have been working from home, with the additional burden of having to take care of children and sometimes COVID-19 ill family members;
- Financial data, e.g., the cost of replacing employees who are on long-term disability leave;
- Health data, e.g., common health problems among the workforce as documented in Medical Aid or corporate health reports. In South Africa, medical insurers produce corporate health reviews annually; such analyses should include mental health conditions; corporate executives responsible for health and wellness should have access to such reports and should request these from the medical aid companies or from the brokers acting on their behalf.

Reviews of the incidence and prevalence of mental health conditions at a workplace could be conducted by analysing medical aid information (in annual corporate health reviews) EAP service provision (annual reports) and internal company occupational health risk assessments and data. Interviews or focus group discussions with key informants, such as employees, their families, managers, and medical personnel within the organization, all make the valuable contribution to understanding the current mental health trends in an organisation.

The needs assessment that follows should outline the gaps from both the quantitative and qualitative analyses compared to a best practice set of standards such as the ISO 45003.[15]

Step 2: Develop the workplace mental health policy

A workplace mental health policy comprises a vision statement, a statement of the values, guiding principles upon which the policy will be based, and a clear measurable set of objectives. Objectives translate the policy vision into concrete statements of what is to be achieved and is a direct response to the needs of the population at risk. They should be specific and achievable within specified timeframes. The vision statement presents a general image of the future of mental health in the workplace, and is usually aspirational, yet realistic, with high standards set, underpinned by values and principles. *"Values refer to judgements or beliefs about what is considered worthwhile or desirable, and principles refer to the standards or rules that guide actions, and should ultimately emanate from the values".*[10]

Step 3: Develop the strategy to implement the policy

We are all too familiar with robust policies that never get to be executed. A workplace mental health policy needs a strategy to be implemented. The specific strategies chosen will depend on the needs of the business and its employees and the resources available. The resources needed might include additional financing (for example, to establish an employee assistance programme) or the reallocation of funds that are currently used elsewhere (for example, negotiating with health clinic staff to conduct a mental health awareness campaign).

List of tasks to execute the strategy:

- Increase employee awareness of mental health issues;
- Support workers at risk;
- Change the organisation of service provision (outsourced, external or internal);
- Provide treatment for employees with a mental health problem;

- Change the organisation of work;
- Reintegrate employees with a mental health problem into the workplace;
- Ensure optimal resource allocation (roles, responsibilities, budgets);
- Project plan to implement the policy – set targets, outputs, deliverables, timelines, responsible individuals.

Step 4: Implement and evaluate

Implementation and evaluation of the programme on an ongoing, continuous basis would be a critical indicator of success, as would clear governance, financial and accountability frameworks. Emphasis is also placed on mental health planning and budgeting in an integrated general health service, in which mental health care is only one component among a range of other health care services. As mental health services are frequently integrated into general health care there may be certain aspects of the mental health budget that are subsumed under the general health budget. For example, mental health nurses at the primary care level may be funded from the general health budget. This means that an understanding of the needs of the population aligned with the best medical evidence and cost benefit analyses, is a key success indicator of such programmes and, when planned, budgeted for and monitored, allows for excellent outcomes in overall health and wellness.[17]

Some practical insights

As health professionals, we have been taught and continue to practice taking a good history of the presenting complaint, past medical history, occupational history (of all jobs held to date along with the exposures), habits and hobbies are all important and yes, a good history on the social determinants of health, completes the picture. As a health professional, a good practice is to be pragmatic and humble in your approach and normalise that reaching out for help and accepting that help, is ok, no stigma accorded. Health professionals are generally trusted individuals. Honour that trust and deliver on it. Go beyond the examination room and ensure that your patients receive the best biopsychosocial solution to their presenting complaint.

And follow up, follow up and follow up on your patients.

Go beyond wherever possible.

As a healthcare or non-healthcare professional working in a corporate setting, be "your brothers' and sisters' keepers". All of the above apply in supporting a colleague, referring a destitute colleague and reintegrating a rehabilitated colleague back at the workplace, through creating a supportive, aware and responsive working environment.

Another good practice is to be a team player. Health and wellness is a team sport. COVID-19 has taught us that so well. No one person can carry the load. It is a shared responsibility, playing the field, whilst focussing on the goals to be achieved.

Do not be afraid of the Boardroom.
Play in the Boardroom.
Be entrepreneurial.
Be innovative.
Be fearless.
Lastly: Remember the CEO's wise words. A gain for one is a gain for all.

Conclusion

The importance of instituting mental health programmes within the broader corporate risk management frameworks, and occupational health and wellness frameworks, has been framed to promote the integration of mental health initiatives into core business practices. The stories over the eras clearly demonstrate that with good, caring leadership and planning, robust mental health services can be integrated into existing health and wellness frameworks.

Let us not forget and not be forgotten like those lepers in Kosi Bay. We have learnt from our past – in the early days of the HIV epidemic, when we were helpless and hopeless without antiretroviral drugs and without EAP and mental health support. Now, in the throes of the COVID-19 pandemic, we are more aware of the tools at our disposal. Let us grasp the opportunities with open arms and hearts that do not prejudice the stricken individuals who need this support desperately. The COVID-19 pandemic will certainly not be the last one of its kind. We need to do all we can now to protect, prevent and preserve our mental health for eons to come as we tackle all our epidemics, past, present and future, with zest and energy.

Chapter 3

Trends in mental health in the workplace

Navlika Ratangee

South Africa, and South African corporates in specific, have seen an increase in mental health concerns over the recent years. According to the World Health Organisation (WHO)[1] 1 in every 4 people will struggle with a mental illness at some point in their lives. Of these people who struggle with mental health concerns, 75% don't get the treatment that they need.[2] It is no secret that South Africa has limited resources when it comes to the treatment of mental health, let alone the multidisciplinary approach and holistic treatment that is required for mental health. The global median of government health funding to mental health is less than 2%. The percentage of government health department expenditure devoted to mental health in South Africa is not known at a national level because budgets for mental health are integrated into general health budgets, particularly at primary care level. Of the 3 provinces (out of 9) that can report on mental health expenditure, spend was on average 5% of health budgets.[3] Mental health costs South Africa 2.2% of GDP.[4]

Looking more specifically at direct costs to the workplace Mall, et.al.[5] measured 'days out of role' (the inability to work or carry out day-to-day activities) and put the average individual figure at 28 days per year for anxiety disorders and 27 days per year for depression. What about the indirect costs; those who are not taking days off but are likely to be struggling with presenteeism in the workplace? It has thus become incumbent of employers to not only take more proactive steps in the management of employee's mental health, but from a productivity perspective to also play a role in the prevention of mental health concerns and preservation of a healthy work environment to support an employee's mental health. This has been noted as a complex task as one's mental health is a subjective experience. Furthermore, the complexity escalates as organisations find themselves dabbling between the virtual and physical workspaces. The advent of COVID-19 has further served to catapult the mental health and wellbeing agenda into every boardroom meeting. In fact, global megatrends highlight that mental health concerns will be a reality for 1 in every 2 people in the future.[6]

With the rising concern of mental health conditions that are prevalent in society and within the workplace and the increased attention that mental health has received as a result of the pandemic, this chapter intends to cover the main trends that organisations in South Africa are seeing with regards to the mental health of their employees. The understanding of such trends may assist organisations to revaluate their current mental health and wellbeing approach in the workplace, target certain areas that may require more urgent attention and look towards proactive steps that may be taken to incorporate employee mental health and wellbeing into the workplace culture, and workplace environment.

To put it into context, an adult spends approximately 80% of their adult lives in the workplace, and thus the workplace needs to be a conducive environment that enables productivity and mental health and wellbeing. This is why employers are paying more attention to this aspect of the workplace environment and workplace culture. Even though many people are working from home due to the pandemic, workplaces have come to acknowledge that in many instances this will be the way of the future for most organisations. In fact, people that still think that they are just waiting for everything to return to normal are considered to be living in denial. There is a need for everyone to move towards a space of acceptance where social distancing, mask wearing, working from home are the new norm. Thus even though employees are not in the physical work environment day-to-day they are inevitably working longer hours at home; feeling more stretched with juggling multiple roles and trying to balance home and work needs; some may even be required to take on a teacher's role with home schooling. These are just some of the factors that requires employers to look beyond the physical work environment as their only responsibility to look after employee mental health. In order to ensure employees can be productive in their work and home environment they need to ensure holistic support for employees to truly make a positive impact on employee health and wellbeing.

The role of stress and mental health

A person exposed to any type of life stressor, and we have all been exposed to some kind of stress at one point or another, may develop symptoms of mental illness. This in turn causes more stressors which cause more mental illness related symptoms. It is a vicious cycle, explaining how it can happen to any person, and can be triggered by the different stressors that one may be exposed to in the home or work environment. This emphasises the role of resilience as a critical area to discuss when talking about mental health which is covered in more detail in Chapter 15. Below is a visual of how the cycle tends to work:

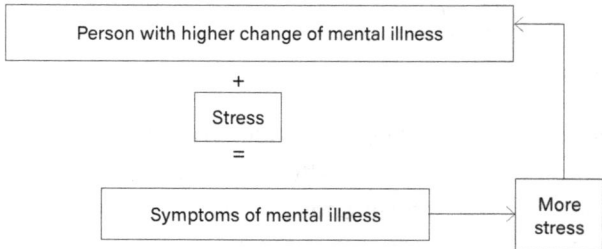

Figure 3.1: Role of stress and mental health

These stressors can often manifest in depression and anxiety related symptoms, which tend to be the most common in the workplace. The below diagram illustrates the workplace challenge in the manifestation of mental disorders, of the multiple reasons why employee seek assistance a huge percentage of them relate to mental health concerns as represented below.

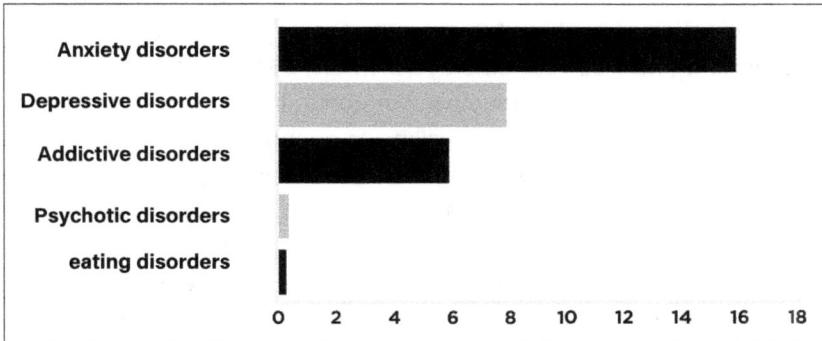

Figure 3.2: Manifestation of mental health disorders in the workplace. ICAS data[7]

This necessitates the need for workplaces to take the mental health of employees seriously as often the workplace is the context in which much of the stressors employees experience reside. In the current context of the pandemic, the workplace is no longer in a physical building but exists virtually as well. The pandemic has put the spotlight on wellbeing which has been welcomed. However, it is also true that wellbeing can be somewhat misunderstood as a destination for employees in the workplace, rather than an ongoing journey. This is an important consideration when thinking about what wellbeing means in the workplace, and what objectives are being put in place when thinking about employee mental health and wellbeing.

Given the above role of stress, it is also important to recognise the positive role a healthy dose of stress can play in maintaining one's mental health. It has been long understood that eustress (the good type of stress) drives one to solve problems, get creative and feel challenged and rewarded. This has a positive impact on feeling like a valuable contributor to the whole and can be considered as a driver of productivity. However, when the type of stress increases or feels completely overwhelming, so much so that it can feel debilitating, this is when mental health can be negatively impacted. Building one's ability to deal with stress and finding ways to self-soothe become an important part of one's resiliency and mental health and wellbeing toolkit. Yet another reason why workplaces need to seriously consider investing in employee mental health and wellbeing and associated stress management programmes within the workplace.

Investment trends in mental health

Wellbeing has been dubbed as the fourth bottom line in the workplace[8, 9], and with good reason. Included under the wellbeing umbrella are aspects of health, spirituality, growth, a deeper sense of self, culture, compassion and purpose. The impact of stress in the workplace and its converse relationship with productivity is increasingly catching the attention of leaders. According to Employee Wellness Industry trends[10] stress is a bottom-line issue for employers where 96% identified employee stress as the biggest challenge to a productive workforce. In the same report it is evident that the majority of organisations are willing to spend more on mental health. This recognises people as the greatest asset in this knowledge economy. The report showcases the top areas that organisations are willing to invest in when it comes to employee wellbeing. For 2021, employers are investing most in mental health (88%) nearly 9 out of 10 employers, telemedicine (87%), stress management/resilience (81%), mindfulness and meditation (69%), and COVID-19 risk intake/wellness passport (63%) programmes. With three out of five rising stars closely linked to mental health, as shown in diagram below, companies are extremely focused on and dedicated to supporting mental wellbeing. Organisations have understood the importance of mental health support and programmes, with the pandemic having accelerated the demand for mental health solutions.

RISING STARS

Percentage Of Employers Investing More

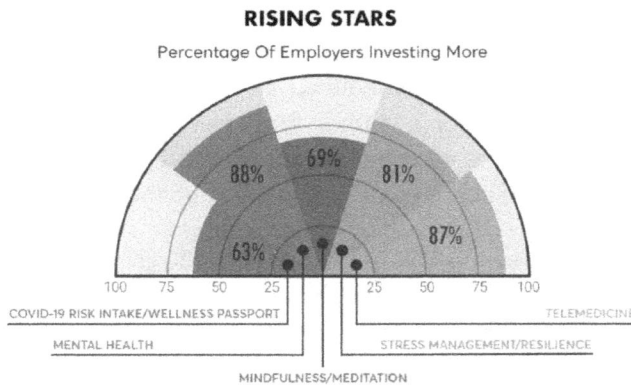

Figure 3.3: What employers are investing in. Employee Wellbeing Industry Trends[11]

Holistic wellbeing

In thinking about these solutions it is useful to bear in mind that support structures need to have a holistic approach. Wellbeing has multiple dimensions including physical wellbeing, intellectual wellbeing, environmental wellbeing, mental and emotional wellbeing, vocational wellbeing, social wellbeing, and spiritual wellbeing.

They all require attention, and they all impact each other. Mental health requires a holistic view and cannot be narrowed under the treatment of mental illnesses only. The focus needs to shift to how to enable individuals to thrive as opposed to managing their illnesses only. These wellbeing dimensions will be discussed in more detail in Part 2 of the book.

A consideration for the workplace in navigating the sphere of creating a space for employees to look after their holistic wellbeing is firstly creating awareness. In addition to the constant awareness it is important to have the space to deal with micro-challenges as they happen. These have a tendency to accumulate and build on one another. The potential to 'explode' on that one additional micro-challenge becomes likely. These micro-challenges take on different forms and triggers individuals in varied ways. This is outside of facing a macro-challenge where you are burdened with a number of life stressors all at once, or one massive blow in your life. The COVID-19 context has put a spotlight on holistic wellbeing, and the impact of both micro and macro challenges that people may be experiencing during this time. Gaining the necessary support when you are feeling wobbly, helps gain the necessary confidence and competence to feel like you can gain control once more, obtain perspective and meet the challenge head on. As human beings, we want to feel in control. When we feel out of control that is when we start to feel anxious. Having the necessary support, gaining confidence in that regard, puts you on a better grounding when the next challenge comes along. Hence the support structures provided by employers, often in the form of support programmes and employee benefits, should always be front of mind for the employee.

We often don't see an approaching threat until it is too late. Employees need to be educated on the signs and triggers for looking after one's own mental health. Workplaces play a role in creating such platforms to enable awareness and then to talk about such issues without fear of discrimination and stigma. Workplaces need to understand the various pain points that they will experience. Pre-empt that employees will be in crisis, help employees to identify these for themselves, and know how to identify employees in crisis. This is going to be critical to ensure employee mental health.

Managers need to be upskilled to pick up when an employee is not coping and requires some additional support. It is increasingly important for managers to play a more active role in the management of employee wellbeing. This becomes a critical skill for managing productivity within an organisation. As it stands many managers already feel crippled and incompetent when is comes to people-management issues. With the advent of dealing with employees remotely this is only overburdening the management layer of an organisation in feeling equipped to deal with employees as holistic beings. The responsibility to take care of oneself and one's wellbeing is hard enough, then to add the responsibility of being able to look after your employees and pick up when they are not coping along so many different dimensions need to be an intentional set of capabilities that an organisation wishes to build on. Something as simple as teaching managers how to meaningfully check-in with their employees can make all the difference. The intention is not for managers to become counsellors, but to educate them on their role in identifying, and sign posting employees to the necessary support. Moreover, it is also about creating the right environment that promotes an individual to thrive in the workplace and enable employee wellbeing. There needs to be a very intentional shift to creating a culture of care, and in the context of the hybrid workplaces that many are working within in, a virtual culture of care.

Remote working and creating a virtual culture of care

In the current context remote working has become the norm for many. It is here to stay as many organisations commit to enabling a hybrid model of working into the future for the next 5 years and beyond. Much is being learnt about enabling the most productive environment in such workplace structures, however one thing is for sure, employees and employers alike have already noted that firstly, remote working is not for everyone, and secondly, it compromises the sense of connection to the company culture, does not create a sense of wellbeing and does not create an environment for learning.[12]

The concept of creating a culture of care for your employees in the workplace has shifted to the virtual world. This requires a rethinking of workplace approaches in employee mental health and wellbeing. What does flexible working actually look like? How does the organisation enable true work-life integration? Some organisations have made structural shifts to facilitate this, others have looked at putting mental health days in place as part of company policy or even as a type of leave that can be applied for. Another idea is that of having meeting-free days, or meeting-free time zones within the day; facilitating getting up and moving during virtual meetings, or even having outside virtual meetings while taking a walk in your garden (where possible). These are not traditional approaches and organisations have been forced to think creatively and think outside of the box in enabling a virtual culture of care. It is an opportunity to get away from best practices and usher in new practices. It is an opportunity for all of us to learn, unlearn and relearn which also happens to be a key capability in how we deal with stressful situations. This can also be created by setting up a platform (structurally or even virtually) to share ideas; ideas on how employees are coping during this time, with the changing demands, with juggling multiple roles, with managing anxiety, etc.

Within the context of 4IR (the Fourth Industrial Revolution), technology has enabled the remote way of working and facilitated ways of connecting using digital platforms. As much as the increase in digitisation increases social isolation and a lack of human connectedness it has also enabled us to stay in touch digitally. Quite the paradox, it being a source of stress and part of stress management. This is the complexity of Generation C, the digital native, the employee that typically turns to the internet first to solve for anything, to get day-to-day activities done, to work and to play. Generation C is not specific to an age group. However, understanding how this group of employees use technology in their lives is a huge focus area in capitalising on how to solve for the challenges of remote working, creating a virtual culture of care and looking after one's wellbeing. It starts to also introduce the shift of 4IR to 5IR which is about putting the human back into the centre of everything, and how technology can enable that.

There has certainly been a change in the way in which people interact with one another, with how they work and play and even how they seek help. The pandemic has allowed the working class to accept the value of telemedicine and some even prefer this modality going forward. This has also paved the way for people to explore virtual counselling as a means of accessing the support they need. Research suggests that the value of virtual means of support is not only more convenient, and safer, it evidences that people go deeper into their issues, and reveal the real issues quicker. It is efficient and effective. Legislation, such as medical aid claim allowances, has further facilitated and enabled the acceptance of incorporating technology as a platform to provide support. These structural changes are here to stay.

The concept of remote working and the impact this has had on employees can also be extended to the rate of technological adoption. In some cases, employees took on the shift to digital platforms easily (less stressed for early adopters) while for others there may have been more resistance resulting in late adoption (more stress), and for some it may have felt like forced adoption (highly stressful). These employees may have felt like they had no choice and felt completely out of control which is not only highly stressful but results in high levels of anxiety as well. This highlights just one complexity in the interplay between digitisation and stress, and the role of technology and mental health. Organisations were mostly ill-equipped and under-prepared in dealing with this as a driver and source of mental health concerns.

Even though a lot more awareness of the impact of the current context on mental health has been created and to some extent has even been normalised on C-suite levels, a considerable amount of work still needs to be done to evolve as individuals and as organisations.

Workplace design and strategy

The workplace design and the workplace strategy require an intentional shift to attend to some of the mental health trends discussed in this chapter. Below are some further considerations in thinking about these shifts:

- Mental health and the responsibility thereof sit with both employer and employee. We all need to be held accountable for our own mental health; however, workplaces need to ensure the necessary support structures are in place which includes the aligning of workplace policies. Policies and procedures need to facilitate the above and protect the rights of everyone. Many organisations have only now looked at implementing mental health policies at work and some are seeing the benefit of writing down the unwritten rules. Mental health is not only HR's responsibility, it necessitates the entire organisation to mobilise resources and work towards creating a culture of care.

- From an office layout perspective, consider the shifts that are required to enhance collaboration on days that employees are in office. This needs to encourage compliance and social behaviour changes but also create a space for connectedness, meaning making and overall wellbeing.

- The concept of social vaccinations needs to be well understood. Whilst most of the world is abuzz with physical vaccinations, social vaccinations need to land with equal importance. The change in social behaviours that are required to adapt and transition is necessary (e.g., mask wearing, social distancing, hand washing, sanitising, etc.). Another focal point is the consideration of what are we doing to socially inoculate ourselves against mental health concerns? Getting employees to own their own journey (by providing the enabling environment and support structures) will help employees to build on their capabilities, gain control and confidence and give themselves back their power.

- The concepts of COVID fatigue, pandemic fatigue and even virtual fatigue are real. Many are talking about a time of "reset" or the new norm as well. Understand how this impacts individuals within your teams and get to know their personal situations and personal spaces (we are already being let into their personal spaces in video meets) in order to signpost them to the relevant support.

- An environment of psychological safety and flexibility needs to be created which includes a culture of understanding, acceptance, and inclusivity (free of stigma). This will also require a renewed focus on leadership style that includes the upskilling of the leadership layer to enable employee wellbeing. Leaders will need to display active and vocal support of mental health with sustained commitment and a preparedness to invest.

- A means of identifying and addressing "psychological hazards" in the workplace (i.e. a risk management framework to ensure risks are effectively identified, managed and controlled).
- Open up the channels for dialogue, concerns to be raised and an opportunity for supporting one another in these difficult times. Create the space to mourn losses. Awareness and education programmes go a long way in facilitating these.
- Programmes that enable individuals to be assessed, treated and/or referred (e.g., EHWP such as EAP, OH programmes). This includes programmes to manage and accommodate those who are disabled by mental illness.
- Communication is key. Consistent communication is important to assist in managing anxieties and uncertainties.
- Organisations would need to shift focus on outputs in the context of employee wellbeing. This will need to be aligned with performance management methods and measurements as well. Business targets would need to be readjusted and communicating this clearly would be useful to alleviate employee anxiety.
- Upon reintegration into the workspace consider the impact of stigma or discrimination that might exist in your employee population.
- Consider that employees find themselves in different spaces, and workplace interventions need to meet employees where they are at. Not everyone will be ready to take on resilience capabilities, some are already at the point of burnout and require a very different type of support to someone who is coping well and looking at how to maintain that. It is important that workplace support is both reactive and proactive in nature. Some are tired of coping ('resilience fatigue') and also need to know that it is okay not to be okay.
- In the context of all of the above, what do employee benefits in the future needs to look like?
- This is a prospect to turn a crisis into an opportunity for long-term organisational growth, organisational health and organisational purpose. Have a short-term view of the measures that need to be put in place, with medium-term and long-term objectives as well.

This chapter covered some of the mental health trends that workplaces need to be cognizant of that are evident in the current context. Some of these concerns arise pre-pandemic, some as a result of the pandemic and some will manifest post pandemic. Living in a VUCA (Volatility, Uncertainty, Complexity, Ambiguity) context there is growing recognition that the V for volatility needs to be replaced with V for vulnerability. We are all vulnerable to mental health concerns and an immediate focus on our wellbeing is required if we are to thrive today and tomorrow.

Chapter 4

The post pandemic context: trauma and fatigue

Navlika Ratangee

Every pandemic in history has shown us that not only is there an increase in mental health issues post a pandemic but that the trauma that remains in the system takes years to overcome. Right now, we are not living in the post-pandemic environment, we are still very much in the throes of the pandemic, the first global mass trauma event for several decades, arguably the first of its kind since World War 2, and likely the first of such severity in our lifetimes.

Trauma is an understated concept. It isn't just a word for something extremely stressful. It doesn't always come from short, sharp shocks like car accidents, hijackings, or house break-ins. It is also not post-traumatic stress disorder (PTSD) on its own. What trauma is about is events and their effect on the mind and what separates it from something merely stressful is how we relate to these events on a deep level of belief.[1] Even though there is debate of the true definition of trauma in such a situation, Jessi Gold, a psychiatrist at the Washington University School of Medicine, in St. Louis, thinks in terms of "big-T trauma" (the officially defined term) and "little-t trauma" (its colloquial cousin). Both meaningfully affect one's mental health.[2] When thinking about COVID-19, though, "trauma", let alone "mass trauma", may not be the first thing that springs to mind. Other frames of reference – economic, political, ecological, scientific – may seem more fitting. Media have tended to focus more on depression, anxiety, loneliness, and stress.[3]

Infectious disease outbreaks have widespread and pervasive detrimental effects on one's mental health manifesting in fear, distress and anxiety, and may further induce symptoms of depression.[4] Quarantine and social distancing is one of the major public health measures that is intended to prevent the further spread of an infectious disease, which has been shown to effectively contain a pandemic outbreak. However, the psychological impact of quarantine, including feelings of uncertainty, exhaustion, insomnia, and detachment from others, is wide ranging, long lasting, and substantial.[5] The ongoing exposure to danger, illness, death, disaster situations, stigma, and discrimination during a pandemic can induce an acute stress response and even cause post-traumatic stress reactions.[6]

What we are facing now in the midst of this pandemic is acute traumatic stress. COVID-19 is a direct threat to our lives or the lives of others we know. We are all either vicariously witnessing trauma, through media or through supporting others, or directly experiencing trauma, by becoming ill, isolated, or experiencing the plight of close others.[7] We all know, in some vague way, that "normal" has changed and the world will never be the same. These acute stress reactions are natural, but it is important to promote self-care, social support, and sleep, in order to prevent prolonged psychological consequences such as post-traumatic stress disorder and depression. These serious reactions are more likely to occur in people with a history of trauma, especially childhood trauma, but we can take steps to protect ourselves and minimise the negative consequences. Resilience and healing from trauma is something that happens best in the context of supportive relationships. This chapter focuses on the manifestation of trauma during and post pandemic and provides some detail on the protective factors in place that can result in post-traumatic growth as opposed to post-traumatic stress.

The stressed brain and fatigue

Given the context of stress, acute stress and even post-traumatic stress that people are being exposed to, it is useful to understand why this is the case. Human beings are wired to deal with stress. We all have a Threat Response System, even though the threshold for activation is different for different people. Some manage it more effectively than others and it also relates to our life experiences and learnt behaviour.

In a situation where we are not under stress, the prefrontal cortex is in action and directs decision making (the thinking part of the brain). See Figure 4.1 below. When faced with a stressful situation the prefrontal cortex shuts down and the primitive part of the brain takes over (the stressed brain). The Threat Response System is the instinctive way our brain and body react when we perceive a real, potential or even imagined threat. This is the sensible way to react as it ensures our survival when dealing with a threat in order to reduce the threat (fight, flight or fright response).

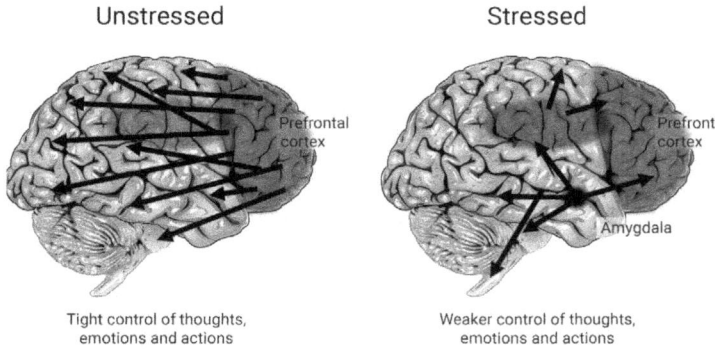

Unstressed   Stressed

Prefrontal cortex

Prefront cortex

Amygdala

Tight control of thoughts, emotions and actions

Weaker control of thoughts, emotions and actions

Figure 4.1: The brain's response to unstressful and stressful situations

In stressful situations we have weaker control of our emotions and typically experience emotions such as fear and anxiety. This is the natural response. Hence, in the context of the pandemic, it is normal to feel anxious and stressed at a time like this. The anxiety itself is actually adaptive, as it's there to try and warn us of danger and to tell us to do something quickly to react, to try and become safe. However, the difficulty is that we are not wired to deal with constant stress and the heightened state of arousal. We need to be able to move into an "unstressed" situation to feel like we can 'think' clearly again. The constant state of stress is not sustainable, and this results in one feeling overwhelmed and having mental health concerns.

As human beings we need to have a sense of control, and have our prefrontal cortex in the driver's seat. When we have lost our sense of control, which is one of the feelings resulting from the pandemic, there is an increase in uncertainty which causes an increase in anxiety. This also relates to the fatigue that many people are feeling. We also refer to 'pandemic fatigue' that people are experiencing, where they are tired in being in the heightened state of arousal (the stressed brain).

The experience of trauma in the context of the pandemic

Many people have been exposed to multiple traumatic scenes as a result of COVID, either real or through media from all over the globe. The emergence of mental disorders in vulnerable individuals is guaranteed. The most common disorders seen after a catastrophe are major depression, post-traumatic stress disorder, and anxiety disorders. Increases in alcohol and drug use and suicidal thoughts are also observed.[8] According to Mari and Oquendo[9] the different effects of the pandemic affect our mental health in different ways:

- The first impact of the virus was the acute stress reaction it brought on due to the fear of the unknown, the fear of contracting the virus or of passing it on to others. The pandemic itself can be considered a traumatic event.[10]

- The next impact on our mental health was the need to quarantine. While quarantine is necessary for fighting the pandemic, the sudden change in routine and the confinement can lead to feelings of helplessness, boredom, anxiety, anguish, irritability and anger at the loss of freedom. These reactions can be simply a situational adjustment to the new reality and not necessarily pathological. After all, being depressed and anxious is a normal reaction to the existing insecurity. Nonetheless, the mental health effects of quarantine themselves are remarkably similar to those of traumatic events.[11] The CDC survey data reported that nearly 41% of respondents are struggling with mental health issues stemming from the pandemic.[12] The issues are related to the pandemic and to the measures set up to contain it, including stay-at-home orders and social distancing.

- Another major impact on our mental health relates to the high numbers of deaths resulting from COVID-19 – overwhelming hospitals, mortuaries, and funeral homes. Without the usual farewell rituals, such as spending time with the person as they are dying or having funerals, cases of complicated grief with depression and risk of suicide may increase.[13]

- The individual perceptions of those that have been admitted to intensive care units have been further impacted with some developing future episodes of major depression, post-traumatic stress disorder, and other psychiatric conditions. An estimated one-fifth of the virus' millions of patients require hospitalisation and this is experienced as a considerable trauma.[14]

- Financial impact and loss, unemployment, food insecurity, and increased social inequality are all generating acute stress likely to become chronic stress for many.[15] This increases the risk for mental disorders.

The population most severely exposed to stress during COVID-19 are the health professionals on the frontlines. They are subject to significant physical and emotional demands, often with insufficient assistance or personal protective equipment to guarantee safety. This population is placed at further risk due to the daily suffering witnessed, and the difficult ethical decisions to be made.[16]

Trauma is also being experienced in other ways including invisible losses, secondary trauma, survivor guilt, the impact of 'long COVID' (referring to the ongoing impact of COVID physically and mentally on an individual). The invisible losses refer to a communal sense of grief at the loss of how things were, and anticipatory grief at the threat of loss of life.[17] Another common feeling is moral distress and outrage, expressions of anger at witnessing injustice and poor management of our national crisis.[18] There may be an increase in the risk of burnout and secondary trauma if organisational leadership struggles to provide support to their employees during the pandemic.[19]

Collective trauma or mass trauma occurs when an entire society feels this intense threat or overwhelming amount of stress that exceeds one's ability to cope.[20] It takes place when the same event, or series of events, traumatises a large number of people within some shared time span. The COVID-19 pandemic is considered collective trauma due to the intense threat experienced by many that we or our loved ones will become seriously ill and die and are experiencing related concerns about our ability to access resources, maintain employment, care for others, and manage ongoing physical isolation.

After the pandemic ends, the effects of the mass trauma it has inflicted will linger across societies for years. Trauma impacts our ability to make meaning, the lens through which we see and experience is interrupted when we experience trauma and extreme feelings of helplessness. Of critical importance here, is children's experience of mass trauma. Their view of the world being a terrifying place, adults that are not coping, may permanently colour their worldview.[21] This can lead to intergenerational problems once they grow up and have kids of their own. Trauma can be transmitted through unconscious imitation and conscious conditioning.[22]

Post-traumatic stress disorder (PTSD)

Let's home in on PTSD. Post-traumatic stress disorder (PTSD) is a potentially debilitating mental health disorder which affects an important minority of people exposed to events involving actual or threatened death, serious injury or sexual violence. The COVID-19 pandemic is unfortunately providing multiple opportunities for people to experience traumatic situations which may lead to PTSD.[23]

Pre-pandemic about six million South Africans 'could' be suffering from post-traumatic stress disorder (PTSD).[24] A study by Yuan, Gong, Liu, et al.,[25] on past pandemics showed that the estimated prevalence of PTSD on the general population after a pandemic is between 22% and 26%. Only a few studies of mental health problems among patients hospitalised with COVID-19 have been published, with more to come. A study of hospitalised but stable patients found a high prevalence of post-traumatic stress symptoms (PTSS) of 96.2%.[26] Davydow, Gifford, Desai, et.al.[27] reports that up to 20% of intensive care unit survivors go on to develop PTSD. These results indicate that PTSD is common in individuals who experience infectious diseases outbreaks, which may persist over a relatively long period of time. With the spread of the COVID-19 pandemic, the global estimate of burden of PTSD following a pandemic is vital for the development of intervention and management strategy.[28]

PTSD or a recent traumatic experience can also cause brain fog. 'Brain fog' is a loose term which describes a feeling of mental fatigue characterized by a lack of mental clarity (as described by the 'stressed brain'), feeling emotional, tiredness, forgetfulness and difficulty concentrating. It can also be caused by experiencing chronic stress, chronic fatigue, diet, hormonal changes, certain medications, medical conditions, and mental health difficulties.[29] One of the reasons that PTSD causes brain fog is that the brain is not functioning optimally if you have PTSD (refer to discussion of brain response in Figure 4.1).

PTSD can also result in an increase in stress hormones moving around the body. This can disrupt our sleeping patterns and quality of sleep. PTSD affects memory making our mind and body feel as if it is still under threat. When you are trying to sleep your mind and body still thinks and feels as if it is trying to fight off a potential threat. This can result in fatigue caused by the stress or fight or flight response being permanently turned on.

Moral injury

Another important risk factor for PTSD is moral injury, which is defined as the psychological distress, including feelings of deep shame and guilt, resulting from doing, or not preventing, events that someone believes are "wrong".[30] Individuals experience moral injury when they are not able to act in ways that are in line with their core values due to the pandemic.

Moral injury is an important framework to help understand the mental health impact associated with the current coronavirus pandemic. It can predispose people to developing PTSD as well as making it less likely that they will seek treatment if they do.[31] Around 20% of healthcare workers face post-traumatic effects through moral injury by virtue of the work that they do and the daily decisions they have to make.[32] Feeling unable to deliver high-quality care or having to make hard choices about who will and who will not receive a given intervention due to shortage of available equipment, have become somewhat commonplace, especially when the rates of hospitalisation are high.

Moral injury is also a relevant concept outside of work environments. Many individuals have had to make difficult choices that contrast with their morals and values during this pandemic. Some may have made decisions that they regret, resulting in another high risk-person being infected with coronavirus and becoming seriously ill or dying. Others may have ongoing guilt, linked to the survivor guilt mentioned earlier, because they needed to make decisions that resulted in others losing their jobs when they had families to support.

Experiencing grief and loss

The pandemic has caused loss of everything we are familiar with, including our daily structure, and for some, jobs and social contacts. It had led to serious financial despair, illness, and death. There are thus a range of emotional responses including grief, loss, and mourning resulting in a number of mental health concerns.

Grief is normal and requires a period of mourning. There is no particular timing to grieve. In fact, grief can begin even in anticipation of loss (anticipatory grief), or it might be delayed for some time. When considering how grief shifts shape over time, it is important to recognise that we are never "done" with it, just as we are not done with whomever or whatever we have lost.[33] Grief isn't predictable. It doesn't involve clearly defined stages. It doesn't unfold linearly. It doesn't necessarily end in acceptance (hence the stages of grief are not being addressed here). It carves long, meandering, and varied paths that popular myths do little to prepare us for.

Grief relating to the loss of a loved one has its own complications. Each death leaves an average of nine close relatives bereaved.[34] Prolonged grief, which affects approximately 10% of bereaved people, is characterized by at least six months of intense longing, preoccupation or both, with the deceased; emotional pain; loneliness; difficulty re-engaging in life; avoidance; feeling life is meaningless; and increased suicide risk.[35] These conditions can also become chronic with additional comorbidities, such as substance use disorders.

The opportunity for post-traumatic growth

With the impact of stress and trauma on individuals and groups it is necessary to understand that there is an opportunity for post-traumatic growth as opposed to post-traumatic stress. Post-traumatic growth refers to the transformative process that leads to recovery and positive changes in perception and relationships as a person creates new meaning out of a traumatic experience.[36] It takes an update and reframing of your beliefs and sense of self, a new round of "meaning-making", to work through the trauma's impact.

Early screening and timely evidence-based interventions and social support should be applied to potentially mitigate post-pandemic PTSD and related psychological problems during COVID-19 and future pandemics.[37] Job satisfaction was associated with lower PTSD symptom scores and positive coping.[38] Other practical measures that create opportunities for post-traumatic growth or act as protective factors include:

- Using strategies to reduce stress throughout the day, including statements that support a resilient mindset (see more in Chapter 15), as well as mind-body exercises that reduce stress reactions such as breathing exercises, meditation, physical activities (with physical distancing).

- Ensuring adequate PPE, handwashing, decontamination of surfaces, and practising safety behaviours assist in managing anxiety (and play a role in reducing moral injury).

- Developing personnel policies that reassign at-risk medical personnel away from high-risk sites assists with exposure management.

- Some mental health care advocates believe the general population may be suffering from various levels of vicarious traumatisation, although strictly speaking, this would not qualify for PTSD's Criterion A for trauma exposure.[39] Czeisler, Lane, Petrosky, et al.[40] stressed the need to identify at-risk individuals to develop policies to address health inequities, and to increase resources for identifying mental health problems and offering new treatment options, including telehealth treatments.

- Manage the overflow of media, and impact of incorrect information. Switch off when you can and recognise the impact social media has on your anxiety and energy levels.

- Stress the importance of self-care as a key protective factor. Take rest when you can.

- Access to support services such as psychological services. Telehealth services have proved to assist in identifying and treating mental health conditions, including depression, PTSD and other trauma-related disorders, substance use disorders, and suicidal ideation.

- Workers should have adequate rest and breaks, encouraged to check in on themselves and their mental and emotional wellbeing, be excused from less-essential tasks, and have regular information and feedback sessions with managers and the community.

- Stay connected to support systems with precautions of physical distancing or by using interactive internet-based platforms, to ward off the negative impact of social isolation.

- Confine your workspace to a specific clear area in your home so your job doesn't intrude on your personal needs. Use this same space regularly to work. This will focus your mind and increase your productivity. End the work day with clear boundaries. Put away electronic devices and work tools at the end of your work day and set clear hours in the day for work. Easier said than done; however try to implement some of these boundaries to manage levels of anxiety and fatigue.

- Be extra kind to yourself. This is a hard time for everyone. Humans across the world are sharing this experience with you. We are all in this together and we may all emerge with a renewed appreciation for our interconnectedness. Helping others in need is both critical to get through this well, and creates more purpose to our days and wellbeing.

- Perhaps more than anything else, though, the lasting social dangers of mass trauma consist in forgetting. When it goes unprocessed, undiscussed, perhaps actively repressed, the group's social issues remain disturbed and unhealed. National commemoration, art, literature, and memoirs, for example, are frequent keystones for remembering and may even assist in our preparedness for future crisis.[41]

Conclusion

This chapter looked at the impact of stress, trauma and fatigue within the context of the pandemic and post pandemic. It is clear that there are multiple factors at play that will result in an increase in mental health concerns. Bereavement, isolation, loss of income, and fear are triggering mental health conditions or exacerbating existing ones. Encouragingly, employers are taking notice (Employee wellbeing trends report) and recognising the importance of providing adequate support for employees to deal with these issues.[42] Certain individuals are more at risk than others for the multitude of reasons discussed above. However, the statistics show a considerable number within the population has been and will be affected. Trauma is not so simple. This not only has serious implications on workplace productivity, but also has intergenerational impact.

Chapter 5

Reflections on the relationship between mental health, work, and the workplaces

Angela Whitford du Plessis

For many decades – until around the 1980s in South Africa – the worlds of work and mental health did not intersect in an organised way. Students trained in Counselling Skills, both within the professions of Psychology and Social Work, were largely not taught to interrogate the work and work-life experience of clients in either the diagnosis or treatment of mental health issues. Instead, family relationships, both current and past, were focused on. Thus, a great deal of information was lost in the belief that mental health issues arose from early relationships and experiences. Indeed, the work milieu provides a visible environment in which workers engage in roles, tasks, routines, and relationships. Any deviations away from expected behaviour can offer valuable diagnostic information. In the same way, the dynamics of the workplace can be adapted to facilitate and sustain interventions in mental health problems.

Gradually, over the years, the worlds of work and mental health became closer and begun to intersect. A detailed historical overview of this is beyond the scope of this chapter; suffice it to say that several national challenges coalesced in a way that encouraged conversations and problem solving between workplaces and mental health practitioners. The challenges included high levels of alcohol and drug dependency (in which SANCA played a pioneering role) and the HIV/AIDS epidemic. Together with these factors, there followed an acknowledgement of widespread mental health issues such as PTSD, depression, and anxiety disorders in the lives of working people. Employee Assistance Programmes mushroomed from the mid-1980s onwards and are now the norm for medium and large employers.

Another variable that played a role in building relationships between workplaces and mental health professionals was the fact that many HR and IR professionals were trained in psychology which helped create a mental health agenda at some workplaces. Early initiatives included programmes for preparing employees for retirement as well as support services for retrenched employees. Psychosocial problems resulting from the migrant labour system were apparent over many decades and social work professionals were employed in large numbers at the hostels in the mining sector.

Workplaces are important sites for the delivery of mental health services for several reasons. Two major arguments are proffered here. The first is that workplaces comprise many people from all walks of life. At some stage during their employment, they, or someone in their family, will face a mental health issue. Many of these are common stressful events encountered at different life stages and would include divorce, health issues such as cancer, depression following the death of a family member, physical injuries following an accident, and so on. Making mental health services accessible to workplaces simply makes good sense.

The second argument is that work itself – and/or relationships at work – may cause or exacerbate mental health problems. A wide array of dynamics experienced at the workplace and within specific work teams can influence the mental health of people, either in a negative way, or, indeed, the opposite – in a positive way. Such dynamics are important in the diagnosis and treatment of mental health concerns of employees.

On the positive side, many employees find meaningfulness in their work which can become a tremendous source of self-validation as well as a confidence booster. Factors which would play a role in this positive scenario would be a supportive manager, healthy relationships with colleagues, interesting and challenging work, as well as a feeling of being adequately rewarded. It is perhaps trite to say that the way an employee experiences his/her workplace dynamics is clearly subjective. Some employees may thrive in a highly stressful environment with stretched goals, while other people would find this too challenging.

Expanding on the above point about subjectivity, a useful and simple concept is that of intent versus impact. This can be enormously helpful in diagnosing the source of conflict in interpersonal relationships at work. Simply put, a well-intentioned comment or action may land badly on the recipient given several factors – unconscious bias, cultural differences, differences in values – to name but a few. A common scenario is, for example, a white manager commenting on a black subordinate's command of the English language ("Your English is really very good"), or perhaps a manager failing to greet an employee for whom greeting is a significant sign of respect. For the employee, the interaction may be experienced as a "Micro-Aggression". If such experiences persist, the affected employee may feel extremely aggrieved, hurt and disrespected and that could lead to a crisis of self-confidence.

Related to the above point, which can also have implications for feelings of self-worth, is the concept of "inclusivity". Diversity and inclusivity are terms used frequently as drivers of healthy teams. In practice, it is easy to see that central to the concept of inclusivity is the feeling that the person representing a form of diversity, or "difference", within a team feels genuinely welcomed and is made to feel comfortable. What is important here is new employees feeling supported by all team members while they transition into a new position if this is the case. Central to feeling welcomed is the amount of curiosity and interest the manager has in the employee – where they literally (and figuratively) have come from and what their aspirations are. Should employees feel "unwelcome" at their workplace, this too can lead to outcomes that include a crisis of self-confidence, depression, helplessness, and anxiety, as well as a loss of confidence in their competency.

So, paradoxically, work can boost, or detract from, one's sense of self-worth and consequent mental health concerns. A theme that is noticeable in practice is the role work can play in changing a person's "script" about themselves with some surprising results which may be positive, or negative, for the employee.

Scripts are the messages we get about ourselves that, consciously or unconsciously, play over and over in our heads. These messages are shaped by what we are told about ourselves as we grow up – from parents, teachers, and society in general. At a simple level, there are two basic messages which are "I am good enough" or "I am not good enough". People with intact beliefs about themselves may literally unravel due to experiences of being incompatible with a manager, team member(s) or with a workplace culture that shatters the person's belief in themselves and their competencies.

And yet, the opposite effect may occur where people with low self-confidence, get boosted at work due to positive interactions with their manager and team members because they are made to feel welcome, are given meaningful work, receive positive feedback, are promoted, and generally affirmed as valued contributors.

The major focus of this chapter will be on real examples from practice that illustrate many of the points made thus far and highlight other dynamics within workplaces that may impact on employees' mental health. The final section looks at the idea of having difficult conversations in the workplace as this can often be a barrier to sorting out hurtful dynamics. Such conversations include giving feedback to a manager or a colleague on how their actions and behaviours are negatively impacting on them, causing hurt, harm or feelings of being harassed.

Before going on to examples from practice, it is important to clarify the author's understanding of "mental health issues" at the workplace. These issues may not be dramatic breakdowns which end up in an employee being stretchered out of the office (although this can happen). Often, the mental health issue may be a low-grade masked depression, feelings of helplessness and of being trapped in an unhappy work environment or feeling sad or regretful about achievements at the workplace, or perhaps life in general as well as feeling shamed or harassed or filled with self-doubt. In the language of labour relations practitioners, the symptoms of these mental health afflictions may be found in increased disciplinary cases, grievances, resignations, interpersonal workplace disputes as well as disengagement and the withdrawal of labour.

The following sections will look at several scenarios that have led to many of the problems highlighted so far. They cover experiences of poor leadership, sexual harassment, racism, and incompatibility.

Poor leadership

The majority of employees would agree that the most important relationship at work is with the person to whom you report. It is also common knowledge that when employees resign, the major reason for this has to do with a troubled relationship with their superior. It is also known that most leadership training interventions begin with leaders getting to know themselves better and an important aspect of this is gaining an insight into their impact on their team members.

The two scenarios that are described in this section deal with the experiences of two teams with leaders that, unfortunately, had no insight at all into their leadership style, with consequent negative effects on their team members.

The first team belonged to a large organisation and was based at their Head Office. The team, comprising professionals who performed well, eventually approached a senior manager to discuss their unhappiness with their leader. A huge concern was that a high proportion of the team had had to be hospitalised (some more than once) for stress and depression. An outside consultant with a mental health background was asked to interview all the team members and furnish the organisation with a report diagnosing the team dynamics.

To sum up the findings, before going into some detail of the dynamics, the leader had created an extremely hostile environment for his team – the exact opposite of what a leader should do.

There were four main dynamics that lead to the team's distress, the symptoms of which included both physical and mental health issues. The first was that the manager simply gave no support to team members. He repeatedly told them that they were not "Head Office" material. He showed no interest in his staff and would blame them for his errors. The second dynamic was that he simply had no respect for his staff. He often belittled their long tenure in the organisation and simply gave them no feedback at all on how they were doing. He displayed little trust in the team and would often bang his fists on his desk and shout at his staff during fits of anger. He never walked around to meet or greet his staff.

The third dynamic was his bullying and undermining behaviour, some of which has already been described. He constantly reminded his staff that he was the "boss". When a team member entered his office with a query or in need of guidance, the manager did not listen to them, changed the subject, went off at a tangent and would proceed to lecture his staff like school children. They would leave his office distraught and frustrated.

The fourth tendency of this manager was that he simply gave no direction in respect of the team's work. He never called team meetings to look at forward planning and when new team members joined, he did not introduce them to the rest of the team.

When interviewed by the external consultant, the manager never mentioned his role in the team's level of distress. He blamed the culture of the organisation which he said led to employees' disengagement from their roles and he mentioned that bullying of staff was organisation-wide and that the tough environment created anxiety. He saw the team dynamics as a reflection of the bigger system. The manager also commented that his saying that his team members were not Head Office material was "supportive", while the impact on the team was a total undermining of their self-confidence.

The consequences for the team were enormous. In a typical flight/fight response, some were planning to leave and staff who had tried to fight, felt exhausted and depleted. The manager had created a crisis of confidence within the team as they were questioning their own competencies which had never happened to any of them before. All people in the team lived with high degrees of anxiety and fear. In addition, some staff suffered from migraines, as well as the anxiety and depression that required in-patient treatment. One employee's medical team suggested that as part of his recovery, he be removed from his current role in the organisation.

The external consultant reported on the above to members of the executive team but was not involved in any intervention and thus does now know what the outcome was.

The second scenario concerned a small team with a female manager. This manager's technical work was praised by the organisation's Head Office and she had the support of the CEO. An outside consultant was asked to undertake a team process and, as part of the preparation for the intervention, all members of the team were interviewed separately to see what they would like to get out of the team process to maximise the time together.

The employees all had one major concern – that of their leader. Her style of managing had a very deleterious effect on the team members individually. Everyone experienced the working environment as unsafe and hostile. Their fears of being victimised were very real as each team member had indeed been victimised. All team members were silenced as they were afraid to speak up. The leader simply disregarded her staff's feelings, and their family responsibilities were minimised. She set totally unrealistic deadlines and would wait until the last minute to brief her team members on upcoming work. She would forbid some staff members from leaving their seats to go to the bathroom or leave the office for lunch. She often remarked that work, not reflecting on feelings, was the primary aim at the office. She would "listen" to staff but then simply do what she decided was the correct action, often citing her rank as leader.

One of the most concerning issues was that problems that arose in the office were individualised. For example, if staff raised issues around their treatment at work, they would end up being referred for counselling or coaching. The leader did not like it when staff gathered, even in two's, to "chat" for fear that they were plotting something or talking about her. At one stage she forbade conversations between staff and said that all conversations had to go through her and commented that staff must not get involved in others' dissatisfactions. Thus, she avoided dealing with issues collectively. Her style was that of 'Critical Parent' which of course automatically hooked 'Angry or Withdrawn' Child(ren)[1] One of her favourite remarks which she repeated frequently was "You guys are so relaxed, it could lead to discipline".

However, if the leader was ever confronted, she immediately felt victimised and betrayed.

All of the above dynamics within this office left employees feeling disempowered, angry and frustrated. Many of them suffered from health problems which were either caused or exacerbated by their work environment.

The following are some direct quotes from the team:

"To work here, you have to say goodbye to your inner peace."

"She kills my passion."

"You have to obey her."

"If you speak your mind, you will be side-lined and not greeted."

"I dread coming to work."

Sexual harassment

The next topic to be dealt with is Sexual Harassment and the mental health consequences for those who experience this scourge at the workplace. The author has dealt with many cases since the mid 1980s and has personally seen the negative effects on both the victims as well as bystanders and an organisation as a whole in which the harassment has taken place.

There are four related descriptors that can be used to summarise sexual harassment cases – Emotional, Complex, Disruptive and Divisive. These will be the themes of this section, as will become apparent in the content. Although it is known that men are also victims of sexual harassment, most cases that are reported concern women. Before going on to some case scenario's, some general remarks about sexual harassment are proffered.

The effects of sexual harassment are common across most cases. Being sexually harassed is experienced as unwanted, humiliating, degrading and distressing. Often victims suffer harassment over a long period of time with quite severe mental health consequences. An important consideration is that frequently, victims are silenced and may take some time to report their harassment. This is because, for many victims, once they experience harassment, they feel some guilt and shame. The first question they frequently ask themselves is: "Did I do anything to encourage this?" Many years ago, a manager took his PA out for lunch and in the car coming back to the office, he placed his hand on her thigh, making his intentions quite clear. Despite being encouraged to report this, she refused and said: "I think I smiled too much at lunch." One of the worst cases of silencing of victims the author has encountered was three very senior women who sat on the Exco of their company (they worked for the same employer but at different operations). All three had been severely sexually harassed by male colleagues over long periods of time. One of the victims eventually plucked up the courage to tell their functional director who probed and identified the other two victims. What is so unexpected about this was that these women had agency to talk up and yet were silenced. Many victims are not senior in an organisation and may thus feel powerless to act on their own behalf. The three women in this case all had lived with guilt, shame and depression for a long period.

The reasons for victims feeling silenced include secondary trauma in not being believed or wanting to avoid facing cross-examination in a formal legal process, including a Disciplinary Inquiry at work. Some people fear that they will be seen as a "troublemaker" or harm the career of the harasser, as well as present as a reputational risk to their employer.

The definition of Sexual Harassment is broad, ranging from touching, innuendos, unwelcome enquiries into a person's sex life all the way to assault and rape. It also covers the telling of offensive jokes and remarks about people's appearances. One of the complicating factors here is that it is the impact on the victim that is regarded as important, as opposed to the intention of the harasser. This means there is a subjective element in assessing what is offensive behaviour. Five people may witness someone's behaviour or something that is said and there could be five different responses, ranging from indifference and mild offence, to feeling highly degraded or humiliated. This can cause disruption in an organisation when, for example, people know that a colleague has reported an action or utterance as sexual harassment and there is disagreement as to whether the action indeed falls into the definition of sexual harassment. Often colleagues fall into different camps and take sides with either the victim or harasser and this can lead to a great deal of discomfort in a work team or an organisation.

Related to the above, are two scenarios that may play out, both with mental health implications. An employee may choose not to report a matter because they fear being isolated by work colleagues as the perpetrator is a powerful and/or popular member of staff. They may choose to resign or put up with the harassment, rather than being seen as a pariah. The second scenario is when a person does report sexual harassment, the very people who should support them, in fact do not. Their experiences may be minimised or trivialised, not believed, or the victim may be encouraged to leave the organisation.

Just to expand on what can be dreadful consequences for the victim of sexual harassment, the author some years ago did a series of talks on Sexual Harassment Awareness Raising. During question time in one session, a senior woman shared the following story. She had been sexually harassed at her previous employer and had chosen to resign and take her ex-employer to court. Five years later her case was still in the court process and she continued to receive calls late at night with threats to harm her children if she pursued the court case.

The next case was a very unusual scenario. It touches on a subject that is extremely sensitive – that of false allegations of sexual harassment in the workplace. It is sensitive because some people believe that if this topic is raised, it will feed into the misperception that many cases are indeed false accusations. This is not the case. In dealing with sexual harassment for over three decades, the author has encountered false allegations on two occasions.

In this case a woman accused her boss of sexual harassment. Two in-depth investigations revealed the claims to be unsubstantiated. Indeed, the employee was herself guilty of sexual harassment. The case had dragged on for many weeks. What is important for this section of the chapter is to reflect on the disruptive impact this had on the management team. In the words of the CEO, "*She broke the team*" and "*she chose stuff that breaks families down*". The employee knew she was going to be dismissed for poor performance and had said to her manager (the accused): "*I know that I am going down, but I am not going alone and am taking you down with me.*"

The final topic on sexual harassment covers a concept which the author has described as "Dealing with the Fallout". As has been shown in the above paragraphs, sexual harassment cases can be very disruptive in a workplace. People take sides, groups become polarised, bystanders are often quite negatively affected and frequently there are rumours and half-truths abound, about what has happened. If a disciplinary case goes ahead, people will be divided on whom they believe was fairly, or unfairly, treated. There may be correct or incorrect information about who gave what evidence at the hearing. In one organisation, three years after the harasser had been dismissed, feelings remained strongly polarised and there was a lot of misunderstanding about who supported whom during the hearing. One way of dealing with this, is to identify those people affected and assist with debriefing them so that they know the correct facts and have an opportunity to ask questions and hear people debunking some of the myths that may hang around an organisation for such a long time. Such debriefings may take place with an individual or with a team or group of employees. This must be done considering the principles of confidentiality, which may differ from case to case.

Racism/allegations of racism

For any person at a workplace who feels marginalised because of their race and experiences both direct and/or indirect discrimination will find this situation extremely challenging. It would be hard to find any workplace in South Africa in which such dynamics have not been raised – formally or informally. Some victims of racism at work will choose to leave their environment but many people are not able to do this and find themselves stuck in difficult circumstances that may include daily humiliation.

One insight that makes dealing with racial disputes very tricky is the fact that people with rank (power and privilege) do not know they have it. It is simply taken for granted. If pressed, the person may concede that they have privilege but then will argue that anyone else could have these too, if they work hard enough. This is simply to misunderstand structural racism.

Many years ago, a team went away for a day's facilitated session to deal with the issue of racism in their team. Shortly after the session began, the pattern of communication got stuck as it had so often before: black employees told their white colleagues that there was both overt and covert racial discrimination in their team and within their organisation. Then, as commonly experienced, their white colleagues denied this and told their black colleagues they were being too sensitive and exaggerating their experiences. A frequent refrain in this team was that black consultants had to work "212%" harder than their white colleagues to get the same recognition. This was raised again and once more the white colleagues said this was untrue. Then a white male colleague stood up to what was being said as factually correct. He had two consultants report to him and the black consultant definitely had to work twice as hard to get the same recognition. Suddenly the white colleagues believed what was being said as it came from a white "voice".

The fact is that people who have never felt marginalised, and always been part of the "in-group", struggle to pick up subtle and nuanced (as well as quite direct) forms of discrimination and can remain unaware of the hurtful impact of an interaction they may witness or indeed be part of. The effect of working in such an environment can be quite cataclysmic – feelings of helplessness, deep frustration, depression and resignation that may all have mental health implications.

In mediating racial disputes at workplaces, white employees often argue that apartheid has been gone for over two decades. One of the many ingredients missing from that simplistic notion is intergenerational hurt and indignity that their parents and grandparents (and indeed all their ancestors) had to suffer before and during the years of systematic institutionalised discrimination which, no matter the current circumstances of their family, are distressing and humiliating. When someone comments: "Would you expect Jewish people to forget about the Holocaust?" there is often a long silence. Any group of people who have faced systematic discrimination listen with "wounded ears" that make them extremely sensitive to any verbal or other interaction which may contain perhaps anti-Semitic or racial slurs. The impact of such comments or behaviour may go unnoticed by people who have not experienced being part of a marginalised group.

Recently, the issue of Unconscious Bias has received some attention at workplaces. As South Africans, many people are aware of their conscious biases but, by their very definition, unconscious biases are those we are not aware of – our "blind spots". Awareness programmes around these dynamics have sprung up but often do not have a lasting effect in a workplace. People may have gained some insight in the moment, but this has often dissipated after a few days. What may happen though is that individuals from different races who work together may develop a friendship and begin to be curious about the other person's life. Too often it is simply easier to judge a person from another race group according to a set of stereotypes. As someone once wrote in a popular magazine: *"If you don't like someone, get to know them better."*

Previously in this chapter the concept of "Micro-Aggressions" was briefly mentioned. It is worth elaborating on in the context of racial disputes and of course it can be useful in all sorts of other "isms" – sexism, ageism, homophobia and so on. Micro-Aggressions refer to comments or actions that subtly, unconsciously, or unintentionally express a prejudice towards a marginalised group. But the "rub" lies in the fact that the perpetrator is not able to see this and will insist that he/she does not possess such biased attitudes. The person emphatically denies that they hold such attitudes, and this makes changing their behaviour, or perhaps mending a relationship, exceedingly difficult.

Mental health practitioners who are involved in interventions across racial divides will know that words chosen in difficult conversations are important. Many people were brought up on the saying: *"Sticks and stones may break your bones, but words will never hurt"*. This is not true. Another related set of homilies says that over 90% of the impact of a verbal interaction is the non-verbal dynamics, including tone of voice. However, when unpacking the source of interpersonal conflict in many workplace disputes where there are allegations of discrimination, it has been one word, or a few words, that have led to a deterioration between, say, a manager and a subordinate. Some examples may be found during Performance Management feedback sessions where a white manager is telling a black subordinate that his/her performance is not at an acceptable level. In one example, an outside consultant was facilitating a conversation in which the manager was attempting to give feedback on the subordinate's performance. The intention was to give positive feedback and it went something like this: "You really did such good work with the client who in turn gave you are very high rating and that was really good, because when you started here, you fumbled..." All the black subordinate heard was the word "fumble" and that signalled the end of their relationship. In such cases the message will confirm a script that the person has of not being "good enough" or that it could be interpreted as being "stupid". This may have devastating consequences and lead to a crisis of confidence.

In many race disputes there seems to be common theme of two intersecting stereotypes: white South Africans seem to want to "catch" black South Africans being incompetent while black South Africans similarly want to "catch" white South Africans being racist. This can set up an unhelpful, almost self-fulling prophecy, of the confirmation of these stereotypes.

Leaders of teams and organisations in which racial conflagration flares up require the ability to deal with the complexity that comes along with these disputes. Too often, leaders demonstrate binary thinking which is too simplistic. In complex disputes, an "either/or" way of thinking is not useful; more useful would be a "both/and" approach diagnosing what is going on in their organisation. Paradoxes can abound, old thinking patterns seem obsolete and the capacity to hold two contradictory "truths" at once is important. This may be challenging as all human beings naturally want to defend themselves. Intervening in such tricky disputes may feel like walking through a minefield.

Incompatibility

When the Labour Relations Act was promulgated in 1996, it only outlined three grounds for dismissal – misconduct, incapacity (poor performance or illness and injury) and operational requirements (retrenchment). As time went on, it became clear that there is a fourth ground – that of incompatibility. This refers to two main scenarios. The first is that of a personality clash with a manager and the second is where an employee simply cannot adapt to the employer's culture. Because of the disruptive nature of such incidents within a team, labour law experts say that incompatibility is a form of incapacity as it impacts on work performance.

A personality clash between a subordinate and their leader/manager/supervisor can certainly disrupt efficiency within a team as well as relationships at the workplace, all which can lead to consternation and conflict.

Some years ago, a younger consultant joined a team within an organisation where client service was of utmost importance. The clients were largely wealthy and demanding and the "deal" was that their consultants were available to them outside of normal work hours to attend to their needs and queries. The consultant was doing alright until he got a new team leader who made it clear that she did not approve of his work rate and level of performance. Gradually he deteriorated in his role and towards the end of his time with this employer, switched off his cell phone between the hours of 5 pm and 8 am. This was so antithetical to the culture of a very hard-working team that he was counselled out of his position by an internal mental health practitioner who was extremely concerned about his declining mental health. He was anxious all the time as well as afraid of his team leader and experienced extremely high levels of discomfort. On leaving this organisation he found a position at another employer and flourished in his new role with the support of his manager.

At another employer, a highly specialised senior female manager was appointed to run a team of people in her profession. Then, due to a restructuring, the manager was given another team to manage. Relationships between her and the larger team deteriorated, and allegations of victimisation were made. Outside consultants were brought in to investigate these allegations and held in-depth interviews with each member of her team. There were numerous examples of the manager's behaviour that had an enormously negative impact on people reporting to her. Examples included silencing her employees, ruling by fear, bullying, and condescending behaviour as well as the use of her positional power to control others. The manager took perceived disobedience personally and exhibited extreme displeasure when challenged. This created a hostile environment in which many of her subordinates were simply terrified to interact with her and dreaded being called into meetings with her. In sum, for those who know Berne's theory of Transactional Analysis,[1] she came across as the "critical parent" and therefore automatically "hooked" the angry or withdrawn child in her subordinates. Thus, people attempted to avoid her, or they fought with her.

The manager's behaviour was very antithetical to the culture of the organisation which emphasises valuing its people by demonstrating respect, trust, and collaboration.

Employees reporting to the manager reacted to the hostile environment in different ways. A recently appointed specialist with an excellent track record had felt so undermined by her that he was contemplating leaving. Another employee simply refused to work for her. Other members of her team had physical symptoms of distress such as migraines and back problems. Another relatively senior person resigned, citing being unable to function in the hostile environment that the manager's style had created and that she "simply could not take this anymore" and was burnt out and exhausted.

Many mental health practitioners would concur that in instances where work and the workplace either create or exacerbate mental health issues for employees, one of the critical missing ingredients in dealing with stressors at work is the fear of having courageous or difficult conversations that are required to give feedback either to colleagues or managers concerning whatever is causing problems for the person. There are many reasons for this which have been mentioned in the examples of poor leadership, sexual harassment, racism, and incompatibility. Frequently people simply fear the repercussions of these tough interactions such as victimisation, being labelled as a troublemaker or even perhaps being asked to leave. Some of the dynamics discussed under the above four headings include silencing people and eroding people's self-confidence to the extent that they feel unable to confront giving tough feedback to another person.

Thus, the final section of this chapter will focus on "Courageous" or "Difficult" conversations to offer guidance and outline what comprises such conversations. The input outlined below is based on the work of Stone et al. of the Harvard Negotiation Project.[2] Courageous conversations are simply those tough conversations that many of us avoid both in our work and personal lives: mostly this is due to fear – fear of hurting someone or being hurt and of the intended and unintended consequences of the content and process of the conversation.

Very often, conversations where there is actual or potential conflict, Stone et al[2] describes it as a *"battle of messages"*. This comprises two main elements, namely, trading positions or demands and blaming. Stone et al[2] contend that in a Courageous Conversation, we need to move towards a "Learning Conversation" – simply put, from expressing your positions and demands to being open to hearing the other party which will lead to an understanding of the following 4 factors:

- The complexity of the interplay of perceptions and intentions
- The joint contribution of each party to the problem (as opposed to blame)
- The importance of feelings
- What the issue means to each person's self-esteem and identity

Stone et al[2] contend that in Courageous or Difficult conversations, there are in fact three levels of communication or conversation happening simultaneously.

a.   The "Fact" Conversation – that is, what happened? This may seem like a simple dispute of fact that can be solved by referring to a document, contract, clipping or other sort of record. For those people working in high-conflict disputes with a lot of mistrust, even at this level, the mediators who facilitate conversations will agree that there is room for vehement disagreement.

In these conversations, there are three assumptions:

- The Truth Assumption – that is, I am right, and you are wrong
- The Intention Invention – the impact we have on another person (that is, the way our message "lands" on them), may not have been our intention. Our intention, we will argue, came from a benign or even well-meaning place.
- The Blame Game – it is useful to distinguish between blaming the other party and the idea of a joint contribution to the problem by both parties. It is common cause that when a person feels blamed, he/she will become defensive and closed to the other party. Talking of joint contribution instead will come across as more neutral and will indicate that both parties have a role in the resolution of the conflict.

b.   The "Feeling" Conversation – feelings of both parties are ever present but are simply ignored, denied or minimised. Rather, feelings need to surface and be managed. This may be hard if the level of trust between the parties is low, or one party's real intent is perceived or experienced as malicious. If feelings are not shared, there is no opportunity to understand their mutual impact.

c.   The "Identity" Conversation – each difficult conversation a person has will impact on their sense of self, self-image and self-esteem. Often the trigger is feedback that seems to in some way confirm that the script, or self-talk, a person has of being "not good enough" established in childhood is now being re-echoed.

In this conversation, we look inward and see the impact of the message on our sense of self and our self-beliefs. This is often felt in disputes that involve minority groups whose experiences of overt and covert discrimination has meant they have a hypervigilance to identify messages that confirm their view of being regarded as "not good enough", or "inferior" in some way.

There is another helpful set of insights which are taught in Negotiation Skills Training. The metaphor of an iceberg is used to differentiate between what lies above the water line and is thus visible, versus what lies below. When parties are negotiating, they frequently get stuck and fight over what is above the waterline – their demands and positions. A good negotiator will encourage the parties to look at what lies beneath the water, which are the parties' needs, interests, fears, and concerns. Getting beneath to this other "agenda" allows the discussion to go to "what really matters" conversations.

By way of illustration, a management and a union party may get stuck on the percentage increase of wages the union is demanding (20%) vs what management is offering (7%). They will get stuck in a "battle of messages" until the negotiation moves to looking at what lies behind these stated positions. For the union, this may include dwindling membership, the high cost of living, members not being able to afford their children's school fees and the rapidly rising cost of both transport and food. For the management party, their fears and concerns may be loss of market share, increases in the price of electricity and the impact of the COVID-19 pandemic on their bottom line.

Courageous or Difficult conversations are often eased by using a mediator or facilitator to guide parties through the giving and receiving of tough feedback such that the relationship between the two parties can continue and be enhanced.

This chapter has focused on the relationship between workplace experiences and mental health and has argued that the mental health of employees may be improved by positive experiences at work, while the opposite, clearly, can happen as well. Four topics were chosen as examples of dynamics that can play out at the workplace with negative consequences for employees' mental health. These were Poor Leadership, Sexual Harassment, Racism, and Incompatibility. The chapter concluded with giving some insights into Difficult or Courageous conversations to encourage parties in workplace disputes to hold transformative dialogues. The objectives here would be to point out intentional, or unintentional, impacts of behaviour on people at the workplace so that hurtful and damaging dynamics may be resolved. This chapter also highlights the importance of having a broader view of the concept of mental health, not just as mental illness, and the role that the workplace plays in fostering the mental health agenda. It can no longer be ignored that the workplace needs to work towards creating healthy workplace environments (physically and virtually) and that this will go a long way in working towards the sustainability of the organisation by creating mental health awareness, upskilling of leaders and managers, creating a culture of care, and providing various interventions for mental health support and resiliency.

Chapter 6

Toxic relationships in the workplace

Dr Jopie de Beer, Dr Karina de Bruin, Dr Renate Scherrer

Introduction

There is no shortage of research regarding the importance of healthy relationships at work and how these relationships actively support the health, wellness, productivity, innovation and engagement of individuals[1], the context of which was also discussed in the previous chapter. The inverse, however, is unfortunately also true. Outside the concepts discussed in the previous chapter relating to negative experiences and relationships in the workplace, this chapter is specifically homing in on dealing with toxicity in the workplace. Regularly dealing with a toxic co-worker or manager can create a substantial amount of distress and negatively impact the physical health and wellbeing of employees. Having to continuously operate in an environment where relationships are negative can lead to serious mental health issues and a significant reduction in performance, typically in several areas of life beyond work[2]. When we consider the impact of the COVID-19 pandemic, where the stress and fear of possible loss of life, loss of income, loss of physical touch and family coincided with social, political, and environmental turmoil and disruption, it is no surprise that two thirds of employees report that during the pandemic, their mental health issues have affected their performance on the job, and at least 40% are battling with burnout[3].

Although work environments presented with various stressors prior to the pandemic, the situation has intensified their effect on individuals, teams, and organisations. Much work is to be done to understand how stressors, such as toxicity, will manifest and impact work environments during times of added uncertainty. Toxicity does not exclusively manifest in real-life or non-virtual interactions. Employees will behave online very much as they do offline. Once toxicity is identified in the workplace, it should be accepted that the same toxicity will probably be presented on social media and elsewhere. Toxicity is contagious – also online – and it can fester over prolonged periods of time. Before the pandemic, about 20% of workers reported that they considered their work environment to be toxic[4]. One can only guess as to what the prevalence will be after the pandemic subsides and employees continue to work virtually. For organisations, the double impact of the pandemic and a toxic work environment may well be lethal since toxicity and toxic cultures negatively impact the ability to attract, retain and develop the talented employees that can enable performance and growth over time.

When considering the impact of toxic relationships in the workplace, several questions come to mind:

- Will there be more toxicity given the high levels of emotionality in the workplace? If so, how may it present?
- Will the impact of toxicity be less because of virtual work arrangements?
- Will tight-knit team structures be able to buffer some of the impact of toxicity?
- Which data/metrics will be most helpful to identify and quantify the presence of toxicity?
- What will toxic leadership look like in the digital context?
- How can workers be supported in a context of toxicity?
- How can organisations limit their risk of employing or promoting toxic workers?

To formulate some thoughts on the above, we need to understand what toxicity is, where to look for seeds of toxicity in the workplace, and how to prevent or limit its prevalence in work environments.

Toxicity in the workplace

The signs and symptoms of toxic relationships in the workplace are typically categorised as interpersonally deviant behaviour. This is typically voluntary behaviour that threatens the wellbeing of others through incivility, harassment, bullying and other types of interpersonal abuse[5]. Much of the impact of this deviant behaviour depends on the position and corporate power of the toxic person, and is most often associated with people's personalities, attitudes, habits, and behavioural patterns. Even though, most companies would not purposefully create or support toxicity, the fact is that toxicity has always been, and still is, very prevalent in the workplace, and tens of thousands of people all over the world experience it every day.[2]

The disastrous impact of toxicity is illustrated where studies report on the following:

- 80% of workers are disengaged.[6]
- 56% of workers report that they work for a toxic boss.[6]
- About 75% of workers report that the worst and most stressful aspect of their job is their immediate supervisor.[7]
- 65-75% of the existing managers are alienating their staff.[7]
- Between 30-50% of all executive-level appointments end in firing or resignation.[7]
- Estimates for the rate of management derailment or leadership failure are as high as 7 in 10.[7]
- 38-50% of CEO's will fail within the first 18 months after their appointment.[8]

"Seeds"/sources of toxicity in the workplace

Toxicity in the workplace stem from various sources – some possibly less harmful, but always dangerous.

General antagonisms, irritations, and misunderstandings

The following behaviours, when displayed continuously, are often viewed as being toxic: gossiping, complaining, criticising, and blaming of others; laziness, helplessness, lying (overtly, or covertly by withholding information), not keeping promises, purposefully undermining others, slow responses, late coming, poor communication, abuse, lack of acknowledgment of others' contribution, and lacking boundaries.

Although some of these interpersonal perceptions may truly be sources of toxicity, it could also be due to personality or even cultural differences. Some of these colleagues may, on a spectrum of the intensity of toxicity, be more of an irritation than truly toxic. Those working with them may "roll their eyes" and find "work arounds", rather than having to rely on and work with them. In a highly emotional context where resilience is low, personality differences may result in full-blown conflict as well as simmering and contagious toxicity.

Incivility

Civility is an interpersonal skill that refers to being polite and showing respect and courtesy to others. It is made up of "thin slices" that consist of listening, saying please and thank you, sharing credit, smiling, showing warmth, care and humility, and being helpful. Civility from leaders have positive results with workers being 55% more engaged.[9]

Over the last decades, there has been a steady rise of incivility in the workplace. One possible explanation is that civility may be perceived as a weakness, something to take advantage of, it is not leader-like, and those who treat people rudely, are seen to be more powerful. In this regard, 40% of people in a study about the returns of civility indicated that they prefer not to be civil at work and about 4% of people claimed to be uncivil just because it is fun, and they can get away with it.[10]

Incivility can do real harm and lead to toxicity in the workplace. Rude leaders cause emotional arousal in employees who observe and are on the receiving end of the rude behaviour. When unchecked, incivility affects individuals' ability to do their work well, problem-solve, and make good decisions. It also destroys trust in teams, impacts the cohesiveness of the team negatively, and puts the reputation of the company at risk when such bad behaviour starts to impact client relationships.[10]

"Fit" or "misfit"

For organisations to remain competitive, they need to hire and retain the best talent. These employees need certain technical competencies and skills, but they must also be a good "fit" for the job, the team, and the organisation.

On an individual level the consequences of not fitting in presents as dissatisfaction, frustration, stress, anger, and a low mood. There is an absence of job satisfaction and a negative attitude toward the job, the leadership, and the organisation. Such negativity can be highly contagious, and the "misfit" appointment may start to play the role of an enabler of toxicity in the workplace. If allowed to simmer, the contagiousness of toxicity could infect more people and teams in the organisation. It could affect the relationship with clients, sales, income, and reputation of the organisation.[11]

Technology, boundaries, social media, rumours, and false news

The pandemic has forced most businesses to rapidly adopt technology. This has facilitated increased communication and efficiency, and opened opportunities for innovation that may not have been possible before. Adopting technology has however also increased the tempo and volume of work. Acquiring new technology-related skills, managing the added complexity technology brings, and seeking solutions to new risks associated with technology are challenging to workers and organisations alike. Prior to 2020, 76% of employees reported burnout at least sometimes at work[12], but recently many more employees have reported a rise in burnout risk given the "always-on" culture and a difficulty in setting boundaries between home and work.

In 2017, users of social media have spent on average more than two hours per day on social media and messaging services[13]. In addition to the reality of a possible social media addiction that may affect productivity in the workplace, the impact of cyberbullying, online firestorms, privacy abuse, and false news on the emotional resources of workers, should not be ignored. The contagious toxicity of false news and conspiracy theories seems to find a receptive audience, particularly amongst those who feel helpless, angry, and frustrated.[14] Social media could present with new sources of toxicity, a challenge to mental health and wellbeing, and a risk to organisations.

Leadership

Leadership plays an important role in setting the example and emotional tone at work – particularly during difficult times. Failed managers and destructive leaders are often at the heart of organisational crises, creating a toxic workplace where fear, stress, and anxiety are exacerbated with employees feeling marginalised, incompetent, or unimportant.[15]

Leadership failure is typically not due to a lack of technical competence or social skills, since it is often these attributes that help to progress the leader. At its core, leadership failure is due to personality-related aspects. These include arrogance; low self-awareness; the lack of willingness to listen, understand, or learn; finding it difficult to build relationships; being authoritarian, insensitive, tactless, or impulsive; and having low integrity.[7] Toxic behaviour, characterised by disrespect, harassment, bullying, exploitation, lies, betrayals, and manipulation destroys trust, respect, and even the humanity of workers.[16]

Toxicity in teams

Effective teamwork requires members that are co-operative, adaptable, proactive, innovative, and networking oriented. Behaviours that cause distrust, for example gossiping, purposefully undermining others, withholding information, continued criticism, and innuendo can immobilise a team and destroy the working relationship.

"The single most important factor in team success or failure is the quality of relationships in the team. In fact, 70% of the variance between the lowest performing teams (saboteur teams) and the highest performing teams (loyalist teams), correlates to the quality of the team relationships, thus, one toxic team member is all it takes to destroy a high-performance team".[17]

Corporate culture, ethics, and toxicity

Organisational culture reflects the shared beliefs and values that guide acceptable behaviour in the workplace. It clarifies, usually by example and endorsement of leadership, what is right and wrong, or acceptable and unacceptable behaviour.[18] Organisational culture and organisational relationships are closely intertwined – culture reflects the dynamics in relationships, and the relationships affect the culture.[19]

Signs of a toxic culture include the following[4]:

- excessive self-promotion and misuse of power by leadership
- situations where nobody disagrees, true thoughts are not shared, thoughts are underplayed to make sure you fit in, lies are told to appease those in power, nobody outside the core leadership group is asked for input, and absolute conformity is required
- a lack of accountability, and in fact, rewarding incompetent behaviours
- a lack of integrity and moral direction
- low levels of innovation and energy

- negativity, hostility, blaming, paranoia, gossip, bullying, abuse, and distrust
- less priority on vision, but more on personal benefit and being the winner
- insensitivity and resistance to feedback
- an absence of employee support, training, coaching, and mentoring
- pressure to overwork
- human resources data that indicate progressive signs of distress, anger, betrayal, anxiety, physical disease, depression, and trauma among individual employees

A culture of integrity stands in contrast to a toxic culture. Bad behaviour such as abuse, lying, manipulation, fraud, corruption, or unfair discrimination will not find a foothold in cultures where integrity is entrenched. A strong and ethical culture provides resilience and stability not only to the company as a business and its reputation, but specifically also for the employees.

A scientific perspective on the root cause of toxicity

As indicated in this chapter, there are many potential sources of toxicity in the workplace. From an iceberg metaphor perspective, some of the elements are at the surface level and visible as signs and symptoms of toxicity at work. Figure 6.1 below provides a view of personality as a below-the-surface root cause of toxic behaviour at work since:

1. deviant behaviour flourishes when it is acceptable in the organisational/team culture,
2. leaders determine the culture, and
3. the leader's style is an expression of personality.

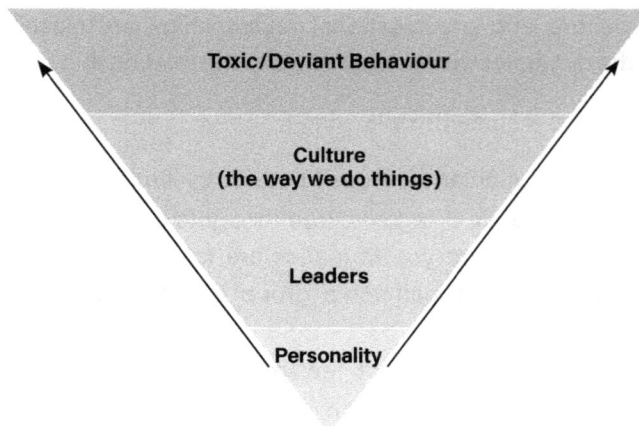

Figure 6.1: Personality as root cause of toxicity

The good, bad, and downright ugly side of personality

Definition and description of personality

Personality is defined as *"the configuration of characteristics and behaviour that comprises an individual's unique adjustment to life, including major traits, interests, drive, values, self-concept, abilities, and emotional patterns. Personality is generally viewed as a complex, dynamic integration or totality, shaped by many forces ... various theories explain the structure and development of personality in different ways but, all agree that personality helps determine behaviour."*[20]

We need to recognise that:

- there is a distinct difference between using personality information that focuses on style preferences and differences, and working with core personality traits,
- personality is relatively stable allowing for the fact that past behaviour will tend to predict future behaviour, and
- personality has two "sides" – what people know and understand about themselves (identity) and what others observe and know about them (reputation) (p. 8).[7]

Personality style, frustration, conflict, "out of character" behaviour, and toxicity

Carl Jung's well-known Personality Type Theory provided a useful understanding of personality style differences. Isabel Briggs Myers and Katherine Briggs, who also developed the Myers-Briggs Type Indicator (MBTI), translated Jung's theory into an easy-to-understand format. According to this theory, people differ vastly in their preferences on four polarities: how they source and channel their energy (introversion or extraversion); the information they prefer to work with (sensory or intuitive); their basis for decision-making (thinking or feeling); and how they prefer to structure their work and personal lives (perceiving or judging).

The variability of these personality styles often leads to misunderstandings and conflict in the workplace. Management of such misunderstandings can be relatively easily remedied with interventions to create awareness and as such limiting the risk for possible development of simmering toxicity.

Under stress and duress, most people will react in both typical and atypical ways. Typically, people may respond by intensifying or overusing their natural styles, such as becoming quieter (introversion), more critical (thinking), or more preoccupied with detail (sensing). This response to stress is generally temporary. Should the stress and pressure however remain, people may behave outside their natural character, causing significant discomfort to co-workers because the nature of the response seems and feels "out of character", irrational, immature, inappropriate, and unpredictable. This response to stress may feel toxic and would tend to become highly contagious, disruptive, and harmful to relationships and trust.

If misunderstandings in the workplace are due to ordinary personality differences and a variety of responses to stress, the solution is relatively easy. By facilitating a process of self-awareness and interpersonal awareness, an understanding and management of these differences can become much easier and will strengthen individual and corporate resilience during stress and turmoil. When workers habitually respond to stress and exhaustion outside their natural personality preferences, individual attention should be given to the sources of stress.

"Bright" and "dark" personality traits

Personality traits, in contrast to personality preferences, can be described as stable, consistent, and enduring characteristics that are inferred from patterns of behaviour, attitudes, feelings, and habits in the individual. These traits can be useful to summarise, predict, and explain an individual's conduct.[20]

Robert Hogan's definition of leadership as the ability to build and maintain a high-performance team[21], illustrates one of the core requirements of successful managers and leaders. In contrast, leaders who fail in this, have poor judgment, cannot build teams, have troubled relationships, cannot manage themselves, and do not learn from their mistakes.[22]

Managing relationships relies on both the "bright side" and "dark side" of the personality of a leader. The "bright side" with appropriate social skills and charisma could mask the "darker side" of personality. The "dark side" refers to the impression and impact people make when they perceive a threat, feel stressed, feel sick, tired, or exhausted, or be challenged with too much change and complexity. In such situations, they may become more impulsive, let down their guard, overreact, and show poor judgment, their biases, and self-protective beliefs. In interpersonal contexts the "dark side" of personality and behaviour can be perceived as both offensive and toxic.[23]

Hogan's taxonomy of "dark side" derailers

Personality derailers represent strategies people use when they interact with others, and whilst it may sometimes provide short-term benefit, it ultimately damages relationships when frequently used. During times of stress, change, ambiguity, and turbulence, or when people stop monitoring their behaviour, they often over-rely on these derailment strategies. This often results in toxicity and perceptions of low integrity in the workplace.[24]

Hogan's taxonomy of dark side personality dimensions describes eleven different derailers, each relating to behaviours that can alienate co-workers, disrupt teams, and undermine group/company performance.[25] Examples of the overuse of derailers include overreaction (excitability), becoming overly critical and defensive (skeptical), or being slow and resistant to change (cautious). Particularly dangerous derailment combinations and personality traits are discussed next.

The dark triad

Various personality and other traits are associated with effective leadership, but the presence of subclinical traits or true pathology can derail the otherwise competent and skilled leader. Some subclinical traits may have short-term advantages, but a long-term negative impact on the organisation.[26]

The "Dark Triad" refers to three distinct, yet related personality constellations, namely psychopathy, narcissism, and Machiavellianism. The presence of any of these in the workplace can create significant turbulence and toxicity, particularly if it is represented in leadership.

Psychopathy	
Marked by	Egocentricity, impulsivity, and lack of emotions such as guilt or remorse.
Some research findings	• Women leaders with psychopathic tendencies tend to be penalised, whilst men are rewarded for psychopathic tendencies. The boldness and fearlessness of those with psychopathic tendencies could be perceived as confidence; their self-centered impulsivity and arrogance as courage; and their cold-heartedness and meanness as being rational and business-focused.[27] These misperceptions will remain up to the point that enough power is provided to them to create harm. • *"... their hallmark is a stunning lack of conscience, their game is self-gratification at another person's expense, many spend time in prison, but many do not".*[28 (pp. 1-2)]
Narcissism	
Marked by	Excessive self-love or egocentrism
Some research findings	• Because their decisions are driven by egocentric needs and arrogance, it can reflect in risk-taking, unilateral opinion, and in general, poor judgment. Overconfident, narcissistic, and erratic leadership styles produce toxic environments that can break down relationships and derail the whole organisation[29].
Machiavellianism	
Marked by	Calculating attitude toward human relationships and a belief that the ends justify the means.
Some research findings	• Known to be low on ethical behaviour and do not care about the impact of their actions on the future survival of the organisation.[25]

Toxic leaders thrive in chaos, ambiguity, and toxic systems. They work hard at catching people off guard and creating anxiety and fear. To further drive intimidation, they build coalitions of like-minded characters, which usually consist of a combination of conformers or colluders.[16] The conformers may follow and support the toxic leader because of anxiety and fear, together with a belief that authority must be complied with, without question. The colluders may be those who have a similar personality and who share the views of the leader. They may be opportunistic, believing that they may share in the benefits of the leader.

The level of emotional and social skills (EQ) in the workplace

In addition to understanding the impact of personality on the development of toxicity in the workplace, the importance of being able to work efficiently with emotions should be highlighted. Emotional intelligence refers to the ability to identify and process emotional information and apply it in reasoning and other cognitive activities to function effectively in the workplace and beyond. EQ skills include constructs such as self-awareness, self-regard, empathy, mood management, reality testing, and impulse control.[30] These skills are essential in self-management and play an equally essential role in how relationships are managed – as such then, essential in understanding and managing the risks of toxicity in the workplace.

The opposite is also true. Workers who lack in self-awareness and have a limited ability to understand, monitor, and manage their emotional reactions, present a risk of derailing into the darker sides of their personality and creating toxicity in relationships.[23, 31]

Presenting with good social skills could possibly conceal and even sometimes compensate for derailment episodes. However, with heightened work demands and additional pressures, chances are good that repeated incidences of dark behaviour will occur, leading to disrupted relationships and becoming offensive and toxic.[22]

Ongoing attention to the emotional resources and skills of leaders is therefore essential given their responsibility to calm down and focus emotions constructively, bring hope, acknowledge mental health and wellbeing of workers as priorities, and consistently challenge toxicity in the workplace.

How to mitigate and manage the risk of toxicity in the workplace

According to the World Economic Forum,[32] the impact of the pandemic on the mental health of workers is expected to be "severe and persistent". In such stressful times, the potential for increased toxicity in the workplace is real and this can further destroy individuals, relationships, and organisations. Leadership that shows compassion and empathy in addition to being able to formulate strategy, drive innovation, manage risk, and ensure the survival of the business will do much to reduce the high levels of stress and anxiety. The following suggestions per focus area should help to limit and reduce toxicity in the workplace.

Selection and recruitment

- Understand the personality structure of a candidate to see past the misleading charisma and social skills that he/she may present with.
- Optimise the "fit" between a candidate and the job, culture, and values of the organisation. *"Talent should be regarded as personality in the right place."*[29]
- Screen out "bad apples" by using evidence-based and well-validated assessments. Overwhelming evidence shows that personality assessments that measure both the "bright" and "dark" sides of personality predict work-related outcomes, job performance, and leadership.[33]
- Given the potential harm of not fully understanding the mental health and the wellbeing of all, hire for humility, civility, and emotional intelligence.

Development and promotion

- Avoid promoting people with prominent dark sides into leadership.
- Provide continuous learning opportunities to develop self-awareness, emotional management, stress management, resilience, purpose and meaning, allocation of responsibility and blame, interpersonal skills, and constructive relationships.[34] Also create awareness of derailment, conscious and unconscious biases, and self-defeating behaviour. Align these with corporate values and modelling from leadership.
- Offer workshops on managing workload, high volumes of information, workplace boundaries, internet, and social media usage and dependency.
- Look out for those who do not feel they fit their job, team, or company to support their development by, for instance, job rotation rather than leaving them to turn toxic.
- Offer coaching and use 360-feedback, particularly for those leaders who resist feedback.
- Educate managers about the causes, impact, and cost of toxicity in the workplace.

HR metrics/data

- Create dashboards to collect relevant data on the teams, departments, and the functioning of the workers.

- Act swiftly on metrics that can indicate stress and possible toxicity in the system, for example, data on absenteeism, mental health, turnover of staff.

Culture

- Culture is ever-evolving, but we should always give attention to building a strong, fair, and ethical culture where employees who stand up against a manager or colleague, will know that the organisation supports fairness.[2]
- Continuously evaluate the impact that change and disruption in the organisation may have on the culture and the quality of relationships.
- Continuously communicate the ground rules, values, and norms of the organisation whilst ensuring strict consequences for incivility and toxicity.
- Provide anonymous feedback channels where employees can speak up about abuses of power and position.
- Provide opportunity for whistleblowers and follow through on actions. Given the fact that low self-awareness and low empathy for others may be a source for toxicity, ensure ongoing opportunities to enhance self-awareness, and to learn how to work with people who are hardwired in a different way.

Leadership

- Provide opportunities for feedback and discuss how leadership behaviour is perceived by others.
- Provide opportunities for coaching and self-driven development, particularly on their own biases, recognising dark behaviour in self and others, and recognising and managing the coalitions that some destructive leaders build around themselves.
- Teach and reinforce leadership behaviours that allow for empathy and understanding of wellbeing, mental health, individuality, stress, and the "emotional architecture" of the organisation, whilst ensuring business strategy and viability.[35, 36]
- Establish a pipeline of leaders throughout the layers of the organisation and help them to be prepared for complex leadership responsibilities. Preparing people for leadership is a process and requires, amongst others, transitioning from managing self, to managing others.[37]

Governance

- Embed fair, decisive, and consistent responses to toxicity-related challenges in policies, disciplinary codes, and other checks and balances to keep unacceptable behaviour at bay.

- Respect and provide safety to whistle-blowers.
- Implement codes of conduct, policies, and standard operating procedures to guide ethics and values, fair work boundaries, and the use of social media and the internet.
- Support policies and procedures with ongoing communication and everyday examples of civil and ethical conduct.
- Formulate clearly, and enforce fairly and consistently the consequences of toxic, uncivil, and unethical conduct.

Conclusion

The intensity and speed of change brought on by the pandemic, the implementation of technology and automation, the economic hardship, and fear and anxiety of people about whether they will be able to survive, had a severe impact on all aspects of mental health and wellbeing.

Toxicity presents in different contexts and in a variety of ways. Essentially, toxicity is driven by emotion and presents itself in relationships. An understanding of personality provides valuable insight into the diversity of human behaviour and potential reasons for the toxic behaviour in the workplace. The overuse of strengths, derailment, and destructive leadership behaviours further explain how much damage can be done to organisations and employees if the wrong people are placed in positions of power and authority.

To conclude, let's get back to the questions posed earlier in this chapter:

- *Will there be more toxicity given the high levels of emotionality in the workplace? If so, how may it present?*

  Should the disruption and speed of change persist, people will keep on presenting with the overuse of strengths and derailment. It is important to provide them with opportunities to become more self-aware and learn how to manage stress and other emotions.

- *Will the impact of toxicity be less because of virtual work arrangements?*

  Toxicity is essentially emotional and carried into relationships in a way that is predicted by the personality of the people in the relationship. Virtual work arrangements will still experience toxicity but in ways that technology allows it to. In this regard, the use of social media to facilitate cyberbullying, privacy abuse, spreading of false news, and conspiracy theories can cause real damage to individuals, relationships, and organisations.

- *Will tight-knit team structures be able to buffer some of the impact of toxicity?*

  Healthy teams, characterised by resilience, trust, and mutual support, can compensate for external sources of toxicity. If, however, the source of toxicity is within the team, the impact can be destructive.

- *Which data/metrics will be most helpful to identify and quantify the presence of toxicity?*

  Individual metrics and survey data related to productivity, absenteeism, mental and general health complaints, and turnover may require a closer analysis of the department or teams.

- *What will toxic and destructive leadership look like in the digital context?*

  Toxic leadership in a virtual and digital context may make extensive use of social media, internet, and electronic messaging means to intimidate, bully, and harm relationships.

- *How can workers be supported in a context of toxicity?*

  Effort should be made to establish a strong culture that allows for regular and open communication.

- *How can organisations limit their risk of employing or promoting toxic workers?*

  Ensure that there is a thorough understanding, not only of the technical skills and abilities, but also of the risk of derailment and destructive leadership behaviour before promotion and/or appointment.

Given the pandemic context, there is little doubt that most employees are currently in a chronic "fight-flight" mode which makes them more susceptible to physical, emotional, and mental symptoms associated with stress. This is, in addition to the fact that pre-pandemic, it was accepted that the workplace and work relationships impact the mental health of workers. Workers can also transition from mentally well and healthy, to being mentally unwell, when the work environment and relationships become toxic.[38] Toxicity will always be a risk in organisations. However, with the current information available, much can be done for early identification, management, and mitigation.

Chapter 7

Burning the candle on both ends: Dealing with burnout

Joanna Kleovoulou

What is burnout?

As mentioned throughout the book thus far, globally, mental health matters have become dramatically topical. Burnout, workplace stress and working hours have highlighted the negative sequalae that have accompanied a lack of organisational focus on mental health matters. Individuals and organisations are recognising the implications on a personal wellbeing perspective as well as the massive fall-outs and costs associated with conditions such as burnout across most vocational fields in the workplace.[1] With the COVID-19 pandemic gripping the globe, the consequences for mental health as another mounting pandemic, has been emphasised and experienced. Research illustrates the global financial burden of burnout to be approximately $300 billion annually due to factors such as loss of productivity, absenteeism, employee turnover, medical, legal, insurance and compensation costs.[2] Another 2018 review[3] commissioned by the Health Programme of the European Union estimates the annual cost of burnout to EU enterprises to be at €272 billion.

The World Health Organisation[4] has included burnout in the 11th Revision of the International Classification of Diseases (ICD-11) as an occupational occurrence. However it is not classified as a medical condition and can be defined as:

"A syndrome conceptualised as resulting from chronic workplace stress that has not been successfully managed. It is characterised by three dimensions:

- feelings of energy depletion or exhaustion;
- increased mental distance from one's job, or feelings of negativism or cynicism related to one's job; and
- reduced professional efficacy."

Since burnout was first described in the early 1970s, thousands of empirical studies have focused on this phenomenon and it is evident that burnout is non-discriminatory and occurs cross-culturally, is pervasive in all genders and is prevalent across a variety of occupations and in numerous fields.

Burnout is indicative of employees not having sufficient resources to deal with the demands and expectations of their jobs, leading to impaired job performance and poor work functioning. A systematic literature review executed on burnout and objective performance, identified high levels of exhaustion with low levels of role performance, and higher levels of exhaustion resulted in lower customer service ratings.[5] In addition, burned out employees may be less able to be attentive, collaborative and empathic – characteristics that have been associated with higher consumer satisfaction.[6]

Worldwide studies showcasing the impact of burnout

In a longitudinal study of 3,895 employees working in a large industry corporation[7] found that burnout predicted future sick leave, even after controlling for the effects of age, gender, occupation, and previous absence. High levels of burnout increased the risk of absence related to mental and behavioural disorders, as well as diseases of the circulatory, respiratory, and musculoskeletal systems.

The consequences of the recent global economic crisis, recession and the COVID-19 global pandemic, have required many enterprises to downscale so as to remain competitive, by way of outsourcing, subcontracting, restructuring, downsizing, merging and substantial layoffs. These changes cause uncertainty, resentment and reduced opportunity to grow within the organisation.[8] Many employees who are retained may experience survivor guilt towards their colleagues who have been dismissed and are required to face increased workload, perform new tasks, longer working hours, role confusion and a sense of lack of control. Literature suggests that the consequences of burnout can be severe and far-reaching. Employees who experience burnout often experience impaired emotional and physical health and a diminished sense of wellbeing.[9] Another study in Finland investigated the relationship between job-related burnout and depressive disorders in 3,276 workers in Finland. It was found that individuals with mild burnout were 3.3 times more at risk of having MDD (major depressive disorder), and those with severe burnout were 15 times more likely to have MDD. The risk of having a major depressive disorder with severe burnout was greater for men than for women, with the risk of a major depressive disorder tenfold for women and almost thirty times more for men.[10] An interesting find from Sora and colleagues[11] showed that individual feelings of job insecurity can become contagious within an organisation, especially one with a strong organisational culture, impede employee interactions and may lead to employee withdrawal, both of which are also synonymous with symptoms of burnout.

The negative impact of chronic workplace stress and resulting burnout on both employees and their organisations is well-documented especially in helping professions, like nursing, psychology, teaching and social work. In a sample study of service workers in a Swedish city which included physicians, nurses, social workers, occupational therapists, physiotherapists, dentists, dental hygienists, administrators, teachers, and technicians, burnout was associated with increased depression, anxiety, sleep problems, impaired memory, neck and back pain, and alcohol consumption.[12] In a recent healthcare workers' study in India, it was found that there was a significant prevalence of burnout during the COVID-19 pandemic, specifically with doctors and support staff. Female respondents had higher prevalence. The doctors were twice as much and the support staff were five times more likely to experience pandemic-related burnout.[13] In an Italian study[14] levels of depression, anxiety, psychological stress, professional quality of life (compassion satisfaction, burnout, and compassion fatigue) and attitudes toward psychological support were measured. Significantly higher levels of stress, burnout, secondary trauma, depression and anxiety and lower levels of compassion satisfaction were observed among professionals working with COVID-19 patients.

In developing countries such as South Africa, with high levels of job uncertainly and high rates of unemployment,[15] the issue of over-worked employees aggravates the necessity to stretch expectations, work performance and capacity, manifesting a breeding ground for a burnout pandemic. Statistics South Africa on 29 September 2020 indicated 23,3% of the population are unemployed. Burnout is not isolated to certain roles but is prevalent across industries and professions, nor does it discriminate on age. An 'always-on' culture where an employee is available online after normal work hours, is encouraged and even unintentionally overvalued, praised contributes to burnout. Nathan Rogerson highlighted the phenomenon called Millennial Burnout,[16] where he links digital over-consumption to an 'always-on' culture, which negatively influences the ability to have down-time which in turn affects brain functioning as it cannot adequately replenish itself which ultimately impacts performance. In a country where the socio-economic situation is tenuous and the prospects of finding new employment easily are low for most, the situation becomes ripe for employee exploitation as employees have little option but to acquiesce to being 'always-on' as well as heavy workloads and demands due to job insecurity. The sudden onset of the COVID-19 restrictions enacted across the world meant significant shifts occurred to people's ordinary working and home life.[17] A significant element in research on stress and burnout in work-home stress and burnout is gender. Pre-pandemic studies consistently showed that women experienced higher levels of stress and burnout due to role overload and lack of support from work and partners and more work-family conflicts and especially for women in part-time employment and from lower socio-economic classes.[18]

A recent study highlighted that South African workers have some of the longest working hours in the world.[19] These long working hours do not correlate with higher productivity measured by the average contribution to the economy per hour of work by an employee. Working such long hours over a prolonged period of time without sufficient rest, increases the chance of experiencing burnout and negative consequences on performance. The International Labour Organisation data tells the story that although South Africans work longer hours, they are not on par with the productivity levels of developed nations who work less.[20] Although the majority of workers fall within a 40-48 hr work week, 21% of the workforce work 49 hrs per week or more. Deloitte's recent external marketplace survey on burnout[21] of 1,000 full-time US professionals explored the drivers and impact of employee burnout, while also providing insight into the benefits and programmes employees feel can help prevent or alleviate burnout versus those their companies are currently offering. The findings indicate that 77 percent of respondents say they have experienced employee burnout at their current job, with more than half citing more than one occurrence. The survey also uncovered that employers may be missing the mark when it comes to developing wellbeing programmes that their employees find valuable to address stress in the workplace. The survey also revealed that:

- 91 percent of respondents say having an unmanageable amount of stress or frustration negatively impacts the quality of their work. 83 percent of respondents say burnout from work can negatively impact their personal relationships.
- 87 percent of professionals surveyed say they have passion for their current job but 64 percent say they are frequently stressed, dispelling the myth that passionate employees are immune to stress or burnout.
- Nearly 70 percent of professionals feel their employers are not doing enough to prevent or alleviate burnout within their organisation. 21 percent of respondents say their company does not offer any programmes or initiatives to prevent or alleviate burnout.
- One in four professionals say they never or rarely take all of their vacation days.
- The top driver of burnout cited in the survey is lack of support or recognition from leadership, indicating the important role that leaders play in setting the tone.
- 84 percent of millennials say they have experienced burnout at their current job, compared to 77 percent of all respondents. Nearly half of millennials say they have left a job specifically because they felt burned out, compared to 42 percent of all respondents.

Many of the organisational variables[22] impacting psychological health and safety in the workplace are the same variables that have been identified as contributing to workplace burnout. It has been shown that burnout is greater when employees feel that they are not making an adequate contribution to their organisation, or do not feel their efforts are appreciated, have role conflict, work overload (even when they say they can handle it), or a lack of predictable and clear expectations. Management or support positions should become aware of the signs and symptoms of burnout, as well as what they can do to prevent or respond to burnout.

Signs and symptoms

The majority of employees experiencing burnout remain at work. This is a concern as this negatively contributes to decreasing levels of productivity and possibly toxic work culture due to the cynicism involved.

Being aware of changes in attitudes and energy can help with early identification. Employees may not realise that they are dealing with burnout and may instead believe that they are just struggling to keep up during stressful times. Stress, however, is usually experienced as feeling anxious and having a sense of urgency while burnout is more commonly experienced as helplessness, hopelessness, or apathy. Employees may not be aware of the negative impact on their performance, such as increased mistakes or lowered productivity. Employers and co-workers may attribute the changes to a poor attitude or loss of motivation.[23] The negative effects of burnout can increase significantly before anyone recognises or addresses the problem and unaddressed burnout can increase the chance of developing clinical depression or other serious conditions.[24] Left unaddressed, burnout may result in a number of outcomes:

Physical:

- Chronic headaches
- Chronic stomach or bowel problems
- Lower resistance to illness
- Exhaustion
- Depleted energy levels
- Complete neglect of personal needs
- Unexplained pain
- Back and neck pain
- Dizziness

Mental:

- Behavioural changes
- Pessimistic outlook on work or life
- Mental and emotional fatigue
- Increased risk for clinical depression and anxiety
- Feeling empty inside
- Rumination over life's problems
- Self-doubt
- Taking everything personally

Social:

- Social isolation
- Desire to "drop out" of society
- Desire to move away from work or friends/family
- Detachment in personal relationships
- Communication breakdown

Career:

- Time away from work
- Demotivated
- Detached from your work
- Decreased productivity
- Increased absenteeism
- Poor workplace morale
- Reduced job satisfaction
- Making careless mistakes
- Feeling like a failure at work
- Rumination of work problems
- Increased chances of staff turnover

Mental (continued):	Spiritual:
• Re-introducing a bad habit • Inability to concentrate • Being constantly bored • Development of an escapist mentality • Self-medicating with alcohol and other substances • Sarcasm and irritability • Suspiciousness and cynicism • Depersonalisation • Increased risk of accidents	• Lack of meaning • Disillusionment • Feelings of not making a contribution to work and society

Five stages of burnout

Many people experience burnout syndrome in different stages. Researchers classify the number and extent of these stages in different ways, however. One of the most common models outlines five stages. The diagram below depicts these phases so one can review their own situation and identify the potential risk of burnout. Many employees commence at stage 1 and fall into the trap of not reaching out for help sooner as they may be unaware of having reached stage 4.

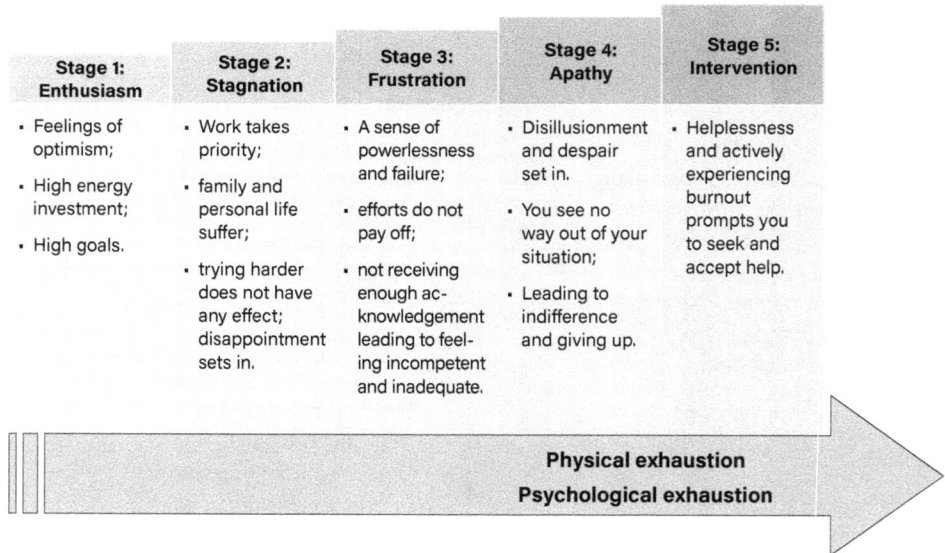

Stage 1: Enthusiasm	Stage 2: Stagnation	Stage 3: Frustration	Stage 4: Apathy	Stage 5: Intervention
• Feelings of optimism; • High energy investment; • High goals.	• Work takes priority; • family and personal life suffer; • trying harder does not have any effect; disappointment sets in.	• A sense of powerlessness and failure; • efforts do not pay off; • not receiving enough acknowledgement leading to feeling incompetent and inadequate.	• Disillusionment and despair set in. • You see no way out of your situation; • Leading to indifference and giving up.	• Helplessness and actively experiencing burnout prompts you to seek and accept help.

Physical exhaustion

Psychological exhaustion

Figure 7.1: Stages of burnout (Schwabe)[25]

Burnout is having a growing impact on workplaces,[26] in particular during times of economic downturn. Because it is chronic in nature, affecting both the health and performance of employees at all levels of organisations, prevention strategies are considered the most effective approach for addressing workplace burnout. Burnout is more likely when employees:

- Expect too much of themselves.
- Never feel that the work they are doing is good enough.
- Feel inadequate or incompetent.
- Feel unappreciated for their work efforts.
- Have unreasonable demands placed upon them.
- Are in roles that are not a good job fit.

The remainder of the chapter focuses on how taking control and changing perception has a positive impact on working against burnout with some useful ideas on what one can practically do to combat burnout.

Quantum physics – Wellness through a microscopic lens

Conventional Western medicine was seen as the only scientific medicine, based upon a materialistic model drawing on Darwin's evolution theory, Newtonian physics, chemistry, anatomy and physiology. However, science has evolved through the study of the behaviour of subatomic particles. Quantum physics emerged as a new scientific model to understand our reality. It has revolutionised our society on many levels, sparking discussions of science versus consciousness/spirituality.

Through the principles of quantum physics it can be explained how ancient healing traditions (Acupuncture, Ayurvedic Medicine), Homeopathy and Naturopathy work with the body's subtle energy systems such as prana or vital force energy. A leading quantum physicist, Amit Goswami, PhD., has already laid the foundation for this in his book, The Quantum Doctor, a physicist's guide to health and healing.

Integrative Quantum Medicine is said to be the key to solving the current healthcare crisis, and it will lead to a new vision of integrative healthcare based on the full potentiality of the individual rather than focusing on disease. Our understanding of wellness and the human body will expand to include the body's subtle energy systems, with mental and emotional connections to the physical body.

Scientists now understand how energy fields react with other forces and have proved that everything that exists is made up of particles of energy that vibrate. Quantum physics has opened the door to the primary role of mind and how we should not only look and believe what is visible, rather that there is much more. These are new intersections that are changing the face of physics, psychology, neurology, biology and many other fields. The work of epigeneticists has discovered that genes are merely codes that give each cell its structure and functions. It has been discovered that cell activity is not dictated solely by our genes but responds to the environment it is in.[27] This environment includes lifestyle choices such as nutrition, responses to stress, thinking styles and emotions. Genes can be turned on or off depending upon the environment of the cell and the environment of the organism, in our case, the human illness or wellbeing is not a genetic issue but has more grounding in the emotional and physical environment we live in. Our responses to the environment are controlled by our perceptions which, in turn, are based on past experiences and what has been learnt. As such, they can interact with our body's cells and activate or inhibit the cell's function just as the medical devices can. There is the case of a construction worker in the UK, who stepped on a nail. It went right through his boot and came out the other side. The pain was excruciating to the point where he needed morphine just to remove the boot. Once the boot was removed it became clear that the nail had completely missed his foot and had gone in between his toes.[28] When people expect something to happen to their bodies, such as side effects of medication – it often does. If people believe something has happened to their bodies, such as happens with sham surgery – it often feels like it has. It seems that our expectations, thoughts and beliefs are impacting our health.

Quantum physics is all around us and the universe runs on quantum rules. When one can apply three of the universal laws to one's wellbeing as fundamental life principles one is freed to make expanded healthier choices, and that which is presented as dis-ease is a reflection of a co-creation with self and one's environment.

Universal law of conservation

Energy cannot be created nor destroyed. It can change form. Energy is. Existence is made up of energy and matter and while material forms may appear to come and go, the energy remains, transformed and enlivening some new form of matter. Human traits, a type of current, are conserved through time. They may change appearances and show up in different ways, but they always exist. They do not come and go, they transform. Perceptions that something's missing – in you or someone else – are merely illusions. When you know that this law governs all energy, you are set free from your limiting viewpoint to see myriad forms of all things. Nothing is missing, and nothing is gained or lost. Everything remains. Energy is.

The law of polarity

This law states that everything (including light particles in physics) can be separated into two opposite parts and that each of those still contains the potentiality of the other. Up exists with down, white has black, slow is also fast and fast can be slow.

The same holds true for elation and depression, infatuation and resentment, kindness and cruelty, generosity and stinginess. No event is solely beautiful or tragic, just as no person is just good or bad. Labelling things this way may help us talk about them but it does not bring you to the heart of love. Realise that every time you allow yourself into an extreme, you create the equal experience of the opposite. When we acknowledge that one-sidedness is merely a function of perception, not the full truth, it opens the doorway to seeing the rest of what is and when you allow yourself to perceive the whole of anything, you are open to the divine perfection of the universe. Nothing is one-sided; everything contains its opposite. All is.

The law of equilibrium

Sir Isaac Newton revealed that any action has an equal and opposite reaction. Forces come in pairs. In life, what goes around comes around. Things have an inherent balance. Although something may appear one-sided in the moment, in time you will see that there is an equal and opposite reaction in the same moment. If someone is criticising you and attempting to tear you down, you can count on the fact that simultaneously you will recognise someone is complimenting and building you up. If you look in the moment, and even over the vast spans of time, you see great order. The universe maintains equilibrium and synchronicity.

We live our lives according to a prioritised set of values, according to Dr John Demartini.[29] The hierarchy of your values determines how you perceive and act upon the world and therefore your destiny. What you perceive to be missing (in fact nothing is ever missing) becomes "important" or valuable in your world. Your private voids give birth to your public values. When you feel your values are being supported, you feel "good". When you feel your values are being challenged, you feel "bad". Your set of values is as unique as your finger prints.

To determine your values, ask yourself the following questions:

1. How do you fill your space?
2. How do you spend your time?
3. How do you spend your energy?
4. How do you spend your money?
5. Where are you most organised?
6. Where are you most disciplined?
7. What do you think about most?
8. What do you visualise most?
9. What do you internally dialogue most about?

10. What do you externally dialogue most about?

11. What do you react to most?

12. What goals do you set the most?

These are the seven areas/values which can be expressed powerfully:

Spiritual	Spiritual mission
Mental	Mental genius
Vocational	Vocational fulfilment
Financial	Financial wealth
Family	Familial stability
Social	Social network
Physical	Physical vitality

Using the 12 questions and determining your perceived voids, list your 7 values in order of priority:

1 _____

2 _____

3 _____

4 _____

5 _____

6 _____

7 _____

Every person is responsible for planning their life so that it is balanced and they can reach their full potential in every area. However, many frequently focus only on their work or home to the exclusion of other important parts of human life. One of the most important characteristics of an emotionally intelligent person is their ability to manage their lifestyle. This implies that they are able to maintain a balance between all facets of life, that is composed of physical, psychological or emotional, vocational, family, spiritual, intellectual and social. The balance may differ from person to person, but it is essential for self-actualisation. If a person does not have balance, they may manifest symptoms causing pain in these components, such as unpleasant feelings, physical pain or disease, mental anguish, which are indicative of unfulfilled needs.

An integrated and holistic way of understanding wellness is by looking at all the dimensions of wellness to ensure overall health, life satisfaction, meaning and the prevention of burnout and ultimately disease.

Wellness dimensions

Wellness is the pursuit of continued growth and balance in the seven dimensions of wellness. Many people think about "wellness" in terms of physical health only. The word invokes thoughts of nutrition, exercise, weight management, blood pressure, etc. Wellness, however, is much more than physical health. Wellness is a full integration of physical, mental, and spiritual wellbeing. It is a complex interaction that leads to quality of life. Wellness is commonly viewed as having seven dimensions. Each dimension contributes to our own sense of wellness or quality of life, and each affects and overlaps the others. Each of these areas also impact on mental health in specific which is covered in the following chapters of this book. At times one may be more prominent than others, but neglect of any one dimension for any length of time has adverse effects on overall health and certainly on one's mental health. The next part of this chapter covers all wellbeing dimensions with suggestions on how to achieve this practically. These all contribute in mitigating and dealing with burnout and the overall maintenance of mental health.

Physical dimension

Health experts believe that 40-70% of premature deaths could be prevented if people changed their personal habits and took better care of themselves. Stress-related health issues are associated with increased healthcare costs, mental-health decrements, and poor wellbeing. Stress activates physiological responses encompassing changes in the nervous and immune systems, such as an increased level of cortisol, increased heart rate and blood pressure. With persistent stress, these physiological changes can lead to chronic health conditions, such as an elevated blood pressure and a dysregulated immune system, cognitive complications and mental illnesses including depression.[30]

Watching what we eat, avoiding drugs and alcohol, wearing seat belts, and exercising are great places to start. But, as life gets frantic and stress sneaks in, the physical dimension is usually the first to go. We get too busy ruminating about what needs to get done or, for example, we over-stretch ourselves in other areas of our lives in fear of losing our jobs. We are too busy to exercise, we do not have enough time to eat lunch, we rely on quick pick-me-up stimulants like coffee, sugar and nicotine and we compromise on restful sleep. The more stimulants you use, the more you are unable to maintain an even blood sugar level which causes a rapid release of sugar into the blood and your blood sugar level then drops too low. The cycle of craving more stimulants to attempt to keep your energy level up causes unpleasant symptoms such as fatigue, irritability, reduced stress tolerance, sleep disturbances and anxiety. These are all things that we do that are detrimental to both our physical wellbeing and other areas of life as well. Physical wellness means learning about and identifying symptoms of disease, getting regular medical check-ups, identifying destructive habits of attempts to cope, and protecting yourself from injuries and harm. For example, alcohol consumption is often a short-term stress-reliever as it increases energy levels by raising blood sugar, and releases our natural brain tranquiliser, a neurotransmitter called GABA. This only occurs for an hour, then alcohol suppresses it, triggering anxiety, depletes you of vital nutrients (Vitamin B and Magnesium which are essential for mental wellbeing) and disrupts your sleep (affecting REM dream sleep which is essential to rebalance in order to feel vital and creative upon waking) – and thus the cycle of drinking continues. Developing healthy habits today will not only add years to your life but will enhance the enjoyment and quality of those years. It also includes the environment you place yourself in. It is an awareness and an involvement of the state of our earth, the effects our daily habits have on the physical environment and being socially responsible.

Table 7.1: Tips for optimal physical wellness and prevention strategies

Exercise	• Physical activity is an adaptive coping strategy and effective in reducing stress and related symptoms. It has the ability to burn off excess adrenalin. In one particular study where joggers were compared to a sedentary control group,[31] the joggers were found to be consistently more emotionally stable and less depressed. Exercise types include strength, endurance, functional, balance and flexibility. Adults need to undertake at least 150 minutes of moderate-intensity exercise per week to maintain their fitness and health. Moderate exercise increases one's heart rate and breathing; specifically, it prompts 40%–60% of heart rate reserve (jogging and bicycle riding slower than 10mph low to moderate exercise intensity) is associated with favourable status on coronary artery disease and other stress-related risk factors. For stress reduction exercising at least three to five sessions per week of at least 15 minutes duration at moderate intensity can be very helpful.[30]
Nutrition	• Maintaining energy levels will stop stimulant cravings and leave you feeling more able to cope with stress, more relaxed and fulfilled. Start your morning with a larger breakfast. Consult a dietician for the best fit for your dietary. It is suggested an oat-based, unsweetened live yogurt with banana, ground sesame seeds and wheatgerm or an egg. Eat slowly, regularly, and control your meal portions. Exclude sodium (salt), drink alcohol in moderation (no more than 1 glass 3 times a week), and limit caffeine. • Replace stimulants with peppermint tea or green tea as they have less caffeine and more anti-oxidants. Stop smoking and protect yourself against second-hand smoke. • Drink 6-8 glasses of water. Eat fresh fruit, vegetables (dark green leaves), fish, nuts and fibre.

Relaxation	• Jacobson's technique or Progressive muscle relaxation: the key to this technique is to tense each muscle group and hold for 5 seconds. Then, you exhale as you let your muscles fully relax for 10 to 20 seconds before you move on to the next muscle group.
	• Doing yoga unites (yoga meaning 'union' in Sanskrit) the mind, body and the breath to bring you into a natural state of balance and calm. Meditate. Enjoy aromatherapy as this reduces stress since the sense of smell is directly connected to the "emotional brain". In a study done in New York essential oils were sprayed in some carriages in a subway and it was found that those sprayed with essential oils had decreased aggression.
Activities	• Maintain a healthy lifestyle. Follow up medical problems and learn to recognise early signs of illness. Take up a sport. Slow down. Sing to your own voice or listen to music – it has been shown that music helps to heal, improves mood, influences your heartbeat and is energising. Certain brain waves (electromagnetic activity) are pulses of energy at a specific vibration and can be activated through sound and music. Take control of your weight. Use seat belts, helmets, and other protective equipment.
Rest	• Restful sleep is the ultimate relaxant and pivotal to mental health and wellness. We need at least 7 hours uninterrupted good quality sleep a night as it allows for REM sleep which assists with feeling rested upon waking, better memory, increases serotonin thus less likely to get depressed; retains learning and helps with longevity. Snooze for twenty minutes. Avoid sleeping in front of the television, telephone or cell phone because of electromagnetic fields and avoid listening to news and scary movies prior to going to bed. Magnesium, valerian, chamomile or hop tea can be used at night to promote sleep. Create a space in your home that feels serene and peaceful.
Nature and natural light	• Nature has an incredible ability to put things into perspective, to ground us and get us to see the hidden order in all things and that we are not alone. The magnificence of its perfection brings forth gratitude to be alive and to be a part of this bigger picture. Being in nature allows for the left brain (analysis paralysis) to settle and to move towards more lateral thinking (creativity, feelings, intuition). Being surrounded by nature also allows us to move from our minds and to the senses, getting the mind to relax to a meditative state (with the same electromagnetic field of the earth). Receive enough natural light to stimulate Vitamin D which enhances mood and promotes sleep. Surround yourself with natural materials like plants, wood and cane.
Colour	• Add blue and green to your environment as this is important for optimal brain functioning. Spend time in nature.
Physical touch	• Hug and touch. Acknowledge the importance of sensual and sexual needs.
	• Having a massage increases oxytocin and a sense of safety, decreases stored negative tension and feelings, and a healing energy exchange. In Japan, companies are using a form of "healing exchange" called *johrei* with 2 people exchanging energy which increases T-cell count (an indicator of good immunity).

Emotional dimension

Emotional wellness means understanding how we feel, accepting our feelings, and learning how to express and cope with our emotions. It is a dynamic state that fluctuates frequently with your other wellness dimensions. Being emotionally well is typically defined as possessing the ability to feel and express human emotions such as happiness, sadness, disappointment and anger. It means having the ability to love and be loved and achieving a sense of fulfilment in life. Identifying the obstacles that prevent us from achieving emotional wellness and taking appropriate steps to cope with such problems is also important. Emotional wellness encompasses optimism, self-esteem, self-acceptance, and the ability to share feelings. It is a human condition to store memories of life experiences, particularly ones that evoke negative feelings such as betrayal, fear, anger, sadness, loneliness and disappointment. We often keep things inside, leaving things unresolved possibly as a way to feel justified in our hurts or self-righteous in our position, instead of releasing or expressing these in a healthy way.

Table 7.2: Ideas for optimal emotional wellness and prevention strategies

Interpersonal skills	• Verbalise feelings and learn to communicate more effectively your needs and wants.
	• Improve self-knowledge. Exercise emotional control. Be accepting. Have a sense of humour. Be resilient. Invest in me-time as there is one relationship you are in for life and that is with yourself.
Awareness	• Tune-in to your thoughts and feelings in order to become more self-aware.
Attitude	• Cultivate an optimistic attitude, as an attitude of gratitude can evoke a sense of hope, happiness and fulfilment. Give yourself a gift on your birthday or other holiday event.
Seek and provide support	• Mental wellness is very much dependent on accessing support and gives us a sense of fulfilment when being there for someone in need.
Acceptance and forgiveness	• If you find you are struggling to let go of past hurts and pain, psychotherapy can assist.

Intellectual dimension

Intellectual wellness is characterised by the ability to make sound decisions and to think critically. It includes openness to new ideas; motivation to master new skills; and a sense of humour, creativity, and curiosity. Striving for personal growth and a willingness to seek out and use new information in an effective manner for personal and social development are also part of intellectual wellness. The intellectual dimension encourages creative, stimulating mental activities. Our minds need to be continually inspired and exercised just as our bodies do. People who possess a high level of intellectual wellness have an active mind and continue to learn. An intellectually well person uses the resources available to expand one's knowledge and improve skills. Keeping up to date on current events and participating in activities that arouse our minds are also important.

Table 7.3: Ideas for optimal intellectual wellness and prevention strategies

Review	• Focus daily on your accomplishments. Avoid criticising yourself unnecessarily. Think and perceive; assess assumptions, personal values and needs. Take a course or workshop. Learn a foreign language. Seek out people who challenge you intellectually. Read. Learn to appreciate art. Learn time management skills. Practise stress management techniques:[32]
	• Guided imagery helps you use your imagination to take you to a calm, peaceful place. Because of the way the mind and body are connected, guided imagery can make you feel like you are experiencing something just by imagining it. Use deep diaphragmatic breathing exercises as breath is the link between the mind and the body and circulates more oxygen which means more vital energy; do 5 minutes of this breath work before breakfast daily.
	• Meditation helps to quieten the mind, improves mental focus, and is a wonderful antidote to the effects of stress. It has been shown to decrease blood pressure, slow heart rate, stabilise brainwave patterns; improves the body's' responsiveness to recovery, stressful events, increases immunity, decreases cortisol levels, decreases anxiety and depression. Meditating a few minutes daily (like physical exercise) will help you feel connected and calm.
Reformulate	• Channel thoughts and attitudes and do a reality check; change thinking and reframe positively.
Responsibility	• Blaming your circumstances is one of the biggest toxins in keeping you stuck, in denial and helpless. Accept responsibility for your own life and take responsible action. Set realistic goals and learn to time manage your lifestyle.

Family dimension

This area involves connecting with our family and loved ones, committing and contributing to the expectations and demands of our personal roles, developing intimacy, and creating a support network of family members in the way we care and communicate.

Table 7.4: Ideas for optimal family wellness and prevention strategies

Commitment	• Real, long-term relationships are built on more than chemistry and compatibility. Commitment is the essential ingredient that keeps it all together and serves as a promise or a guarantee of that personal agreement you made with your partner. Creating and conveying trust means to be honest. Teamwork indicates commitment as it demonstrates your willingness to compromise and recognise your partner's needs.
Care & Communication	• Demonstrate respect and appreciation for your partner through words and actions. Kind communication – by giving praise and showing gratitude – will leave your partner feeling cared for. Be supportive of their feelings and encouraging them will help them feel like they can always turn to you for advice and comfort. • Set boundaries for yourself in terms of what you will and will not do and be okay with saying no. • Allocate quality time together connecting and doing activities that are nurturing and fun-loving.

Occupational dimension

This may include the actual work that you do, the roles that you play and/or the responsibilities that you have as a full-time parent or student. Being occupationally well means seeking opportunities to grow professionally and to be fulfilled in your "job" whatever that may be. Occupational/Vocational wellness involves preparing and making use of your gifts, skills, and talents in order to gain purpose, happiness, and enrichment in your life. The development of occupational satisfaction and wellness is related to your attitude towards your work. Achieving optimal occupational wellness allows you to maintain a positive attitude and experience satisfaction/pleasure in your employment. The occupationally-well individual contributes her/his unique skills/talents to work that is meaningful and rewarding. Values are expressed through involvement in activities that are personally rewarding for you and make a contribution to the wellbeing of the community at large. It means successfully integrating a commitment to your occupation into a total lifestyle that is satisfying and rewarding.

Table 7.5: Ideas for optimal occupational wellness and prevention strategies

Development	• Create opportunities to develop and learn by being open to change and learning new skills.
	• Connect with a mentor to give you guidance and support. Consider opportunities for the employee to help or support others, keeping in mind that this may not be a great strategy if that was a regular and difficult part of the employee's job prior to their burnout. By taking the attention away from what they are not doing well, and instead using their strengths to mentor or coach someone else, you may help reduce apathy and cynicism. Stop multi-tasking by focusing on one thing at a time. Work at a reasonable, steady pace. Help organise and prioritise work into manageable and clear expectations. by breaking down seemingly overwhelming tasks and projects into smaller achievable parts. Recognise and celebrate your small steps along the way. Communicate to your manager that you want to be successful at your job and ask him/her how they would measure that. Provide clear expectations for all employees and obtain confirmation that each employee understands those expectations. Make sure that employees have the necessary resources and skills to meet expectations. Provide ongoing training to employees to maintain competency. Help employees understand their value to the organisation and their contributions to the organisation's goals. Encourage social support and respect within and among work teams. Support physical activity throughout the workday. Strongly encourage the taking of breaks away from the work environment.
Boundaries	• Set reasonable and realistic expectations. Organisations should be clear as to which activities require the highest standards and when it is okay to lower the bar and still meet business needs. Enforce reasonable work hours, including, if necessary, sending employees without good boundaries home at the end of their regular work day. Help assess workload for those who feel pressured to remain working beyond normal business hours. Learn to set boundaries by ensuring you take your leave days, not working overtime perpetually, and leaving work at work, and not working on your off days. Avoid toxic people and situations. Learn to keep your work space neat, tidy and organised. Learn to be comfortable with saying, "I don't know" if you do not know. Take regular assigned breaks. Even if you must provide contact information in case of emergency, try as much as possible to stay disconnected from work during vacation time. Setting of boundaries becomes even more important in the work from home environment.
Workplace Plan	• Develop a workplace plan with a practical strategy to support an employee who may be experiencing burnout. As part of any plan, ask the employee how best to recognise their successes and victories. This could include immediate and personal praise, opportunities for growth and development, public recognition, or incentives. It is important to understand what is most valued by the employee. This may help as employees experiencing burnout often have a significant loss of confidence in their overall competency.

Career Planning	Visit a career planning/placement office and use the available resources. Explore a variety of career options. Create a vision for your future. Choose a career that suits your personality, interests, and talents.

Social dimension

Making contact and reaching out to others can be difficult, but very rewarding. Communication and sharing are important to your social life and vital to your sense of wellbeing. Social wellness refers to our ability to interact successfully in our global community and to live up to the expectations and demands of our personal roles. This means learning good communication skills, developing intimacy with others, and creating a support network of friends and family members. Social wellness includes showing respect for others and yourself. Contributing to your community and to the world builds a sense of belonging.

Table 7.6: *Ideas for optimal social wellness and prevention strategies*

Develop interpersonal skills	• Practise listening, self-assertiveness, self-disclosure, facilitative questioning, positive reframing, empathising, validating, restoring relationships, forgiving. Attend to social support systems. Cultivate healthy relationships. Get involved and participate. Contribute to your community. Share your talents and skills. Communicate your thoughts, feelings, and ideas.
Personal coping	• Eliminate circumstances that cause problems; keep consequences within manageable boundaries (direct/indirect, active/inactive).

Spiritual dimension

No matter what religion you practise, your spiritual sense of wellness is the part of you that develops values. Everyone creates their own rules that provide a sense of who they are and why things work the way they do. A spiritual centre can allow you to answer tough questions like: "Am I on the right track?" It can give you something to turn to during hard times. Just a few minutes a day of quiet time to gather your thoughts can have powerful results. Spiritual wellness involves possessing a set of guiding beliefs, principles, or values that help give direction to one's life. It encompasses a high level of faith, hope, and commitment to your individual beliefs that provides a sense of meaning and purpose. It is willingness to seek meaning and purpose in human existence, to question everything and to appreciate the things which cannot be readily explained or understood. People can derive meaning and purpose through nature, art, music, religion, meditation, or good deeds performed for others. Spirituality transcends the individual to create a common bond with humanity. A spiritually well person seeks harmony between what lies within as well as the forces outside.

Table 7.7: Ideas for optimal spiritual wellness and prevention strategies

Self-reflection	• Existential questions by pondering on the purpose and meaning of life – Why am I here? Explore your spiritual core. Be inquisitive and curious. Be fully present in everything you do. Listen with your heart and live by your principles. Allow yourself and those around you the freedom to be who they are. See opportunities for growth in the challenges life brings.
Meditation/ prayer	• Spend time alone and meditate or pray regularly or surround yourself in nature by nurturing your spirit.
Gratitude	• Being grateful allows for giving perspective and leaving us feeling uplifted, content and happier. Write daily in a gratitude journal to help refocus your mind on those things that are positive in your life.
Volunteer	• Allocating time for a meaningful cause can make you feel fulfilled and give you a sense of purpose and fulfilment – that your life matters in the bigger picture.

Achieving a balanced sense of wellness is an ongoing fluid process. You can better enjoy all that life has to offer by being well-rounded and healthy. Each small change you make in one area will have a positive effect in all the other dimensions. Organisations need to shift to a more collaborative methodology by dialoguing with their employees in developing individualised solutions to prevent burnout and focus on their wellness as a part of integrating it into their working lives. Creating a workplace plan that focuses on specific solutions to past, current and potential work-related issues, with ways to assist employees will be beneficial and will help to avoid crisis interventions in the long-run. The employees' involvement in the creation of a workplace plan will get their commitment to the plan's success and overall wellbeing, job satisfaction and retention within the organisation with a compound positive effect in all dimensions.

Burnout is a common workplace phenomenon affecting every aspect of life. No organisation, including its employees are immune to this. Thus in closing, it is imperative for organisations to provide a work environment where every employee feels happy, motivated with the necessary tools and support needed to succeed, and each employee has the insight to be aware and mindful of how their beliefs, thoughts and actions contribute to managing one's mental health and wellness in the workplace.

Chapter 8

Depression and anxiety – A big deal in the workplace

Joanna Kleovoulou

Five of the 10 leading causes of disability worldwide are mental health problems, major depression, schizophrenia, bipolar disorders, alcohol use and obsessive-compulsive disorders. These disorders, including anxiety, depression and stress, have a direct impact on any working population and should be addressed within that context. They may also develop into long-term disorders with accompanying forms of disability.[1] Four out of every ten people suffering from mental disorders such as depression, intellectual disability, alcohol use disorders, epilepsy, schizophrenia, and those committing suicide are living in low- and middle-income countries (LMICs).[2]

The ability to work productively is crucial to health and psychological wellbeing. Mental health involves the individual's capacity to cope with internal needs as well as external demands, such as roles within employment. Common Mental Disorders are associated with reduced workplace productivity. It is anticipated that this impact is greatest in developing countries. Furthermore, workplace stress is associated with a significant adverse impact on emotional wellbeing and is linked with an increased risk of common mental disorders.[3]

Depression and anxiety are among the most frequent causes of occupational disability.[4] The burden of mental disorders is under-recognised in developing countries, despite strong evidence regarding its social impact.[5] Depression is expected to be the second most common disorder across the world behind ischemic heart disease by 2020 and is expected to account for 15% of the total disease burden.

The first part of this chapter goes through the details on the clinical diagnosis of depression and anxiety including the criteria to be met for diagnosis, the symptoms and the triggers. The balance of the chapter address the manifestation of depression and anxiety in the workplace together with some practical ideas of addressing these issues and seeking help.

Depression and the DSM-V

Clinical depression, otherwise known as major depressive disorder (MDD), is a common and serious mood disorder. *The Diagnostic and Statistical Manual of Mental Disorders* Fifth Edition (DSM-V) is the handbook used by health care professionals in the United States and many other counties worldwide as the guidebook to the diagnosis of mental disorders. DSM contains descriptions, symptoms, and other criteria for diagnosing mental disorders.[6] Depressive Disorders classified under the latest DSM-V are: Disruptive Mood Dysregulation Disorder, Major Depressive Disorder, Single and Recurrent Episodes, Persistent Depressive Disorder (Dysthymia), Premenstrual Dysphoric Disorder, Substance/Medication-Induced Depressive Disorder, Depressive Disorder Due to Another Medical Condition, Other Specified Depressive Disorder and Unspecified Depressive Disorder. The DSM-V outlines the following criterion to make a diagnosis of depression. The individual must be experiencing five or more symptoms during the same two-week period and at least one of the symptoms should be either (1) depressed mood or (2) loss of interest or pleasure.

1. Depressed mood most of the day, nearly every day.

2. Markedly diminished interest or pleasure in all, or almost all, activities most of the day, nearly every day.

3. Significant weight loss when not dieting or weight gain, or decrease or increase in appetite nearly every day.

4. A slowing down of thought and a reduction of physical movement (observable by others, not merely subjective feelings of restlessness or being slowed down).

5. Fatigue or loss of energy nearly every day.

6. Feelings of worthlessness or excessive or inappropriate guilt nearly every day.

7. Diminished ability to think or concentrate, or indecisiveness, nearly every day.

8. Recurrent thoughts of death, recurrent suicidal ideation, without a specific plan, or a suicide attempt or a specific plan for committing suicide.

To receive a diagnosis of depression, these symptoms must cause significant distress or impairment in social, occupational or other important areas of functioning. The symptoms must also not be a result of substance abuse or another medical condition. A person suffering from depression feels sad or hopeless about most things and loses the ability to experience joy or pleasure.

What are the triggers?

Depression is a complex illness with many contributing factors. There are internal and external variables that predispose a person to triggering clinical depression.

Internal triggers

Genes: A family history of depression may increase the risk. The genetics of depression, like most psychiatric disorders, are not as simple or straightforward as in purely genetic diseases such as cystic fibrosis. It is well-documented that there is a genetic link to depression. Children, siblings, and parents of people with severe depression are somewhat more likely to have depression than are members of the general population.

Serious illnesses: Depression may occur comorbidly with a major illness or may be triggered by another medical condition. A chronic illness is one that lasts over a long period and usually cannot be cured completely. Some examples of chronic illnesses that may cause depression are heart disease, diabetes, lupus, arthritis, HIV, hypothyroidism, multiple sclerosis and kidney disease.

Gender: Women are about twice as likely as men to become depressed. Gender inequality in mental health and diagnosis is still common practice. Women are found also to be lonelier and more devoid of support than men. Hormonal changes that women go through at different times of their lives may play a role. Some studies indicate that women are generally more emotionally vulnerable as compared to men and they are more likely to hang on to a negative thought, reveals several studies. This can increase the risk of depression. Higher testosterone levels in men were linked with lower sensitivity, while feminine attributes were associated with higher sensitivity.

Age: People who are elderly are at higher risk of depression. That can be made worse by other factors, such as living alone and having a lack of social support.

Chronic pain: Not only is chronic pain unpleasant, it is disruptive to sleep, affects mobility and exercise, triggers feelings of discouragement, demoralisation, amotivation, lowered mood, withdrawal and it impacts overall functioning in terms of relationships and work productivity.

Biology: Researchers have noted differences in the brains of people who have clinical depression compared with those who do not. The hippocampus, which is a small area in the brain that is used to store memories, appears smaller in some people with a history of depression which means fewer serotonin receptors. Serotonin is a neurotransmitter that allows communication across brain circuits involved in processing emotions.

Studies have also found that the stress hormone cortisol is produced in excess in depressed people and believe that cortisol has a shrinking effect on the development of the hippocampus.

External factors that trigger clinical depression

Abuse: Physical, sexual, emotional and financial abuse can make one more vulnerable to depression.

Conflict: With persons with a biological vulnerability to depression may result from personal conflicts with family or friends.

Major events: Job loss, relocating, death, divorce, retirement or even starting a new job can trigger depression.

Medications: Certain medications may increase the risk of depression. Medications such as benzodiazepines, barbiturates, and the acne drug isotretinoin, have been linked with depression. Corticosteroids, opioids such as codeine and morphine, and anticholinergics taken to relieve stomach cramps can sometimes cause fluctuations in mood. Even blood pressure medications (beta-blockers) have been linked to depression.

Substance misuse: Nearly 30% of people with substance misuse problems also have major or clinical depression.

Anxiety under the DSM-V

The former DSM-IV category of Anxiety Disorders became three separate categories in DSM-V. These three categories are:

1. **Anxiety Disorders:** Separation Anxiety Disorder, Selective Mutism, Specific Phobia, Social Phobia, Panic Disorder, Agoraphobia, and Generalised Anxiety Disorder, Substance/Medication-Induced Anxiety Disorder, Anxiety Disorder Due to Another Medical Condition, Other Specified Anxiety Disorder, Unspecified Anxiety Disorder.

2. **Obsessive-Compulsive Disorders:** Obsessive-Compulsive Disorder, Body Dysmorphic Disorder, Hoarding Disorder, Trichotillomania/hair-pulling disorder, Excoriation Disorder/skin-picking disorder, Disorder Substance/Medication-Induced Obsessive-Compulsive and Related Disorder, Obsessive-Compulsive and Related Disorder Due to Another Medical Condition, Other Specified Obsessive-Compulsive and Related Disorder, Unspecified Obsessive-Compulsive and Related Disorder.

3. **Trauma and Stressor-Related Disorders**: Reactive Attachment Disorder, Disinhibited Social Engagement Disorder, Post-Traumatic-Stress-Disorder, Acute Stress Disorder, Adjustment Disorder, Other Specified Trauma- and Stressor-Related Disorder, Unspecified Trauma- and Stressor-Related Disorder.

Generalised Anxiety Disorder (GAD), Obsessive Compulsive Disorder (OCD), Panic Disorder, PTSD and Social Phobia will be discussed as they are prevalent in the workplace.

- **Generalised Anxiety Disorder**: GAD is characterised by chronic anxiety, exaggerated worry and tension, even when there is little or nothing to provoke it.
- **Obsessive-Compulsive Disorder**: OCD is depicted by recurrent, unwanted thoughts (obsessions) and/or repetitive behaviours (compulsions). Repetitive behaviours such as hand washing, counting, checking, or cleaning are often performed with the hope of preventing obsessive thoughts or making them go away. Performing these rituals provides only temporary relief, and not performing them significantly increases anxiety.
- **Panic Disorder**: is characterised by unexpected and repeated episodes of intense fear accompanied by physical symptoms that may include chest pain, heart palpitations, shortness of breath, dizziness, or abdominal distress.
- **Post-Traumatic-Stress-Disorder**: PTSD can develop after exposure to a terrifying event or ordeal in which grave physical harm occurred or was threatened. Traumatic events that may trigger PTSD include violent personal assaults, hijackings, natural or human-caused disasters, accidents, or military combat.
- **Social Phobia**: (Social Anxiety Disorder) can be described by overwhelming anxiety and excessive self-consciousness in everyday social situations. Social phobia can be limited to only one type of situation, such as a fear of speaking in formal or informal situations, or eating or drinking in front of others. In its most severe form, a person experiences symptoms almost anytime they are around other people.

Risk factors related to anxiety disorders

Researchers are finding that both genetic and environmental factors contribute to the risk of developing an anxiety disorder.[7] Although the risk factors for each type of anxiety disorder can vary, some general risk factors that may develop an anxiety disorder for all types of anxiety disorders include:

- Temperamental traits of shyness or behavioural inhibition in childhood;
- Early childhood exposure to stressful life events in early childhood;

- Genetic factors – a history of anxiety or other mental illnesses (depression) in biological relatives particularly with a parent with anxiety;
- Some physical health conditions, such as thyroid problems, irritable bowel syndrome, heart arrhythmias, or caffeine or other substances/medications, can produce or aggravate anxiety symptoms; a physical health examination is helpful in the evaluation of a possible anxiety disorder;
- Personality type such as high-strung, busy people with type A personalities have a greater risk of developing an anxiety disorder;
- Another comorbid anxiety disorder;
- Unresolved or exacerbated stress has shown to increase the chances of developing chronic anxiety;
- Trauma: Severe trauma, such as child abuse or military combat, increases your risk of developing anxiety. This can include being the victim of trauma, being close to someone who's the victim of trauma, or witnessing something traumatic.
- Sex or gender: Women are twice as likely as men to have generalised anxiety disorder and other related conditions.

A combination of psychotherapy, medication, support groups and overall lifestyle enhancements can assist in relieving and managing depression, and improving overall functioning. As health care professionals gain a better understanding of the causes of depression, they are able to make better tailored diagnoses and recommend more effective treatment plans.

Prevalence

Mental and substance abuse disorders are important causes of disease burden, accounting for 8.8% and 16.6% of the total burden of disease in low-income and lower middle-income countries, respectively. Unipolar depressive disorder is the third leading cause of disease burden accounting for 4.3% of the global burden of disease. Out of fifty million people suffering from epilepsy, 80% live in low- and middle-income countries; of the sixty-six million people suffering from depression, 85% live in low- and middle-income countries; of the twenty-four million people with an alcohol related problem, 82% live in low- and middle-income countries; of the 1 million people who commit suicide each year (rates for attempted suicide are 10 to 20 times higher), 84% of these suicides are committed in low- and middle-income countries. In low-income countries unipolar depressive disorder represents almost as large a problem as malaria (3.2% versus 4.0% of total disease burden); but funds being invested to combat depression are tiny compared to those allotted to fight malaria. In middle-income countries unipolar depressive disorders are the biggest contributor to disease burden, accounting for twice the burden of HIV/AIDS, yet funds are not being directed to address this priority.[8]

One of the most important reasons for higher morbidity and mortality rates among people with mental disorders is the inequitable care and treatment that these individuals receive for both mental and physical illnesses. Between 75% and 85% of people with severe mental disorders are unable to access the treatment they need for their mental health problem in low- and middle-income countries, compared with 35% and 50% of people in high-income countries.

Treatment rates for physical health problems are much higher than for mental disorders, and in low- and middle-income countries there was a marked discrepancy (92% and 47%, respectively), wider than in high-income countries (76% and 35%).[9]

Mental disorders have diverse and far-reaching social impacts, including homelessness, higher rates of imprisonment, poor educational opportunities and outcomes, lack of employment and limited income-generating opportunities. An increased risk of becoming homeless is as a consequence of a mental illness, lack of treatment thereof and few opportunities for income-generation.[10]

This evidence of strong links between poverty and mental disorder provides weight to the argument that mental disorders should be an important concern for development strategies implemented by government, NGOs, bilateral agencies, global partnerships, private foundations, multi-lateral agencies and other stakeholders.

Depression and anxiety in the world of work

Depression and anxiety manifest in many different ways within the workplace and the impact scales across the entire workforce. With the increase in stress that so many employees are exposed to today, there is a resultant impact on one's ability to cope. This renders the employee more stressed due to a lack of coping and more vulnerable to depression and anxiety-related symptoms. The fast pace of change and the move towards digitisation is said to play a pertinent role in the increased levels of depression and anxiety in the workforce.

Work environments also play a critical role in the mental health of employees. In the context of the COVID-19 pandemic and work from home structures, this has led to a breakdown of workplace support and social isolation. This also plays a role in the increase in depression and anxiety symptoms felt by employees. The work environment forms the foundation of an employee's perception of coping and thriving in such an environment. If this environment is felt to be distrusting, punitive, competitive (unhealthy levels of), unjust, etc. this all contributes to a rise in depression and anxiety in the workplace.

Panelists at the Global Forum called out the need for employers to not only provide mental health resources through employee assistance programmes and employee resource groups, but also to consider how to proactively foster connection and remove the stigma around mental health.

Many studies have shown the reluctance of employers to employ people with mental illness. A study in Uganda revealed that people with mental illness are denied access to credit services due to the belief that they have impaired functioning, are unable to meaningfully engage in productive work and are thus incapable of paying back loans. This discriminatory practice denied people the opportunity to escape poverty through income-generating activities.[11]

The variables of the impact of mental illness on work productivity include loss days, or the number of days during which respondents were unable to do their usual activities; cutback days, or the number of days during which activities were reduced; and extra effort days, or the number of days during which individuals were able to function normally but only with significant effort.[12] The cost of working days lost in the European Union due to stress-related illness is estimated to be on average 3–4% of GDP. Estimates are that in the UK stress in the workplace causes a loss of 6.5 million working days a year.[13]

It has been found that employees may not recognise that they are suffering from anxiety or depression, and may lack motivation to seek assistance. Furthermore, even if the employee recognises that they are suffering, they may be fearful of negative consequences if they reveal their condition to their employers.[14]

To seriously address the current mental health crisis there needs to be more evidence-based interventions. At the same time that businesses are coming to understand the urgency of implementing workplace mental health programmes, many are also facing budget constraints or under-performance as a result of COVID-19. As with any smart business decision – and especially in challenging times – employers need to know that their investments are proven effective and backed by data. Researchers at the Global Forum emphasised the need for a larger 'menu' of evidence-based workplace mental health interventions – along with comprehensive training and implementation plans. Telehealth services and other digital therapies are filling a key gap in the availability of care.[15]

A note on depression and suicide

In South Africa alone there are approximately 23 suicides per day and at least 10 to 20 attempts for every successful suicide.[16] Teen suicide is on the increase. According to WHO, a suicide occurs every 40 seconds and an attempt is made every three seconds.[17] There is a close relationship between depression and suicide. Although the majority of people who have depression do not die by suicide, having major depression does increase suicide risk compared to people without depression. The risk of death by suicide may, in part, be related to the severity of the depression.

Longitudinal research on depression shows that 2% of people treated for depression in an outpatient setting will die by suicide, and this doubles (4%) for inpatients.[18] Those who have had suicide ideation or have had suicide attempts in the past, this risk increases to 6%. We also see that men are four times more likely to die by suicide then women are. Another way to understand the relationship between depression and suicide, is about 60% of people who commit suicide had struggled with a mood disorder (this includes depression, bipolar disorder, dysthymia).

These statistics are important as it is one of the top causes of death around the world, especially in young people, and yet suicide can be preventable. Most people who commit suicide don't really want to die, however they do want to end their pain. Often the pain they feel is unbearable and is spoken about in this way, sometimes they may also feel like a burden on others. When someone talks about suicide or dwell on the topic of death and dying, they should be taken seriously. Don't be afraid to ask questions around their thoughts and how you can listen or support them or help them to obtain the relevant support. Many people who commit suicide also plan the steps they will take and take the opportunity to say goodbye to others, if you feel uncomfortable around the person's behaviours especially if they become withdrawn, talk to them and seek guidance. In some cases, there is a correlation between substance misuse, depression and suicide. In such cases, the substance misuse is used to try and numb the pain, or it is used to harm themselves. In any event, being intoxicated or under the influence can increase the chances of suicide purely by accident.

For many losing a loved one to suicide can be quite traumatic and can result in a complex bereavement, often because it is difficult to gain closure with more questions than answers related to the suicide and what the person was going through. Talking about mental health openly whether it be at home or at work increases the likelihood of those who are struggling to obtain support rather than suffering in silence. Those who have lost loved ones due to suicide often face stigma and discrimination as well, which could make them feel isolated and refrain from the support that they require to heal. We need to create dialogue around mental health taboos to create awareness and more importantly to direct people to the support that they need.

Dealing with depression and anxiety

Only 25% of those struggling with depression and anxiety seek treatment. This means that 75% of people struggling are not getting the help that they need. There are a number of things we can do ensure people are directed to the relevant support from both a personal and a workplace perspective. Below are some frameworks to consider.

Take the lead in mental health

The subjective experience of high-quality relationships with supervisors (i.e. Leader–Member Exchange) is one of the protective factors against psychological health issues at work and this effect is mediated by psychological empowerment.[19]

- As leaders it is vital to create a positive work environment that results in better outcomes for all employees – including those battling depression. Remember not to personalise and keep in mind that depression is an illness and can be treated. By helping an employee with depression, you ultimately help your team and your organisation as a whole, which demonstrates strong leadership.

- Ensure your employees have the resources they need to be productive. Many companies have Employee Assistance Programmes (EAPs) or other resources available to employees free of charge. By sharing these resources often, you become an approachable leader and your team members will see you as an enlightened manager. This increases the likelihood that they may approach you when they experience problems – and before these problems seriously compromise their work performance.

- Identify your employees' strengths and utilise them. If your employees feel like tasks are designed for them, they will be more likely to view the tasks as important, complete them more quickly, and experience a sense of achievement and validation.

- Focus on supporting and acknowledging achievements rather than highlighting failures. Motivation in depressed employees drops in the face of threats and punishment. People who are depressed are usually highly self-critical. Moreover, research shows that people who are criticised by someone whom they perceive as highly critical of them are less able to activate neurocircuits that control negative emotions.

Self-care for the employee

For people who have a pre-existing mental health condition such as anxiety, depression, OCD, PTSD, social anxiety or panic, the COVID-19 pandemic may have triggered and intensified the symptoms. Some basic guidelines to keep you resilient during these times:

- Recognise what is in your control, and let go of what is out of your control. If we can learn to surrender to the fact that although we would like to feel in control, we do not really have control of what happens next. In surrendering to this fact, uncertainty does not feel so daunting.
- Uphold a daily routine as it creates some mental sense of regularity, momentum and structure which relieves stress, and gives us a sense of purpose.
- Use your extra time to discover new parts of yourself – for example, starting up sewing, or knitting, gardening or learning to be more tech savvy.
- For those (especially parents) who have had to take on multiple roles, learn to ask for support, get your family working together for a common goal and, to alleviate your responsibilities, lower your expectations about your children's performance and do the best you can. Remember that we are all experiencing a crisis.
- Do not repress feelings and find a trusted family member or friend to reach out to.
- Remember to do something self-loving to fill up your own cup.
- Avoid watching too much COVID-19 media coverage as this perpetuates anxiety and creates a sense of dread.
- Keep connected with your loved ones, extended family and friends that care.
- If you are a chronic patient, remember to take your medication and to stay in touch with your specialist.
- Change and uncertainty are difficult for most of us to deal with, and can affect our mental health and wellbeing, potentially leading to increased stress, depression and anxiety. Uncertainty is one of the most anxiety-provoking experiences, as it feels like a threat to our wellbeing and survival, as well as the feelings of helplessness, both of which are being evoked in most of us during this pandemic, which poses a real threat of risk to health, and other potential losses.
- Find a new routine that works for you during lockdown, and find constructive ways to release frustrations such as exercise – walking, yoga, breathing and mindfulness, journaling, kicking a ball against a wall etc.

In conclusion, targeted programmes in the workplace are needed to break the cycle between stress and mental illness. These must include measures specifically addressing the needs of people with mental disorders, such as accessible and effective services and support, facilitation of education, employment opportunities and housing, and enforcement of human rights protection. It also includes stress-management support, and conducive working environments. Many organisations have identified mental health as an important issue, yet lack resources, expertise, workplace education and workplace policies to address the problem. Financial investments have not always been used efficiently; for example, minimal spend is considered for employee wellbeing support. Having mental illness on the agenda of organisations will be a critical step in the right direction. Important barriers to employment such as stigma and discrimination must be overcome.

The impact of COVID-19 will eventually lessen, but untreated psychological damage can have lifelong effects. It is important that as employers and employees alike, know when to intervene and seek additional support. Reach out for help. The COVID-19 pandemic has not limited your digital access to doctors, psychologists, social workers, to your loved ones or to your church and community. The cost and impact of depression and anxiety in the workplace are only going to continue and immediate action needs to be taken.

Chapter 9

"Dis"traction and "dis"ease

Ashika Pillay

As you sit at your computer, laptop open, climbing onto your Zoom call, phone nearby, maybe even your tablet open somewhere nearby, the pings, alerts and WhatsApp notifications come streaming in. Perhaps this started since you opened your eyes to turn your alarm off this morning? As the meeting starts, with your camera off, you feel the insatiable urge to turn the phone around, unlock it, read the message and perhaps even to respond. Even as you read this, you may be aware of your attention being pulled in many directions?

Nassim Nicholas Taleb, author of the famous book, *The Black Swan*, says that the difference between technology and slavery is that slaves are fully aware that they are not free. Even though this may seem a bit facetious, it does beg the question of whether we have really become hooked and enslaved by technology and gadgets. If we have, this is not a chance occurrence. It may be a fight for market share of a very scarce resource – human attention. In his book *Hooked, How to Build Habit-Forming Products,* Nir Eyal[1], says that the route to making products "sticky" is basically to create a habit around use, using the "hook model" which makes them addictive.[1] Once you are "hooked" your behaviour has become a habit – an unconscious repetitive sequence that does not need you to think. This is what companies use as a model to build products that grab our attention. And grab our attention they do!

According to statistica.com there are about 3.96 billion people using digital media as at August 2020 and the average global internet user spends 144 minutes per day on social media sites.[2] While another study by RescueTime, of 11 000 users shows a whopping 3 hours and 15 minutes of daily use.[3] It is clear that we need technology – it is ubiquitous and part of what makes life easier for us. During this pandemic and the lockdowns that ensued it has become a way to ensure business continuity. Additionally, many organisations have used the opportunity to evolve their offering to more online and virtual. While we can acknowledge the leverage and advantages that technology affords us, the question is really about who or what is in control? The reality is that we are living in the attention economy, where our attention is a scarce and valuable resource, and where products are designed to attract our attention, find the hook and habituate to keep us coming back.

The advent of limitless connectivity and the "always on" environment creates an imperative for us to be able to embrace technology and social media and still work with it in a way that serves our wellbeing, work and purpose in life. Social media is not to be vilified and painted as a monster in whose clutches we are the helpless victim because it is a tool that serves a purpose. The question is: What is the skill level of the artisan using this tool? The intention of this chapter is to understand distractibility and its impact on our wellbeing so that we can be in control of our attention, time and health in an intentional, deliberate and causative manner.

The relationship between distractibility and wellbeing

Harvard psychologists Matthew Killingsworth and Daniel Gilbert conducted a study with 2 250 subjects in 2010 and used an iPhone to track firstly, what they were doing at a particular time and secondly what their minds were focused on at that time. What they found was that, of those studied, their minds were not present, or on task 47% of the time.[4] They also found that this mind wandering was linked to a general state of unhappiness.[5] It is in the nature of the mind to wander, and the human mind is often naturally in a state of mental chatter, moving from one random thought to another quite reflexively. The so called "monkey mind" grabs onto the next thought, which can pull you into ruminating about the past or planning the future. Bring a global pandemic into the mix with unprecedented levels of uncertainty, health concerns, managing working from home or grieving for loved ones that have passed on, has really only amplified the mind's capacity to be distracted and restless leading to an increase in mental health concerns. These states can create a low level of "dis" ease where we are neither depressed nor anxious but have a sense of restless unfocussed energy. Sound familiar?

So, if this is the "normal" state of how the mind works, adding the pings and vibrations of your phone can only fan the flames of the proverbial fire that is already simmering in the underground, adding to the state of "unhappiness" of the wandering mind.

Continuous partial attention, a term coined by Linda Stone (1998), formally of Apple and later Microsoft consultant, is a state of being attentive to several things at once, but with nothing really getting all of our attention, which can lead to a constant state of stress and hyper-arousal with an increase in stress hormones in the body.[6] With a steady flood of cortisol and adrenalin, the downstream impact of chronic stress is well known – from a reduction in immune system effectiveness, to impacting the cardiovascular system, to gut conditions, anxiety, depression and the list can go on. Additionally, the cognitive overload created by digital distractions erodes our self-control, of course, making it much easier to then engage in other unhealthy behaviours like unhealthy snacking, as an example.[7]

This, as early as 1998, was already a mental health concern, and has now been further amplified by the pandemic. The time that we spend on devices, video calls and online interaction has increased many fold, and we've amplified this level of restlessness, and state of "dis"ease that is bubbling just beneath the surface. Moreover, the boundaries between work and home are so blurred that it's challenging to know when to "switch off" from one mode to the next.

Much has been written about the impact of technology on sleep, which we now know is a crucial element of wellbeing. Research has shown that sleep balance is crucial – that it is not just quantity, but quality as well. When we sleep we help the body to reset, restore and heal as it has an impact on us mentally, emotionally and physically. To elaborate, mentally, we have better memory, cognition and logical thinking, while emotionally it calibrates our emotional circuits. As one study done in 2018 showed, loss of sleep can actually trigger anxiety.[8] Physically, sleep helps strengthen the immune system, fight malignancy, balance insulin and glucose, regulate appetite and the cardiovascular system, among many other benefits. In his book, *Why We Sleep: Unlocking the Power of Sleep and Dreams*[9], Matthew Walker says that "sleep is the single most effective thing that we can do to reset our brain and body health each day".[9] However, several studies cited by Gazzaley and Rosen[10] show that our devices are impacting both the quantity and quality of our sleep.[10] The blue light impacts the melatonin response in our brains which starts 2-3 hours before we even go to sleep, thereby interrupting our circadian rhythm. The results of poor sleep can impact mental functioning, induce anxiety, impact memory and our capacity to pay attention during the day.[10] On the other hand, when we are able to focus and get work tasks done, be present for meaningful conversations with work colleagues, family and friends, complete home chores to the best of our ability, we can get a sense of presence and accomplishment, positively impacting our sense of happiness and wellbeing.

Social media on its own, not used correctly, may also have an impact on wellbeing. In his book, *When Likes Aren't Enough*[25], happiness researcher and psychologist Dr Tim Bono, quoted in *Healthista*, says that social media, can lead to social comparison.[11] Constant scrolling through FaceBook, Twitter or Instagram, watching others' lives unfold, can make us unhappy, depending on our own personal situations.[11] Robust data is certainly missing on the actual impact of social media on mental wellbeing. However, anecdotal evidence and some studies have seen an impact on social connection, physical wellbeing (sleep), and mental wellbeing (attention span). The other question is 'How "social" is social media?' While true social connection has been shown to be one of the key determinants of health and longevity, demonstrated quite unequivocally in a Harvard Study[12] by researcher Robert Waldinger, this is not what we get with social media despite the likes, retweets and number of friends on Facebook.[12] The rise of the "Digital Detox" with people self-reporting the need to go offline is certainly evidence that people are feeling the need to have time away from social media, and its impact on themselves and their relationships.

The anatomy of distraction

One of the main reasons that we see these impacts on wellbeing is because reflexive and 'uncontrolled' use of technology impacts our focus and attention by the distraction that they tempt. There are essentially two types of distraction – sensory and emotional. The first is basically anything coming up from your sensory input like pain, temperature, touch, taste, smell and sight. The second, emotional distraction, is probably more challenging for us especially during this time.[7] Concern, worry and anxiety can pull for our attention and lead us down the rabbit hole of rumination.

By contrast, selective attention or focus is how we learn best. In this state we are "phase locked" on what we are doing, forming a mental model of what we are reading and having deeper insights into and reflections on our work. In the context of technology, providing a constant source of both sensory and emotional distraction can materially challenge our focus, clarity and capacity for deep work.[7]

Can we multitask?

As you sit there, contemplating the response to the WhatsApp, while the meeting has started, you might think that it's completely possible to multitask and that you can kill the proverbial two birds with one stone. Not according to neuro-scientific research. While the brain is totally capable of parallel processing information, with activities that need cognitive control, what it's actually doing is task switching.[10] Task switching is costly – both in terms of accuracy as well as time efficiency. You make more mistakes and it takes longer, and if you do a lot of task switching you can lose up to 40% of your productivity in a day.[13]

Here is a simple and practical example of demonstrating task switching that you can try out (adapted from Gazzaley and Rosen)[10]

- First, count from one to ten out loud
- Now, recite the alphabet from A to J
- Now, try to combine them by superimposing the two so A1, B2, C3

You will notice that the first and second steps were easier and faster, and that there was significant slowing in the third step.

The cost of multitasking as highlighted by Gazzaley and Rosen[10] ranges from lower productivity, higher stress levels, lower cognitive capacity and the increased effort required.[10] These authors note several studies which demonstrate that workplace interruptions result in additional work time, due to the time it takes to gather attention back to the original task. In some cases it took workers more than half an hour to return back to the what they were busy with. The real cost of this it seems, is not just the time lost, but higher workload, frustration, stress and time pressure.

What does technology and social media give us? Why do we do this?

The accessibility of cost effective technology and bandwidth, has probably created some of the temptation. Another, according to Gazzaley and Rosen, is that we have an "innate desire to seek information".[10] There is another theory, backed by research that every time we look at our phones, read an email or see a "like" to our post, we activate dopamine in the brain, and get a dopamine "hit" and that this reward-based behaviour gets hardwired over time, building a habit.[14]

Additionally, with the advent of the pandemic and lockdowns emotional wellbeing has taken one of the biggest knocks. The emotional state that many are in is fear and anxiety, and neuroscientists label this as "frazzle". In this state, our executive centre (prefrontal cortex) goes offline, and the emotional centre (amygdala) lights up. So the capacity to pay attention is limited when the focus is on worries about jobs, working from home, finances or the health and safety of family. In this state it is much easier, using less cognitive energy, to scroll through your social media than to deal with the work in front of you.

Why do we need to focus and what is that?

Focus, defined as selective attention, works much like a spotlight on our cognitive control. When we focus our senses are honed in, enhancing some, and inhibiting others depending on what it is we would like to focus on.[10] Importantly, focus needs a goal and an intention.[7] In the real world what this means is that for that Zoom call, the goal needs to be clear, that this is indeed an important goal for you.

Have you ever experienced a time when you were doing something that you enjoyed, that tested your abilities or challenged you to the right level, where you were so immersed in the activity that a few hours passed without you realising it? It could be a physical activity, a creative process or working on a work project. *"The best moments in our lives are not the passive, receptive, relaxing times . . . The best moments usually occur if a person's body or mind is stretched to its limits in a voluntary effort to accomplish something difficult and worthwhile"*.[15] Mihaly Csikszentmihalyi, author of *Flow: The Psychology of Optimal Experience*[15] and one of the founders of Positive

Psychology describes flow as a state of being totally immersed in an activity that is challenging and *"the holistic experience that people feel when they act with total involvement".* The dimensions of flow that he names are:

- clear goals
- a balance between challenge and skill
- action and awareness
- focused concentration
- sense of potential control
- loss of self-consciousness
- time distortion

Importantly, he labelled this as the optimal experience and that it is linked to happiness and wellbeing. In the age of distractibility, we have to consider how we achieve this state of alert focus and intentional goal orientation more often, and what is preventing us from achieving this. How do we find and refine our sense of control and focus so we can truly live up to our potential by managing internal and external distractions appropriately? In the context of the pandemic, managing attention and focus can be strongly linked to a sense of wellbeing, productivity and balance, noting the multidimensional nature of the challenges that we are facing.

And... enter willpower

When we practise self-restraint vs self-gratification, our attention seems to be needed in triplicate. So, the phone buzzes and a WhatsApp pops up, while you are at last quite engaged in finishing a report. You feel that reflexive urge to unlock and read the message. Three things need to happen, according to Goleman[7]:

1. You need to disengage from the phone that is powerfully pulling for your attention, and "ignore" it.
2. Second is to keep your attention on the report at hand.
3. And third you need to focus on the goal which is the completed report[7]

*Adapted example of the Marshmallow test

According to Goleman[7], this trio is what adds up to willpower. Importantly, ignoring and filtering out (step 1) is not a passive process, but a very active one and requires considerable brain resources. So ignoring the buzz or the ping of the WhatsApp is an energy-consuming event.[7]

How can we gain focus, harness energy and create the conditions for wellbeing and optimal performance?

Manage energy: The opposite of distraction is not focus

In his book Indistractable, Nir Eyal[16] says that the opposite of distraction is not focus, but traction. He proposes that *"Traction is an action that moves us towards what we really want"*.[16] Dr John DeMartini of the Demartini Institute is often quoted as saying: *"If you do not fill your day with high priority actions that inspire you, your day will fill up with low priority distractions that will not. If you do not bring order to your life, disorder will rule your destiny".* [17] What both are essentially saying, is that we are not slaves to, in this case, technology.

Distractions will always be present in our lives. At this point the distractions happen to be the ever accessible gadgets with their multiplicity of uses. Understanding what is important to us, being clear on our goals, having clarity of purpose for our lives sits at the core of wellbeing. In the famous adage by Lewis Carroll, *"If you don't know where you are going, any road will get you there",* means that from a practical perspective, setting out your day, your intentions and what you would like to achieve, casts the way to navigate your day. Do you understand what your values are? What is your purpose and vision for the life that you want? Placing our attention into our values, and acting on those values, is what will lead us to fulfilment and living up to our true potential.[18]

Create awareness: A distractibility audit

Go about your day, as you normally would for one or two days. Start a task, and notice what gets you "off task". Is it the message notifications on your phone? Are the email alerts on when you are finishing a report or on a call, or meeting? Is there something on your mind that is an internal trigger? Doing this audit will help you create awareness of which tech, tools or apps are not helping your productivity and impacting your wellbeing, and perhaps also about what's on your mind.

Next, look at the amount of time you are spending on these apps – some phones have that available as well as the amount of screen time you are having per week. How much more productive time could you have if you had more focus?

Manage the environment: Clear the clutter

Now that we understand how labile and scarce human attention is, it is important to help this distractible and wandering mind, so that it can use its resources more productively. First, how can we manage the physical environment? Look at your workspace. How conducive and optimal is it to minimising external triggers like sights, sounds and smells while maximising focus?

Here are a few tips:

- Clear your work space so that it has only what you need to work.
- Pack away unnecessary books and office equipment out of sight to enable laser focus and attention.
- Put a sign on your door or tell people around you that you have some deep work time for the next 60 – 90 minutes.
- Clear your phone of unnecessary apps that you don't use, and file them so you know where to go. It's easy to take a scroll down Facebook Lane or Twitter Avenue when you feel that twinge of boredom, so see if you can move the apps so that they are not so easy to get to, or delete them altogether if you really feel like you spend too much of time on them. You can also just keep them on your desktop and not your phone.
- In managing the organisational environment, companies need to look at the culture that they are potentiating. Is it the "always on, respond immediately, emails at 2am" culture in one breath, and then "employee wellbeing and mindfulness sessions" in the next? As tongue-in-cheek as that may sound, culture is the feeling that employees experience when the values are lived and have meaning. It is therefore important to take a step back and assess how much meaning we really place on true wellbeing. The cost to an organisation is not just absenteeism when employees are not physically well, its presenteeism when they are mentally not ok i.e. present in body, but mentally and emotionally disengaged because of stress, or worse, burnout.

Manage your calendar intentionally

Diaries can also become full and cluttered. Here are some ideas of looking at this and planning for focus and productivity:

- Conduct a calendar audit and note where you are spending your time versus what your priorities are
- What meetings are truly necessary and is your company in the "meeting mania" where there's a meeting for everything?
- Nir Eyal suggests that instead of "to do lists", you create "time blocks" of designated tasks that are important to you.[16] So, for example, schedule "Report" from 9 – 11am.
- It is also important to plan every day, to be deliberate about how you are going to "spend" your time. Do this planning every evening so that when you wake up you are not in the abyss of choice, and wasting energy and attention.

Managing emotions: Understanding the triggers of boredom and anxiety

Sometimes distractions of technology could be the symptom for deeper emotions like anxiety, boredom and stress. Even though we are not speaking of addiction per se, which is the other end of the spectrum, we could be finding emotional relief from mindlessly using our phones or Facebook. Gabor Mate, renowned addiction expert, speaker and author on trauma, addiction, stress and childhood development, says that an addiction is an attempt to escape suffering and pain.[19] Is distraction a way of avoiding an emotional state that is painful or uncomfortable? Check in with yourself the next time you find yourself reaching for the source of distraction.

At its extreme, distractibility can become a habit, an unconscious repetitive pattern that becomes automatic. Jud Brewer, American psychiatrist, neuroscientist and author says that we are biologically rewarded by checking feeds, posts and likes and get a "jolt of excitement" from the positive affirmation.[14] Understanding this neuro-chemical process can help us in managing emotion and the urge to check our device.

- Notice when you have the urge to check your phone or feed.
- Become aware of what that feels like in your body and allow the urge to pass.
- Called "surfing the urge", Brewer says that this "urge" shifts as we watch it mindfully rather than act on it in the "unconscious" way, and break the habit.[14]

Practising mindfulness and meditation has demonstrated in many studies to have a positive impact on managing emotions, attention, memory and executive functioning. Starting a mindfulness practice can help you to alleviate stress, be more present and less reactive, as well as become more focused, creative and compassionate (See chapter on Mindfulness for more detail).

Managing your body so that your biology can work for you

Sleep

Good quality sleep is crucial not only to physical wellbeing, but definitely to paying attention and being able to focus. You would also want to look at how you prepare for sleep – dimming lights, cooling your bedroom and moving away from screens and devices a few hours before bedtime. Activities like reading (a paper book), listening to music, having conversations with your loved ones a few hours before bed help you wind down your nervous system and align to the natural circadian rhythm of the body. Avoid caffeinated drinks and stimulants up to 7 hours before bedtime.

Diet

The mind and body are intimately integrated and what you eat, when you eat and how much you eat will influence not only how you feel, but also how well you can focus. There are many "diets" on the market, and there's definitely no one-size-fits-all approach as we are all so genetically unique. One thing that's for sure is that a diet high in processed food, high in refined sugars and fat is not good for your body. Additionally, sugar-laden drinks and juices are also what is called "empty calories" and can lead to a spike in blood sugar and then the dreaded low. Most of us inherently know what we should and should not be eating. *"Eat food. Not too much. Mostly plants"*, is a quote ascribed to Michael Pollan, a food writer in the USA and is good practical advice in 7 words.[20] However, if you have a particular medical condition it is important to consult with a health care professional to work on the appropriate foods that will nourish your body for better health, wellbeing and performance. See more on the role of diet in Chapter 11.

Exercise

If there's one "pill" that we can prescribe for almost anyone, of any age its exercise – a universal tonic. This is not just the so-called "runners' high" after a high-intensity cardio workout. In the book *Spark, the revolutionary new science of exercise and the brain*, written by Associate Clinical Professor of Psychiatry at Harvard Medical School, John Ratey, we see evidence that exercise increases blood flow to the brain, changes the cocktail of biochemicals in the brain and can increase the connections between the brain cells themselves.[21] Research has shown that it can help with anxiety, depression, improve mood, enhance cognitive function and memory. The American Heart Association recommends *"150 minutes per week of moderate-intensity aerobic activity or 75 minutes per week of vigorous aerobic activity, or a combination of both, preferably spread throughout the week."*[22]

"And we change our brain chemistry almost immediately. Exercise increases all the neurotransmitters that we target in psychiatry for depression, anxiety and attention, as well as helping deal with cravings and addictions. It also makes us much more social, makes us much more eager to connect to other people"[23] says Ratey. Short bouts of exercise can also help you focus better. So when you have long days at the office or working online, fit in even 10 minutes of movement and notice the difference in your ability to focus and be present. Consult with a health care practitioner if you have any medical conditions so you can tailor your movement to your body and lifestyle. If not, get moving!

Conclusion

Nobel Laureate Herbert A. Simon, defined attention as the *"bottleneck of human thought"*.[24] Living in the "attention economy" where technology, their apps and social media are fighting for one of the scarcest pieces of real estate, human attention, means that in order for us to be conscious, awake and thoughtful about our lives, our wellbeing and that of our loved ones, we must not become "slaves of technology". We need to wake up to intentionally focus and direct our minds, thoughts and energy. The distracted mind can move us into habitual patterns, where we can sleepwalk through our lives, and not wake up to that which we are blessed to have, or to be able to effect change in our wellbeing. Distraction does not have to bring disease. On the flip side, attention and focus can help us wake up to the life that we have, or wish to have, and most importantly do the work that we need to do, add our contribution to making the planet a better place than we found it.

Part 2

Mental health is not an island: Wellbeing is holistic and has multiple dimensions

Chapter 10: The impact of nutrition on mental health

By: Kim Martin

Dietician Kim introduces that we should consider food as the basis of our mental and physical health throughout our lives. This chapter not only covers the link between diet and mental health but explains in detail the biochemical pathways that contribute to various mental health issues. In investigating these pathways one can find clues as to where specific vitamins, minerals, antioxidants (or even dietary patterns) can intervene positively. With this information the guidelines for using nutrition to influence mental health can then be deduced. Dietary patterns that have been researched to improve mental health are included for your consumption. The chapter concludes with some insights on nutritional interventions in the workplace and at home with the advent of so many working from home.

Chapter 11: Link between mental health and physical wellbeing

By: Dr Nikki Connellan

This chapter begins with an explanation of mental health and physical health. There is such a strong interplay between physical health and mental health – some of the statistics may surprise you. Understanding the links between mind and body is the first step in developing strategies to reduce the incidence of co-existing conditions and supporting those already living with mental illnesses and chronic physical conditions. Dr Nikki Connellan unpacks some of the conditions that are highly interlinked with mental health concerns, and also discusses the role of social factors and the power of optimism. This chapter highlights the importance of looking after our mental health in order to look after our physical health and vice versa.

Chapter 12: How financial stress impacts mental health

By: Val Leeming

No one is exempt from experiencing financial stress at some point in their lives. This of course has been further exacerbated as a result of the COVID-19 pandemic, with many feeling the negative impact of job loss and general financial impact on personal and family lives. The chapter details the kinds of factors that escalate financial stress and highlights how this in turn plays a role in worsening mental health. The reverse is also true. Those with mental health concerns also find themselves in situations that exacerbate financial concerns. Case studies are used to showcase the relationship and impact of financial stress on mental health. Interesting concepts such as 'black tax', money memories and personalities are unpacked. The advent of money disorders which is a chronic pattern of self-destructive financial behaviours, and the link this has to mental health is also discussed. The sad reality is that many of these stressors can be avoided by creating a greater awareness and with more education. Financial education is very limited, and this is often where workplaces can play a valuable role is assisting employees to make improved decisions related to their finances.

Chapter 13: What can workplaces do to create a culture of care around mental health?

By: Namhla Tambatambata

Mental health needs to be a focus area within organisations and needs to be housed within a culture of care. This chapter highlights the complexity and importance of designing a culture of care and environment for employees to thrive with regard to their mental health within the context of the future world of work imperatives which include workplaces that are innovative and high performing. The point is made that the organisational response on mental health is a shared responsibility and requires participation from all functions. In addition, employees also need to take responsibility to show care and support to one another as leaders alone cannot change the culture. Creating a culture of care and a culture of looking after one's mental health is a very important aspect of a successful business now and in the future and must be a priority in order to have healthy businesses.

Chapter 10

The impact of nutrition on mental health

Kim Martin

The impact that nutrition can have on mental health is often grossly underestimated and overlooked. The global mental health crisis has negative effects not just on social functioning, but on physical wellbeing and nutritional status. Likewise, nutritional status has an effect on mental health issues. Mental health issues incur significant burden on the individual, but also on society as a whole through the high economic cost of lost productivity and the demand on healthcare services. Similarly, poor physical health and more importantly poor diet quality are associated with increased risk for mental health disorders.[1] The further one delves into these issues, the further one is confronted with the proverbial "chicken and egg" conundrum as both mental health and nutrition are closely intertwined and directly influence one another. Regardless of the angle from which you examine it, dietary and lifestyle interventions are key to improving outcomes whether they be mitigating risk for mental health disorders or improving the health status of those already diagnosed.

We should consider food as the basis of our mental
and physical health throughout our lives.

Two challenges of modern life: Poor diet and poor mental health

You may think that our modern diet must surely be better for us than that of our ancestors. We have greater access to food today than ever before in history. There are shops on almost every corner, and you can even purchase groceries at your local petrol station. Our modern food environment has seen the rise of the industrial and globalised food industry – and this may not actually be entirely to our benefit. Food companies recognised more than 100 years ago that food products with a longer shelf life could be produced cheaply, and that people would buy them for their taste and convenience. They also realised the value in adding scientifically targeted amounts of the key flavour determinants – salt, sugar and fat. This means our food environment has rapidly evolved into what public health experts call "obesogenic", that is, an environment that promotes weight gain, poor health and ultimately obesity.

Poor diet is now the number two risk factor for early death across the world. Diets considered to be poor are those higher in "junk" foods such as sugar-sweetened drinks, fried foods, pastries, doughnuts, packaged snacks, and processed and refined breads and cereals. This is also known as a more "Western" diet. Across the world in 2016, the number one risk factor for death in men and second highest risk factor for death in women was a diet low in fruits, vegetables, wholegrains, nuts and seeds, fibre, and good-quality fats from fish and plants, and/or a diet high in processed meats, salt and sugar-sweetened beverages.[2] This eating pattern contributes to early death by increasing risk for non-infectious chronic diseases of lifestyle such as diabetes, heart disease, hypertension, stroke, obesity and many forms of cancer. Those living with chronic conditions often experience emotional stress and chronic pain, both of which are associated with the development of depression and anxiety – which brings us full circle back to the mental health challenges we're faced with today.

There are challenges to good quality nutrition in individuals with mental health issues. For example, we know that appetite changes are common in people with depression. Whilst some will lose their appetite, others may crave foods that are sweet and fatty. Furthermore, those with depression tend to have less energy to perform activities of daily living related to nutrient intake such as grocery shopping and preparing meals. This combination can lead to malnutrition either by a lack of sufficient calories in the diet, or by an increased reliance upon take-aways which are often laden with excess salt, refined sugar or fat. This in turn can lead to further decline in both physical and mental wellbeing. Only through targeted and appropriately supportive nutrition and psychological intervention can we hope to break this cycle and initiate positive change.

To better understand the relationship between mental health and nutrition, one first needs to get an overview of the biochemical pathways that contribute to various mental health issues. In investigating these pathways one can find clues as to where specific vitamins, minerals, antioxidants (or even dietary patterns) can intervene positively. With this information the guidelines for using nutrition to influence mental health can then be deduced.

Mental health and associated biochemical changes: Areas for nutrition intervention

We now know that the diet quality influences both the risk for and outcome of mood disorders, with much of the available research focusing specifically on depression.[1] Standard treatments for depression will often include the administration of medications alongside counselling with a trained psychologist. However, based on the evidence now available, standard treatments are more effective when they include nutritional intervention as well.

Major depression has not one cause, but rather a myriad of factors that may contribute, namely environmental, psychological, genetic and biological pathways. The clinical presentation may also be complex, with many dysregulated pathways and biochemical changes which provide key areas for nutrition intervention. As we understand it today, depression may present as a neurotransmitter (chemical messenger) of imbalance, hypothalamic-pituitary-axis (HPA) disturbances, inflammation, increased oxidative stress, neuroprogression (cell changes in the brain), and mitochondrial disturbances.[3] A brief overview of each of these alterations will be given. However, it is important to note that they can occur simultaneously.

Neurotransmitters

Neurotransmitters are chemical messengers made by nerve cells that transmit signals from one cell to another. These neurotransmitters include the most commonly known serotonin (the mood stabilising hormone), dopamine (the pleasure hormone), noradrenaline (the hormone that increases heart rate and blood pressure), and glutamate (the hormone that helps with learning and memory). The most extensively studied of these neurotransmitters is serotonin. Low levels of serotonin are commonly found in individuals with depression and anxiety, which is why these individuals are often prescribed medications to increase the availability of serotonin, noradrenaline and possibly dopamine.

The pharmaceutical treatment to neurotransmitter imbalances can be well complimented with dietary intervention. Diet quality is important in the production of both serotonin and dopamine. In order for the body to produce serotonin there needs to be sufficient quantities of available tryptophan, which is an amino acid found in both protein and carbohydrate foods.[4] In fact, when you restrict dietary carbohydrate and protein, we see a decrease in serotonin levels.[3] It's important to note that dietary carbohydrate refers to whole food options such as fruits, vegetables and wholegrains, and not the simple sugars such as fruit juices or sweets. We actually see serotonin levels decrease following consumption of refined sugars, and this same effect is found when the diet habitually contains large levels of refined sugars and dietary fats (as in the regular consumption of fast-foods).[3] Other nutrients that have an effect on tryptophan and overall neurotransmitter functioning include folic acid, zinc, vitamin B12, vitamin B6, Iron, and Omega 3 fatty acids.

HPA disturbances

Our hypothalamic-pituitary-axis is based in our brain, and functions much like a manager in a business. It oversees both the production and flow of resources (in this case hormones) from one area of the body to another. The HPA is responsible for maintaining homeostasis, or balance in the body. One of the major hormones regulated by the HPA is cortisol (our stress hormone). Cortisol often presents as elevated in individuals with depression, with the degree of elevation corresponding to the severity of the condition.[5]

There are three main lifestyle factors that influence cortisol levels namely diet, sleep and exercise. Regular exercise and high-quality sleep are fantastic ways to decrease elevated cortisol levels, but diet can also play a role. A high intake of dietary fat and especially saturated fats (like those found in butter, coconut oil, baked goods, animal fats, and more) can negatively influence cortisol levels, whilst a Mediterranean-style diet based around whole foods is associated with improved HPA functioning. Some investigations into higher intakes of dietary Omega 3 fatty acids (through the ingestion of fatty fish such as salmon or through fish oil supplementation) have also shown benefit in terms of decreasing cortisol levels.[3]

Inflammation

Dietary patterns that are considered to be pro-inflammatory are associated with a significantly higher incidence of depressive symptoms even among undiagnosed individuals. [2] Increased levels of inflammation in those with major depression has been confirmed in multiple meta-analyses.[3] Acute inflammation is not always a bad thing for the body, as it is necessary for healing – for example, after a small cut. Prolonged inflammation is however harmful. When you have chronic inflammation, your body's inflammatory response can eventually begin damaging healthy cells, tissues, and organs. Over long periods of time, chronic inflammation can lead to damage to your DNA, tissue death, and internal scarring. All of these are linked to the development of several diseases. It is important to note that inflammation has been suggested to be at the root of many of the biochemical changes listed in this section. It is currently a hot topic in the literature, and whilst we cannot conclude that it is in fact the main cause, we know that addressing inflammation in depressed patients yields positive results.

The very best strategy to address inflammation in the body is to change your diet and lifestyle. There is strong evidence to demonstrate that a Mediterranean based diet is associated with decreased inflammation in the body.[3] The main components of a Mediterranean diet include:

- Daily consumption of fruits, vegetables, wholegrains and healthy fats
- Weekly intake of fish, poultry, eggs and beans
- Moderate portions of whole dairy
- Limited intakes of red meat

The Mediterranean diet differs from other approaches through the specific inclusion of lifestyle changes. Other important elements of the Mediterranean diet are sharing meals with family and friends, enjoying the occasional glass of red wine, and being physically active on a regular basis.[6]

Further strategies to address inflammation include higher intakes of dietary omega 3 fatty acids, and the consumption of anti-inflammatory compounds such as curcumin (an extract of the spice turmeric).[3]

Oxidative stress

Aging, cardiovascular disease, Alzheimer's disease, Parkinson's disease, cancer and more, are diseases that are initiated in part by oxidative stress. Oxidative stress arises when there is excess oxidation in the body as a result of stress, trauma, toxins and infections. Oxidation is a natural process that happens when our bodies metabolise oxygen, and our cells produce energy from it. As a by-product of oxidation, free radicals are produced. Free radicals are necessary components to some degree as they tell the body to initiate repair processes. However, when free radical production overwhelms these repair processes we arrive at a state of oxidative stress.[6] One repair process our body employs to alleviate oxidative stress is to use antioxidants such as vitamin C, vitamin E, and coenzyme Q10. These work to bring about homeostasis in the body by decreasing the free radicals circulating in the body. Patients with major depression have been found to have not only higher levels of oxidative stress, but a decreased antioxidant status.[3]

Whilst we will all likely experience oxidative stress at some point in our lives, the best defence is to be proactive with improving our antioxidant status. Research has yet to identify the ideal amounts of each antioxidant to fully counter oxidative stress, however, there are global food trends associated with improved antioxidant status. These include a high raw food intake (by this they mean fruits and vegetables – not necessarily sushi), increased fibre intake, olive oil use, and decreased use of high-heat cooking methods such as grilling or deep frying. Furthermore, improved antioxidant status and decreased oxidative stress has also been seen in obese and overweight individuals who embark on a weight loss protocol. The research tends to hint that a "normal" body mass index (BMI) also decreases oxidative stress in the body.[3]

Neuroprogression

Neuroprogression is a complex term for what is essentially alterations to the cells of the brain both physically and functionally. Individuals with major depression have been found to have compromised neurogenesis (new brain cell production) and neuronal plasticity (the ability of the brain to change its structure and/or function). This loss of certain functionality leads to stress-induced changes to the brain. Certain antidepressants have been shown to be beneficial in countering neuroprogression, however diet quality and overall physical health also play a valuable role. Importantly, obese people – even children – show deficits in memory, learning and executive functions when compared to those within the healthy weight range. What remains unclear is whether this is due to the obesity, poor diet, or a combination of both.[7]

Following a dietary pattern that emphasizes a high refined carbohydrate intake, high fat intake and that essentially drives excess weight gain, increases the rate of neurodegeneration (brain health decline). Conversely, placing individuals onto a Mediterranean-based diet that is rich in plant foods, wholegrains and fish and encourages a healthy BMI, improves markers of brain health. Going one step further, omega 3 fatty acids themselves have been studied in order to determine their role in countering neuroprogression. Omega 3 fatty acids seem to play a beneficial role when supplemented for 3 months in patients with post-traumatic stress disorder. Further research is warranted in this area.[3]

Mitochondrial dysfunction

The mitochondria are known as the energy powerhouses of the body. They are found in every human cell and are responsible for producing the energy currency of our bodies, Adenosine-Triphosphate (ATP). Depression is associated with mitochondrial dysfunction, and many patients reporting reduced energy levels have been found to have low levels of ATP in biopsied muscles. Likewise, patients who have mitochondrial dysfunction for reasons other than mental health dysfunction often develop depression. This isn't a difficult concept to understand, as we can all relate to having a higher bar for joy when fatigued (parents of young children most especially!) – and this is without diagnosed mitochondrial dysfunction. Essentially, if you're feeling more energetic you are more likely to report positive feelings.

Good quality nutrition can significantly improve the health of your mitochondria. Eating a high fat diet and consuming excess calories on a regular basis has been shown to decrease mitochondrial function. Conversely, healthy calorie restriction (under the guidance of a healthcare practitioner) can actually boost the health of your mitochondria. Increasing your intake of antioxidant-rich foods (through eating more fruits, vegetables, nuts and seeds) can also improve mitochondrial function. As is not often the case with these pathways, specific nutrients have also been investigated for their benefit to mitochondrial function. Coenzyme Q10, Vitamin B2 and L-carnitine have all been shown in the literature to influence mitochondrial metabolism positively.

Does gut health play a role in mental health?

The bacteria living in our gut are not separate entities from our bodies. In fact, they are integrally involved in a number of aspects of our physical and mental wellbeing. Our gut microbiome is part of a bi-directional communication pathway with our central nervous system, named the microbiota-gut-brain-axis. This system is believed to regulate various processes in the body including the immune system, inflammation and even behaviour. Disruptions to the gut bacteria have been correlated with several psychiatric disorders including Parkinson's disease, autism, schizophrenia and depression. While we are unsure of the exact mechanism of this correlation between poor gut health and mental health disorders at this stage, we do know some of the causes of gut microbiome dysregulation.[20]

There are a number of risk factors for poor gut health. These include the use of antibiotics, obesity, stress, high fat and high sugar diets, environmental influences, and exposure to heavy metals and pesticides.[20] Our gut bacteria, when in a healthy state, should be diverse and have a balance between health-promoting strains of bacteria as well as some level of bacteria that we typically refer to as pathogenic such as Enterococcus coli (E.Coli). Poor gut health refers to a gut microbiome that has been depleted in some way and has an increased number of pathogenic bacteria relative to health-promoting strains.

There are two main methods to employ in order to address a dysregulated gut microbiome, namely probiotic supplementation, and a diet rich in prebiotics (found in fibre-rich plant foods) or prebiotic supplementation. Probiotics are widely available on the market, and the research is yet to define exactly which strains should be employed to specifically address mental health issues. What we do know is that biodiverse gut microbiomes are associated with improved health outcomes, and for now this should be the target of dietary intervention – beginning with increasing intakes of plant foods, and considering the addition of probiotic supplementation. A number of studies have shown benefit in supplementing with probiotics in order to encourage biodiversity in the gut. There is also promising evidence that probiotic supplementation increases cognitive function in those with major depression, alleviates stress in adults with anxiety and depression, and lowers anxiety in women with postnatal depression.[20] Further research is still warranted, but this is an exciting area of research to pay attention to.

Overall dietary patterns associated with improved mental health

When you examine the influence of nutrition on individual pathways that can become dysregulated in mental health disorders such as depression, there are some clear trends. As much as society would love for nutrition experts to come up with an exciting and new dietary strategy to revolutionise mental health, the literature steers us consistently back to certain dietary practices that have been preached throughout the decades.

The dietary pattern that comes up most often in the literature with having a positive impact on mental health, is the Mediterranean Diet. It is considered one of the healthiest dietary models worldwide. It was first described by Ancel Keys as a dietary pattern based on low intakes of fat oils, and high intakes of vegetable oils as practised in Greece and the South of Italy during the 1960s.[8] The Greek Dietary Guidelines, the Mediterranean Diet Foundation, and Oldway's Preservation and Trust have all proposed dietary guidelines based around the same principles that we now collectively know as the traditional Mediterranean Diet.[9,10] These guidelines recommend respectively a) olive oil, vegetables, fish, bread and cereals > 6 servings per day; eggs, legumes and nuts 3 – 4 servings per day; b) olive oil at every meal, vegetables, fruits, fish, legumes and cereals > 2 servings per day; and c) olive oil, vegetables, fish, legumes, cereal and bread at every meal. The Mediterranean Diet may also include a moderate consumption of fermented dairy products, a low intake of red meats, and moderate consumption of red wine during main courses. Traditionally this type of diet tended to be home cooked and consumed with friends and family in a relaxed setting. It is likely that this in itself provides benefit. Importantly, whilst the Mediterranean Diet is the dietary pattern with the most research behind it, it is certainly not the only dietary approach that may be beneficial or even appropriate for every individual. When choosing a dietary pattern, it is important to first discuss the options with your personal healthcare practitioner.

Recent clinical trials on the Mediterranean Diet and mental health have shown positive findings on the improvement of depressive symptoms and remission rates when following a healthy dietary regime.[8] From a nutritional point of view, the Mediterranean Diet is low in saturated and animal fats, rich in fibre and antioxidants, rich in monounsaturated fats, and shows a balanced intake between omega 3 fatty acids and omega 6 fatty acids. Therefore, the overarching benefit to human health can most likely be attributed to the high intake of antioxidants, fibre, monounsaturated fats and omega 3 fatty acids. Does this mean that the Mediterranean Diet is the only approach that may benefit patients with mental health issues? Certainly not. There are in fact a few dietary approaches whereby we can achieve emphasis on the same nutrients listed above.

We have a thousand-and-one diets on the market today. It's no wonder the public have become confused as to whether they can eat eggs for breakfast, or whether they can (heaven forbid) have a slice of toast with them. Whilst the Mediterranean Diet is the most well-researched dietary strategy, we cannot discount the benefit of a personalized approach. At the end of the day, adherence and acceptability are two of the most important factors of any dietary intervention. We cannot expect for a vegetarian or vegan to simply adopt the Mediterranean Diet of which animal products are a component. What we can do however, is modify the approach to suit the individual whilst still fulfilling the core components, namely a large emphasis on plant-based foods, omega 3 fatty acids (which you can obtain from either fish or plant-sources) and fibre. Personalised nutrition has been shown to be more effective in changing health behaviours, and so should be incorporated into interventions.[13]

The challenges of nutrition research and diet recommendations

Research into dietary habits and their impact on health is exceptionally tricky. The majority of the diet recommendations that we have are based on epidemiological or observational studies. These involve collecting information from large groups of people in a specific population and then using statistics to test hypotheses as to which risk factor is related to which health outcome. One major limitation is that in every individual there are countless confounding factors that might influence both diet and mental health, and it's not always possible to capture all of these, or their nuances and subtleties, through questionnaires. The other major challenge to "measuring" an individual's dietary intake is that most people are pretty awful at accurately remembering or recording their food intake. This is most true when it comes to estimating their overall calorie intake. The more overweight an individual is, the more likely they are to under-report calorie intake.[7] When discrepancies are seen in the data, it's quite likely to be caused, at least in part, by measurement error.

The most reliable research data comes from randomised controlled trials, however, it's simply not practical to run these for most big nutrition questions. Take the Women's Health Initiative study, which was one of the biggest and most costly nutrition studies ever undertaken. Women were randomly assigned to one of two groups. Group one was told to eat a regular diet, and the other a low fat diet, for two years. When researchers collected their data, it was pretty clear that no one did what they were told, and the two groups had basically followed similar diets. Randomised controlled trials can however be used to assess short-term outcomes of nutrition interventions, for example to measure cholesterol changes over a short period of time. The results are limited in that they may not be reflective of changes over long periods of time. Researchers have to extrapolate results to infer what the long-term health effects might be, which is essentially educated guesswork.

Research challenges aside, there are so many studies in the field of nutrition and mental health now and, with very few exceptions, they point to the same conclusion: diet is an important component in the risk of developing common mental health issues throughout the one's lifespan.

Individual nutrients and their impact on mental health

There are a few individual nutrients worth highlighting for their role in ensuring good mental (and of course physical) wellbeing. These nutrients include folate, vitamin D, omega 3 fatty acids, B vitamins, and antioxidants.

Folate

Low folate levels are common in many depressed adults, particularly in women.[4] Folate is important for the production of red and white blood cells, the health of our DNA, the metabolism of carbohydrates, and is crucial during phases of rapid growth such as pregnancy, infancy and adolescence. The recommended daily intake for adults is 400mg, however, this can be obtained through a variety of dietary sources. The very best sources of folate are brewer's yeast, mushrooms, spinach, broccoli, brussels sprouts, asparagus, kale and other leafy greens, legumes, liver and orange juice.

Vitamin D

Vitamin D affects countless genes in the human body and is recognised as an important vitamin for brain health and skeletal health. Vitamin D can by synthesized from sunlight, and so adequate and frequent sun exposure is a great way to maintain mental health. Clinical research has associated Vitamin D deficiencies with the presence of mood disorders, as well as with increased risk for depression in adults. The recommended daily intake for adults is 600IU. As sunlight is one of the best sources of vitamin D, it is important to recommend this first as it is free and (weather dependent) easy to achieve. Taking a 10-minute coffee break outdoors for example is very achievable for many people. You can also obtain vitamin D from the following dietary sources: oily fish, egg yolks, fortified foods such as cow or soy milk, and fortified cereals (although the doses tend to be low).[6] The prudent approach is to include a vitamin D blood test as part of your annual check-up, or as routine in individuals presenting with mood disorders. If vitamin D levels are low and sunlight exposure is not feasible for any reason, supplements may be warranted.

Omega 3 fatty acids

Omega 3 fatty acids are important for the maintenance of cognitive function with age. Research suggests that those who consume more fish and seafood during their lifetime have better cognitive function as they grow old. Some research has shown that eating fish or supplementing with omega 3 fatty acids improves cognition and the onset of dementia. The dietary recommendation for consuming adequate omega 3 fatty acids is to ingest fatty fish (such as salmon, trout, halibut, sardines and pilchards) at least twice per week. In individuals with mood disorders however, it is recommended that a minimum of 1g of omega 3 fatty acids be consumed daily via a supplement, with an upper level of 3g per day in severe cases.[6] Fish oil and cod liver oil supplements are fairly easy to obtain, with vegetarian algae oil supplements increasing in availability with demand. It is important to note that omega 3 fatty acids consist of two active components, namely eicosapentaenoic acid (EPA) and docosahexaenoic acid (DHA). Research demonstrates that consuming both EPA and DHA is important for improved mental health outcomes, with more EPA relative to DHA being necessary for clinical intervention. The limitation with vegetarian-based omega 3 supplements is that algae oil only contains DHA, for which the research has yet to demonstrate provides benefit on its own in relation to mental health.

B Vitamins

The B family of vitamins are knowns for having positive impacts on brain health, and sufficient intakes are important for individuals with mood disorders. B vitamins play a role in maintaining overall health and wellbeing, and help to prevent infections. They have a direct impact on energy levels, brain function and cellular metabolism. Three main B vitamins are often associated with improved brain health: (i) folate (covered previously), (ii) vitamin B6, and (iii) vitamin B12. They help to break down homocysteine, high levels of which are associated with an increased risk for dementia and Alzheimer's disease. B vitamins as a group also help produce the energy needed to develop new brain cells.[6] Dietary sources of B vitamins include animal meats, milk, eggs, fish, some enriched cereals and breads, and dark green vegetables such as spinach and kale.[6] In individuals with diagnosed psychological conditions, it may be prudent to suggest a comprehensive multivitamin or simply a vitamin B complex to provide sufficient daily amounts of B vitamins.

Antioxidants

Plant-based foods rich in bioactive chemicals, antioxidants, make important nutritional and biochemical contributions to mental health and normal brain functioning. Antioxidants are found in foods such as berries, citrus fruits, spices and green tea. Certain antioxidants known as the flavonols, anthocyanins and flavanones are reported to be protective of brain cell structure and brain cell metabolism.[6] One of the newer antioxidants that is showing exceptionally promising results in the treatment of depression is a compound called Curcumin, which is extracted from the brightly coloured spice turmeric.

Curcumin has been found to have the potential to improve a number of health conditions, including depression. Curcumin works to scavenge free radicals that can create inflammation. As discussed earlier, a connection has been made between depression and inflammation although it's unclear yet whether depression causes inflammation or vice versa. Nevertheless, it is thought that antioxidants such as curcumin can fight chronic inflammation and relieve symptoms of depression. In 2017 a review looked into all of the research on curcumin for treating depression, and it was found to be a safe and effective natural option.[19] Most studies have used a compound called BCM-95ä at a dose of between 250mg – 500mg daily, but we need further data before we can recommend this as the optimal dose.

Key takeaways:

Mental health can be driven by biochemical changes in the body in a variety of different systems.

- Inflammation may be at the root of these biochemical changes, but further research is needed to confirm this.
- A diet rich in whole grains, fruits and vegetables, olive oil, fatty fish and dietary omega 3 fatty acids, and low in refined products and saturated fats, is beneficial to mental health.
- A high intake of refined sugars and saturated fats is associated with increased risk for mental health issues.
- The most well-researched dietary approach in relation to improving mental health outcomes is the Mediterranean Diet.
- Paying special attention to nutrients such as folate, vitamin D, omega 3 fatty acids, B vitamins, and antioxidants such as curcumin, may give individuals added protection against mental health issues.
- Probiotic supplementation in individuals with depression, stress and anxiety may be beneficial.
- A diet rich in plant foods encourages biodiversity in the gut.

Successful strategies for improving the nutritional and mental health of workers

Work for most people can be stressful and mentally draining – their schedules may be unpredictable, tasks varied, and they are surrounded by others who are inevitably influencing their behaviour. As most of us are creatures of habit with our daily routine centred around work demands, the workplace could actually be considered an ideal channel for promoting change in large sections of our population. In the workplace we have a large, captive audience, and interventions can be offered repeatedly which increases the likelihood of inspiring change.

The modern shift away from the traditional office setting and towards a remote work model provides a unique set of challenges to nutrition and mental health. On the one hand it comes with a host of benefits from increasing available free time (that would have been lost to travel for example) and increasing the availability of potentially high-quality nutrition. Provided that the employee purchases high-quality food options for their home, they have every opportunity to eat well. On the other hand, schedules and routines may be harder to implement when working from home, and the lines between "home" and "work" spaces may become blurred. This can add an extra layer of stress to the individual, and we know that stress is associated with poorer food choices. Fortunately, with the telecommunication options available to employers, there are still opportunities for nutrition education and interventions to take place.

Eating well in the workplace (whether this be at home or in the office) can have a significant effect on overall health and wellbeing. Nutrient-dense foods can boost concentration and cognitive function, improving an employee's performance. It is well documented that happier and healthier employees are more creative and more productive. The World Health Organization (WHO) have found that nutritious foods can raise productivity levels by 20%.[14] Healthy employees are happier, more engaged, less stressed, sleep better and get sick far less often.

Nutrition interventions in the workplace

Nutrition intervention, whilst obviously the best way to improve the health of employees, does require both time and financial investment to implement. These are resources that many companies do not wish to part with unless they are assured of positive outcomes. Fortunately, in 2009, South African researchers examined a number of workplace nutrition interventions in order to determine the most effective strategies. They evaluated the success of an intervention using the following criteria: (i) change in nutritional knowledge, attitudes, self-efficacy, intentions and stage of change; (ii) change in dietary behaviours; (iii) changes in clinical markers such as body weight, BMI, blood pressure, or cholesterol; and (iv) process and/or policy outcomes. Their findings highlighted the following key success factors for nutrition interventions in the workplace:

- Dietitians are involved in the nutrition education process.
- Both nutrition and physical activity were encouraged.
- Changes were implemented to the staff cafeteria to increase the availability of healthy food options, and healthy foods were advertised.
- Personalised feedback on diet and any clinical outcomes was given to participants at the start of interventions, and at various intervals thereafter.
- Employees were involved in both the planning and management of programmes.

- Prices of available healthy food options were slightly reduced to encourage employees to purchase them.

- The Stages of Change Model was used in order to assess readiness of participants to make changes.[12]

Nutrition programmes can serve an important role in fostering employee mental health, wellness and productivity. The comradery of partaking in a programme alongside your colleagues means that there is accountability, which is often a determinant in long-term commitment to a programme. So how does this work in the era of the "work from home" movement?

Nutrition interventions when working from home

A range of positive benefits are associated with remote work. These include improved family and work integration, improved productivity and reduced levels of fatigue.[15] Working from home, theoretically at least, should allow for greater time and energy to be spent on one's personal health status. Employees have gained back valuable travel time, as well as potentially time previously spent getting ready for work in the morning or preparing lunch boxes. This translates into more available time for exercise, grocery shopping and food preparation. However, the blurring of home and work environments can also negatively impact a person's mental and physical wellbeing due to extended hours, unclear delineation between work and home, and potentially limited support from the employer or organisation.[15]

The impact of remote work on actual nutrition status remains unclear as there is limited research in this area. One research paper from 2020 examined the effect of remote work on two specific health-promoting behaviours: (i) the production of food at home, and (ii) the consumption of home-cooked meals. A slower eating speed and increased consumption of home-cooked meals has been associated with decreased risk for weight gain, and a higher quality diet.[16] A higher frequency of home-cooked meals is associated with a higher intake of fruits and vegetables, overall lower consumption of calories, fat and sugar, and an overall higher quality diet.[17,18] This is, however, affected by time constraints depending on the demands of their work. For those with demanding work hours, cheap convenience foods and ready-to-eat meals may still be appealing alternatives.

Nutrition interventions remain beneficial regardless of the in-office or remote-work model used by companies. Simply the nature of the intervention would need to be altered. Fortunately, with the rise of telehealth, access to nutrition and even exercise professionals is arguably greater than ever. Through employing the advice of these professionals, workers can still gain access to high-quality nutrition education as well as advice on exercises that can be done in a home environment. Whilst we may not have key success factors established for this model as yet, remote work is only predicted to increase and it remains in the best interest of the employer to ensure the health and mental wellbeing of their employees to improve business outcomes.

Assuring good mental health and overall wellness

We can all relate to feeling symptoms such as lethargy, bloating, and heaviness after an over-indulgent meal, and these aren't ones we associate with general health and wellness. Likewise, many people will experience periods of anxiety or a depressed mood whether or not they end up receiving a diagnosis or requiring medical intervention. Whilst good food may be only one aspect of a lifestyle that truly promotes mental wellness, it is a practical place for any person to start.

Our bodies are designed to run on high-quality, whole food sources that allow us to perform at our very best. Rather than focusing on treating illness when it crops up, we should be preventing disease through making conscious healthy choices. Consistently nourishing your body with whole foods that are packed full of vitamins, minerals, antioxidants and fibre is the very best strategy to assure good mental health and overall wellness.

Conclusion

Food and nutrition are fundamental to every single aspect of our functioning. What we put into our mouths really matters, both in the short term and long term. As a recurring theme throughout this chapter, choosing a diet that is rich in whole foods is key for improving mental health. Whilst the majority of the research has been conducted on depression, the benefits seen through dietary intervention are certainly not limited to this condition alone. Based on the literature, the traditional Mediterranean Diet has by far the strongest evidence base for health benefits, including mental health. This doesn't mean however that it is the only dietary approach, and the decision to follow any one particular pattern should be first discussed with your healthcare practitioner. The key takeaway here is to encourage a dietary pattern that includes mostly whole, unprocessed foods, with an emphasis on plant foods, lean and unprocessed animal foods (such as fish and lean meats), healthy (unsaturated) fats from plant and fish sources, and wholegrain cereals.

Good nutrition certainly has a role to play in the workplace. The literature clearly shows that healthier employees tend to be happier in their jobs and more hardworking. It is in the best interest of employers to put nutrition interventions into practice whether this be in the physical workplace itself or conducted via telehealth communication.

Chapter 11

Link between mental health and physical wellbeing

Dr Nikki Connellan

Introduction

As a medical practitioner, working primarily in the field of Absence, Incapacity and Disability, it has become increasingly apparent that a clear distinction is often made between 'mind' and 'body'. But when considering mental health and physical health, from a clinical point of view, separating these two is deleterious for both patient and clinician. There is no doubt that mental health and physical health are fundamentally linked. There are multiple associations between mental health and both acute and particularly chronic physical conditions that significantly impact people's quality of life, demands on health care and other publicly funded services, and generate consequences to society. In fact the World Health Organization (WHO) defines: *health as a state of complete physical, mental and social wellbeing and not merely the absence of disease or infirmity.* The WHO states that *"there is no health without mental health".*[1]

Poor physical health can lead to an increased risk of developing mental health problems. Similarly, poor mental health can negatively impact on physical health, leading to an increased risk of some conditions.[2]

The current COVID-19 pandemic has highlighted this disconnection between physical care and mental health care as never before and there is an increasing call on healthcare professionals to consider psychological wellbeing when treating the physical symptoms of a condition and vice versa. As the physical risks are better managed, the permanent impact of the pandemic weighs heavy on our mental health. The SA Society of Psychiatrists predicts that mental health is the biggest threat in 2021. Globally, mental health professionals predict that the pandemic is going to impact significantly on the mental health of the population with an increase in cases of depression, suicide, and self-harm due to COVID-19, and other related symptoms reported internationally.

Although statistics from South Africa have not been released as yet, a study conducted by the Indian Psychiatric Society showed a 20% increase in mental illnesses since the coronavirus outbreak in India. A meta-analysis on mental health and COVID-19 among the general population in China estimates the prevalence of anxiety to be around 31.9%, and depression around 33.7%.[3]

In Georgia a survey amongst 2088 respondents observed high levels of symptoms for anxiety (23.9% women, 21.0% men), depression (30.3% women, 25.27% men), PTSD (11.8% women, and 12.5% men), and adjustment disorder (40.7% women, 31.0% men). Factors significantly associated with increased COVID-19 concerns included stressful household economic situation, larger household size, non-communicable diseases (NCDs), symptoms of anxiety, adjustment disorder and post-traumatic stress disorder (PTSD).[4]

It is clearer than ever before that the promotion of positive mental health can no longer be overlooked when treating a physical condition and vice versa.

What is mental health?

As described earlier in this book, the broad definition of mental health refers to the wellbeing of an individual on emotional, social and psychological levels. The state of someone's mental health has significant influence over the way they act, process emotions and make decisions. A person in good mental health can maintain healthy relationships, express a wide range of emotions and manage the difficulties of change.

The World Health Organization (WHO) defines mental health as the state of wellbeing where every individual realises his or her own potential, manages the normal stresses of life, works productively and fruitfully, and can contribute to her or his community.[5]

Most people think of mental health as the absence of diagnosable disorders, but mental health is best represented as a continuum. On one end of the spectrum are people who exhibit active resilience and are capable of taking life's uncertainties in stride. On the other end of the spectrum are individuals whose disorders cause severe impact on daily functioning. If someone falls in the centre of the spectrum, they would likely describe their mental health as "fine."

Mental Illness   Mental Health

It's possible, even common, for people to fall somewhere in the middle. Even if you don't have a diagnosed condition and feel you function well enough in your day-to-day life, you may lack the resources to cope with a sudden change. These are some of the signs that someone's mental health is shifting:

- Changes in sleeping and eating patterns
- Withdrawal from friends, family and activities
- Loss of energy
- Increasing irritability and mood swings
- Loss of performance at school or work

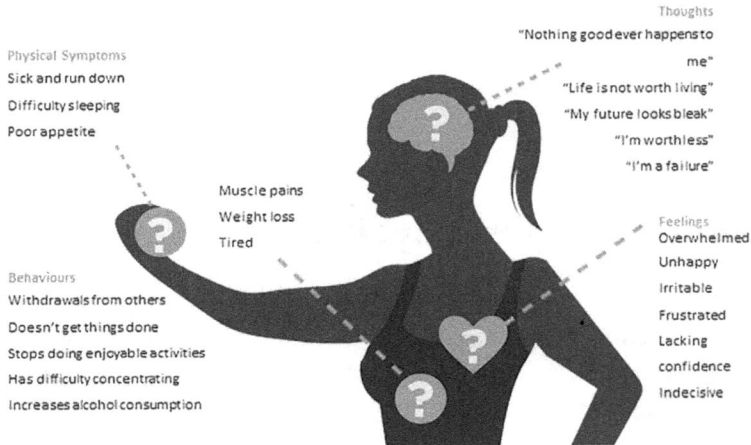

Physical Symptoms
Sick and run down
Difficulty sleeping
Poor appetite

Muscle pains
Weight loss
Tired

Behaviours
Withdrawals from others
Doesn't get things done
Stops doing enjoyable activities
Has difficulty concentrating
Increases alcohol consumption

Thoughts
"Nothing good ever happens to me"
"Life is not worth living"
"My future looks bleak"
"I'm worthless"
"I'm a failure"

Feelings
Overwhelmed
Unhappy
Irritable
Frustrated
Lacking confidence
Indecisive

These symptoms indicate a decline in mental health and potentially point to a developing psychological disorder. Some of the most common disorders in children and young adults include:

- Depression
- Anxiety
- Bipolar Disorder
- Impulse Control Disorder

What Is physical health?

Physical Health represents one dimension of total wellbeing – the term refers to the state or overall physical condition of your physical body and how well it's "operating". A person who has good physical health is likely to have bodily functions and processes working at their peak. Physical health is thus the "soundness" of the body, freedom from disease or abnormality and the condition of optimal wellbeing. Physical wellbeing is thus the ability to maintain a healthy quality of life that allows us to get the most out of our daily activities without undue fatigue or physical stress.[6]

Physical wellness involves making good choices when it comes to:

- Illness prevention
- Nutrition and hydration
- Physical activity and body movement
- Maintaining a healthy weight/BMI
- Alcohol and smoking
- Sleep
- Sexual health
- Stress management

How mental and physical health are related

The difference between physical and mental health is not as pronounced as you might think. For years, researchers have been asking a complex question – how do mental and physical health interact? The answer is predictably complicated, but we do know that mental illness impacts physical health directly and indirectly.[7]

1. Depression and the immune system

Depression, the most common mental disorder in South Africa, doesn't just impact mood and motivation. It can directly affect the immune system by suppressing T cell responses to viruses and bacteria, making it easier to fall ill and remain ill for longer. A weakened immune system can also, for example, increase the severity of allergies or asthma.

Some research suggests that it may be the other way around, and the immune system may actually cause depression. Stress – especially chronic stress – triggers an immune response within the brain itself. That inflammatory response may be a driving cause of depression.

A recent study on immune inflammation and depression involved the manipulation of immune receptors in mice. Researchers exposed the mice to repeated stress and observed that stress caused the mouse brains to release cytokines. Cytokines are a type of protein associated with inflammation, and their release led to damage in the medial prefrontal cortex, a part of the brain that plays a critical role in depression. In other words, the researchers were able to trigger depressive symptoms as a result of the immune system's response to stress.

A strong immune system is a hallmark of physical health, but the addition of stress increases the chances of depression. In turn, depression may further weaken the immune system, resulting in a discouraging cycle.

This case illustrates the fact that many health problems have both a physical and a mental element.

2. Mental illness and fatigue

Depression, anxiety and other mood disorders often result in persistent feelings of tiredness and exhaustion. All too often we hear the inappropriate suggestion that "it's all in your head," but research shows this is not the case. Mental fatigue leads to physical fatigue.

A study from Bangor University in Wales, the United Kingdom, had participants ride a stationary bike until they reached the point of exhaustion. They defined exhaustion as the inability to keep up with a pace of 60 revolutions per minute for five or more seconds. [8]

Participants performed the test in two different situations. In one situation, they rode the bike like usual. In the second setup, participants first engaged in a 90-minute task with elements drawing on memory, fast reactions and inhibiting impulsive responses to stimuli.

After participants engaged in the mental challenge, they reported feeling tired and a little listless. Most importantly, the participants reached the point of exhaustion 15 percent earlier.

Mental illness is closely linked with fatigue, and that persistent tiredness can easily lead to declines in physical health. When someone is chronically depressed or anxious, they are less likely to engage in exercise and to quit early when they do. Fatigue from mental illness can also interfere with basic hygiene, increasing vulnerability to disease.

3. Anger, anxiety and heart health

Angry outbursts and the stress of anxiety are bad for the heart. An Australian study set out to see if acute emotions can cause heart attacks "like you see in movies" – and unfortunately, the cliché' is true.[9]

Dr Thomas Buckley, lead author of the study, said, *"Our findings confirm what has been suggested in prior studies and anecdotal evidence...that episodes of intense anger can act as a trigger for a heart attack."*

In the two hours following a bout of intense anger, which the study defined as tense body language, clenched fists or teeth, and feeling "ready to burst," a person's risk of heart attack becomes 8.5 times higher.

In the case of anxiety, the risk of heart attack increases 9.5 fold in the following two hours. While youth are generally a long way away from having to worry about heart attacks, anger and anxiety involved in impulse control disorders can negatively affect their growing hearts.

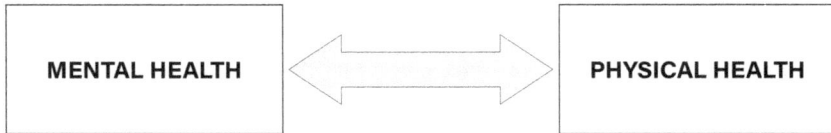

Figure 11.1: Mental health and physical health have a bi-direction and complex relationship

How mental health affects physical health

There are various ways in which poor mental health has been shown to be detrimental to physical health.

People with the highest levels of self-rated distress (compared to lowest rates of distress) were 32% more likely to have died from cancer. Depression has been found to be associated with an increased risk of coronary heart disease.[10]

Schizophrenia is associated with:

- double the risk of death from heart disease
- three times the risk of death from respiratory disease.

This is because people with mental health conditions are less likely to receive the physical healthcare they're entitled to. Mental health service users are statistically less likely to receive the routine checks (like blood pressure, weight and cholesterol) that might detect symptoms of these physical health conditions earlier. They are also not as likely to be offered help to give up smoking, reduce alcohol consumption and make positive adjustments to their diet.

Severe mental health issues and cardiovascular disease

An international study lead by King's College London in 2017 found an increased risk of cardiovascular disease in people suffering from severe mental health conditions. The study analysed data collected from 3.2 million patients with conditions including schizophrenia, bipolar and major depression. They found that people suffering from any of these were 53% more likely to develop cardiovascular disease than those without underlying mental health issues. In addition, the risk of dying from cardiovascular disease is 85% higher in people with mental health conditions compared to other people in the same age range.[11]

Lifestyle factors

These lifestyle factors can influence the state of both your physical and mental health.

Exercise

A major variable that seems to contribute to mental wellbeing, but is often underestimated, is exercise.

"Exercise is something that psychologists have been very slow to attend to," says Michael Otto, Ph.D., a Boston University psychology professor. *"People know that exercise helps physical outcomes. There is much less awareness of mental health outcomes – and much less ability to translate this awareness into exercise action."*

Counsellors, like psychologists, may see results in their clients' wellbeing when exercise is encouraged. A paper published in *The Personnel and Guidance Journal* in 2012 went as far as to call physical health an *"expanding horizon for counsellors".*[12]

The American Psychological Association reported that the benefits of exercise include:

- Lessening anxiety
- Improving mood
- Enhancing mental health

Adults are not the only people affected by exercise. According to a 2012 study by the Economic and Social Research Council, a survey of 5 000 adolescents between the ages of 10 and 15 revealed that those who lived a healthier lifestyle were happier than those who indulged in unhealthy habits such as drinking, smoking and eating junk food. The council also found that the more hours a week the participants played sports, the happier they considered themselves, Economic and Social Research Council (ESRC).[13]

According to Dr Michael Craig Miller, assistant professor of psychiatry at Harvard Medical School, exercise and physical activity can be as effective in treating some depression as therapy or medication: *"For some people it works as well as antidepressants, although exercise alone isn't enough for someone with severe depression".*

The reason exercise can be so effective in alleviating the symptoms of depression and anxiety is both chemical and mental. Exercise releases a number of feel-good drugs (endorphin and serotonin), helping you feel good in the short term. Low-intensity exercise sustained over time can promote the production of neurotrophic proteins. These proteins cause nerve cells to grow and form new connections and as a result can improve brain function, making you feel better in the long term. Exercise can also give people a sense of achievement and self-esteem, and also lends itself well to improved sleep hygiene.

Physical activity means any movement of your body that uses your muscles and expends energy. From tending your garden to running a marathon, even gentle forms of exercise can significantly improve your quality of life. Even a short burst of 10 minutes brisk walking increases our mental alertness, energy and positive mood.

Exercising outside and in nature can have additional benefits as well. Numerous studies have shown that spending time in nature and green spaces can significantly reduce stress levels as well as alleviate symptoms of anxiety and depression. There is also evidence to show that children who spend time around nature and green spaces are less likely to develop mental health issues.

It's increasingly challenging to ensure children get enough exercise and physical activity. With the proliferation of screens in every area of life, children and young adults are becoming more sedentary. Many guidelines recommend youth ages 6 to 17 get 60 minutes or more of physical activity each day; the majority of children don't get anywhere near that.

TV is one of the biggest culprits when it comes to creating a sedentary lifestyle. Children who watch three or more hours of TV per day are 65 percent more likely to become obese than children who watch less than one hour a day.[14]

Other components to physical health include regular dental and vision checks to monitor development as well as ensuring kids get enough sleep to fuel their growth. Your child's regular check-ups are the perfect opportunity to bring up any questions you have regarding physical health and catch any developing issues early on.

Diet

As discussed in the previous chapter, good nutrition is a crucial factor in influencing the way we feel. A healthy balanced diet is one that includes healthy amounts of proteins, essential fats, complex carbohydrates, vitamins, minerals and water. The food we eat can influence the development, management and prevention of numerous mental health conditions including depression and Alzheimer's.

Good nutrition is essential for everyone, but growing bodies need even more resources. A host of vitamins and minerals is essential to physical health, as are the right amounts of protein and carbohydrates. Balancing your child's diet gives them a much better chance of remaining physically healthy.

Smoking

Smoking has a negative impact on both mental and physical health. Many people with mental health problems believe that smoking relieves their symptoms, but these effects are only short-term.

- People with depression are twice as likely to smoke as other people.
- People with schizophrenia are three times as likely to smoke as other people.

Nicotine in cigarettes interferes with the chemicals in our brains. Dopamine is a chemical which influences positive feelings, and is often found to be lower in people with depression. Nicotine temporarily increases the levels of dopamine, but also switches off the brain's natural mechanism for making the chemical. In the long term, this can make a person feel as though they need more and more nicotine in order to repeat this positive sensation.

Sleep On It

Sleep is intrinsically tied in with both physical and mental health. Although the specific timing may change, when a person sleeps they cycle through two forms of sleep every 90 or so minutes. The first cycle, sometimes known as "quiet sleep" sees a person move through a number of stages of progressively deeper sleep. During these stages heart rate and breathing become slower and body temperature lowers. The deepest level of quiet sleep can effect physiological changes that strengthen the immune system.

The other cycle, REM (Rapid Eye Movement) sleep is where people dream. Heart rate, respiration and temperature are essentially the same as if you were awake. This sleep cycle helps improve learning ability, forming and retaining memories, and improving emotional health. Disrupting the sleep cycle can play havoc in the brain, impairing emotional response and coherent thinking. In short, not getting enough good sleep can exacerbate mental health issues. Of course, the reverse is also true.

There are a number of sleep disorders that can affect the length and quality of your sleep. Depending on the cause, you may have to see a doctor or specialist to explore what might be happening. Even so, there are a few simple things you can try to increase the quality of your sleep and practise good sleep hygiene.

- Remove all distraction from your bedroom – including TV, computer or the like.

- Reserve your bedroom for sleep and sex only. Think of other places in the home that you can designate for reading, watching TV, listening to music or the like.

- Keep a regular sleep schedule – go to bed at the same time every night and get up at the same time every morning.

- Keep your room as dark as possible.

- Regular exercise can also increase the quality of your sleep.

Get support

Your social circle is also a vital aspect to preventing a decline in mental health. But mental health can be a difficult topic to discuss with peers. This often prevents people from seeking help. Don't be afraid to reach out to friends and family for support.

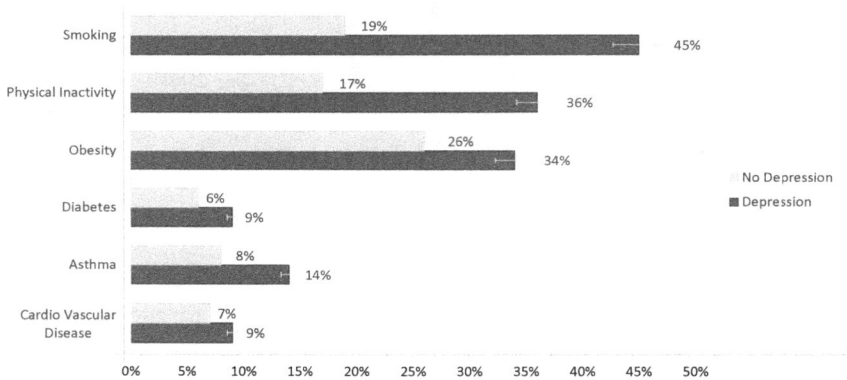

Figure 11.2: Prevalence of health risks and chronic diseases by depression status[15]

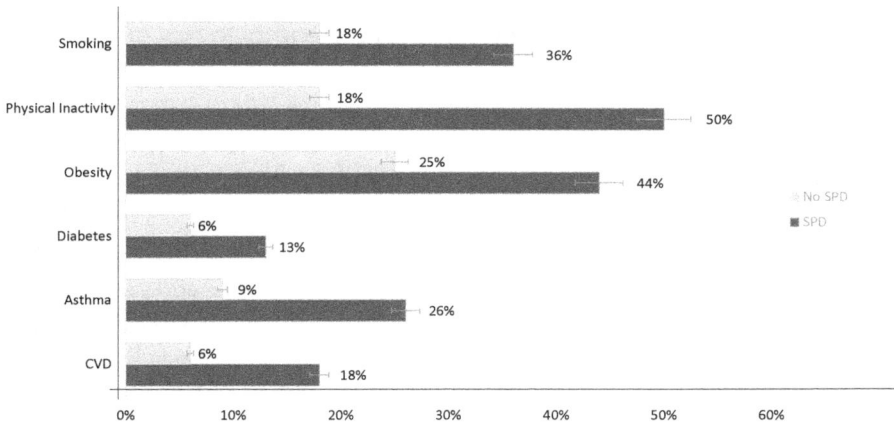

Figure 11.3: Prevalence of health risks and chronic diseases by serious psychological distress[15]

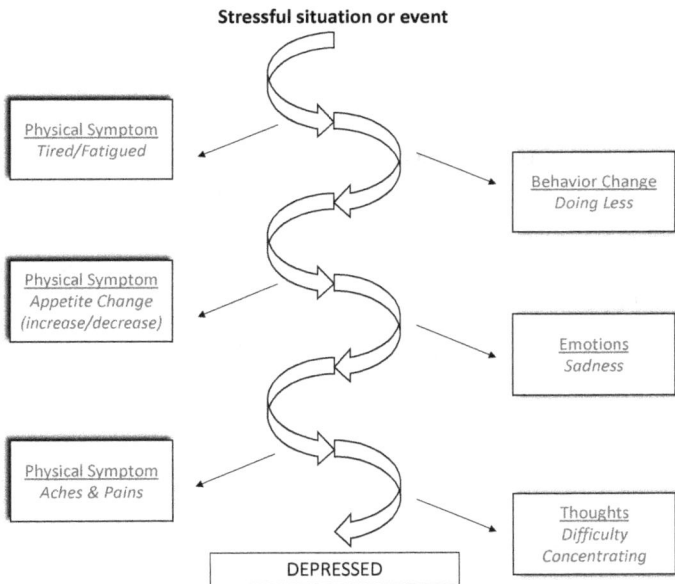

Figure 11.4: The Depression Spiral

Long-term/Chronic health conditions and mental health

Nowhere is the relationship between mental and physical health more evident than in the area of chronic conditions. The associations between mental and physical health are:

1. Poor mental health is a risk factor for chronic physical conditions.

2. People with serious mental health conditions are at high risk of experiencing chronic physical conditions.

3. People with chronic physical conditions are at risk of developing poor mental health.

The social determinants of health impact both chronic physical conditions and mental health. As referred to above the key aspects of prevention include increasing physical activity, access to nutritious foods, ensuring adequate income and fostering social inclusion and social support. This creates opportunities to enhance protective factors and reduce risk factors related to aspects of mental and physical health.

Understanding the links between mind and body is the first step in developing strategies to reduce the incidence of co-existing conditions and support those already living with mental illnesses and chronic physical conditions. The promotion of positive mental health can often be overlooked when treating a physical condition, particularly a chronic medical condition.

Psoriasis, for example, is one such condition in which the effects go beyond the visual signs and symptoms, impacting psychological wellbeing and quality of life. Psoriasis is a condition which is commonly characterised by red flaky sores on the surface of the skin, but its effects go beyond the physical signs and symptoms. Psoriasis is an auto-immune condition commonly triggered by stress. It affects 1.8 million people in the UK and can impact on emotional as well as physical wellbeing.

- Up to 85% feel annoyance with their psoriasis
- Approximately one third experience anxiety and depression
- 1 in 10 admit to contemplating suicide
- 1 in 3 experience feelings of humiliation about their condition
- 1 in 5 report being rejected (and stigmatised) as a result of their condition
- 1/3 experience problems with loved ones

Yet, a recent report from the British Association of Dermatologists (BAD), highlighted that only 4% of Dermatology Units have access to a counsellor. The physical and psychological impacts can be cyclically linked: the condition can cause emotional distress which can trigger a psoriasis flare and, as a result, cause further distress. Some people with psoriasis can feel that their GP regards psoriasis as a minor skin complaint and are dismissive of the emotional aspects, leaving many to continue unaided on the isolating and emotional journey associated with psoriasis.[16]

The following chronic medical conditions are associated with a higher risk of mental health conditions:

1. Diabetes

    - Major Depressive Disorder 2x greater risk
    - Panic Disorder
    - Generalized Anxiety Disorder
    - PTSD

2. Arthritis

    - Mood Disorders
    - Anxiety Disorders

3. Heart Disease

    - Anxiety and Depression
    - Phobic Anxiety
    - Panic Disorder

4. Obesity

    - Clinical Depression
    - Eating Disorders

5. Gastrointestinal Conditions

    - Anxiety and Depression
    - Cancer
    - Bipolar Disorder
    - Schizophrenia

6. Asthma

    - Anxiety and Depression

Stress about medical symptoms

Medical conditions can lead to pressures and changes of lifestyle that patients finds unpleasant. These unplanned and unwanted lifestyle changes can lead to stress and often the patient feels worse than anticipated resulting in acute stress that interferes with physical recovery.

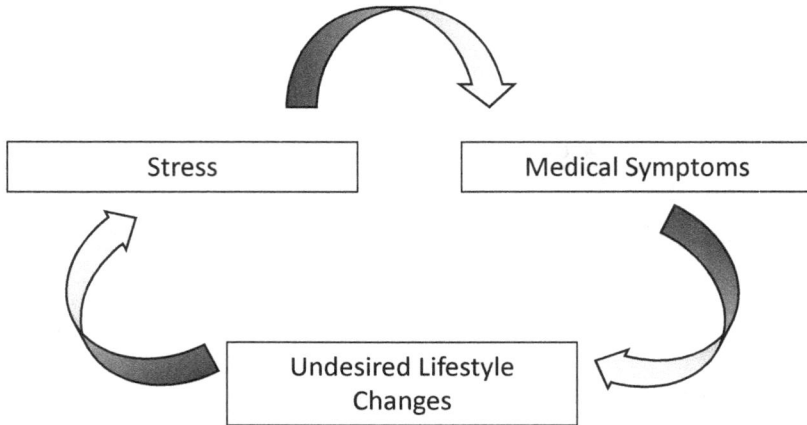

Figure 11.5: Medical Symptom-Stress Cycle

Physical/Mental health impact

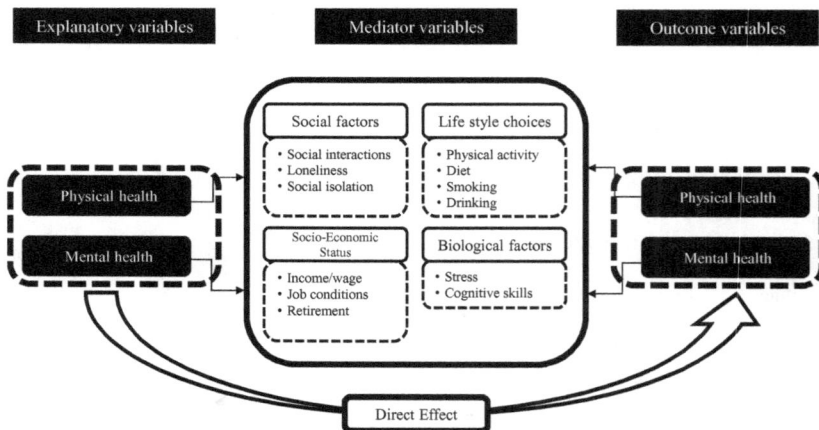

Figure 11.6: The direct and indirect effects between physical and mental health

The effect of mental health on longevity

One of the clearest places that the link between mental and physical health is illustrated is in longevity. Many studies have found that those with mental health challenges, such as schizophrenia or even depression, tend to live shorter lives when compared to those who do not have these conditions. In fact, the Mental Health Foundation reported that schizophrenia is associated with a tripled risk of dying from a respiratory disease and a doubled risk of dying from a form of heart disease.

Depression has been linked to a 50 % increase in a person's risk of dying from cancer and a 67% increase from heart disease. These conditions have a significant impact on life expectancies.[17]

Researchers hypothesize that one reason for the increase in respiratory disease, heart disease and cancer risk is that individuals with mental health conditions are less likely to seek care for their physical health.

However, there are other ways that mental health can affect longevity. Researchers are finding that a person's sense of optimism also has an impact.

The power of positive emotions

According to a 2012 Harvard University meta-analysis of 200 articles, optimism may correlate with cardiovascular health and may even decrease the rate of the disease's progression.[18]

"The absence of the negative is not the same thing as the presence of the positive. We found that factors such as optimism, life satisfaction and happiness are associated with reduced risk of cardiovascular disease regardless of such factors as a person's age, socioeconomic status, smoking status or body weight," said lead author Julia Boehm.

Boehm, a research fellow at Harvard School of Public Health's Department of Society, Human Development and Health, additionally stated that the most optimistic individuals, when compared to their less optimistic counterparts, had approximately 50 % less risk of an initial cardiovascular event.

Whereas positive emotions correlate with a person's mental state, the opposite is also true: negative emotions correlate with deficits in a person's physical wellbeing. Stress is the perfect example. While chronic stress can wear down the body over time, even short-lived spurts of minor stress, such as temporary stomach aches, can have an impact, it has been reported. Negative emotions such as anger have been found to correlate with heart attacks and other physical problems that sometimes can lead to death.

Conclusion

It is clear, that as healthcare professionals, it is our duty of care to our patients to adopt a bio-psycho-social approach to the management of those individuals who consult us for help.

This model views health and illness behaviours as products of biological characteristics (such as genes), behavioural factors (such as lifestyle, stress, and health beliefs), and social conditions (such as cultural influences, family relationships, and social support). Health psychologists work with healthcare professionals and patients to help people deal with the psychological and emotional aspects of health and illness. This can include developing treatment protocols to increase adherence to medical treatments, weight-loss programmes, smoking cessation, etc. and focus on prevention and intervention programmes designed to promote healthier lifestyles (e.g., exercise and nutrition programmes).

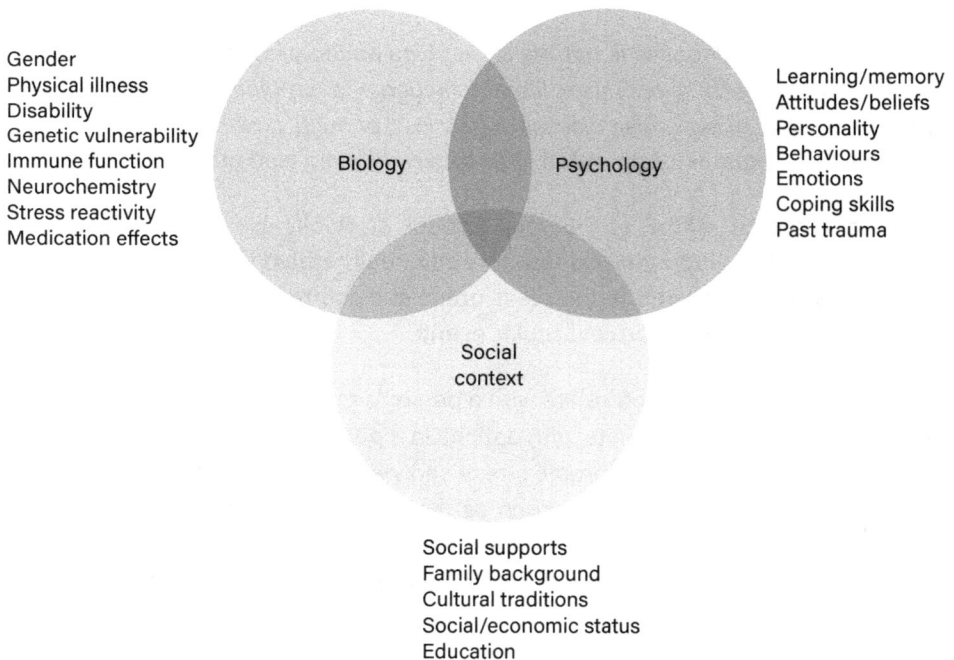

Gender
Physical illness
Disability
Genetic vulnerability
Immune function
Neurochemistry
Stress reactivity
Medication effects

Biology

Psychology

Learning/memory
Attitudes/beliefs
Personality
Behaviours
Emotions
Coping skills
Past trauma

Social
context

Social supports
Family background
Cultural traditions
Social/economic status
Education

Figure 11.7: Biopsychosocial approach to understanding health

Chapter 12

Link between mental health and financial wellbeing

Val Leeming

How financial stress impacts mental health

The ability to earn a living to take care of ourselves and our loved ones is one of the core motivators for working. Sadly, most employees lack the skills to manage their money, making them prone to experiencing both financial stress and the impact it has on their mental health.

Financial stress impacts men and women alike, and it affects people regardless of the position they hold or the amount they earn. In fact, research[1] spanning 18 years suggests that only 20% of people never worry about their personal finances: the other 80% of us experience financial stress at some point in our lives, and are susceptible to its effect on our mental health.

This chapter explores some of the key questions around financial health and wellness, including the mental, physical and emotional impact of financial stress on individuals, their relationships and their work. We also look at some of the causes of financial stress, including socio-economic factors such as debt, family responsibility and unemployment, as well as other causes like money memories, money personalities, money disorders and other mental disorders.

Better understanding financial stress will enable employers to identify whether an employee is struggling with financial stress. This chapter also provides insight into how financial stress can be managed and how companies can provide relevant support for their employees that will benefit all concerned.

Many people have similar challenges and experiences around money, financial stress and mental health. Some of these common experiences of how money problems can affect mental health, physical health and even relationships are shared in this chapter, with names and personal details changed to protect confidentiality.

Financial stress and mental health

"Are you feeling overwhelmed by money worries?"

When asked this question, the large majority of people answer "Yes", regardless of the organisation or industry in which they work. But when do money worries turn into financial stress that impacts mental health and when do money problems become money disorders?

Let's start by defining these financial terms.

What is financial health and financial stress?

Financial health can be defined in different ways[2,3] depending on the sources consulted, but one that combines various ideas is most helpful: ***Financial health and wellbeing*** *is:*

- the ability to make informed decisions about your personal finances,
- the ability to manage your finances on a day-to-day basis and
- being able to formulate a plan for your financial future.

Sadly, numerous studies over the years, including the 2019 research released by SALDRU[4], confirm that financial literacy in South Africa is concerningly low, leaving millions of South Africans unable to make informed decisions regarding their personal finances that will result in financial wellbeing.

As a result, most people experience the opposite of financial health, which is ***financial stress.***

It can be defined as feelings of worry, fear and anxiety about your personal financial situation.[5] Most of us have experienced some form of stress when it comes to money, and know exactly what this feels like. This stress can result in physical symptoms like insomnia, headaches, fatigue, depression, anxiety and more.

What is the impact of financial stress?

Like any source of stress, financial stress can take its toll on a person's mental health, physical health, emotional health and relationships.

Money worries can have an impact on everyday life, leaving a person feeling scared, angry, ashamed and fearful. This in turn impacts sleep patterns, and insomnia is a common side effect of financial stress.

Financial coaches at Interface[6], based on 18 years of coaching and mentoring employees from diverse companies in South Africa on a range of financial issues, confirm that financial stress has a significant impact on mental health, evident in the anxiety, tension, worry and insomnia it causes.

Financial stress also impacts a person's self-esteem. Research[7] shows that one of the causes of low self-esteem is financial problems and difficulties. Many employees who reach out for help seem to feel ashamed about their financial situation and doubt their ability to find a solution. Very often, personal finance is also seen as a taboo subject and people feel a sense of fear, anxiety and even embarrassment when discussing their personal financial concerns and issues.

In some instances, money problems can cause more than just feelings of despair and anxiety – it can cause feelings of hopelessness and depression that may even lead to suicidal thoughts for a person who feels that there is no way to resolve their financial problems.

Financial problems are definitely a trigger when it comes to depression and anxiety. The South African Depression and Anxiety Group (SADAG) reports[8] that as many as three out of every ten people in any given workplace experience symptoms of depression, while among managers the statistics are one in three. According to SADAG[9], financial problems are also among the causes of suicide. The organisation notes that *"in South Africa's present financial situation, chronic and acute stress as a result of financial pressures are critical considerations in suicidal behaviour".*

These concerning statistics have been aggravated by the economic climate caused by the COVID-19 pandemic. According to a Human Sciences Research Council (HSRC) report[10] on the mental health implications of COVID-19 in a developing country *"stressors that contribute to an already high risk for mental illness are highlighted and exacerbated: health worries, crowded living, lack of access to basic services, financial stress, food insecurity and the risk of violence".* More and more people seem to be suffering from insomnia, anxiety, anger, and depression, these feelings are exacerbated by fear of infection, and of financial loss.

Many people are fearful of losing their jobs, and do not have savings to fall back on. During the initial period of lockdown, the South African government stipulated that no evictions were allowed, which provided a level of welcome relief for many whose income may have been affected and who were already feeling the stress and anxiety linked to potentially losing their homes. Similarly, all the major banks offered short-term debt relief for consumers whose income had been affected to counteract the resultant stress related to job loss and reduction in income.

How financial stress affects relationships

Financial problems are often linked to other issues too, and many people can attest to how financial problems affect their relationships. The reason for this is that partners often have different financial backgrounds and different money personalities, and do not communicate with each other about their personal finances and struggles.

Sadly, because many couples do not work through their financial problems, financial issues are one of the top ten reasons for divorces[11], both in South Africa and around the world.

Case study – Saving a relationship

John had been working for his company for many years. When his performance dropped concerningly, his manager suspected that it was due to financial stress and suggested he reached out for assistance from a financial coach. It was clear how financial stress was impacting him, physically and mentally, while also affecting his relationships.

John's story is not unique: he had gotten into a significant amount of short-term debt, mostly due to unconsciously spending money and living beyond his means. John was married, but his wife and teenage children had no idea how deep in debt he was. He was feeling highly stressed and anxious, and this significantly affected his work performance.

During a coaching session, John had an opportunity to explore his relationship with money and his money personality. Like many people, he had an 'ostrich' money personality, tending to bury his head in the sand when it came to his personal finances. After getting to grips with his current financial situation – by reviewing his budget and his credit report – John felt ready to share his financial situation with his wife. In the couple's first financial coaching session, it became very apparent that his wife had a completely different money personality and had strong financial skills. Although she initially felt hurt and betrayed by John's financial infidelity, as a couple they agreed to start talking about their money situation and to tackle their financial difficulties together, working as a team.

Within a few weeks, John started to feel less stressed and anxious and his performance at work improved. Within 18 months, they managed to close several of their retail accounts. With careful planning, they had made considerable progress and had moved into a much better financial space within three years. By the end of five years, they were free of debt and able to save actively towards their retirement goals.

> *The intense financial stress and the adverse impact it had on John's mental health, work performance and relationship had been transformed into a positive and empowering experience that also improved his marriage.*

What causes financial stress?

It is important to understand the common causes of financial stress, as well as to identify which of these factors are within our control and which are outside of our control.

Financial stress may stem from socio-economic conditions, including job loss, escalating debt, unexpected expenses, black tax or family support, or a combination of factors. It may also be affected by your money memories, your money personality, money disorders and mental health problems. All these issues have also been exacerbated by the COVID-19 pandemic.

Socio-economic causes of financial stress in South Africa

According to Interface[12], there are seven common reasons for financial stress, all of which have been intensified due to COVID-19:

1.   Too much debt

2.   Spending more than you earn

3.   Poor planning

4.   Not having savings to fall back on

5.   Carrying the debts of partners and family members

6.   Job loss

7.   Unemployment

It is important to note that the first five of these seven reasons are within a person's control, and only two – job loss and unemployment – are outside one's control. Let's look at some of these causes more closely.

Too much debt

Right at the top of the list is too much debt.

We all know how stressful and overwhelming it is to receive overdue letters and final notices, and to get phone calls from debt collectors who threaten and intimidate. A person faced with too much debt can feel utterly alone and helpless. In fact, research[13] indicates that financial stress adversely impacts mental health, and impaired mental health can cause and exacerbate financial problems, which causes worsening mental health problems.

The 2020 Old Mutual Savings & Investment Monitor[14] confirmed that 58% of households are facing high or overwhelming financial stress. Similarly, a 2020 survey[15] by debt counselling company, Debt Rescue, found that approximately 85% of all South Africans need help financially, emotionally or both as a result of the COVID-19 pandemic. The study found that a further 55% required financial assistance but had no access to credit, and an additional 96% were stressed about their health, finances or both.

Job loss and unemployment caused by COVID-19 and the lockdowns have resulted in many households getting into even more debt in order to make ends meet. Despite the prime lending rate in 2020 being 7% – the lowest it has been in 45 years – the income-to-debt ratio in South Africa is still at 72,8%. This means that, on average, for every R100 earned, around R73 is spent on debt repayments!

Case study – The impact of over indebtedness

A manager in his late fifties, who is the sole breadwinner in his family, struggled with feelings of depression and suicidal thoughts before eventually reaching out for help. One of the triggers causing his stress and anxiety was financial: he had taken out a significant loan to invest in a business opportunity, which later turned out to be a fraudulent scheme, and he lost everything.

His financial situation had spiralled out of control, and by the time he was referred to a financial coach, he had over R520,000 in short-term debt, with an average interest rate of 21%. As a result, his debt repayments exceeded his net income by thousands of rands, leaving him utterly desperate and contemplating suicide.

His financial coach immediately set out to renegotiate his debt repayments through a formal debt counselling solution and, in this way, reduced his interest rate to less than 4% and his debt instalments to an amount he could afford each month.

The net effect was immense relief from a substantial debt burden and the crippling financial stress it caused, and transforming his depression, desperation and suicidal thoughts into renewed confidence that he was able to provide for his family and to pay off his debt.

No savings

The 2020 Old Mutual Savings and Investment Monitor (OMSIM) COVID-19 Special Report[16] confirmed that South Africans' personal financial situation was worse than a year ago. A key finding of this report, which was conducted during full lockdown when only essential services were permitted to operate, shows that 40% of those currently employed only have enough funds to survive for one month or less should they lose their jobs, and as many as 66% of the respondents stated that they are constantly worried about losing their job or income.

Similarly, during the period between March 2020 – November 2020, thousands of people in many companies in South Africa were trained by local employee wellness provider Interface[17] on building financial resilience and managing their personal finances through the pandemic. One of the interesting polling questions asked of attendees was "Do you have a savings account to tap into in the event of an emergency?" and over 75% of attendees answered "No" to this question.

The COVID-19 pandemic is the perfect example of an unplanned emergency. The reality is that financial stress can be reduced if we promote a savings culture. One of the key benefits to a savings account is peace of mind, something that money cannot buy!

Family responsibility

Family responsibility increased significantly during the COVID-19 period, and according to the OMSIM[18] report, 52% of respondents have adult dependents living at home – a significant increase from 35% in 2015.

Similarly, more people in their 30s to 50s find themselves in the Sandwich generation, a term coined for those who are 'sandwiched' between supporting their children and caring for elderly relatives. These numbers too have grown from 34% in 2019 to 42% in 2020.

Statistics[19] show that just 6% of South Africans are able to retire. It is not surprising then that a 2017 Old Mutual Savings and Investment Monitor[20] found that 70% of working South Africans are already supporting, or foresee that they will have to support, older family members in the future. Responsibility for family members is extremely complicated and can be linked to many emotions, from guilt to anger and even fear. This responsibility can become overwhelming and can take its toll mentally and emotionally.

The amount of family support varies, but Interface research[21] indicates that as many as 40% of people are spending as much as 25% of their income on family support.

In other cases, the situation is more dire. In one instance, a young lady shared how her mother insisted on having full access to her salary through her ATM card. She had no control over her own hard-earned income, with her mother controlling her finances. Another young graduate admitted to sending the lion's share of her salary to her parents, leaving herself struggling to buy food for the remainder of the month.

Many young professionals feel financial pressure to support family members who, for example, made meaningful sacrifices to provide for their education, and feel that they do not have a choice when it comes to what is often colloquially referred to as "black tax".

Case study – Sandwich generation

The story of a dynamic and professional working woman, let's call her Ann, provides a fitting example. Ann is in her early 40's, and she is married with three children. She works as a manager at an IT company and her husband is self-employed. The family relies on Ann's income as her husband's income is sporadic.

Ann also has two elderly parents, who have very limited income and rely heavily on Ann to manage their personal finances. Although Ann has two siblings who she had hoped would assist in financially supporting her parents, she had to ask them continuously and they often had excuses as to why they were unable to provide support.

Ann's situation is not uncommon, and she is sandwiched between caring financially for her children and for her parents. Her income can only stretch so far and so certain sacrifices need to be made to ensure that all family members are taken care of. This situation often causes stress, anxiety and guilt for the supporting child, who feels overwhelmed by the pressure to provide for all family members. This stress often leads to depression or mental health issues.

Education is key to ensuring that people are empowered with skills to deal with situations like these – enabling them to support their families without crippling themselves financially. The safety rules on an airplane provide a fitting analogy: *"make sure you secure your own mask before helping those around you".* It is important that people first pay themselves and get their own finances in order before they provide financial support to their extended families.

Job loss and unemployment

Unfortunately, job losses and unemployment rates have increased dramatically and have been compounded by the COVID-19 pandemic. The unemployment rate stood at 32,5% in the fourth quarter of 2020, according to the South African Reserve Bank.[22]

Even employed South Africans are also affected by these job losses and unemployment rates, as they struggle with their own reduced incomes and also increased support to extended family members who have lost their jobs and face unemployment.

Money memories and money personality

When considering the causes of financial stress, it is important to explore money memories and money personalities, because these affect our responses to financial issues and could lead to mental health problems.

Better understanding your current financial situation requires taking a step back into the past to identify your personal money memories and answering key questions such as:

- How old were you when you first received money?
- How much money did you receive?
- Who gave you this money?
- How did it make you feel?
- What did you do with this money?

This exercise is often used in both financial training for groups as well as individual coaching sessions. It is a powerful exercise, as it explores your first experience of money. Many people share how they received money from parents or grandparents, or from the tooth mouse or fairy. Some people say that money made them feel good or powerful or happy, and others recall that they feared losing the money. Many spent this money on sweets or goodies and some immediately saved the money in a money box.

Our money memories are shaped by our financial role models, and by the environment in which we grow up. Uncovering often forgotten money memories allow people to identify why they do what they do when it comes to making financial decisions.

Case study – Money memories

Sandy grew up in a big family, with six older sisters and two older brothers, so 'hand-me-downs' were definitely a way of life in their family!

Sandy recalled her mom preparing a long row of lunchboxes for school, putting a simple sandwich in each. As such, one of her childhood memories is comparing her lunchbox to those of her classmates.

> *Thirty years later, Sandy finds herself over-compensating with her own children's lunchboxes, spending more than necessary to ensure her children have the best lunchboxes. In this case, it is clear how Sandy's money memories affect the money decisions that she still makes day by day.*

Our money memories shape our money personalities. Understanding your money personality is vital for having a healthy relationship with money. There are many different money personalities and our money personalities affect how we respond to money situations on a daily basis. One way to understand your money personality is to answer truthfully how you would respond when faced with a money situation, such as the example below.

Imagine you are having a casual dinner with a group of friends. It is not a special occasion, nor is it anyone's birthday. When the bill arrives, how do you respond?

- Pay the bill in full
- Pay for your share after working out the amount with a calculator
- Split the bill equally among the friends
- Avoid the situation by going to the bathroom
- Ask a friend to pay for you
- Feel anxious and unsure

The way in which you react to the situation provides insight into your money personality. People who disappear to the bathroom, may have an 'ostrich' money personality, burying their heads in the sand when it comes to personal finances. The 'big spender' money personalities will pay the bill in full, regardless of whether they can afford it or not. Those with an 'accountant' money personality will calculate and pay only their fair share.

There is no right or wrong answers – there are literally hundreds of money personalities. The exercise simply provides insight into how our money personalities affect our response to different money situations and how this could impact our mental health.

Money disorders and mental health issues

It is also important to explore the difference between money problems and money disorders. A money disorder is defined as *"a chronic pattern of self-destructive financial behaviours"* by financial psychologist Dr Brad Klonz[23], a leader in the field of money disorders.

Beyond simply struggling to manage money, a money disorder can be identified when a person's money management has become destructive – potentially resulting in severe financial consequences, including negatively impacting physical health, mental health, personal relationships and work.

In his book, *Mind over Money*, Klontz outlines 12 money disorders[24] under three main categories. Each category can be broken down further into more specific conditions, like overspending, workaholism and pathological gambling.

Avoidance disorders, such as compulsive hoarding, can be seen as a symptom of Obsessive Compulsive Disorder (OCD) or Obsessive Compulsive Personality Disorder (OCPD). While being careful about how you spend your money is good, too much scrimping and being frugal can be considered a symptom of OCD.

The term 'workaholic', derived from the word 'alcoholic', describes those who work so unreasonably hard that it becomes a problem, affecting their sleep, health, social relationships, and even their family life. This workaholism may stem from anxiety and depression about personal finances, worry about poor money management, fear that there will not be enough money or concerns about losing a job.

One of the most common money disorders is 'financial denial'. It is common among those with an 'ostrich' money personality, and the symptoms of this disorder include, for example, ignoring bills, delaying filing tax returns, and not taking calls from debt collectors.

Another disorder that is quite common – and even acceptable – in our consumer-driven society is overspending or compulsive buying. Symptoms include constant spending to boost 'happiness' levels. Unfortunately, while this form of retail therapy provides some temporary relief from anxiety, another shopping fix is soon required.

Relational money disorders are identified when financial problems are interwoven with relationships with family and friends. An example of this is 'financial infidelity' in which partners in a relationship lie about their finances and even hide financial transactions from each other.

In addition to these money disorders, other mental health problems can also negatively impact financial wellness. For many people who are struggling with mental health problems, it is difficult to manage money. This leads to stress and anxiety about money, which in turn aggravates their mental health issues. In the US, the Money and Mental Health Policy Institute[25] confirms that people with mental health problems are *"more likely to be in debt"*. Similarly, in the UK, a 2019 Money and Mental Health Policy Institute survey[26] found that nearly 5, 500 people – a convincing 86% of respondents – said that their financial situation had made their mental health problems worse. According to the Institute, a UK-based independent research organisation, *"people with mental health problems are three and a half times as likely to experience financial stress and debt problems".* The research further indicates that people with debt problems are significantly more likely to experience mental health problems, and 46% of people who are experiencing debt problems also have mental health problems. The diagram below illustrates the vicious cycle and relationship between financial difficulty and mental health problems.

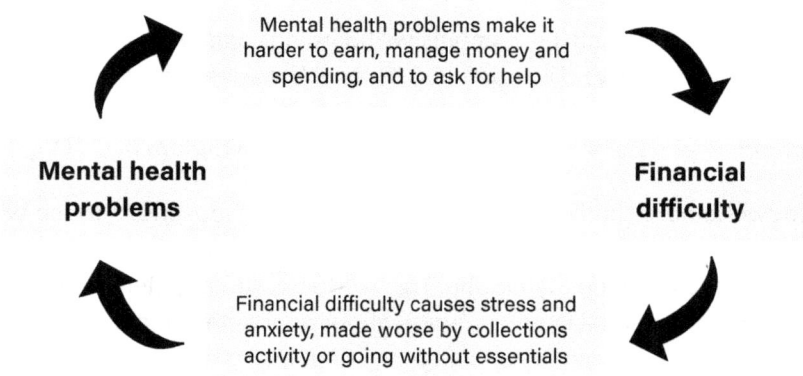

Mental health problems make it harder to earn, manage money and spending, and to ask for help

Mental health problems

Financial difficulty

Financial difficulty causes stress and anxiety, made worse by collections activity or going without essentials

Figure 12.1: The cycle of money and mental health problems[26]

Who is most affected by financial stress?

People from all over the world and from all walks of life are having to deal with financial stress and uncertainty, and this has been exacerbated by the COVID-19 pandemic and its devastating economic impact.

Financial stress is one of the most common stressors in modern life. An American Psychological Association (APA) study[27] in 2015 found that 72% of Americans feel stressed about money at least some of the time.

In South Africa, the National Credit Regulator's report[28] also indicates financial stress, confirming that just 63% of South Africans are in good standing or one to two months in arrears with their debt, while 36% are three months or more in arrears. A Sanlam study in 2017[29] also showed just how pervasive financial stress is among middle-class workers.

In a 2020 study by Interface[30], 4261 people who were employed at the time, completed financial health assessments. One of the questions in this confidential assessment was: "Do you feel anxious or stressed about your financial life?" Half (50%) of the respondents answered "yes" to this question, 20% answered "sometimes", and just 30% said they don't feel stressed. This means that 70% of the employed population surveyed feel some level of anxiety and stress when it comes to money.

The interesting reality about financial stress is that it affects people of all demographics and income levels. It is often assumed that financial stress only affects lower income earners, but this is not true.

Financial stress and money worries impact and affect people regardless of colour, culture or language, across all types of companies and industries, and across income levels – from entry-level positions to senior management.

Certainly, financial stress impacts men and women alike, although women tend to use financial wellbeing programmes more often than men do. However, because of the greater financial pressure since the beginning of 2020, more men are also reaching out for assistance in dealing with financial problems.

According to psychiatrist Dr Dora Wynchank[31], many South African men are struggling with emotional issues. However, as they are socialised to be 'strong' and not express emotion or sadness, they often have no outlet or support system. Men are under enormous pressure to perform in the competitive workplace and are frequently judged on their occupational and wealth status. When they are in a difficult financial situation and can no longer provide for their families, feelings of helplessness can result in mental health issues. Recent economic hardship, unemployment and the financial crisis are all reasons that men have more stress to contend with, and an increased incidence of depression. SADAG[32] have reported an increase in businessmen reaching out for psychological help because of financial problems during this time of crisis.

It is also true that financial stress affects people regardless of the positions they hold or the amount of money they earn. For example, a 2018 Profmed survey[33] of 2,500 of Profmed's young professional membership base revealed the stress levels and causes of stress for young professionals. "More than 50% of young professionals said they were more stressed in 2018 than the previous year. The rise in financial stress is not surprising, considering the economic conditions which continue to take their toll on every sector of South African society. A cause of concern is the increase in the number of professionals who said they experienced higher levels of stress-induced anxiety and depression, with approximately 40% of young professionals claiming to feel detached and wanted to be left alone."

One of the reasons why young professionals put up with the stress, is to earn a large salary at the end of the month. However, it is concerning to note that despite working hard in order to earn a substantial pay cheque, financial problems are the top cause of stress, with 91% of respondents saying that financial issues were the leading cause of stress followed by health, work and family pressure.

Addressing financial stress

One of the ways to address financial stress is to provide people with education, empowerment, support and tools. *"Remember that during times like these, knowledge plays a crucial role in the financial decisions we make,"* says John Manyike Head of Financial Education at Old Mutual Limited. *"Equip yourself with financial understanding to ensure you make the right decisions."*

Sadly, few people are taught financial skills at home, and although it is part of the school curriculum in Life Orientation, it does not become fully relevant until you are working and earning a living.

Many more companies in a wide variety of sectors are now taking the matter of financial stress very seriously. These companies recognise how financial stress can impact productivity and the health of their organisation and understand the need to start a conversation around financial stress.

Companies that focus on empowering their employees with financial skills and support reap the dividends. By improving their money matters, employees experience less financial stress, which has a positive impact on their mental health. This also reduces absenteeism and improves employee productivity.

Empowering their employees with financial skills and support can be achieved through employee wellness programmes that encompass financial education, ranging from one-on-one coaching to classroom-based training and online and virtual training, as well as assistance with financial matters such as budgeting and debt management. These programmes are designed to help employees to build financial resilience – the ability to bounce back from financial challenges and setbacks – and cover important aspects such as exploring your relationship with money and understanding your money personality.

When it comes to teaching financial literacy and resilience successfully, a trainer who is the right fit for the organisation and who can connect with the employees is vital, as is customised training for each company, based on their benefits and remuneration.

Many employees need personal guidance to manage their financial challenges, and this is where financial coaching can play a useful role. Financial coaching is quite different to financial advising – the role of a financial coach is to create a safe place and to assist without any judgment, no matter where a person is in their financial life.

Financial coaches, unlike financial brokers or advisors, do not sell any financial products or services, but rather coach and mentor a person to reach a better financial situation. Financial coaches are trained to assist people to understand their financial "now" or current financial situation, and then to define a financial goal or financial "wow" they want to achieve.

People reach out to financial wellbeing programmes from all walks of life, from all levels within an organisation, from entry-level positions to managers, and even partners, directors and executives.

Managing financial stress in the workplace

Financial stress impacts employees regardless of age, gender or position, and this chapter has demonstrated the link between financial stress and mental health.

Financial stress among employees also has a significant impact on a company's bottom line. Addressing financial stress among employees can unlock major benefits for companies.

Research on absenteeism[34] conducted by AIC Insurance in South Africa in 2009 confirms that absenteeism is reaching staggeringly high levels, and could be costing the country's economy as much as R12 billion per year. In the average company, approximately 4,5% of the workforce is absent on any given day!

One of the reasons for absenteeism is financial stress. Some years ago, one organisation in South Africa experienced a payroll issue which resulted in employees' salaries being delayed. This resulted in about 20% of their workforce being unable to come into work, as they simply did not have money for transport! In another South African company, a payroll glitch resulted in employees being overpaid, and 25% of these employees were unable to return the funds. This is because the funds were immediately detected and collected from employees' accounts by tracking and collection software to cover outstanding debt repayments.

Employee morale and motivation is also affected when the workforce is overwhelmed with too much debt. In some instances, employees don't feel motivated or inspired to work for their income as they are only working to pay off lenders and loan sharks.

In some organisations, these loan sharks are not even outsiders, but work colleagues! Despite this being illegal, inter-employee lending is rife, with employees in some companies creating a second income or side hustle through a loan business, lending their co-workers money at astronomical rates of up to 60% in interest. Desperate employees see no other option but to take these short-term loans. Taking a R1,000 loan on the first of the month, they face having to pay back R1,600 on payday: the R1,000 capital plus R600 in interest. This is not only illegal but can be very damaging to inter-employee relationships.

Financial wellbeing programmes can also mitigate against loss of valuable employees, who resign in order to access their pension/provident fund monies. This is probably one of the worst financial mistakes employees can make. However, due to extraordinary financial stress and anxiety, they may feel that this is the only solution open to them.

Managers who proactively refer employees to the financial wellbeing programme when faced with a resignation can save these employees from making poor financial decisions while also reducing the company's costs in replacing such employees.

Case Study - Resigning to access a pension monies

When Sue, a top performer, resigned from her company in order to access her pension monies due to the financial stress she was under, her manager refused to accept the resignation until she had engaged in financial coaching and received assistance from their financial wellbeing programme. During the financial coaching meeting, alternative solutions were found to Sue's financial distress through the debt counselling process. Her financial coach worked with her to restructure her debts so she could then afford her monthly debt repayments, save herself thousands in interest charges, keep her job, and preserve her retirement savings – a real win-win solution for employee and employer.

Many companies of all sizes and across industries are becoming more proactive, dynamic and innovative in their quest to support employees in every aspect of their lives, from their physical health to their mental and emotional health and their financial health.

Financial wellbeing programmes – either as a part of an employee assistance programme or as a stand-alone programme – send a strong and powerful message to employees that a company cares about its people and about improving their quality of life by improving their finances.

Through financial education and literacy programmes, financial coaching and support, employees have access to best of breed advice and assistance that will reduce financial stress and improve the mental wellbeing, health and wealth of employees now, and into the future. By focusing on financial empowerment, education and support, companies can achieve a measurable return on investment.

Chapter 13

What can workplaces do to create a culture of care around mental health?

Namhla Tambatamba

There are guiding design principles that organisations can consider as design principles in solving for mental health. In today's world, talent engagement and employee experience is centred around providing employees with choices, equipping them for the dynamic world of work, breaking barriers of access to several health and wellbeing solutions. Generally, organisations are interested in considering programmes and practices that promote holistic wellbeing, however, the journey and the end-goal on organisational-employee health is not always clearly defined. Through multiple perspectives, we know that protecting and caring for mental health requires an integrated approach for compelling employee support, but at the same time we cannot overlook the view or the fact that the mental health topic can be overwhelming and/or up-in-the-air. Its presentation in the workplace may also differ depending on industry dynamics. Therefore, a focused prioritisation on what the starting point is and establishing partnerships is necessary. Influenced by the future world of work imperatives, organisations are continuously recognising the need to create a working environment that promotes creativity and high performance, yet it can be cumbersome to correlate the extent of mental health required for people to thrive. Fortunately, in an era of big data, people and health data analysis provide direction and serve as a good basis for business conversations.

In this chapter, a more practical-action-based approach is provided to guide organisations and prompt action for improved mental health support. Organisational response on mental health is a shared responsibility and requires participation from all functions. The topic itself is layered, and its implementation can be robust. Due to the complexity of mental health, conversations around it must be continuously reflective, sensitive and should be followed by responsible actions. Role players from different contexts can benefit from broad recommendations made herein.

Employers must be reflective towards the overall context of employees to inform actions of care

It is a matter of fact that by now, key role players in corporate environments have better awareness of the rising concerns on mental health conditions, at work and society in general. Organisations are transitioning from just caring for typical/ traditional business metrics to recognising the importance of being a catalyst for change concerning the wellbeing of communities they operate in. This has come with much awareness that for businesses to survive and be sustainable, it is critical to sustain communities and their livelihood. Some do this for continued economic activity and some, as part of their purpose. However, up to now, the view that is typically applied towards mental health as a critical aspect of holistic wellbeing has often been related to business productivity and performance, which on its own can constrain (or limit) the broader impact organisations can achieve to address or truly recognise mental health as a pandemic. In certain instances, it seems as though the motive in addressing and supporting mental health is self-serving (thus somewhat narrow) and can be seen to be less about care and sustainable livelihood.

The growing trend on mental health has driven a collective response and responsibility on mental health and with much emphasis being placed on organisational leaders. By now we know, with so much awareness and advocacy by global and local institutions, there is a need to recognise poor mental health as a costly pandemic because of its prevalence, yet it is complex to manage even at a national level. Typically, it is almost impossible to win the battle against unmanaged mental conditions if the responsibility is placed on the one part, and not the other. We must also recognise that workplaces are part of broader society; as such it must be acknowledged that when individuals interact in other areas of their lives, they remain exposed to aspects of poor mental conditions, directly or indirectly. Organisations need to evolve from just supporting mental health with an internal perspective.

Another reflection point is for organisations to recognise that while workplaces provide financial relief for most and meaning or purpose for the selected few, there should be strong acknowledgement that the exposure of mental health conditions remains a high possibility in a working environment due to a couple of triggers that may arise from the workplace. This can create a vicious cycle, to some extent. It may seem as though workplaces are not doing enough, or they are not totally addressing mental health conditions. The bottom line is, mental health is a societal problem, irrespective of where the trigger comes from.

The dialogue and actions on mental health require everyone involved to un-learn limiting or instigating behaviours that perpetuate mental health challenges and re-learn behaviours that support mental health. The working environment can encourage good mental health; however, this must be done with an understanding that an individual's life is not defined by work and work is just a small aspect of a person's life. So there can't be mentally healthy workplaces without healthy societies. The World Health Organisation (WHO)[1] is clear on this: organisations support mental health because we want sustainable communities that can function and participate in creating wealth, prosperity, peace. So, those in business inversely benefit from this but the support of good mental health should be for a greater good.

In speaking about mental health, even the language used in academia and generally in business writing has been normalised to give a promise that seems to be solely built on driving performance as the main carrot. Yet, performance is an obvious end-result if people are cared for and are well. Perhaps the practical commercial benefit of good mental health cannot be ignored, because it is the basis for economic participation and progress for organisations and for individuals; however, the more the language is unchanged, the more difficult it becomes to get people to relate to the topic of mental health.

Now more than ever before, individuals must navigate a changing and a highly digital environment. On the one hand this is intimidating; on the other, it is dynamic and exciting. The changing society, business environment and even the changing human behaviours are calling for people to be resilient and adaptable to change. Often, these aspects are 'forced' on people's lives. COVID-19 has led to new ways of working, new ways of living, introduced higher levels of stress and anxiety for many reasons. There has been an aspect of loss and trauma, helplessness and even hopelessness. People have formally and informally reported high levels of fatigue and exhaustion, consistently. Adherence to COVID-19 protocols has meant that individuals generally have limited options and their lives have been greatly shifted by the pandemic. The social connection with loved ones, community and religious gatherings have largely been limited, which could introduce a certain level of emptiness and distance, yet closeness is so much needed for mental health. Generally, the working class is continuously aware of the changing nature of work, with the introduction of digital transformation in many business processes across sectors. While this shift is at different cycles in the business environment, at an individual level, people's minds are tossing between being impacted or affected by these changes and having fears for job security. This places a huge responsibility on organisations to think deeply around how the necessary organisational change and management thereof trigger mental health conditions.

Acknowledge the presentation of mental health conditions in the workplace

Mental health problems, such as depression, mood disorders, anxiety, substance abuse and job stress are common in a working environment, affecting individuals, their families and co-workers, and the broader community. In addition, they have a direct impact on workplaces through increased absenteeism, reduced productivity, and increased costs. In emerging economies, very few individuals seek treatment for mental health related conditions even though mental illness can be treated at nearest clinics, hospitals and/or any other health provider. In fact, there seems to be general lack of awareness at an individual level and where there is some awareness, acting on mental health care is often the least of the concerns people have. The majority of individuals are often concerned about societal challenges and the impact on their lives. These can include high levels of unemployment that exist in poor communities, socio-economic constraints, poverty, crime and trauma. Generally, individuals carry on with life with the hope to first address the basic human needs more than an urgency to act to address mental health conditions.

Presentation of poor mental health conditions is often invisible, misunderstood, and if expressed, stigmatised. There are also cultural and religious reasons that may limit access and acknowledgement of a mental health condition. In certain cultures, it is common to associate mental health conversations mainly with the weak, and seeking help is at times interpreted as a weakness. This is not surprising, because mental health problems are the result of a complex interaction between biological, psychological, social and environmental factors. Therefore, both the content and context of work can play a role in the development of mental health problems in the workplace.

Generally, people complain about workload which can be excessive or insufficient work, lack of participation and control in the workplace; the nature of work which can include monotonous or unpleasant tasks. Currently, organisations value collaboration, yet in certain instances, ways of working may not be adequately structured, resulting in role ambiguity or conflict. Some inequality may exist, often accompanied by lack of recognition at work, which results in poor interpersonal relationships amongst teams; and poor working conditions. Therefore, the role of a leader is, and it must be acknowledged that poor leadership engagement and communication makes it even harder for employees to trust and to be empowered in managing conflicting priorities in their lives. All stakeholders should be empowered to understand that poor mental health presentation at work can include cognitive changes which can be expected to be part of the condition. This can affect work motivation and interest in performing tasks. In an increasing digital working environment, some are working remotely and others in offices; therefore ways of engagement and working have shifted. This shift requires extra-sensitivity in supporting and protecting mental health. For businesses, it is an opportunity to create efficiencies in a time where there is already a perception and even a trend that organisations tend to do more with less, and of course this has an impact on how the employee approaches work and the psychological contract itself.

Acknowledge the meaning of mental health statistics in South Africa

We have an opportunity to accept that the role of statistics to track and understand mental health conditions should be used as directional and indicating trends for policy considerations and implementation of supportive programmes. The nature of mental illnesses and its effect on people, continues to be hidden. At the same time, as we are in a data-driven world, for most organisations, being guided by statistics is still a golden rule through which there is confidence to react and respond. Looking at the complexity, confidentiality and stigma attached to mental illnesses, it is time for organisations to be comfortable with this ambiguity and support mental health with rigour while at the same time containing it.

Organisations could consider being less preoccupied by specific internal data and ensure their response is guided by emerging data and, more accurately, statistics from national mental health institutions and related bodies as adequate to propel action. Within academic structures, the mental health conversation is rich, accessible and information is easy to consume for organisations to structure the care and support required. For instance, the narrative stated through the *Wits News* publication[2]; Robertson thinks that mental health support is under-resourced and under-funded, where the WHO[1] notes 0.4 public sector psychiatrists per 100 000 people in SA but has no figures for other mental health specialists and there is also a dire shortage of specialist nurses. It is further indicated that according to the South African Depression and Anxiety Group, there are 11 mental health conditions covered by the Council for Medical Schemes' prescribed minimum benefits that medical schemes must provide to their members. But there are only two conditions, bipolar mood disorder and schizophrenia, that are classified as chronic, and cover for these conditions vary based on the medical aid.

Goudge says, *"the level of specialist care available varies significantly, both between provinces and areas of SA. In some areas of Gauteng there are primary healthcare nurses who can deal with severe mental illness with specialist support. It is important for organisations to understand the impact of skills shortages on the overall health of employees, therefore supporting mental health requires a multi-sectorial approach; and employers can within their mental health programmes, co-ordinate not only for internal campaigns but also include offering primary healthcare which looks at the provision of mental health services. This should link to the use of psychologists, social workers and occupational therapists".[2]*

Organisations should actively drive behaviours through supportive interventions that demonstrate care for mental health, on an ongoing basis

Generally, the first point of contact to enter a workplace environment is through human resources and in certain instances the hiring/line manager. With mental health conditions being prevalent in communities, it is time for key role players in organisations to demonstrate social acumen in the way individuals are introduced to employment. There is an indirect, yet significant responsibility placed on organisations to be cognisant of basic psychological needs, to appreciate the connection that individuals form as these relate to their self-esteem to being employed. Recognising these basic human needs will help segment and come up with the appropriate response in supporting mental health.

For most people, the first and foremost pursuit is about earning a living; yet employment is not only about a pay cheque. In fact, the pay cheque is an enablement for the livelihood of the employed individuals, and through pay the individual can provide for his/her family. In South Africa where unemployment levels are high, individuals may have unspoken vulnerability to hold onto employment at all costs due to the mindset of scarcity and yet it is a necessity to have income. In this context, there is a clear role played by people practices, as these are a vehicle to communicate and demonstrate organisational values and essentially a culture of care. Therefore, understanding the initial employee-employer engagements as a contribution to the culture of care in the workplace can influence the basic benefits and remuneration practices that the organisations will have in place. People practices are meant to enable the employee with experience which, over time, has evolved and has been stated to be directly linked to customer experience and productivity.

So, we must appreciate that the invitation to be a part of an organisation is often mutually beneficial. On the one hand, it is clear that individuals mostly join the workplace to earn a living and very rarely for career progression or meaning. On the other hand, organisations will hire individuals to fulfil a certain function so that their business objectives are met. This is an exchange. However, the onus to support mental health is largely placed on organisations, recognising their capabilities and generally less is said about individuals having to act and prioritise their mental health. We can appreciate the narrative that seems to be leaning on organisations to do more; therefore, these are some of the initiatives organisations can do:

Shift and review people policies and practices that support mental health, introduce progressive practices and reduce restrictive practices

Organisations with a standalone wellbeing strategy tend to take a fairly holistic approach, promoting all aspects of employee wellbeing particularly physical health, mental health and good lifestyle choices. There is a need to make it a standard to introduce mental health policies and guidelines that include:

a. Clearly expressing an organisational stance as a response to mental health challenges and to support the notion of psychological safety for employees;

b. Promote a culture of acceptance for individuals who may be struggling with mental health conditions;

c. Tactics on encouraging access, transparency and individual actions; articulate the nature of care the organisation provides and ensure general understanding amongst employees and leadership;

d. Directionally, CIPD Survey report, 2020[3] indicates an opportunity for organisations to put in place absence management processes that normalise reasons related to mental illnesses as is the case with physical illnesses. On a positive note, some organisations are taking some action to manage employee mental health at work. The most common approach is to offer a phased return to work and/or other reasonable adjustments, return to work interviews (RTW), and often these are used to manage both short- to long-term absence. However, in other instances there is a gap in policy provision leading to lack of genuine reporting, which is largely driven by stigma and discrimination that still exists in the workplace. This means there should be emphasis on creating awareness to support disclosure.

e. In certain contexts, mental health admissions are in the top ten reasons for hospital admissions and are increasingly becoming the leading cause for disabilities. Thus, as part of supporting recovery, the RTW process should be guided by the expertise of an occupational therapist. This support often enables an independent view for individuals to understand how mental health problems interfere with the capacity to engage effectively and for people to be appropriately guided on the use of resources.

Offer a mental health menu on ways of working and rituals that employees-line managers can jointly do and own, even virtually

In simple language but with consistency, the potential impact of implementing team habits can go a long way. There is no 'one-size-fits-all' approach to designing mental health tips and habits; introducing behavioural habits that will enhance mental health should be based on the individual's unique needs and characteristics. An old saying, 'Know your Employee', is still relevant today, to avoid developing initiatives and interventions that are far-removed from the reality that people live in. The start could be incorporating positive words or language in regular interactions for basic yet essential positive feelings or experiences that people commonly need. These could include the following values:

a. **YOU BELONG:** Team rituals to forge a culture of collaboration, team work and connection.

b. **WE SHARE AND LISTEN:** Culture of trust and open engagement.

c. **YOU MATTER:** Open to differences, respect and welcome different perspectives.

d. **FREEDOM:** Autonomy to negotiate, set boundaries to manage workload or expectations and openness to share work challenges and explore opportunities.

e. **ENERGY THROUGH MOVEMENT:** Physical exercise tactics to stimulate hormonal activity to improve mental health.

f. **TEAM EATING HABITS:** The brain has a direct effect on the stomach and intestines. Psychosocial factors influence the actual physiology of the gut as well as symptoms, in other words, stress (or depression and psychosocial factors) can affect movement and contractions of the gastrointestinal tract.[4] This highlights the power of nutrition to influence mood and physical health. Workplaces that offer canteen/staff restaurants, including catering for functions or team meetings can make it a habit to incorporate and normalise healthy eating and lifestyle options to improve mental health.

g. **TAKE CHARGE OF YOUR MIND AND FEELINGS, IN THE MOMENT:** According to the mental health foundation; mindfulness is an integrative, mind-body based approach that helps people to manage their thoughts and feelings. There is a need to incorporate mindfulness practices throughout the organisation, while being sensitive to and respecting religious and cultural contexts. These can be further designed and selected at a team level and be implemented in times of high stress.

Shift the leadership practice approach to be open to change, to continuously and consistently encourage a *hearty* leadership behaviour

There are many approaches and innovations that continue to shape leadership behaviours that are essential for the current and future world of work. With distributed and virtual teams, there is an increased focus on leadership conversations taking place globally, it is also an exciting time that now, and in the future, there is readiness or interest to lead comfortably and effectively in environments where mental health is a continuous threat.

Peter Northouse[5] refers to work done by Kouzes and Prosner (1987, 2002) which is centred on transformational leadership, which in a nutshell is a broad-based perspective that encompasses many facets and dimensions of the leadership process. Indirectly, this approach discredits a single-minded leadership success story, and is simply emphasising leading with empathy. Different schools of thought have been articulated, emphasising the need for leaders to shift from simply focusing on the bottom line, to also delivering business results that have a broader societal benefit. Enough said, it is time for organisations to execute on this by considering:

a.   **Leaders as social architects:** being interested and involving themselves in the culture of the organisation and shape its meaning. A key aspect to this, is understanding the leadership role in providing guidance, direction on how people contribute to the greater purpose of the organisation for shared meaning. With a workplace that espouses trust and collaboration, there is automatically psychological safety that is created. This is essential in fostering care and supporting mental health. People tend to feel better about themselves, their contribution and in turn remain engaged. This approach is an obvious answer in a time where the majority of organisations must manage virtual teams.

b.   **Leadership style that encourages openness about mental health:** is effective at supporting people with mental ill health and actively promotes good mental wellbeing. A leadership style that is willing and prepared to explore creative ways to support an employee's recovery, which could include flexible/adjusted working hours, demands, conditions and/or working remotely when needed. This should be the backdrop of understanding the necessity for support of an employee who is struggling with mental health; there are already more people affected as they interact with the individual. So, the impact of support is not only narrowed to the employee but for the benefit of many, at work and outside work. This could sound burdensome and transformational at the same time.

c. **Build leadership capability** so that leaders are effective in holding wellbeing conversations with confidence, which largely include matters related to mental health. The enablement approach is largely dependent on the culture and sector; however, the most common leadership behaviours include empathy and more than ever before puts the people and the heart at the centre of the business.

d. **Consider reverse empathy:** the responsibility for leaders to be empathetic in protecting mental health has grown and has been made known. However, it is also about time to appreciate that workplaces are made up of leaders and employees. Therefore, there is equal responsibility for employees to be trained to demonstrate more empathy amongst each other and towards their leaders. The current reality is that society at large is navigating a pandemic, and most will feel the impact of the pandemic in years to come. Resources are stretched and depleted, therefore it is not sustainable to expect a selected few to lead supportive behaviours for a healthier and caring workplace. Everyone needs support, and everyone can play a role in protecting and supporting mental health.

Provide organisational mental health support capabilities that benefit and/or impact communities

Organisations should contract Employee Assistance Programmes (EAPs) that offer holistic psychosocial counselling and multichannel support. This offering could be extended to other partners/community-based groups in partnership with Corporate Social Responsibility (CSR) initiatives. While the social impact of this is clear, commercially this needs to be implemented in a sensible and affordable manner.

Revolutionise EAPs to be integrated and proactive: in a time where mental health challenges are most common, EAP programmes are likely to transition to play a more prominent role for individuals. This can be characterised by a continued journey of having a go-to-person (that being a therapist), on an ongoing basis. Perhaps it is time to come up with a system that shifts from offering short-term counselling, on a reactive basis, to ongoing counselling and self-development proactively. Within the network of counsellors, there will need to be diverse expertise to cater for non-traditional needs that mirror societal ills. For instance, a much more elevated offering on:

1. **Appropriately defined career support and health:** For the most part people in workplaces struggle with job security, jobs are changing, there is increased digitalization, threat of under-employment and entrepreneurialism for survival and meaning. One can expect that largely, individuals are preoccupied by these factors and their mental health is at risk. Other than the typical human resources process, individuals could benefit from an independent and safe space for dialogue and support in this regard.

2. **EAPs are effective to support mental health problems:** Raise awareness on current employee assistance programmes and emphasise that these programmes are effective in supporting and addressing mental health problems, including coping with mood disorders, bipolar, depression and work-stress. Perhaps there is an opportunity for role players and consumers to appreciate the role played by EAPs going forward.

Implement diverse empowerment and enablement tactics

Educate employees on poor mental health, especially how cognitive functioning or ability as a result of a mental health condition can affect work performance. **Psychological language** used in matters of mental health is specialised; and could create limitations in understanding and relatability on mental health matters. It can be intimidating and, in some way, farfetched for certain contexts. At an organisational level there is an opportunity to translate and put things simply in a relevant and relatable manner.

Business language: it has been interesting to observe that over time, in most practices there has been a significant shift towards introducing practices that are purpose-led and sensitive and sustainable to the broader society. While this is a progressive shift in a corporate environment, there is room for improvement, that is to see mental health and support as means to respond to the societal livelihood that will cause a catastrophe for businesses.

If this remains unmanaged the hidden costs will continue to rise. Mental health support is one of the ways in which organisations can indicate a shift into thriving for purpose.

In addition to psychological counselling offerings, traditional and spiritual advisors are widely spread in most African contexts, and are knowledgeable of the cultural norms, and their advice is sought, believed and acted upon by people in general. Organisations should recognise the significant role played by religious and traditional leaders in the treatment of mental health and be willing to engage and understand the nature and the meaning of the support provided. This would reflect a diverse way in which mental health can be supported, shifting from being rigid towards most commonly used (and advocated) approaches, which have been mainly psychologically focussed.

Provide preventative health solutions and practices

We must recognise that underlying mental health conditions often create other health vulnerabilities. With COVID-19, it has been mentioned that individuals with high levels of stress, have an immune system that is compromised and as such, they are prone to being severely affected by the virus. During and post the recovery period, it has been indicated that individuals continue to have lingering symptoms, some related to mental health. However, the most common stress assessments conducted in workplaces tend to be behavioural and somewhat subjective at a point in time.

So, with work stress being the most common and persistent aspect of mental health, organisations can look at contracting medically proven stress screening as part of health risk assessments which are mostly delivered through wellness days by most companies. Dr Makiwane[1] says, while stress is necessary in our day-to-day living to push us to higher heights, excessive longstanding stress (toxic stress) has a detrimental effect to health because it leads to:

1. A cascade of hormonal disruptions leading to adrenal gland over-activity, excessive adrenaline and cortisol production

2. Immune system depletion

3. Impaired Psychosocial Systems

In addition, prolonged high levels of cortisol play a pivotal role in development of chronic diseases like obesity (diabetes mellitus) leading to high homocysteine, Hypercholesterolemia, Stroke, Coronary Artery Disease leading to Heart Attacks (Myocardial Infarction), Depression and Anxiety.

High adrenaline increases heart rate and blood pressure. Dr Makiwane further states that, studies show that depression and anxiety predispose people to unhealthy behaviours like dysfunctional relationships, poor diets, sedentary lifestyle, substance abuse, excessive alcohol consumption, violence, suicidal thoughts and actual suicide.

Therefore, in collaboration with medical aid schemes and their healthcare network systems, organisations can include proven stress assessments of which the recommended tests would be testing morning cortisol levels for employees:

Therefore, in collaboration with medical aid schemes and their healthcare network systems, organizations can include proven stress assessments of which the recommended tests would be testing the following tests:

1. Morning cortisol levels- high in chronic stress

2. Fasting Blood Glucose- impaired glucose (pre-diabetes mellitus) or high indicative of diabetes mellitus

3. Hemoglobin A1c- high in impaired glucose or diabetes mellitus

---

1   Dr Unati Makiwane- Dr M Health Corner, Family Physician in Canada

4.   Lipid Profile – high sometimes

5.   White Cell Count- normal or high

6.   hsCRP- when high, it means higher risk of developing coronary artery disease

7.   Homocysteine- an amino acid in the blood which is usually high amongst people with diabetes mellitus, poor diet, chronic stress, substance abuse, excessive caffeine intake in turn increasing risk of heart disease.

Stress assessments should not be done in isolation. Typically a referral process between role players will provide holistic care and support to employees. This intervention would need to be part of the health risk assessment or screenings that most organisations do.

In instances where an employee shares their struggle with a mental illness, they should be effectively referred to a mental healthcare professional and be reassured of confidentiality and treatment. Research shows that, while most organisations collect absence data, few use it to inform mental health activity. Moreover, a substantial proportion of organisations do not attempt to identify the causes of stress, in order to align their efforts to address these issues.

Managed Care Programmes through the medical aid benefit offering can be effective towards improving recovery and cost of mental health conditions. Such programmes can be paired with support that EAP provides, to offer a basket of choices for individuals.

Explore organisational diagnostics to manage health risk and 'connect the dots'

To target mental health support, activity and the accompanying policy, organisations should have a wider focus on key metrics. The most common include reducing absence, manage health risk, measure levels of engagement, better retention, improved customer service, enhanced performance.

Through seasonal surveys there is an opportunity to include specific questions on mental health, pulse check on a regular basis for employees to keep track of their mental health status and this could include overall sense of wellbeing as necessary.

Clearly, mental ill health is a significant and growing challenge for organisations despite their increased focus in this area. Hopefully higher awareness in some organisations is contributing to a higher reporting level, but organisations still need to do more to target the right support to those who need it.

The impact of mental health on the bottom line of the business – that is, profitability – cannot be ignored. There is a direct impact on the financial performance of the business due to mental health challenges that employees might face. Organisations must create financial reporting and tracking tools that identify this impact, and find solutions to minimise the loss on the bottom line. Healthy employees lead to higher profitability without a doubt.

Conclusion

In conclusion, the challenges of mental health conditions are undeniable and clear for all to see. On the other hand, the solutions to the mental health conditions in the workplace and society at large are accessible and require the willingness of the organisation's leadership in collaboration with their employees to engage and apply the most appropriate solutions, taking into account the unique situations they find themselves in. Mental health is a very important aspect of a successful business now and in the future and it must be a priority to have healthy people in businesses.

Part 3

Coping mechanisms: Towards a way forward with mental health

Chapter 14: Strengthening plasticity for wellbeing and welldoing at work

By: Ingra Du Buisson Narsai

In understanding current mental health trends, the impact the pandemic is having on our mental health, the escalating concerns related to the increase in mental health, and the multiple dimensions impacting mental health, this chapter focuses on the power of the brain. It is a great follow-on that encapsulates relevant techniques that can be used to build new neurological pathways and enhance existing ones in order to build one's mental health. It proposes that understanding the neuroscience fundamentals associated with wellbeing can help build behavioural flexibility and human flourishing at work and in life. These fundamentals serve as primary prevention for mental health risk mitigation. With a detailed explanation of some of the mechanisms of brain processes, one can cultivate a sense of wellbeing and welldoing in the workplace and in life. Wellbeing involves a set of skills that can be deliberately and explicitly cultivated and developed through education and with appropriate support. This chapter has proposed five dimensions of wellbeing and welldoing that can be strengthened through intentional training. Using and practising these techniques in day-to-day life can be lifechanging!

Chapter 15: Coping mechanisms: more than resiliency, towards building prosiliency

By: Navlika Ratangee

Resilience is often a buzz word that has been used over the past few years and more so now in the context of surviving and thriving through the impact of the pandemic. This chapter unpacks resiliency and the importance of resilience in coping with the future world of work. Resilience can be learnt, built on and developed as individuals. However, workplaces play a critical role in creating the optimal environment to develop resilient individuals which is a key ingredient enabling organisations to deal with the rapid pace of change and to encourage innovation. Strategies to build resilience as individuals and how workplaces can support the building of resilience is incorporated under the context of creating an environment of psychological safety. Social vaccinations are explained in that it needs to land with equal importance as the physical vaccinations if we are to change our response to the challenges of the pandemic context and create an environment to build resilience. Lastly, the concept of prosilience is discussed as a coping mechanism to grow from adversity and have more resilient responses readily available to deal with future challenges. We cannot run away from facing further trials in the future, but we can develop the tools to mitigate the impact it has on our mental health.

Chapter 16: Mindfulness in the workplace: A life skill for today and in the future

By Rakhi Beekrum

The concept of mindfulness has grown in popularity and has been applied to several contexts, including the workplace. This chapter focuses on all the benefits of mindfulness in the workplace and provides evidence for the importance thereof, especially in improving the mental health, wellbeing and performance of employees. It is discussed from the angle of the employee, the employer or leader and the workplace environment itself. Considerations for practical implications of mindfulness in the workplace are provided in conclusion.

Chapter 17: ACTing with purpose to generate adaptive performance

By: Dr Xander van Lill and Dr Rinet van Lill

This chapter offers insights into the use of purpose as a powerful antidote to mental health challenges. Work is an important vessel of meaning and managers can apply goal setting practices as a tool to enforce purpose and combat uncertainty and hopelessness. In this chapter, Acceptance and commitment therapy (ACT) is utilised as a framework to foster alignment between major life goals and specific career development goals. If managers can match broader personal aspirations and organisational goals, employees are more likely to respond with curiosity and display adaptive performance which in turn assists with mental health. The pyramid of purpose is discussed as a model that provides guidelines to achieve purpose through goal setting by adopting committed action and psychological flexibility. Application of the model can assist organisations to cultivate a context of sustained career development and mental health.

Chapter 18: The role of employee support programmes

By: Radhi Vandayar

The role of Employee Support Programmes (ESPs), also known as Employee Assistance Programmes (EAPs) or Employee Wellbeing Programmes of late (EWPs), has seen much transition over the last few years in South Africa. This chapter shares some of the trend lines evident in the growth of ESPs in the South African market over a period to one that is really valued in the current workspace. Mental health, psychosocial stressors and employee engagement and performance have all been key drivers in ensuring effective workplace programmes. There are multiple levels of consequences experienced by the individual and the organisation should employee wellbeing needs not be addressed. Wellbeing models that assist with business priorities are explained within this context. The benefits of effective wellbeing programmes are discussed with specific reference to dealing with mental health and the impact of COVID-19 related challenges. This chapter is concluded with a discussion of some of the technological enablers that need to be considered in ESPs in this digital age.

Chapter 19: The Fourth Industrial Revolution in the workplace: career capital, mental health and wellbeing in the future of work

By: Dr Frank Magwegwe

This chapter, exciting for some, daunting for others, explains the context of the future world of work and the opportunities and challenges it represents for both employers and employees. It also provides guidance on the competencies required for the future of work and evidence-based interventions that could possibly mitigate the impact of 4IR technologies on employees' mental health and wellbeing. Learn more about human literacy, digital fluency, hyper-learning, systems and design thinking within the context of building your own career capital. This is an important framework to ensure you are building skills for the future of work and hereby enhancing your coping abilities in this fast-paced environment in order to support your mental health and wellbeing. The chapter concludes with the discussion of practising positive behaviours and emotions as a risk mitigation factor in the disruptive impact of 4IR technologies in the workplace.

Chapter 14

Strengthening plasticity for wellbeing and welldoing at work

Ingra Du Buisson Narsai

"It is a fair, even-handed, noble adjustment of things, that while there is infection in disease and sorrow, there is nothing in the world so irresistibly contagious as laughter and good humour." — Charles Dickens, A Christmas Carol

Getting started

Mental health and wellbeing are essential to our collective and individual ability as humans to think, feel, engage with each other, earn a living and enjoy life. They directly support the core human and social values of independence of thought and action, happiness, friendship and unity. On this foundation, the promotion, protection, and restoration of mental health can be regarded as a critical concern of individuals, communities, and societies worldwide.[1] However, our current reality presents a very different picture. The COVID-19 pandemic has impacted everybody's wellbeing and has stretched many employees' physical and psychological resources to their capacity. How can we recover from adversity and respond with behavioural flexibility when we have (completely natural) thoughts or feelings like fatigue, frustration, disorientation or even dysregulation?

This chapter proposes that understanding the neuroscience fundamentals associated with wellbeing can help build behavioural flexibility and human flourishing at work and in life. We take an evidence-based approach showing how we can cultivate wellbeing through various methods.[2, 3, 4, 5, 6, 7]

A neuroscience flashlight

Understanding the underlying brain mechanisms of a wellbeing intervention can increase our trust in the intervention and help improve its outcome. For example, in the setting of chronic pain management, there is convincing evidence from multiple randomised controlled trials that "therapeutic neuroscience education" – that is, educating patients about the neurophysiology of pain and how the brain can temper the experience of pain – improves intervention outcomes, such as diminishing the experience of pain and disability.[8, 9] As with physical pain, so too social and emotional distress might be better managed with an improved understanding of the underlying brain mechanisms and strategies that can help mitigate it.

However, we must note that any neurobiological concept of wellbeing (like Flourishing, Languishing, Resilience, Stress, to name a few) can't be narrowed down to a single neurochemical, hormone or peptide but rather is the consequence of the interaction of multiple chemical components working in concert through complex large-scale networks within the human brain.[10]

Relating neurobiological processes to psychological states under the central concept of resilience (as an example) is also problematic. For example, a specific neurochemical may be found to be co-present with psychological symptoms of stress or resilience; however, this co-presence may not be sufficient to show a direct causation. This was demonstrated in a research study titled *"Adapting to Stress: Understanding the Neurobiology of Resilience."*[11]

So, we are not overpromising what Neuroscience can offer as no one level of analysis can tell us all we need to know about mental health and wellbeing in the workplace. Only when rooted within a person's larger context, behaviour, body, feelings, thoughts and social environment does the brain become helpful in understanding mental health. This chapter aims to touch on these variables.

What does wellbeing truly mean? – Capturing the many meanings

Basically, wellbeing is the state of feeling good and functioning well in your life but there are many views:

Views from the human sciences

- The APA defines mental health as *"a state of mind characterised by emotional wellbeing, good behavioural adjustment, relative freedom from anxiety and disabling symptoms, and a capacity to establish constructive relationships and cope with the ordinary demands and stressors of life."*[12]
- One of the most significant conceptual frameworks to explain wellbeing is known using the acronym PERMA. PERMA was put forth by Martin Seligman, the inventor of positive psychology, and consist of five pillars that jointly explain wellbeing.[13]
    - **P**ositive emotions – feeling good
    - **E**ngagement – being fully absorbed in activities
    - **R**elationships – being authentically connected to others

- **M**eaning – living a purposeful life
- **A**chievement – a sense of accomplishment

The PERMA model can be used as an initial diagnostic framework for inquiring into wellbeing in the workplace. It can serve as a point of departure for growing awareness and identifying areas where a wellbeing intervention may be valuable in your workplace.

- Mental health in the workplace can be depicted on a continuum, fluctuating from flourishing to languishing. 'Flourishing' refers to a sense that one's life at work is going well and functioning well.[14] 'Languishing', which is opposite to flourishing, refers to the absence of mental health. A multi-dimensional outlook of flourishing, which includes the dimensions of feeling good (emotional wellbeing) and functioning well (psychological and social wellbeing), appears to be broadly accepted.[15, 16]

- 'Resilience' is a word derived from the Latin verb *resilire*, which means to "leap back".[17] Psychologists define resilience as the *"process of adapting well in the face of adversity, trauma, tragedy, threats, or significant sources of stress – such as family and relationship problems, serious health problems, or workplace and financial stressors"* (*"Building your resilience"*).[18]

Views from the neurosciences

A molecular neuroscientific view on wellbeing is captured in this quote by Eric Kandel.[19]

> *"Down regulating distress and facilitating enriched environments enhances neural proliferation."*

Distress means the brain is regularly experiencing energy deficiency or dysregulation, fear, worry and negativity (a compromised environment). Should this be chronic (always present, it becomes a steady-state where survival becomes paramount, and all other neural functioning suffers. In this state of affairs, the brain does not exert effort to create new neurons. In a compromised environment, the electrochemical ecosystem becomes toxic, causing neurological, physical, emotional, intellectual and spiritual degeneration (allostatic dysregulation). This leads to languishing and suffering and more stress.

Resilience is the ability of the brain/body system to withstand the challenges that threaten its steadiness. Specific, measurable drivers that optimise resilience are: exercise, sleep and wake cycle, feeling socially safe, and silencing the mind.[20]

The good news is that with discipline and repetition, we can change our stressed steady-state to a "new steady-state", and to do this, we need an understanding of the human brain.

The nature of the human brain
– The essential problem

There are a lot of examples of fiction in science. We used to believe that the earth was flat and that the sun circled around the earth. One of the oldest evolutionary stories is that of the triune brain arrangement. In this story, the human brain ended up with three layers – one for surviving, one for feeling, and one for thinking. Emotions, thinking and perceptions are said to be hosted in a so-called "triune brain" that evolved like a layered cake with each new (better) processor loaded on top of the ones that came before. This is a widespread misconception in which much of psychology holds that (1) as vertebrate animals evolved, "newer" brain structures (like the neo-cortex) were added over "older" brain structures (like the limbic system) and (2) these newer, more complex structures gifted humans with newer and more complex psychological functions, behavioural flexibility, and language.

"The brain is not an onion with a tiny reptile inside rather the brain is the world's most proficient accountant"

Essentialism believes that a category of things share a precise nature because they share a deep, immutable core, an unchanging essence. This essential view also claims that we have emotional categories that are biologically hardwired via dedicated neural circuitry or their own neutral substrate. For example, the amygdala, which is part of the limbic system, is implicated in detecting fearful stimuli. The insula is associated with disgust.[21] Basic emotions like fear and anger are innate, fast, trigger behaviour with a high survival value, and less creative.

Though widely shared in society, these misconceptions have long been discredited among neurobiologists and stand in contrast to the clear and undisputed agreement on these issues among those studying nervous system evolution.[22] Perhaps misguided ideas about brain evolution persist because they fit with our human experience: We do sometimes feel overwhelmed with overpowering emotions and even use animalistic terms to describe these states. We know from contemporary science that the brain as a whole is highly complex and intricate, with deep interconnections and cross-connections. Thus our brain is much more like a proficient accountant in which networks, hubs and chemicals are inextricably linked to all other parts of the brain. The key focus is to ensure energy efficiency to the brain and the body.

The nature of the human brain
– emerging discoveries

"To make sense of chaotic inputs, the brain makes educated
guesses as to what generates them" Andy Clark

From all directions in science, there is an emerging consensus that variation is more the rule than the exception in nature and modern human society. This new robust scientific view states that experiences and behaviours derive from populations of time-varying, context-dependent brain states.[23] The brain is also 24/7 preparing what to do next (called predictive processing).

The predictive brain – Surfing uncertainty

A considerable amount of your brain's activity occurs outside your awareness. In every instance, your brain must work out your body's needs for the next moment and implement a strategy to supply those demands in advance. Take, for example, a typical morning routine: as you wake, your brain anticipates the energy you'll need to jump (or crawl) out of bed and start your new day. It proactively trickles your bloodstream with the hormone cortisol, which aids in making glucose available for quick energy.

Your brain runs your body like a budget where deposits and withdrawals are precisely tracked. The budget consists of your body's resources, including water, blood, salt, oxygen, glucose, hormones, and many more biological resources, to keep your body running efficiently – a term called Allostasis. Each *action* that spends resources, such as going for your morning run, sitting down for a virtual meeting, and having a stressful conversation, is like a withdrawal from your account. *Actions* that restock your resources, such as drinking water, eating, sleeping, or laughter, equate to a deposit.

The brain is always preparing what to do next (called predictive processing)

To be more precise, it automatically predicts and prepares to meet the body's needs before they arise. A straightforward example is when you drink a glass of water. The water takes several minutes to reach your bloodstream, but you feel much less thirsty within a few seconds. This is how the brain "relieves" your thirst. It has learned from previous experience that water is a deposit to your body budget that will hydrate you, so your brain reduces your thirst long before the water has any impact on your bloodstream.

This budgetary explanation of how the brain works may seem plausible when it comes to your bodily functions but it may seem obscure to compare your mental life to a bank account of deposits and withdrawals. Be assured that every clever or dull thought you have, every feeling of joy or worry or inspiration you experience, every act of kindness you show and every insult you give or take forms part of your brain's calculations as it guesses and budgets metabolic requirements.

This new understanding of the brain has many implications for how we, as human beings, function. First of all, the body and the mind are highly interrelated. We should not think of ourselves in psychological terms, separate from the body. We often tend to interpret our bodily sensations as emotion – for example feeling fatigued or anxious. It turns out that the primary physical symptom of dehydration isn't thirst. It's fatigue and feeling anxious. So it is a good start to consider both the physical and psychological in explaining our experiences.

Your body's internal state (called interoception), as perceived by your brain, directly affects how you feel today. Your affective feelings of pleasure and displeasure and calm and agitation are simple summaries of your budgetary state. If you feel generally unpleasant and/or agitated, your body budget is unbalanced; if you feel primarily pleasant and/or calm, your body budget is balanced.

Everything you feel and do hinges on the state of your inner budget: The human brain is anatomically designed so that no decision or action can be free of interoception [inner sensations] and affect [raw feelings], no matter what fiction people tell themselves about how rational they are. Your bodily feeling right now will project forward to influence what you will affectively feel and do in the future.

Affect is the general term for the raw experience of feeling or outlook or mood one experiences throughout each day. It is not an emotion but a much unassuming feeling with two features. The first is how pleasant or unpleasant you feel, which is known as valence. Examples include the bliss of feeling the winter sun on your face or the discomfort of a toothache. The second future of affect is how calm (passive) or agitated (active) you feel, also called arousal. For example, the fatigue after a long run or feeling buzzed up with too much coffee or the energised feeling on hearing you got the exam result you hoped for. Gut feelings are also affected.

Each of us maintains our own and each other's body budgets through our concepts, including emotion. We construct instances of emotion to make sense of our body's pleasant and unpleasant moods or raw feelings and different levels of stimulation. Your affect is always some blend of valence and arousal, represented by one point on the affective circumplex, pictured below in Figure 14.1 (established by psychologist James A. Russell).

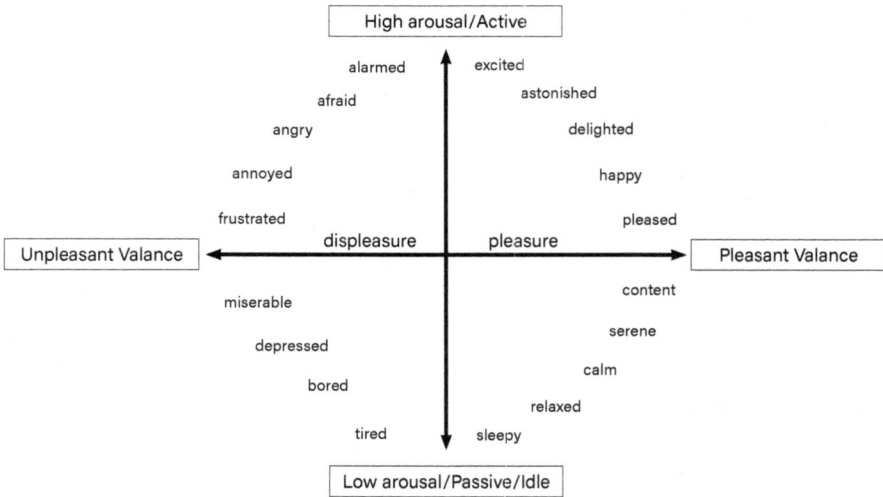

Figure 14.1: Affective circumplex (Source: Russell & Barrett)[24]

When you experience affect, lacking knowledge of the cause, you will probably treat affect as **information about** the world rather than **your experience** of the world. This phenomenon is termed **"affective realism"** since we experience hypothetical (made-up) facts about the world that are created in part by our feelings. Thus, *"believing is seeing" – you see what you feel (i.e. what your brain* supposedly believes). We have much freedom to change our human condition by realising how the brain processes information.

Put in another way: Affect leads us to believe that things and people in the world are fundamentally negative or positive.

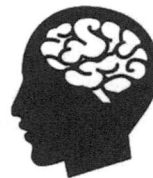

"Your most important relationship is with your inner voice"

Valence and arousal are dimensions of consciousness that are constantly with you, whether you are emotional or not. These basic elements of affect are the feelings that we make sense of with our emotion concepts. You might have a vaguely unpleasant feeling, but through emotion, you experience something much more **specific**: that emotion prepares you to act in a way tailored to the current (in the here-and-now) situation.[25]

In short, your body-budget balance directly affects how you function, feel and think. Our moment-to-moment *physiological state* literally impacts every aspect of our existence or mental experience. Therefore taking care of your body through physical actions like deep rhythmic breathing, changing your lackluster diet that deprives you of essential nutrients, or getting quality sleep, can be transformative in solving problems we usually view as psychological.

A new way to conceptualise and cultivate wellbeing at work

Research has shown that wellbeing may develop over time and contexts. Dynamic exchanges with colleagues, and other stakeholders, various contexts and events in our personal life history may radically change states of wellbeing. Therefore, wellbeing is neither permanent nor innate. Contemporary studies have shown that wellbeing involves a set of skills that can be deliberately and explicitly cultivated and developed through education and with appropriate support.[26, 27]

Our "Wellbeing" is fascinatingly flexible. It is NOT a fixed, innate state

We propose a wellbeing protocol (using insights from neurobiology and psychology) that draws a parallel with physical fitness. It implies that wellbeing isn't just something that happens to you but something you can take responsibility for. It's a skill that you can build, a state and even trait that you can choose to create over time. This idea aligns with the theory of **self-directed neuroplasticity**[28], which means altering the structure of our neural pathways with conscious intent.

"The brain continually reorganizes itself by forming new neural connections throughout life."

This phenomenon is known as Neuroplasticity

The question is really: What can you do, practically speaking, to keep your predictions calibrated and your body budget balanced? To bridge the knowledge versus doing gap in this area, we present a framework on cultivating wellbeing and welldoing in the workplace. Wellbeing skills are generally covered by interventions addressing the development of socio-emotional skills, resilience, self-determination and metacognitive abilities, thus making it easier for your brain to regulate your body. We have called it the "Shift and persist to Wellbeing and Welldoing" framework (see below).

The "Shift and Persist to a Wellbeing & Welldoing" framework

A graphical representation of the "Shift and Persist" framework is shown below. It shows the interrelated physical and psychological constructs contributing to bolstering wellbeing and welldoing. An image of a human brain in the background signifies that the psychological constructs are regulated by the brain via the central nervous system consisting of large scale brain networks, (it cannot be reduced to essential brain regions).

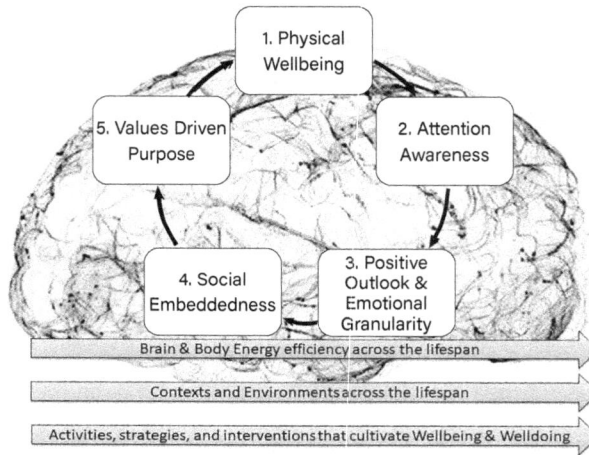

Figure 14.2: Shift and Persist framework

Focus On

1. **Physical wellbeing:** keeping your brain-body budget in good shape
2. **Attention awareness:** making meaning out of sense data
3. **Positive outlook and Emotional Granularity:** knowing what you're feeling and knowing what to do about it

   (WELLBEING)

4. **Social embeddedness:** caring interactions seeded by the "words" you use from your tribe and culture
5. **Purpose:** Doing what really matters (work you love to do congruent with your highest values)

   (WELLDOING)

Focus on physical wellbeing – keeping your brain-body system in good shape

A quality question to make part of your life is: "How aware are you of the impact that your daily activities have on your body budget?" We focus on a few vital activities to keep your brain and body budget in good shape:

Build circadian rhythm into your life

This means giving routine and ritual to your day like "make your bed", "unplug time", "purposeful pauses". Also, learn to down-regulate distress by building perceived control into your life through exercise, nutrition and sleep hygiene. Exercise profoundly reduces the effects of chronic stress, which is the number one enemy to brain performance.

The power of slumber

We may be what we eat, but we are also how we sleep. Sleep deprivation is increasingly used as a badge of honour in a supercharged world of work, and "Why am I so tired?" is one of the most used phrases that we think and talk about. Sleep is indispensable for our nervous systems to work properly. Inadequate sleep selectively impairs those areas of the brain that are important for problem-solving, creativity and emotional regulation. Less dangerous cases of sleep deprivation typically involve short-temperedness, moodiness, illogical thinking and irrational behaviour. Sleep deprivation is a stressor – chronic sleep deprivation increases blood pressure and cortisol levels, insulin, and pro-inflammatory cytokines[29] with negative consequences for the brain and the rest of the body.

Leverage the power of slumber: Go to bed in a state of grace and without light-emitting devices. Gratitude primes the brain for good quality and quantity of sleep. Lack of sleep can increase inflammation in the body, which puts us at risk of getting ill. Take a power nap – as little as a seven-minute nap allows for the regeneration of creative brain circuits and improves mood. Both quality and quantity of sleep remove neural debris and help to consolidate memory (cherry-picking to remember).

The science of the breath

Taking an embodied view of Affect means that it is not easy to change it (read: mood or outlook) because you don't have volitional control over your heart or your lungs (and other core systems), but you do have voluntary control over your breathing, so you can try to practise breathing to calm your heart and control your heart and so on. So the best way that you can quickly, consciously control your body is through the breath. Our breath is mainly automatic and unconscious; by practising conscious breathing, we gradually strengthen the connections between our unconscious, autonomic reactions and our voluntary or consciously chosen responses. Breathing increases the activation in your parasympathetic nervous system that sometimes dampens down your sympathetic nervous system, so if you breathe deeply and regularly, 7-9 second breaths, for a little while, you can calm your body down fairly quickly.

Recent research entitled, "How breathing can help you make better decisions: Two studies on the effects of breathing patterns on heart rate variability and decision-making in business cases"[30] reported that:

- just two minutes of deep breathing with longer exhalation recruits the vagus nerve, increases heart rate variability (HRV), and improves decision-making.
- performing deep breathing exercises diminishes perceived stress after a challenging decision-making task, and
- performing deep breathing exercises improves decision-making task results (nearly 50% more correct problems).

Observing the breath allows us to take a deep look at the nature of conceptual constructions /mental formations such as fear, anger and anxiety. This allows the opportunity to deconstruct it and even reconstruct it into different concepts that serve us.

Slouch less: there is a significant correlation between lack of physical activity and high rates of depression. You can banish depressive feelings and negativity by up to 20 percent simply by exercising three times per week – even if you're taking the stairs and walking while shopping. Eating healthy is also vital to keep your body budget in shape and is discussed in other chapters.

Focus on making meaning out of sense data – Attention Awareness

"Odd as it may seem, I am my remembering self, and the experiencing self, who does my living, is like a stranger to me." Daniel Kahneman. Thinking Fast and Slow. Macmillan[31]

Paying attention in different ways

Attention Awareness, in our "shift and persist" framework, is about deliberate and flexible attentiveness to one's perceptions and impressions of the environment, as well as internal bodily sensations, thoughts, feelings and emotions. A focused state of Attention Awareness is characterised by being solely aware of what one is doing, thinking, whom one is with, and one's own internal states. Being aware of the body is vital as it primarily drives our mood and outlook in life. Choiceless Attention Awareness is when we are loosely paying attention to whatever enters the mental sketchpad but without processing it.

Develop interoceptive sensitivity

The body and mind are deeply interconnected. Understanding our body's inner sensations is central to everything from thought to emotion to decision making and our sense of self. Most of the time, we don't feel sensations from our body in an exact way. If we do, it's in simple terms like raw feelings or "affect". More intense sensations are used to make emotions, whereas less intense ones are used to make thoughts and other things.

Where we focus is where we GO

Attention Awareness practices may foster long-term increases in our ability to attend to interoceptive sensations[32] and even improve cognitive function.[33] Why does mindful Attention Awareness work so well? Firstly, it has a potent effect on brain structure and function. The key regions in the interoceptive and control networks are larger for meditators, and connections between these regions are stronger. The interoceptive network is vital to constructing mental concepts and representing physical sensations from the body, and the control network is crucial to regulating re-categorisation.

> *Attention awareness means paying attention with flexibility,*
> *openness and curiosity. This is not the same as thinking.*

The neural correlates of the process of mindful Attention Awareness were recorded in a ground-breaking neuro-imaging study, where functional magnetic resonance imaging (fMRI) was used to study the two neural modes of self-referencing: 'narrative' focus, or NF, and momentary experience, known as 'experiential focus', or EF, as well as the neural systems supporting these 'modes' of awareness.[34]

These two forms of self-awareness are habitually integrated but can be dissociated through attentional training. The decoupling of these two forms of awareness enables one to choose which mode is required for the task at hand. The narrative focus equates to the conceptual world that is full of descriptions of events, memories, attitudes, and evaluations of people and things. The experiential focus is about tracking how one's body, thoughts and feelings change in an instant to that of a judgment-free awareness of current experiences and intentions. These two modes are completely different, have different neuroscientific underpinnings, and are anti-correlated. Thus, if the one is 'off', the other one is 'on'.

Attention Awareness is about being able to be aware of which mode you are in and then being able to switch to the circuit that is most beneficial for the task at hand. These two modes are set out below.

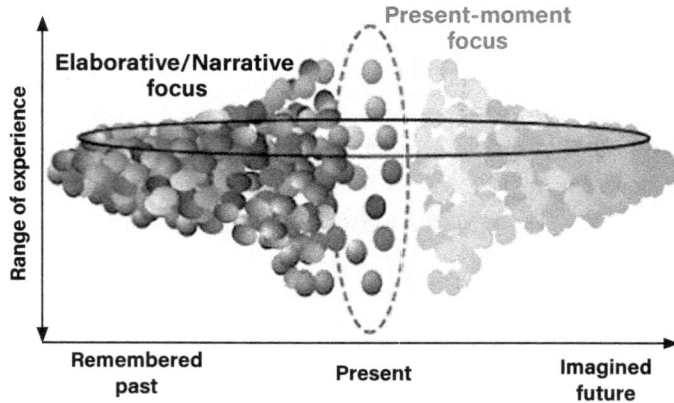

Figure 14.3: The two modes of self-referencing (Adapted from: Farb, et al.[1])[35]

Table 14.1: Summary of the two modes of self-referencing

Narrative Mode – Extended Self-referencing	Direct Experience Mode – Momentary-centred Self-referencing
Making a story about something. Focus is through time (past, present, future)	Processing incoming data as they happen (in real-time)
• Circuitry involved: Conceptual, memory (hippocampus) and limbic (friend or foe decisions) • Metabolically expensive in terms of brain resources	• Circuitry involved: Somato-sensory cortex, Insula (Internal visceral experience) • Metabolically stable on brain resources
This leads to fixation on the story line, constantly running predictions and creating experiences in line with it. This can lead to a state of hyper-arousal	This leads to better self-regulation and the ability to take in more sensory data, which increases affect and mental representations, enables new insights and reduces adverse biological effects like hypertension

Attentional enhancement

Attention Awareness allows you to suspend the predictive process or dial it down. When you are in a mindful state, you are not making meaning of the sense data. You are not detecting or processing prediction error. The reason why this is an important thing to practise to do – and meditation isn't the only way to practise it, but is an important skill to have – is because the more you practise it deliberately, the more practised you get at it and then the more automatically you can use those skills.

---

1   Thank you to Prof. Farb for the permission granted.

If you can master Attention Awareness, you will be able to deconstruct your experience and more easily reconstruct it. This means taking the same sense data and reconstructing it into a different experience; just by changing the meaning of the sense-data facilitates re-categorisation (termed "emotion regulation") and reduces unpleasant affect.

To 'fine tune' your direct experience mode:

- breathe in slowly through your nose and exhale all your breath;
- focus your attention on your body or one part of your body, such as your feet; and
- hold your attention on the direct experience and take in the data – do not process the data.

Examples of how to induce the direct experience mode:

- When you walk up the stairs, be aware of your breathing, your movement up the stairs, the feeling of your feet on the steps, i.e. be aware of the sensations.
- When you get to work, sit in your chair, close your eyes, focus on your breathing and pay attention to your feet, i.e. be aware of the sensations.
- Other '1-5 minutes a day' examples: washing dishes, going for a walk, eating, working in the garden, waiting for a meeting to start, going for a smoke break, any exercise, a mindful shower.

Attention Awareness, once stabilised, promotes a state of wellbeing in that it supports the discovery of new meaning by broadening attention to include previously unattended data. Attention Awareness also gives the opportunity to re-appraise daily life hassles, stressful thoughts, feelings and emotions in working memory, and long-term memory, thereby creating more positive future predictions. But, there are boundaries to Attention Awareness practices, specifically in acute trauma, as trauma may impede one's ability to access and stabilise Attention Awareness. Skilful clinical support practices may then accomplish attention stabilisation.

Focus on positive outlook and emotional granularity

Knowing what you're feeling and knowing what to do about it

Emotions help us steer through our daily lives by providing a quick and reflective answer to the questions: "What am I feeling?" or "How am I doing?". We vary in the degree to which we differentiate our emotions, which is defined as *emotion differentiation* (ED) or emotional granularity.[36] Emotion differentiation is a core skill that facilitates psychological and social wellbeing. Emotion differentiation depends on developing our emotion concepts.[37, 38, 39] Our emotion vocabulary words are linked to the emotion concepts that we use to conceptualise our affective experiences and convert them into more refined, granular emotional experiences.

Don't get emotional about emotions

Imagine a colleague who, when upset at being excluded from a Zoom meeting, reports that he feels angry. Now imagine a colleague who, when upset at being left out of a Zoom meeting, reports that he feels angry, anxious, sad, and disgusted all at once. Whereas the first colleague has a particular emotional response, the second is having a much less specific experience – in essence, he is telling you that he just feels unpleasant. The tendency to experience emotions in a highly specific manner is known as 'emotional granularity'[40, 41] or 'emotion differentiation.'[42, 43]

The evidence base for emotional granularity

- There is evidence that emotional granularity improves mental health. Higher emotional granularity translates to better coping skills and, therefore, fewer maladaptive behaviours such as addictions. Finely grained feelings allow us to be more agile at regulating our emotions and less likely to react aggressively against someone who has hurt us. Relationships also improve when people are attuned to emotions.[44]

- People with the skill to verbally characterise their emotional experiences with granularity and detail are less likely to be overwhelmed in stressful situations. It works as follows: people who respond to their felt experiences with greater differentiation are more aware of their conscious state and find it easier to shift their attentional focus and maintain emotional stability.[45]

- Training individuals to recognise one's emotions as discrete and specific is a core aspect of many cognitive psychotherapies.[46] People who show higher emotional granularity go to the doctor less frequently, use medication less frequently, and spend fewer days hospitalised for illness.

So, learning how to put your feelings into words, label, differentiate, granualise or choose your words with care acts as a circuit breaker for the intensity of negative affect.

Experiential blindness

One of the most thought-provoking consequences of the Theory of Constructed Emotions is that if we do not have a concept to label an emotion, we won't be able to distinguish it. We will still feel the bodily sensations but won't be able to describe them precisely. To put it differently, the range of emotions one can experience is restricted by one's emotional granularity – the capability to construct and categorise more precise emotional encounters.

This might sound like a radical illustration, but picture someone who can only distinguish between "good" and "bad" feelings. They exhibit low emotional granularity. Because they have only vague information about what is happening inside their bodies, it will be tough for them to get a grip on many of life's demands. They will be experientially blind to their own feelings.

Emotion differentiation: Emotional granularity creates a rainbow of possibilities

"Learn new words as a path to greater emotional health, it follows directly from the neuroscience of construction. Words seed your concepts, concepts drive your predictions, regulate your body budget, and your body budget determines how you feel. Therefore, the more finely grained your vocabulary, the more precisely your predicting brain can calibrate your budget to your body's needs".[47] *Please see figure below.*

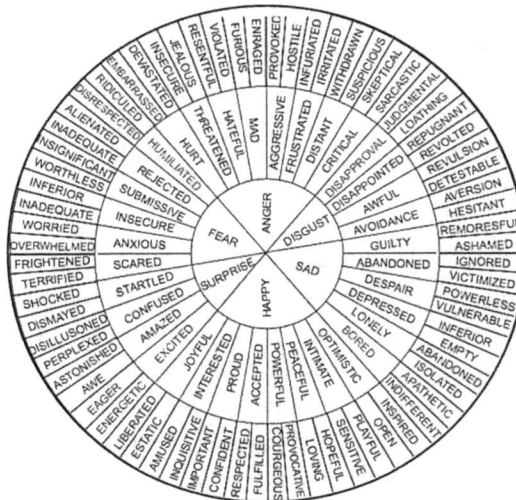

Figure 14.4: Emotional Differentiation (Source Shutterstock)

A way to change the way your brain makes meaning out of your bodily sensations in relation to the world is to increase your emotion vocabulary size. The words that we know for emotion are like tools that our brains use to make meaning of our physical sensations and predict and tailor our actions to specific situations. The more emotion concepts you know, the bigger, more flexible your vocabulary of emotion concepts is, giving you an extensive, more flexible repertoire of emotions that you can construct and perceive in other people.

The paybacks of granularity go beyond being well-spoken. The greater your granularity, the "more precisely" you can experience yourself and your world. Emotional granularity can be enhanced. For example, if you can learn to differentiate specific meanings for:

"Feeling great" like happy, pleased, thrilled, relaxed, joyful, confident, inspired, appreciative, loving, grateful, blissful . . .

OR

"Feeling bad" like fuming, shocked, aggravated, distressed, spiteful, irritable, remorseful, cranky, offended, uneasy, resentful, offended, afraid, envious, woeful, melancholy . . .

Your brain will have many more possibilities for predicting, categorising, and perceiving emotions.

How does it work? The mechanisms of emotion differentiation

Momentary experience is shaped as we categorise incoming sensations from the world (exteroception) and the body (interoception). This categorisation process forms a conceptualisation of the sensations that are linked to the specific context or situation, providing precise predictions for contextualised action (and presumably adaptive coping). Because conceptual knowledge is embodied, it can adjust internal body sensations and lessen intense negative affect, resulting in better emotion regulation.[48]

When one has only basic emotion knowledge (because his or her emotion vocabulary is limited/weakly developed) or does not have the working memory capacity to access emotion vocabulary knowledge,[49] sensory inputs will be conceptualised in a quite undifferentiated way, depriving one of the contextualised knowledge that is needed to deal with the situation at hand. (A quick definition of Working Memory (WM) = WM refers to the temporary maintenance and manipulation of information for use in guiding goal-directed decision-making and action selection).

When one has elaborate knowledge about emotions and uses it, sensory inputs will be conceptualised in a categorised, situation-specific fashion. One will have the contextualised knowledge that is required to deal with the situation at hand. When stressful feelings and bodily sensations arise, instead of letting these experiences govern attention or prescribe how to behave, high differentiators are better able to distance themselves – a concept referred to as defusion.[50] With this psychological distance, there is a greater opportunity to direct effortful behaviour toward personally valued strivings or goals.[51]

Constructing our Conceptual Model: dial-up the positive and dial-down the negative

Whatever you attend to results in the tweaking of your conceptual model, thereby reinforcing concepts about interpersonal experiences and making them salient in your mental model of the world. Each experience you construct is an investment, so invest wisely.

Dial-up the positive

Nurture and grow the experiences you want to construct again in the future. Dial up the positive, spot the good, find the benefits. It's even better if you write down your experiences because words lead to concept development, which will help you predict new moments to cultivate positivity.[52]

Dial-down the negative

Many of the ways in which we attempt to regulate our negative experiences like using self-blame, rumination, catastrophising, and other-blame robs us of energy-efficiency as the overthinking of emotions and thoughts associated with negative events causes fluctuations in body budgets.[53] Rumination especially is a vicious cycle: each time you dwell on (say) a recent disagreement at work, an additional instance to predict with is added, which expands your opportunity to ruminate. Certain concepts about your disagreement, such as your raised voice towards a colleague or the look on your boss's face when she left the virtual meeting, become entrenched in your model of the world. These concepts, as patterns of neural activity, become easier for your brain to recreate, like a well-trodden walking path. You don't want them to become super high-ways.

Learning to recategorise emotions is not easy but, like learning to drive, it can be done. So you can take anxiety and turn it into willpower or exhilaration even. You can take anger and turn it into admiration. *The affect stays the same, but the meaning is what's changing.* And if you practise in advance, you're seeding your brain to be able to do this much more automatically. Change plasticity at its best!

"Words, then, are tools for regulating human bodies"

Focus on your social embeddedness seeded by "words" from your tribe and culture

Social embeddedness refers to a personal sense of care and kinship to other people that encourages helpful relationships and caring interactions. This may happen through positive social practices, such as gratitude, kindness and appreciation, as well as taking a deliberate stance to recognise shared human characteristics like loneliness and burnout and many more.

Social reality – Your conceptual operating system

In short our **social reality** represents our collective agreement and language that make the perception of emotion probable among people who share a culture. The human brain creates a conceptual system into its wiring (a dependable network of concepts) within the first year of life. This "conceptual system" is responsible for all the emotion concepts you now employ to experience and perceive emotions. The brains of babies are very much "under construction" at birth, making babies defenceless against becoming intricately wired to the conditions they're born into. These wiring commands happen through the words and actions of other people and are life-long. The most powerful thing about our families, tribes, and cultures is that they impart the meaning of concepts to us before we're even aware that they're doing it. These concepts, like happiness, anger, or unconscious bias, will seem intuitive and normal to us and hard to escape later in life. Because our cultural concepts feel normal to us, we intuitively assume they do for others as well.

Why do the words we encounter have such extensive effects inside us?

*"Words are, of course, the most powerful drug
used by mankind."* Rudyard Kipling

It turns out that numerous brain regions that process language also control the inside of the body (the default network). This language network guides our heart rate up or down and even adjusts the chemical messengers that are "heard" by immune cells and lead to changes in immune function, including effects on inflammation.

As Rudyard Kipling said above, words are, of course, the most powerful drug used by humanity. The bottom line is that words are tools for regulating human bodies. Part of being a social species is that we impact the ways in which our brains manage the bodily resources we use; occasional disagreements can be like exercise. Brief withdrawals from your body followed by deposits create a stronger, better you. But chronically elevated stress can slowly eat away at the shape and size of your brain and become the root cause of illness in your body. This includes physical abuse, verbal aggression, social exclusion and the countless other ways that we social animals annoy and even torment one another. The workplace is a particularly complex environment. Everything from the tone of your voice, the way you phrase a question, who you direct questions to and more can send messages to co-workers that either boosts brain-body energy efficiency or depletes it.

Whereas evolutionary theories generally suggest that negatively valenced emotions support short-term survival,[54] positive emotions such as joy, contentment, hope, and love have been broadly theorised to increase physical, intellectual, and social capacities, connections, and resources that facilitate survival in the long run.[55]

Scientific studies are unequivocal on this point when you're on the receiving end of ongoing insults and threats, OR if you live in an environment that persistently and relentlessly taxes your body budget, you're more likely to get sick. Also, long term, negative social interactions are linked to inflammation, which can develop into cardiovascular disease, cancer, and hypertension. Harmful partner bonds, coworker bonds, family and friend bonds can also result in low self-esteem, anxiety and depression. Analyses of brain activity revealed a link between pains and pleasures of social life and physical pains and pleasures.[56]

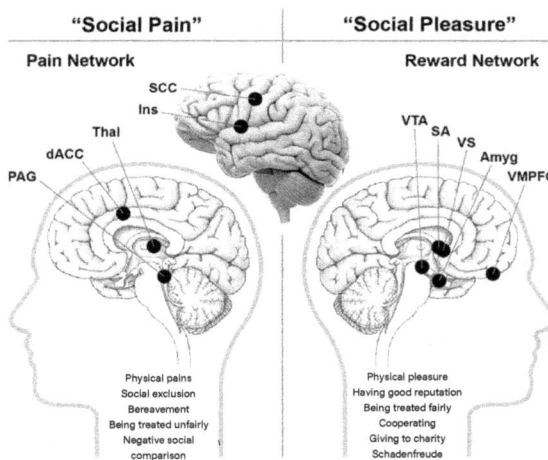

Figure 14.5: Social pain/pleasure vs physical pain/pleasure (Source: Lieberman and Eisenberger)[57]

The diagram above depicts the overlap in brain regions for physical and social pain/pleasure processing and suggest that certain social psychological concerns may have the same motivational importance as other physical survival needs. For every state of deprivation associated with a specific need, there is a pain. These discoveries suggest that the brain may treat abstract social experiences and concrete physical experiences as more similar than is generally expected. Surprisingly, neuroscience research shows that helping others leads to the release of oxytocin in the ventral striatum and ventromedial PFC. So, there are two kinds of social rewards, namely the social rewards we receive when others let us know they like and respect us, and the social rewards we get when we show pro-social behaviour (i.e. 'giving is its own reward').

A convergence of mood and emotions at work

> "If you raise your voice or just your eyebrow, you can affect what
> goes on inside other people's bodies." Lisa F Barret

The emotional states and regulation strategies of others, especially those in positions of power, can have a real and enduring effect on individuals and groups. The existing evidence shows that while all emotions can be contagious, 'negative' emotions have greater power to influence. This can lead to a negative organisational culture. The aim is to create a safe environment for all individuals within the organisation.

The brain's *mirror neuron system* or *resonance circuitry* underpins the construct of emotional contagion. Mirror neurons fire both when we are performing a particular action and when we observe that action. Thus, people in relationships become more emotionally similar over time. This similarity helps coordinate the thoughts and behaviours of the partnership, increases their mutual understanding, and fosters their social cohesion.

Our attentiveness to the social world may sometimes seem like a diversion from more concrete concerns, but more and more, neuroscience is providing evidence in which such attention is actually an adaptive response to some of our most vital concerns. Social reality is the human superpower – and a superpower works best if you know you have it. This can lead to bias, prejudice but also to bonding and belonging.

Focus on what really matters: Clarity of purpose

It is often said that the primary operating premise of the brain is to avoid pain and maximise pleasure. However, concepts of purposefulness, autonomy and worthwhileness are essential to consider alongside feelings like pleasure and pain when measuring experienced wellbeing. If these aspects are not included, a vital part of people's experiences may be overlooked. People do many things because they deem them purposeful or worthwhile, even if they are not especially pleasurable (e.g., reading the same story repeatedly to a child, visiting a sick friend, or volunteering).

Purpose in the "Shift and Persist" Framework refers to a sense of clarity concerning personally meaningful goals and values applicable to daily life. A heightened state of purpose fosters the self-perception that one has both goals and values. This self-perception, in turn, leads one to notice meaning and worth in one's life. Framing purpose as our "hearts desires" to organise and stimulate goals and provide an overarching narrative that helps us make sense of our lives.[58] States of lessened purpose may involve a lack of clarity concerning our goals and values.

Pursuing your goals and changing behaviour is not easy but highly rewarding if it is aligned with organisational, team and individual purpose. This equates to being inspired from within (intrinsic motivation) as opposed to having to be motivated from without (extrinsic motivation).[59] Being clear about the future helps the brain to construct an internal model of itself and the body in the world, minimising adverse effects on energy efficiency (Allostasis).

How to action this? Clarity of Purpose can be enhanced through what neuroscientists call Episodic Future Thinking (EFT). This means imagining doing something specific in the future in a vivid, detailed way. Engaging EFT with high imagery can significantly change the ability to focus on and achieve future goals. It strengthens connections between the anterior cingulate, amygdala and hippocampus.[60] Episodic Future Thinking (EFT) is essential for adaptive functioning[61] as it helps us preserve mental and physiological resources, especially when swimming in a sea of uncertainty like now. Uncertainty is more unpleasant and alarming than assured harm because if the future is a mystery, you can't prepare for it.

Being clear about our future goals with daily action steps to achieve it prevents us from giving in to anxious predictions and fixing where we jump into action and try to get as many small, low-priority tasks done as possible. Persevering to achieve long-term goals has been formally studied as the construct of Grit, and it has proven to be a predictor of one's resilience.[62] Duckworth et al.[63] extensively studied grit and concluded that grit is the most reliable predictor of personal success.

Purpose as a wellbeing dimension is effective provided that the goals are clear and aligned with one's unique values. The only way to hold the Episodic Future Thinking (the why) through time is to keep it in motion (the how). The only way to keep it in motion is to focus on the ever-finer details.

Sharing one's life story (and that of the team and the company) and how that drives one's purpose is crucial to creating a wellbeing culture. Storytelling is a distinctive human ability that played a key role in building and navigating social settings in human evolution. The biomarkers of storytelling show that it increases oxytocin and positive emotions and decreases cortisol and pain.[64] We are all storytellers – and in complex organisational settings, it is a low cost and humanised intervention to build understanding, belonging and shared purpose.

Evidence for action: Wellbeing and welldoing and the link to mental health

The importance of improving wellbeing and reducing mental distress is more apparent today than ever. Unemployment, being disconnected, loneliness, depression, and anxiety are all on the increase, making for an emerging crisis in mental health and a mounting deficit in our joint wellbeing[65, 66, 67] The magnitude of this crisis demands new methods to approach Mental health in the workplace.

Using neuroscience as a flashlight to understand workplace wellbeing at a more granular level pin-points the neurobiological processes that cause higher levels of wellbeing, which, in turn, can inform promising training interventions that can bring about new learnings (neuroplastic changes) and help us live happier, healthier and more meaningful lives.

Mental health clearly results from a multitude of factors. In this chapter, we looked largely at wellbeing. The notion that wellbeing is a binary variable, meaning one either has it or does not, denies its complexity. Wellbeing relies on behaviours, thoughts, and actions that one can develop.[68] We can indeed construct our wellbeing and welldoing through leveraging brain and body plasticity.

Still, it is hard to talk about mental health in the workplace, and to action it boldly is even harder. Multiple levels of analysis show us that we are human before we are workers, professionals, or any other role we might define ourselves by. This chapter has proposed five dimensions of wellbeing and welldoing that can be strengthened through intentional training. These dimensions serve as primary prevention for mental health risk mitigation and can be a starting point for talking about mental health as well as serve as a framework for mental health goals.

Conclusion

All our mental representations – cognition, emotion, perception, and action – are shaped by allostasis. Thus, all decision making is embodied, predictive, and concerned with balancing energy. Therefore, we all walk a tightrope between the mental and the physical. What this chapter has shown us is that the boundaries are porous even when it comes to mental health. To be an effective designer of your life experience, you must differentiate physical reality from social reality and don't mistake one for the other while still understanding that the two are irrevocably entwined. Finally, our emotional concepts are tools for living. The larger your tool kit, the more flexibly your brain can guess and prescribe goal orientations and actions, and the better you can create your life.

Finally, this is a map (not the territory) – may it offer some useful meaning to those striving for enhanced wellbeing, and welldoing at work and in life.

Chapter 15

Coping mechanisms: more than resiliency, towards building prosiliency

Navlika Ratangee

The majority of people who experience stressful events do not end up developing psychopathology or mental illness and this raises the question of resilience playing a role in providing mental health immunity.[1] Building your mental health resilience can go a long way towards offsetting the factors that increase the risk of mental health conditions. Resilience improves your ability to cope with day-to-day stressors, and we have already established that exposure to any kind of stress increases the likelihood of developing mental illness related symptoms, which in turn causes more stress. Thus, working towards positive mental health strategies is key to looking after your mental health and wellbeing. Resiliency can be learnt and developing your resiliency toolkit is within your control. This chapter covers resiliency, strategies to building resiliency and delves into an introduction in taking this to the next step and looking towards building prosiliency. Building prosiliency takes into consideration building positive mental health coping strategies as with resilience, and in addition builds skills and competencies in dealing with the future world of work. This will be a key ingredient for what future employers will be looking for. Organisations are also finding it increasingly important to invest in building resiliency within their workforce to ensure increased productivity and employee wellbeing.

Defining resilience

Even though resilience is a widely used term, there are various definitions and ways to measure resilience. The most common understanding of resiliency is the 'ability to bounce back'. It is also linked to the term GRIT, which is becoming more and more of a buzz word meaning guts, resilience, influence and tenacity. Resilience as a concept has gained more airtime over the recent years as a tool to promote and enhance wellbeing. Historically, however, the general notion of protective factors for mental health dates back to the 19th century notion of mental hygiene defined as *"the art of preserving the mind against all incidents and influences calculated to deteriorate its qualities, impair its energies, or derange its movements"* and including *"the management of the bodily powers in regard to exercise, rest, food, clothing and climate, the laws of breeding, the government of the passions, the sympathy with current emotions ..."*[2]

Some people innately have more resilience than others. However, the good news is that resilience can be learnt. It requires practice. You can increase your resiliency by focusing on developing specific approaches and responses to life's events that promote control-taking responses as opposed to uncontrollable responses. From a neuroscience perspective, as covered in chapter 14, we can build neuropsychological pathways at any point that carves out an altered response as opposed to automated responses to stressful events. It requires focus and intent; reflection (after the event to examine and understand your responses); creating pauses to reflect on immediate responses to a stressful event and practising new approaches to stressful events.

When trying to understand what resilience is, it is also important to understand what it is not. Being resilient doesn't mean that you will never experience difficult situations in your life, or that you will never feel stressed. In fact, in order to build your resilience, it would require experiencing some level of emotional distress. Researchers have found that people who experience some adversity in their lives tend to show more effective responses to stressful events later on.[3]

Social vaccinations

The term 'social vaccine' becomes an important one to understand at this juncture. The world is abuzz at present with the physical vaccination process for the COVID-19 virus to work towards decreasing the severe impact of the virus. Social vaccines are designed to assist the health-promotion movement in arguing for a social view of health which is so often counter to medical and popular conceptions of health.[4] The concept of social vaccines needs to land with equal importance as physical vaccinations akin to mental health and wellbeing needing to land with equal importance to physical health and wellbeing.

The vaccine metaphor is helpful in arguing for increased action on the social determinants of health,[5] and consists of two components. The first being that of social behaviours which includes all the behaviours we have had to change to respond to taking better care of ourselves and prevent or manage exposure to the virus, such as mask wearing, hand washing, hand sanitising, and social distancing. The second component is the idea of what strategies we are putting in place to take better care of our mental health in the time of the pandemic; to 'inoculate ourselves' against mental health concerns. This is tied in quite closely to the idea of practising resiliency, being conscious of adding more tools into your personal toolkit, not just being resilient. According to John and Tharyan[6] social vaccines are made possible through social mobilisation:

- Social mobilisation is a process whereby people are organised in order to enable them to collectively think and act upon their development.

- It can empower populations to resist unhealthy practices, increase resilience, and foster advocacy for change. This can ultimately drive political will to take action in the interests of society.

This is where organisations have a massive role to play in guiding employees by driving a focus on our social behaviours and actions to take care of our mental health. Even for those that are relatively self-aware and emotionally adept, going through stressful situations and challenges can take us by surprise. But learning healthy ways to move through adversity and take control, whether through social vaccinations (group led) or individually driven, can help us cope better and recover more quickly.

Strategies to build resilience

Developing resilience is a personal journey. Different people will use different strategies based on what has worked for them in the past and what they have had exposure to in terms of intentionally trying to adopt new strategies. It is also important to note that how people show resilience, what resilience means to different people, may vary due to cultural difference and cultural influences. Below are practical suggestions for individuals in building their own resilience[7]:

- **Make connections.** Good relationships with close family members, friends or others are important. As the saying goes: "Misery loves company". Thus it becomes important to build a good support system and one that is positive, one that is there to assist you during difficult times, not make you feel worse, or one that can only see the negative in the situation.
- **Avoid seeing crises as insurmountable problems.** You can't change the fact that highly stressful events happen, but you can change how you interpret and respond to these events.
- **Change the narrative.** When something bad happens, we often relive the event over and over in our heads, rehashing the pain. This process is called rumination; it's like a cognitive spinning of the wheels, and it doesn't move us forward toward healing and growth.[8] Focus on looking at the situation through different lenses, the downsides and the upsides – it may not all be apparent at first.
- **Accept that change is a part of living.** Accepting circumstances that cannot be changed can help you focus on circumstances that you can alter.
- **Move toward your goals.** "What's one thing I know I can accomplish today that helps me move in the direction I want to go?"
- **Take decisive actions.** It is easy to get caught up in second-guessing yourself and to try to think about all possible alternatives as a way of being avoidant, before making a decision.

- **Look for opportunities for self-discovery.** People often learn something about themselves and may find that they have grown in some respect as a result of their struggle with loss.
- **Nurture a positive view of yourself.** Developing confidence in your ability to solve problems and trusting your instincts help build resilience.
- **Keep things in perspective.** Even when facing very painful events, try to consider the stressful situation in a broader context and keep a long-term perspective. Avoid blowing the event out of proportion.
- **Maintain a hopeful outlook.**
- **Take care of yourself.** Pay attention to your own needs and feelings. Engage in activities that you enjoy and find relaxing. Exercise regularly. Taking care of yourself helps to keep your mind and body primed to deal with situations that require resilience.

Resilience as a critical skill in the future world of work

In most top Consulting house reports on the critical skills required for the future world of work, resilience is showcased in the top 3. In the ever-changing, competitive landscape employers are looking for employees who can manage the level of change, the ongoing change, and thrive in such environments. This has best been described as a resilient employee. As the world continues to become more complex, resilience is becoming an increasingly important life skill. As the workplace becomes more complex, with the impact of the rapidly changing work environment, being in the midst of a pandemic and post pandemic, the innovation and disruption caused by digitisation, resilience becomes a critical skill to cope in the world of work.

Individual resilience is critical when the world around us is volatile, uncertain, complex and ambiguous (VUCA world).[9] Being resilient in such an environment means we can adapt to difficult situations and not just survive but thrive which is what is needed in the current and future world of work. Unless we do, the stress will overwhelm us, and we will suffer physically and mentally. The future holds an increase in the exposure to stress, and, as discussed throughout the book, an increase in mental health concerns. There needs to be an intentional focus on building the armoury to prepare and withstand the challenges of tomorrow. In the context of the pandemic, futurists say this is the first of many pandemics to come. Thus, it becomes even more critical to ensure we are doing all that we can to shield ourselves from future impact socially, personally and from a workplace perspective.

COVID-19 is forcing young children to cope with stress, loss, and anxiety about everything from in-person school to pandemic-friendly playground practices. Whilst the long-term impact of the pandemic on these children is not yet known, the pandemic may have inherently fostered a resilient generation.[10] Generation C is a term being used to describe the children born during the Coronavirus crisis.[11] However, Generation C was a term coined by Brian Solis in 2012 (before COVID) and it refers to the Connected generation, the digital native, representing a connected society based on interests and behaviour.[12] Generation C is collaborative, community-orientated and its members appear to be good problem solvers. The respondents of a survey as reported on in *Infomentum Report*[13] describe themselves as inventive, 'continually coming up with new ideas and different ways of approaching problems', defining themselves as resilient employees.

Creating psychological safety

Psychological safety is often connected to resilience from a workplace perspective. Workplaces need to create an environment for resilience. This is an environment in which individuals and teams are resilient in the face of constant change. Psychological safety is required to achieve such an environment. Psychological safety and resilience in the workplace promote a culture of ongoing learning, adaptability, and innovation in an ever-changing business environment.[14] In today's world where companies are compelled to be innovative to survive and the role of social media in making or breaking your news (for individuals and organisations), it has become critically important for people to speak up. And, to speak up timeously. A Harvard Business School professor, Amy Edmonson[15] who coined the term "psychological safety", described it as a belief that one will not be punished or humiliated for speaking up with ideas, questions, concerns or mistakes.

In the context of the pandemic and remote working structures the concept of psychological safety becomes even more important. But psychological safety isn't a silver bullet. It's not something that can be implemented overnight. The results, or return on investment (ROI), can be hard to measure, with timelines differing dramatically from immediate, short-term effects to gradual long-term change.[16]

Despite this, promoting psychological safety and resilience in the workplace provides a significant strategic advantage to companies. Research shows that high-performing teams have a sense of psychological safety.[17] High-performing team members are significantly more resilient than those on lower performing teams. Psychological safety underpins all of the keystone attributes that successful businesses strive for – resilience, innovation, teamwork, creativity, engagement, and more. All of these attributes occur faster and more often when your workplace is psychologically safe. Rather than embracing 'fear, uncertainty, and doubt' (FUD), it's time to embrace psychological safety.[18]

Ferris[19] advocates that there is no place for fear in an organisation today if it is going to sense and respond in a world of constant change. There is no place if the organisation is to innovate and experiment. She posited a quick test to understand and measure the levels of psychological safety in your workplace environment. Answer yes or no to the following:

1. When someone makes a mistake in this team, it is often held against him or her.
2. In this team, it is hard to discuss difficult issues and problems.
3. In this team, people are sometimes rejected for being different.
4. It is not completely safe to take a risk on this team.
5. It is difficult to ask other members of this team for help.

If you have answered yes to any of these, focus needs to be given on how to create a culture of trust, and culture of care, and a culture of psychological safety in order for employees to truly practise resiliency.

Various measures can help to foster individual resilience on a collective scale. Jointly discovering levers to foster resilience closely connects people and creates a sense of trust, care and support, fostering the key dimensions we are aiming for: psychological safety and mental wellbeing.[20]

Makarius, Larson and Vroman[21] offer some suggestions of how you can promote psychological safety in your team, especially if you are working remotely.

- **Ask questions.** Proactively check in and show curiosity about your employees' lives outside of work.
- **Show vulnerability.** Share your professional and personal experiences and encourage your employees to do the same.
- **Build a sense of collective responsibility.** Invite team members to participate in meetings by asking: "What do you think?" "What is your perception of this?" "What are we missing?"
- **Encourage risk.** Give employees the latitude to try out new ideas, pitch new projects and processes, and experiment on the fly.

Leading companies have identified the urgent need to address mental health issues long before the outbreak of the current crisis, acknowledging their far-reaching implications.[22] They have further understood the importance of employee psychological safety and mental health. Both are crucial to upholding organisational performance and ensuring sustained business success. In addition, they are also necessary from a human perspective, together representing the backbone of every healthy and flourishing human being. Fahrbach, Weidling and Behrens[23] suggest that resilience is the main ingredient to foster psychological safety and mental health and can also be understood as antifragility. Some things are beyond resilience or robustness. The resilient resists shocks and stays the same; the antifragile gains from disorder and grows from the experience.[24]

The more resilient an individual, team, or organization the better their ability to get through and evolve during circumstances such as the ongoing pandemic and working remotely. Earlier in this chapter, individual strategies to build resilience were discussed. From a workplace perspective, and in aid of creating psychological safety, Fahrbach, Weidling and Behrens[25], suggest that employers and leaders can support individuals by activating the following five levers behind resilience:

1. **Self-care:** the ability to recognise and take care of one's physical and emotional wellbeing, experiencing a range of emotions and acting on their inherent messages

2. **Support:** the feeling of mutual care, compassion and connectedness via a stable network of close people, and via small, but meaningful interactions that include empathy

3. **Meaning:** the conviction that one's work is meaningful and worthwhile, respectively the ability to achieve meaning by acting on what is most important in any given situation

4. **Strengths:** the awareness of one's personal strengths and capacity to deploy them effectively to thrive and remain energised

5. **Perspective:** the ability to look forward with 'realistic' optimism, not by 'smiling when feeling like crying' but by focusing on positive aspects and things within one's control

Towards prosilience

Recognising that we are still to face much adversity, whether it be in the context of the pandemic, in the context of loss and trauma, or the context of the constant change we will experience, all of which may result in mental health challenges, we should equip ourselves by better understanding and evaluating our responses to such adversity. Resilience is reactive. A setback happens and it refers to your ability to then deal with the challenge and recover from it. Prosilience, on the other hand, is proactive, strengthening your responses to adversity so that you are better prepared for many different kinds of challenges in the future.[26]

However, prosilience is not just about being proactive, which requires acting in advance to deal with anticipated problems. The world is often too uncertain to enable us to be proactive, but we can respond to unexpected events by trying to improve our overall situations rather than just reverting to the previous state.[27] In fact, studies show that people with a history of some lifetime adversity reported better mental health than people with no history of adversity, suggesting that one cannot build resiliency or prosiliency without adversity.[28]

A critical mental shift needs to take place to work on developing prosilience. That is, to consider all the small challenges in life as opportunities to practise your resilience.[29] The perception shifts to learning and growth as opposed to challenges being a source of anger and frustration. These 'practice rounds' allow you to create new responses that become more readily available to you when you face larger challenges in the future.

The above suggestions by the American Psychological Association[30] on building resilience is foundational for developing prosilience. In addition, it is useful to evaluate the challenges you face by understanding the source of the challenge (a chosen challenge versus one you had no control over), the duration (moments to decades), impact (how much energy it requires from you to regain balance), how many challenges you may have to deal with at once.[31] Understanding the nature of your challenges in this way allows you to improve your decision making through the process by strategising how you will deal with them. As much as adversity cannot be avoided, it is also useful to think about what steps can be taken to avoid challenges where possible as a first step to preserving your energy and mental capacity.

Lastly, from a coping perspective, it is productive to think about methods you use and can use in the future to calm yourself. This needs to be practised as part of daily life so that it comes to you naturally in times of difficulty. In addition, it helps to create that moment of pause that is required when faced with trials and tribulations to think through your response. It allows the frontal lobe of the brain to take over again, after the initial emotional response to a challenge, so that you are able to exercise your executive functioning to decide on next steps. This gives us back the control and builds confidence, and confidence is very much an important part of looking after our mental health.

Concluding remarks

In summary, this chapter has included the concept of resilience and the importance of resilience in coping with the future world of work. Strategies to build resilience as individuals and how workplaces can support the building of resilience is incorporated under the context of creating an environment of psychological safety. Social vaccinations are explained in that it needs to land with equal importance as the physical vaccinations, if we are to change our response to the challenges of the pandemic context and create an environment to build resilience. Lastly, the concept of prosilience is discussed as a coping mechanism to grow from adversity and have more resilient responses readily available to deal with future challenges. We cannot run away from facing further trials in the future, but we can develop the tools to mitigate the impact it has on our mental health.

Chapter 16

Mindfulness in the workplace

Rakhi Beekrum

Introduction

The term 'mindfulness' which is derived from Buddhism, was coined by T W Rhys Davids in 1910.[1] Rhys Davids translated the Buddhist work *'sati'* into what we now refer to as 'mindfulness'. Mindfulness practices were first used in Western psychotherapy in the early 1980s by Jon Kabat-Zin.[1] For purposes of this chapter, 'mindfulness' will be defined as *the focused awareness of the present moment*. Over the years, mindfulness has been found to be effective in treating both physical and psychological symptoms.

Mindfulness has been applied to several contexts, including the workplace. This chapter focuses on all the benefits of mindfulness in the workplace and provides evidence for the importance thereof. It is discussed from the angle of the employee, the employer or leader and the workplace environment itself. Considerations for practical implications of mindfulness in the workplace are provided in conclusion.

How can mindfulness benefit us in the workplace?

Johnson et al.[2] found mindfulness-based training to be an effective intervention for organisations to improve the mental health, wellbeing and performance of employees. The positive impact of mindfulness-based training has been found to occur both personally and professionally.

Some of the major stressors in the workplace today include heavy workloads, stressful deadlines, competitiveness, toxic work environments and poor boundaries. With the COVID-19 pandemic having affected all aspects of our lives, the workplace had to transform accordingly. Working from home seemed to become the 'new normal' for many organisations. While technological advancement has made this possible, there have been several downsides, including poor work-life integration. The lines have become blurred, and boundaries are often forgotten by individuals and organisations. While working from home might in the past have been an ideal that some dreamed of, the reality that came to light during the pandemic and resultant lockdowns was far from ideal for many.

The primary focus of mindfulness in the workplace has been on improving employee wellness and performance.[3] However, the benefits of mindfulness in the workplace extend far beyond. The benefits extend to the individual, to performance, to stress management, professional relationships, career planning and leadership.

Mindfulness and the individual employee

Focused attention on the present moment means that the employee is able to concentrate on the task at hand and thus make fewer errors. The practical application of mindfulness to daily work means that one is more aware of distractions and able to refocus the mind on the current tasks. A mindful employee is more intentional about how they allocate their time. Focusing on the task at hand increases positive personal and workplace outcomes. When an individual is mindful, they are aware of when they are distracted; and this awareness helps them to refocus. Mindful employees schedule their work more effectively and are able to plan their time better. This means that they are less likely to miss deadlines or fall prey to extreme deadline stress.

Being mindful also means that they are aware of their own physiological and psychological needs, meaning that they recognise when their body needs a break and are able to identify symptoms of stress earlier on. Early recognition of stress means that one can intervene sooner and at a lesser cost, which benefits individuals and the company at large (due to less time off for ill health). This also mitigates the mental health impact of exposure to stressors as discussed in Chapter 3.

A mindful individual listens to their body and this attunement helps to identify when something is off-balance. Investigating and addressing possible health concerns earlier enables one to prevent worsening of symptoms, which not only affects the employee, but has a reverberating effect on their work, their colleagues and the organisation at large.

A mindful employee is also aware of their needs. This is vital because it reduces complaining and promotes problem-solving. The reduction of complaints not only creates a more conducive working environment but also promotes collaboration and ultimately creativity and innovation. Problem-focused employees tend to waste valuable time, whereas mindful employees who are conscious of their needs are able to ask for what they need.

There is also evidence of improved relations with co-workers when employees are mindful. This is because they are more self-aware and are less likely to let their personal issues interfere with work. Mindful employees are conscious of their own tone, choice of words and tend to be better listeners due to their focused attention, hereby improving professional relationships. This promotes empathy[4] and leads to higher levels of emotional intelligence which is often lacking in today's workplaces. Having a better sense of emotional awareness and how emotions affect relationships contributes to a working environment that is characterised by high EQ (emotional intelligence).

Mindfulness and work performance

Van Gordon et al.[5] found that mindfulness training leads to increased productivity and greater positive job outcomes. When employees are trained in mindfulness, they are better able to plan their work and identify obstacles more easily. Mindfulness aids in productivity as it requires focus on the present. This intentional focus on the present, means less opportunity for error. It also means that employees can be more efficient as they are not easily distracted by focusing on the past or worrying about the future.

Bostock et al.[6] found that mindfulness training can reduce job-related strain, work stress and work-life conflict. Mindful employees are more likely to recognise when they are taking strain as they are more self-aware. They are able to identify the source or trigger and take relevant steps to address this. Awareness of the trigger that results in feeling stress and anxiety is always the first step to identifying the steps that can be taken to reduce the negative impact thereof. It is not uncommon for personal issues to impact on work and productivity. Personal and relational stress, loss and other forms of trauma also impact negatively on work. Identifying and addressing such issues means that it is less likely to impact on performance and productivity.

Work-life conflict has been an issue for many; and has recently been exacerbated by the shift to remote working during the COVID-19 pandemic. The boundaries between work and personal life have become further blurred in cases where employees are working from home. This is sometimes due to expectations of the employer, but also commonly due to unhealthy boundaries that the employee may have. Across industries and organisations, more employees are working longer hours, not switching off when they need to, are more available and accessible due to technology and find it more difficult to relax, as the stress of work has entered the home (which might have been their safe haven). Hence the term of the "always on" employee.

Mindful employees tend to have healthier boundaries as they are aware of how they spend their time and how they want to spend their time. This makes them more likely to set healthier boundaries between work and home, including the use of technology and the implementation of multi-tasking. All of which has a positive impact on looking after one's mental health.

Mindfulness and occupational stress

Work and stress seem to be inseparable concepts. Some of the common work-related stressors include job insecurity, long hours, tight deadlines and poor support. These have been heightened in the context of the pandemic. Workplace stress can lead to ill health (both physical and emotional), which in turn affects attendance and output. Stressed employees, in effect, cost the organisation through increased absenteeism, reduced productivity and increased chances of error due to lack of concentration. The relationship between mental health and wellbeing was discussed in Chapter 12.

Another important component of stress management is time management. Many stressed employees cite not having enough time to complete their work, working longer hours or taking work home. Ironically, using time management as a technique can assist in managing one's level of stress better. Mindfulness increases one's awareness of how time is allocated and can thus lead to either allocating time more efficiently or requesting specific resources, once the challenges are well understood.

The wellbeing of employees is therefore vital to the overall success of any organisation. Mindfulness has been found to help develop a powerful mind for work.[7] According to Petchsawang and McLean[8] organisations that arrange meditation courses for employees have higher work engagement. Further, when employees feel valued enough by their organisation through such activities, they are likely to be more engaged in work.[9] The engaged worker plays a critical role in shaping the workplace culture and promotes an environment of creative problem-solving.

Professional relationships

Most employees who seek help for work-related stress cite conflictual work relationships. Such conflict might occur between co-workers or even with superiors. Workplace bullying is an increasingly common phenomenon that employees seek assistance for. Increased awareness of this phenomenon means that more employees are identifying this as a problem in the workplace.

Mindfulness can assist individuals to develop awareness of their own behaviour and reactions that maintain and contribute to workplace conflict. Those with decreased self-awareness are not always able to recognise when their communication and conflict resolution skills are ineffective. Mindfulness practices can enable increased awareness of our own responses, our role in conflict and enable choosing more effective responses. As mentioned earlier, mindful employees are better able to distinguish work and personal issues and maintain healthier work-home boundaries.

Mindfulness at work during a pandemic

The COVID-19 pandemic has transformed the way that we work. While we have made advances in some aspects of work, other aspects have suffered. Job insecurity has become a greater concern, work-life boundaries have become somewhat indistinct and working from home has removed the human element in our workplace interactions. Many employees who have started to work remotely are now realising the value of workplace interactions that they might have previously taken for granted. Having a casual conversation at the water cooler, walking into different venues for meetings, combatting the more sedentary activity of sitting, or brainstorming ideas with a colleague when passing each other in the aisle are examples of activities that we might not have paid much attention to in the past, but were meaningful parts of our work day. These promoted collaboration and a sense of belonging, elements that play a role in positive mental health. Humans are social beings and the lack of workplace social interaction, uneventful as it might have seemed, can lead to feelings of isolation and even exclusion in some cases.

The practice of mindfulness allows for acceptance of difficult emotions – such as anxiety and uncertainty about the future – these being the two most common descriptions of how people are feeling right now. Our inability to sit with our feelings means that we are likely to project these feelings onto other aspects of our lives (including work). When we don't acknowledge and process difficult emotions they can manifest physically (in the form of somatic symptoms), in relationships (e.g., unnecessary conflict with others) or at work (e.g., through reduced concentration and productivity). Mindfulness practice then becomes a valuable tool in processing anxiety in a helpful way. When we are aware of the trigger for our anxiety, we are able to recognise the personal impact of the anxiety, and more importantly, take steps to manage our anxiety (e.g., by rational thinking and problem-solving).

Job insecurity, which has been an existing problem due to the high unemployment rate in South Africa, has been heightened by the pandemic. According to Glomb, et al.[10], mindfulness might be beneficial for organisations undergoing structural change. Organisational restructuring creates stress at all levels in the workplace. Mindful practice can help those at various levels to cope with anxiety and uncertainty, to make more informed decisions and to approach change with compassion. Mindfulness firstly promotes compassion and empathy for those affected by restructuring. Sitting in the shoes of the decision-maker, mindfulness as a skill assists in taking employee wellbeing into account during uncertain times. Human resource teams who deal directly with employees affected by restructuring are more mindful about their own feelings and capacity and are likely to come across as more empathic to employees.

Those who are negatively impacted by restructuring can benefit from mindful practice, as they are more aware of their emotions, more likely to acknowledge what help they require and are able to make better life decisions once they process the emotions and the implications of the changes.

The role of mindfulness in managing mental health

Mindful leaders are more aware of issues such as mental health in the workplace, as they are typically more aware and present. This presents the opportunity to notice changes in employee behaviour and performance.

The benefit of mindfulness in managing workplace mental health is twofold:

1. Employees are more likely to identify when they are not coping.
2. Managers and team leaders are able to identify when subordinates are not coping and intervene appropriately. This is a critical leadership skill and becomes paramount in facilitating healthier working environments.

Employees who are trained in mindfulness are not only more likely to be aware of their emotions but are also more likely to seek help when they realise that they are not coping. Mindfulness techniques, on the other hand, further assist by serving as effective coping skills, for example, mindful breathing or grounding techniques.

Team leaders and managers should ideally be trained to identify when an employee might be presenting with mental health challenges and refer the employee for help accordingly. Often employees are not aware of their deterioration in mental health until it is pointed out to them. This is where the trained manager's role becomes so critical in flagposting such concerns and also signposting the employee to the correct pathway of assistance. This awareness and curiosity on the part of the manager, is likely to prevent unconstructive meetings. Rather, instead of assuming that an employee is just not performing, there is benefit in having a conversation to explore the reasons. Leaders are well-placed to pick up on early signs and symptoms and assist in identifying when there is any change in employee behaviour, such as an employee that is more withdrawn than usual, making more errors, complaining of significantly more health issues or is absent from work more often.

From an organisational perspective, mindfulness creates an environment of awareness of the challenges that might be faced by employees, and therefore ensures that there are more resources available to address issues such as mental health challenges. These resources include employee wellness programmes and appropriate referrals for individual counselling. These form part of the support structures that contribute to overall organisational health.

As mindfulness is considered a protective factor for mental illness, incorporating mindfulness activities is beneficial to individual employees as well as the organisation as a whole. Some of the activities that corporate organisations have found useful are regular mindfulness or yoga sessions, 'coffee chats' to check-in on employee wellbeing and insisting on no work during lunch breaks. Regular mindfulness or yoga sessions protect against mental illness as they promote both physical and mental wellbeing. Such activities require awareness of one's physical and emotional state. They help identify issues that might need to be resolved. Regular check-ins with employees helps them feel valued and normalises any difficulties through mutual sharing. Emphasising the importance of breaks not only shows employees that their wellbeing matters, but also that taking breaks is essential for improved productivity.

Mindfulness as a coping mechanism

It is often understood that depression involves focusing on the past, and anxiety is usually about the future, being present then is an effective coping mechanism. As being mindful requires being present, those who suffer with depression and/or anxiety can benefit in the alleviation of symptoms.

Those who focus on the past are rarely able to solve problems until they refocus on the present. Problem solving is only possible in the present. Those who are anxious are often worrying or overthinking about the future. Grounding themselves in the present decreases anxiety and the chances of panic attacks. Grounding oneself in the present requires focusing one's senses on the present moment – by focusing on what they see, feel, smell, hear and taste. A popular and useful grounding technique involves focusing one's mind in the present by identifying five things that they can see, four that they can feel, three things that they can hear, two things that they can smell and one thing that they can taste. An equally useful grounding technique is focusing the mind on something specific, for example on one's breathing pattern. Mindful breathing is most common and a useful coping mechanism. It helps regulate our parasympathetic nervous system. This slows down one's heart rate and respiration after a stressful or anxious situation. When we are under significant stress, our heart rate and blood pressure increase due to the release of adrenaline. Mindful breathing helps slow down these processes, which, if remain accelerated, can lead to further medical complications. As humans we are built to deal with stress, but we are not built to deal with sustained levels of stress. The good news is that mindful breathing can be learnt by anyone, can be practised anywhere and does not require any special skill or tool. It is one of the most accessible and valuable coping mechanisms but does take time to practise in order to draw on this technique quickly in a stressful situation. The ability of the body to then slow down during a stressful impact, assists in gaining clarity of mind and reduces the negative impact of the stress during and after the event.

Practical application of mindfulness in the workplace

Practical application of mindfulness in the workplace requires organisations and decision makers to understand the benefits of mindfulness as discussed throughout this chapter. This understanding should facilitate organisational rules, policies and mission statements.

The following are examples of how mindfulness can be incorporated in the workplace:

1. Reducing distractions. Organisations can set rules and policies that reduce distraction, which is a productivity-killer. This might involve rules about the use of technology or having quiet zones/relaxation pods for employees to de-stress.

2. Promoting single tasking. While many organisations seem to praise multi-tasking, task-switching is time consuming and the chances of error are increased. Promote prioritising of work tasks and doing one thing at a time (within reason).

3. Promoting wellness at work. This includes taking breaks, providing opportunities to train employees on mindfulness and having zones that promote being mindful. Because many are working from home, mindfulness is equally, if not more, important. Incorporating mindfulness when working from home includes being mindful of working hours, being intentional about taking breaks as if one were physically going to the office, taking screen breaks to prevent screen fatigue, being mindful of ergonomics and switching off on time. Being mindful when working from home is likely to lead to healthier work-home boundaries.

4. Build mindful activities into existing routines, for example, starting the workday with a mindful activity such as breathing techniques, incorporating a mindful activity (such as mindful appreciation) into meetings or having a weekly/bi-weekly activity (such as time in nature or yoga sessions) that promotes mindfulness.

5. Gratitude practices. Encourage gratitude practices in teams so that employees feel valued and acknowledged. This helps to bring people back into the moment, offering an opportunity to reflect as well. This is likely to enhance workplace positivity and therefore, productivity.

It is evident that a mindful workplace benefits individuals and organisations at large. Mindfulness training can benefit our personal lives and work performance. The practical application of mindfulness costs far less than the possible consequences of not being mindful.

Because mindfulness practice benefits individual wellbeing, this in turn benefits the organisation as a whole. So, investing in mindfulness training in the workplace will have a reciprocal effect as employees will have more effective coping skills to help them deal with work and personal stressors. Having such resources means that employees are more present and intentional about their work and are actively participating in looking after their own mental health.

Chapter 17

ACTing with purpose to generate adaptive performance

Xander van Lill and Rinet van Lill

Introduction

"It matters not how strait the gate,
How charged with punishments the scroll,
I am the master of my fate,
I am the captain of my soul."
William Ernest Henley

On the journey through life, no person's path is free from stumbling blocks and hardships. While imprisoned on Robben Island for 27 years, the late president Nelson Mandela found consolation in reciting Henley's poem, *Invictus*. As a freedom fighter and the first president of a democratic South Africa, his life had been a testament to the wisdom of maintaining a greater direction as a guiding light through hardship. As an important ingredient to mental health, purpose can be a powerful antidote to the hopelessness and anxiety that often accompanies difficult experiences.

2020/1 has placed unforeseen challenges in most people's lives. Uncertainty, economic turmoil, changing family routines, and remote work arrangements made it difficult to prevent personal challenges from translating to the workplace. In fact, according to the Gartner's Reimagine HR Employee Survey[1], the COVID-19 pandemic is likely to shift employers' attention from managing the workplace experiences of employees to managing their general life experiences. If employers care about their workforce and the organisation's productivity, they cannot stand indifferent to their employees' mental health.

A greater fusion between work and life in general also creates an opportunity for workplace experiences to offer structure and direction to employees in trying times. Provided the amount of time that people spend performing occupational duties, work has significant potential as an important vessel of purpose for employees. Finding meaning in work to navigate the hardships of life might seem like a tall order to facilitate in the workplace but goal setting is an instrument for practical application. The following discussion will illustrate how an acceptance and commitment therapy

(ACT) approach can guide the alignment between major life goals and specific career development goals to benefit both employees and the organisation. A pyramid of purpose will be proposed to offer guidelines on how managers can facilitate greater purpose amongst employees.

Act as a guiding framework for the pyramid of purpose

The field of psychology has made great progress in establishing interventions that can assist people to overcome challenges and achieve personal development. "ACT is a therapeutic approach that uses acceptance and mindfulness processes, and commitment and behaviour change processes, to produce greater psychological flexibility".[2] Accepting challenging inner experiences instead of trying to eradicate them, while focusing on committed actions to achieve valued outcomes, is the hallmark of ACT.

ACT can be thought of as a general approach that can be incorporated in many interventions rather than a specific treatment. To implement ACT in a therapeutic context requires psychological expertise from people with the appropriate qualifications. However, there are useful ideas, resources, and behavioural strategies that could be applied by managers in the workplace to enhance psychological flexibility and adaptive performance. Goal setting is frequently used by organisations to direct the actions of managers and employees. The current model includes a focus on goals and while ACT typically ascribes to values, major life goals will be employed in this model.

A pyramid of purpose

People are meaning-seeking creatures and many are looking towards their work environment to fulfil this need, especially when considering the amount of time spent on work-related tasks. As a component of meaning, purpose can follow if people direct their efforts towards the achievement of valued goals. If managers can facilitate alignment between broader personal aspirations and organisational goals, employees are more likely to experience purpose, which can promote mental health. When people are pursuing goals that they value, natural curiosity would impel them to acquire more knowledge and skills and solve problems in a creative manner. As a result, the organisation gains a workforce that displays adaptive performance. Figure 17.1 depicts the pyramid of purpose, a model that managers can use to facilitate greater purpose in their workforce. Major life goals are perched at the top point of the model as the highest level of goal achievement, while career development goals form a second level of purpose that is a reflection of major life goals. Committed action and psychological flexibility are the two supportive components that form the foundation of the model.

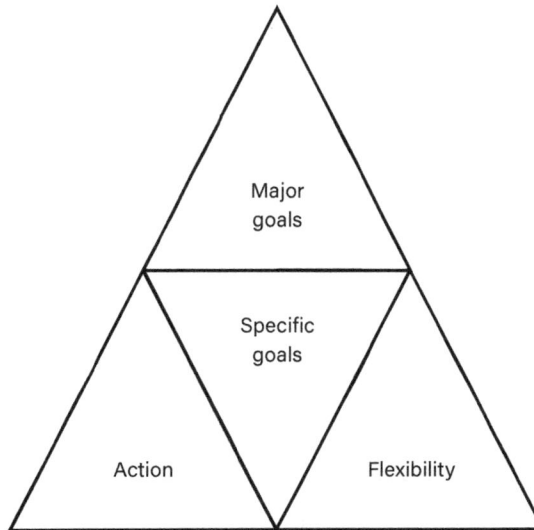

Figure 17.1: Pyramid of purpose

Level 1: Identifying major life goals

The entropic nature of existence ensures uncertainty and, if this phenomenon is not appropriately managed in the workplace, employees who feel out of control could respond with passivity. On the other hand, times of uncertainty could bring about an opportunity for reflection. Revaluating their broader aspirations could assist employees to establish new intentions, which could make them feel more in charge of their work and lives. Major life goals refer to employees' long-term aspirations and the broader agendas they aim to pursue.[3]

Existing literature points to different categories of major life goals,[3] which are presented in Table 17.1. By engaging with employees to identify their major life goals, managers can help them to express the greater purpose they have in life. The ranking of major life goals will also be informed by an individual's personality and interests. If the necessary resources are available, psychological assessments, such as personality or career interest inventories with relevant feedback sessions, can assist employees to identify major life goals. Table 17.1 contains constructs from the Big Five personality traits and the Big Six career interests that are related to each major life goal.

Table 17.1: Types of major life goals and related constructs

Goals	Definition	Related construct
Economic	Having a prestigious career and wealth.	Enterprising Interest
Aesthetic	Making contributions to arts and culture.	Artistic Interest
Social	Promoting the welfare of others.	Social Interest
Relationship	Living in harmony with loved ones.	Trait Agreeableness
Political	Being influential in public affairs.	Trait Extraversion
Hedonistic	Live an exciting lifestyle.	Trait Extraversion
Religious	Devoting oneself to religion.	Social Interest
Educational	Being recognised for expertise.	Trait Conscientiousness

Adapted from Stoll et al., The roles of personality traits and vocational interests in explaining what people want out of life[5]

Clarifying major life goals is a useful starting point to create purpose but it is not a sufficient mechanism to sustain it. More specific career goals can help employees to steer their dedication and subsequent efforts towards committed actions.

Level 2: Setting specific career development goals

Major life aspirations can be daunting and may remain a distant dream if not divided into smaller and more manageable steps. The workplace offers an opportunity to connect major life goals with specific career development goals. For instance, an employee who identified economic and social major life goals can decide to target new potential clients and establish a working relationship with them to offer improved service delivery and increase organisational and personal profits. As employees direct work-related efforts towards major life goals, they are more likely to experience a sense of purpose, which would intensity their efforts when deadlines are challenging and the tasks are cognitively taxing. Even when challenging goals are pursued, this experience of meaning can assist employees to maintain stability in terms of their mental health.

As facilitators of career development goals, managers who instruct their employees to "do their best" when it comes to self-development cannot guarantee subsequent goal achievement.[5] Instead, managers should create a space of growth and development and demonstrate their dedication to employees by engaging in conversations on important goals. Once a career goal has been set, the manager could ask the following questions to enhance commitment to career development goals:

Question 1:   Is the goal challenging enough to motivate you?

Question 2:   Is the goal complex enough to capture your interest?

Question 3:   Is the goal meaningfully aligned with your major life goals?

Question 4:   Is the goal practical in terms of its achievability in both scope and timelines?

Question 5:   Does the goal produce positive emotions, such as excitement?

Question 6:   Does the goals elicit a sufficient level of dedication and intention to work hard to achieve it?

To help employees maintain their focus on goal achievement, it could further be useful to anticipate possible obstacles that might prevent goal achievement.[6] Managers can engage with their employees to deliberately think about specific obstructions and devise contingency plans for their occurrence. Knowing which action strategies to follow when goal achievement is hindered can make employees feel more under control and decrease the demotivating impact of the obstructions.

Level 3: Committed action

Goals shape intentions but sustained implementable actions are required to see goals through. If employees have to actively choose a course of action in line with career goals every time an alternative presents itself, it might deplete their self-control resources. Consider an employee who aspires to an aesthetic major life goal and sets a career development goal to complete an online course on web design with the aim of improving the organisational website. Yet, he finds that there are constantly other tasks that compete for his attention and every time he neglects the graphic design goal, he becomes more frustrated and disappointed. As a remedy, repetition can produce habituation, making it less taxing to act in line with goals. This employee can make an arrangement with his supervisor to set aside strategic times in the week where he would be allowed undisturbed time to focus on web design.

A useful strategy to automise the implementation of specific career goals is by considering when, where, and how action should follow. This could be formulated as an "if statement" followed by a "then" statement[7], for instance: **If** I have an opening in my work calendar (**situation**), **then** I will go to the secluded area (**where**), preferably early in the mornings (**when**), to read a scientific article (**how**). This will further my knowledge about a specific subject (**career development goal**), which will help me to become an expert in my field (**major life goal**). This illustration extends the "if" and "then" statements to incorporate both major life goals and career development goals.

Level 4: Fostering psychological flexibility

The journey metaphor is often used in ACT, and in accordance with the current discussion, major life goals can be regarded as an ultimate destination while career development goals are stopovers along the way. On a journey, people might make new discoveries and experience joy but there will also be parts of the journey that are boring or challenging to the point where giving up might seems like the soundest option. To stay on course, people need to respond with psychological flexibility, a term referring to a person who "(1) adapts to fluctuating situational demands, (2) reconfigures mental resources, (3) shifts perspective, and (4) balances competing desires, needs, and life domains".[8]

ACT subscribes to six core processes that contribute to psychological flexibility and translates into people who are open, centred, and engaged.[9] Openness requires people to view their own thoughts in a non-judgemental way without getting entangled (defusion) and display a willingness to make room for such experiences (acceptance). Being centred implies an attentional focus to the now (present moment) and allowing different perspectives from initial views of the self (self as context). To be engaged, people must be aware of what they deem important (values) and direct their behaviours accordingly (committed action).

There is a growing body of evidence emphasising the relevance of these processes along with practical exercises (i.e. behavioural tasks, stories, metaphors, and experiential activities) proposed by the community of ACT practitioners. Although some of these processes might be more appropriately facilitated in individual therapy with a psychologist, managers can introduce several ACT concepts to enforce psychological flexibility and assist their employees with goal achievement. For instance, if an employee does not believe in his ability to achieve a career goal, a manager can do a defusion exercise to show the employee that his thoughts are separate from his competencies. Writing these negative thoughts on cards and placing them some distance from the employee can help the employee to disentangle from negative self-talk and focus on helpful actions instead. A manager could also ask the employee to imagine these ideas on leaves, flowing down a river, to enhance mindful awareness. Teaching the employee to notice thoughts and accept their presence can prevent the anxiety that comes with the urge to act on them. When obstacles to goal achievement include complicated psychological dynamics, it would be more prudent to refer the employee to a psychologist for further assistance.

The importance of a deliberative style

Managers who are interested in applying the pyramid of purpose with their employees, could benefit from adopting a deliberative management style, characterised by a display of intellectual competence and warmth. Intellectual competence can be demonstrated through stimulating engagements with employees, concerning the complexity, meaningfulness, and practicality of goals, as well as the alignment between major life goals and existing work/team priorities. This approach could encourage employees to have positive expectations regarding the attractiveness and attainability of their own career development goals. Warmth, on the other hand, can be displayed by a concern for the wellbeing of employees, careful attention to employees' views, and conveying respect for employees' concerns. A demonstration of warmth increases employees' sense of self-worth and agency to achieve their career development goals.[10] Greater displays of both intellectual competence and warmth are likely to increase employees' internal motivation (or commitment) to achieve their career development goals and enhance their ability to act in alignment with major life orientations.[10]

Positive outcomes of purpose and its measurement

Organisations often emphasise the achievement of performance goals at the cost of learning or career development goals. However, sustained performance can be compromised when the acquisition of knowledge or the maintenance of mental health becomes a secondary priority.[11] Implementing the pyramid of purpose is a way to ensure an environment of development, and if employees are engaged and acquiring new skills and knowledge, a more adaptive workforce can be cultivated. To measure this return on investment, managers could prioritise outcome measures that focus on adaptivity and not only task performance. Relevant outcomes that are related to adaptive performance are summarised in Table 17.2. Measuring adaptive performance and implementing reward structures are ways to promote sustained career development and mental health, which are more likely to contribute to long-term performance.

Table 17.2: Relevant dimensions tied to adaptive performance

Dimension	Definition
Handling stress	Demonstrating resilience in difficult situations.
Creative problem solving	Generating new ways to think about and deal with existing problems.
Dealing with uncertainty	Easily change actions in response to changing circumstances.
Learning work tasks	Demonstrating enthusiasm for acquiring new knowledge and skills.
Handling emergencies	Reacting with the appropriate urgency to a crisis.

Adapted from Pulakos, Arad, Donovan, and Plamondon[12], *Journal of Applied Psychology*, 85(4), p. 617.

Conclusion

The growing merge between work and life offers an opportunity to bring alignment between employees' major life goals and career development goals. Purpose is an important contributor to mental health and can serve as a healthy psychological barrier against the barrage of uncertainty and prevent the progression of hopelessness and anxiety. By utilising the pyramid of purpose managers can facilitate discussions with employees aimed at setting and achieving meaningful goals. A deliberative approach, characterised by displays of intellectual competence and warmth, could increase employees' motivation to attain goals. The incorporation of ACT principles can assist employees to pursue valued outcomes with psychological flexibility, which could increase adaptive performance and improve mental health.

Chapter 18

The role of employee support programmes

Radhi Vandayar

Introduction

In 2016, Alan Kohll[1] from *Forbes Magazine* wrote: 'Employee wellness is all the rage. More companies jump on the bandwagon each day. Some companies go all in. They invest in their employees, provide wacky wellness perks, and strategise. Others do wellness on a smaller scale and only offer the bare necessities.' The phenomenon of employee wellness globally seemed to be more popular in the recent decade and especially in recent months as a result of the pandemic. Publications such as *Gallup*, *Harvard Business Review*, etc. all seem to cover topics that indicate how employee engagement/employee performance and business success is linked.

Traditionally Employee Wellness (EW) was a clinical or medical service that was hidden and utilised when there was serious need and was not linked to the business functioning itself. However, published articles of the last decade indicate more and more business publications talking about employee wellness and engagement in the workplace. Leadership seems to at last observe the link between wellness and the performance of their people and how this impacts on the bottom-line profits too. Mental health of employees is a key indicator of employee engagement and performance. Therefore, all Employee Wellness programmes address psychosocial matters both proactively (awareness campaigns) and reactively (call centres with psychologists to do counselling).

Today Employee Support Programmes (ESPs) have evolved to so much more than the basic counselling model. Today's programmes look at the ecosystem of a company and aligns the wellness interventions to all stakeholder needs and business priorities to have maximum results or return on value.

Below is an example of a framework that highlights the above mentioned ecosystem and enables business priorities and wellness to work together in driving action.[2]

HLC-7-Cell-Wellbeing-Model™

7. WELLBEING FACTORS

	INFORMATION	MEANS	MOTIVATION
	Output Wise	Method Wise	Recognition Wise
WORK	1. Objectives & Targets / Feedback	2. Processes & procedures / Equipment	3. Partake in setting targets / Output vs reward
	Competence Wise	Job-fit Wise	Motivation Wise
PEOPLE	4. Knowledge / Competency training / Trained trainers	5. Capacity / Job fit / Potential/ability	6. Motives / Personal motivators / Inspiration / Commitment

SUPPORTIVE ENVIRONMENT

SUPPORTIVE ENVIRONMENT

7. WELLBEING FACTORS

HLC-7th-Cell-10-Wellbeing-factors™

Money Wise

Socially Wise — My Health — My Lifestyle — Business Wise

Outer Circle — Inner Circle — Outer Circle

Team Wise — My Meaning — My Mind — Transformation Wise

Work Wise

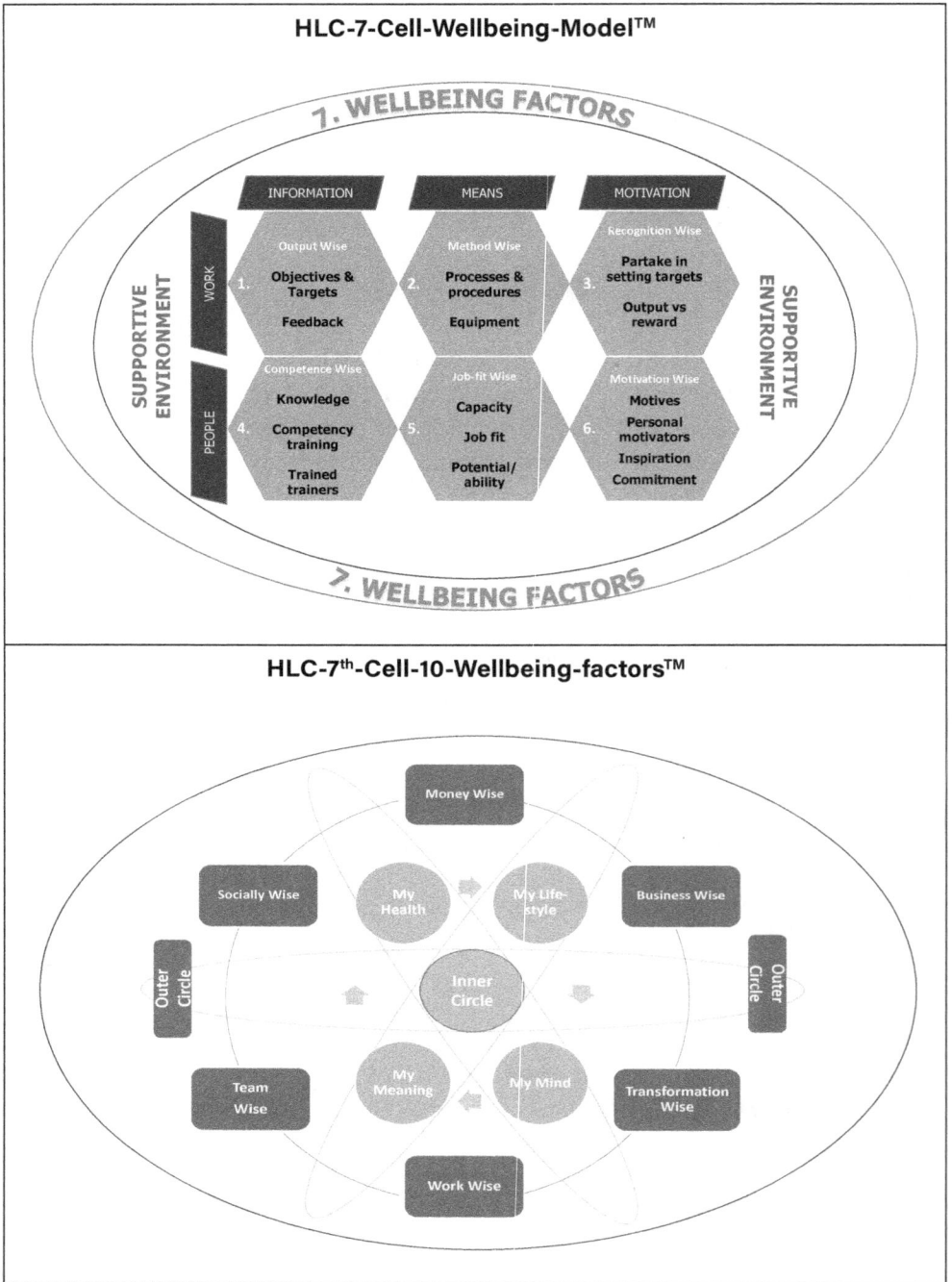

Figure 18.1: The HLC 7-Cell-Wellbeing Model™ is a blend of Thomas Gilbert's Behaviour Engineering Model (BEM)[3] and the Wheel of Life concept created by Paul J. Meyer in 1960.[4]

An experience-based Best Practice adaptation to the Thomas Gilbert's BEM, the HLC 7-Cell-Wellbeing Model™, encompassing the environment for service delivery and human proficiency. It highlights the 6 areas/cells business focuses on with an enveloping cell of wellness to fit into all areas/cells of the business. Numerous models have been developed for identifying and addressing the contributing factors leading to problems in employee performance. However, only one such model has been endorsed by the International Society for Performance Improvement, the leading professional association for human performance technologists.[5] This model was developed by Thomas Gilbert[6] in 1978 and is known as the Behaviour Engineering Model (BEM) (see Figure 18.1).

Thomas Gilbert's BEM focuses exclusively on human competence and behaviour, and includes six hierarchical cells, containing variables that impact performance in the workplace. The BEM is firmly rooted in general systems theory, which identifies employees as an essential part of the organisational system whose performance is affected by environmental factors within the system, as well as the individual characteristics they bring to their job. The strength of Gilbert's BEM is that it provides a comprehensive framework for identifying the underlying causes of workplace performance issues and examines both the environmental and individual influences that have an impact on performance in the workplace. This model allows for business and wellness to align in meeting the outputs of an organisation.

For example in Company X, business delivery which is the output of a procurement team is seriously delayed due to negative team dynamics and individuals functioning less than optimally. The team is expected, according to new management, to decrease their time spent on procuring key equipment to improve their sales and meet new targets. Traditionally, each department, to assist this team, would work in silos. HLC 7-Cell-Wellbeing Model™, advocates that wellness is integrated into all aspects of business and therefore would work with the business leaders to craft a blended solution to meet the output of that team. Wellness then partners with business to work towards the output. The key focus will be the one goal everyone is working towards which is 'decrease their time to procure key equipment to improve their sales and meet new targets.' However, the method to get there would be a blended approach of business responsibility and actions (project management and performance management and process optimisation), and wellness support interventions (counselling at-risk individuals, team alignment trainings and moral building initiatives) in order to ensure the people engagement meets the business demands. This requires a relationship between business and people engagement (HR, wellness, and OD). See the diagram below to visually display this process unfolding in the team optimisation process. The grey bubble indicates the characteristics and expectations of team members that would be needed in order to achieve optimisation. A synergy is needed between business processes and wellness support including change management to obtain these results.

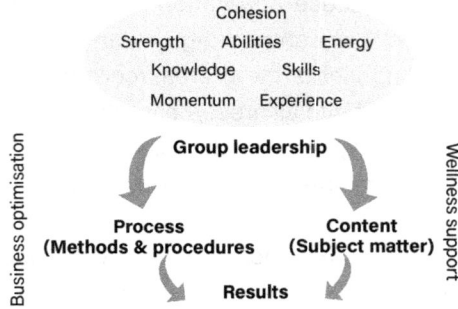

Figure 18.2: Business Optimisation Process

EAP has had a reputation of being a 'nice to have' type of service for many leaders or executives. However, to appreciate this evolution one must understand the journey of these services within the Employee Support space. However, the business case to address wellness far outweighs the cost of a programme:

By not addressing the needs of employees timeously these are the consequences:

The organisational Costs of Human Capital Problems		
Individual Consequences	Organisational Consequences	Organisational Costs
Health problems	Absence from work	Sick pay
Physical:	Sickness absence	
Back, Musculoskeletal, CVD,	Absence for personal	Temporary employee
IBS, Ulcers, Migraines, Skin,	or family issues	replacements costs
Impaired immune function	Arriving late/leaving early	
Mental:	Disability absence	Disability payment
Depression, Anxiety, PTSD,		medical claims
Paranoia, lifestyle diseases	Accidents/errors	
	Increased accident rate	Equipment repair/
Behavioural	Increased error rate	replacement costs
Increased alcohol/drug use		
Poor interpersonal	Supervisory time	Supervisor time/salary
communication	Increased discipline problems	
Eating problems (over/under)	Increased grievance issues	Disciplinary procedure costs
Sleeping problems	More time dealing with	
Increased smoking	employee personal issues	Recruitment costs
Poor home/work life balance		
Increased aggression/	Improving morale/motivation	Training costs
irritability	Team relation issues	
Reduced patience		Redundancy/early
	Loss of employee	pension costs
Cognitive	recruitment costs	
Reduced concentration/focus	Training costs	Loss of customers
Poor judgement/perspective	Loss of knowledge/expertise	
Reduced creativity		Litigation costs
Rigid/obsessive thinking	Additional	
Reduced motivation	Presenteeism	Increased insurance
Reduced commitment	Poor customer relations	premium payments
	Violence at work	
	Vulnerable to litigation	
	Poor company image	
	Quality control problems	
	Property theft	

Figure 18.3: Consequences of unaddressed wellness issues by Andrew Davies[7]

Many of the above consequences can be related to undetected mental health issues.

Mental illness in the workplace leads to decreased productivity, increased sick-related absenteeism, poor work quality, wasted materials and even compromised workplace safety. Despite the significant financial loss to employers and broad economy, many mental disorders fly below the radar in the workplace. A more proactive approach for managing mental illness in the workplace is a strategic imperative for South African employers. Unfortunately, mental health issues in general are still poorly understood and often surrounded by stigma, prejudice, ignorance and fear. Many employees would 'rather die' than admit they suffer from a mental illness. Despite increasing evidence of the connection between physical health and mental distress, when both mental and physical problems co-occur, doctors usually tend to focus on the physical problem. This often means the mental health issue remains untreated. Patients also ignore or downplay mental illness. According to the South African Depression and Anxiety Group (SADAG), less than 16% of sufferers receive treatment for mental illnesses. However, when mental health issues are addressed, many patients report improvements in their physical health.[8]

A well-designed and implemented workplace wellness programme effectively prevents, manages, and significantly minimises the negative organisational consequences of human capital problems, substantially improving organisational efficiency and delivering a significant return on investment. There is also improved employee commitment and engagement, better working relationships and higher overall productivity.

At an organisational level EWPs contribute to reductions in:

- Sick pay and medical costs
- Use of medical aid
- Accidents and injuries
- Compensation claims
- Sick leave
- Disability

Therefore, by addressing the above-mentioned points timeously and effectively, EWPs actively prevent staff turnover resulting from employee personal and/or work-related problems. This results in significant cost savings which are highlighted below:

- The Cost of Staff Turnover (Financial Sector estimates) 1.25 x annual cost-to-company wage including 'hard' and 'soft' costs.
- Exit management costs

- Recruitment
- Vacancies
- Training and development of new incumbent
- Compromised productivity[10]

Other hidden benefits:

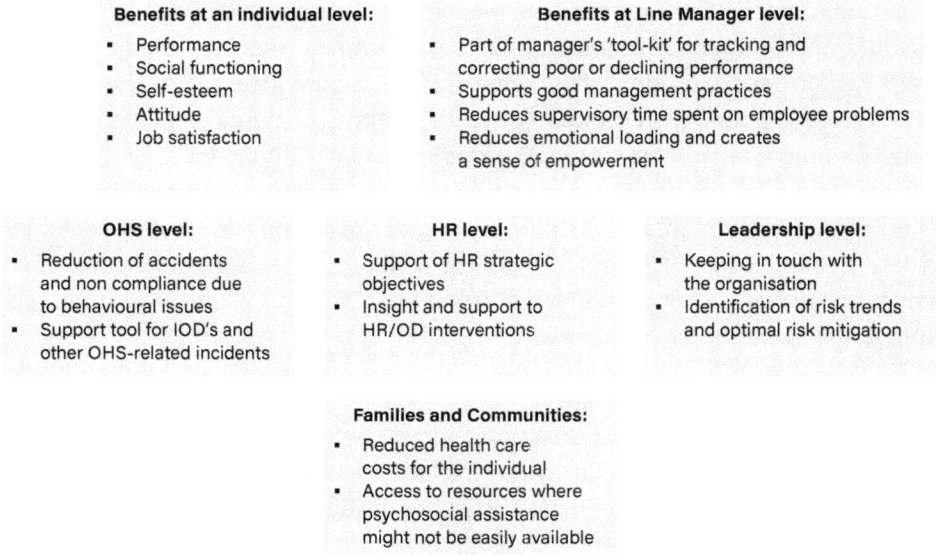

Benefits at an individual level:	Benefits at Line Manager level:
• Performance • Social functioning • Self-esteem • Attitude • Job satisfaction	• Part of manager's 'tool-kit' for tracking and correcting poor or declining performance • Supports good management practices • Reduces supervisory time spent on employee problems • Reduces emotional loading and creates a sense of empowerment

OHS level:	HR level:	Leadership level:
• Reduction of accidents and non compliance due to behavioural issues • Support tool for IOD's and other OHS-related incidents	• Support of HR strategic objectives • Insight and support to HR/OD interventions	• Keeping in touch with the organisation • Identification of risk trends and optimal risk mitigation

Families and Communities:
• Reduced health care costs for the individual • Access to resources where psychosocial assistance might not be easily available

Figure 18.4: Benefits of a wellness programme. Adapted from M Rucker[11] and T Torre[12]

Therefore, in proactively addressing wellness matters and proactively looking at mental health issues organisations are managing their people risk and ensuring better efficiencies to reap higher business results.

The business strategy must be aligned to the people strategy as healthy employees and productive employees means a performing business. EWP is usually positioned within the HR space in many organisations.

To make an effective contribution to an organisation's HR strategy, an EWP must provide a service that will:

- Facilitate lifestyle change and promote resilience in the context of improved productivity and performance (staff optimisation).
- Facilitate the management of risk in service to both the employee and the organisation.
- Incorporate assistance on a broad range of issues, empower and engage individuals and build resilience.

- Meet the challenges facing the organisation, its different people, and the community it serves.

- Evaluate itself and be accountable to the organisation and all its stakeholders (ROI).

- Meet social responsibility and corporate governance requirements (risk management and triple bottom line reporting).

- Include pro-active interventions (where identified and or required).

History of employee assistance (wellness) programmes in SA

The historical development of Employee Assistance Programs (EAPs) in South Africa (SA) has been a complex process. EAPs have evolved in the 90s from Social Welfare – Occupational Social Work, Human Resource Management, Occupational Health and the Mental and Medical Health Fields. Social Workers appear to be the preferred profession in staffing EAPs. They are certainly not the only ones as nurses, psychologists and human resource personnel all play a role. As such, EAPs have become more sophisticated in a short space of time.

The HIV pandemic in South Africa has been a key driver for the emergence and development of EAPs in both the public and private sector. Stigma and discrimination relating to HIV and AIDS resulted in the adoption of the broad-brush approach of EAPs. Many newly born EAPs, traditionally under-financed, used the peer education and peer counselling models to deliver low-cost EAP services ... some still do today.

South Africa at the time of transformation had limited state resources to handle mental health matters. Therefore organisations requiring assistance for their staff had to hire experts (internal or outsourced) to handle employees struggling to cope. This was done mostly by social workers and psychologists employed to do counselling with their employees. This was initially mostly done within the mining sector but spread to all industries over time.[13]

Another influencer in moulding the EAP industry in SA is the well-regulated labour environment as it creates external pressure for employers to take care of employee health and wellness needs and mitigate workplace risks. In the public sector EAPs have been compulsory for all tiers of government departments since a directive was issued in 1996. South African law protects the rights of workers. The Employment Equity Act (EEA) protects employees from unfair discrimination based on illness or disability and the Labour Relations Act prohibits the employer from dismissing an employee because they are disabled or ill. It also implores employers to display a "duty of care". All of which sets up a receptive environment for an employee support programme within the workplace.

There are 3 models of operation in the industry:

- internal division in an organisation
- external to the organisation
- hybrid of internal and external (best practice).

Internal EAP models remain the preference for most organisations although they may not be pure/100% internal models of EAP. Many of these internal EAPs are varying hybrids of combining elements of internal and external models, depending on access to professional resources and funding. The growth of employee support practitioners gave birth to the need for a professional body to regulate the practice in SA. The government, being the largest employer of EAP practitioners, follows a framework of practice prescribed by the Department of Public Service and Administration (DPSA):

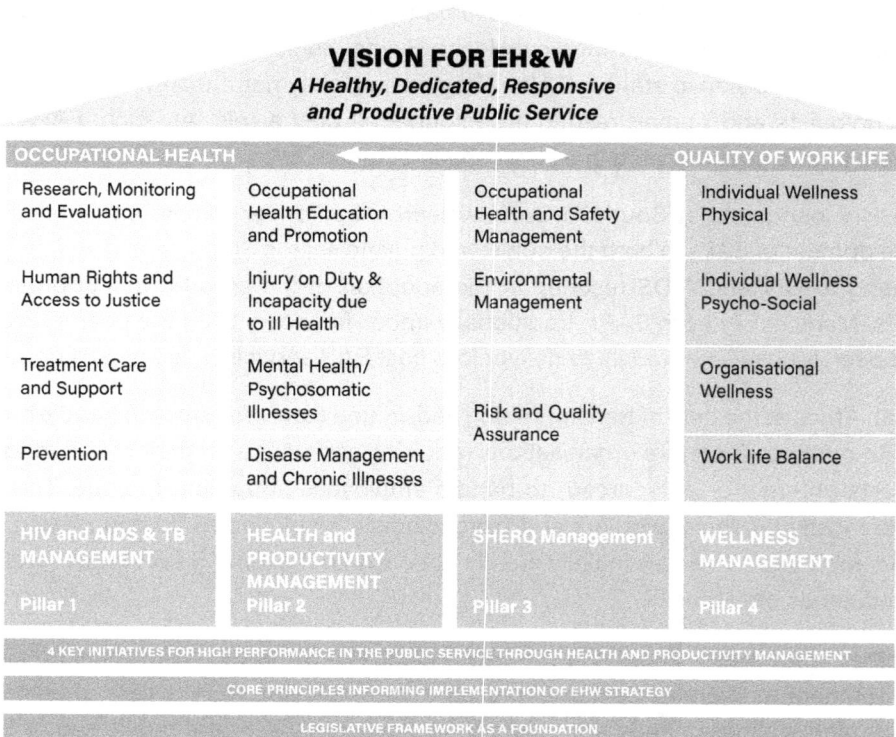

Figure 18.5: DPSA Framework Department of Public Service and Administration (DPSA)[14]

You will note that this framework strives to cover all aspects of an employee's health and wellness requirements. Many corporate companies also endeavour to cover most of these services too. Mental health issues are covered under the "Wellness management leg" of the model where the Individual Psychosocial cell addresses counselling of individuals. It could also be covered in the proactive services to combat mental illness like stress-management campaigns, or work/life education etc. The "Health and productivity leg" allows for the employees to be screened and treated at the occupational health clinics onsite at the organisation for psychosomatic illnesses. Then the Occupational health and safety management will also allow for the legal rights and management of mental health issues within an organisation. Therefore, this model is quite comprehensive in assisting management of an organisation to identify, manage and have prevention initiatives within the mental health space.

The professional body

EAPSA became a formal body and professional association in 1997 according to Prof Terblanche.[15] EAPA SA proceeded to align to the international practice standards to the South African culture and practice while keeping the validity of international ethical and clinical practice.

So, while the 'Core Technologies' have not changed as it's grounded in best practice, the way people have implemented it in the 'here and now' has always been innovative and relevant, evolving to the employees receiving the services.

Ethical practice focus areas of the profession:

- Confidentiality as a cornerstone of practice
- Professional responsibility
- Professional competency
- Professional development so that the professional is up to date with latest research in industry
- Clinical record-keeping
- Client protection
- Professional staffing
- Business practice vs clinical practice
- Related professional relationships
- Neutrality
- Timely intervention
- Managing conflict of interest

By 2015 EAPSA tabled a revised Standards document to ensure their practice is relevant in the field.[15]

So, what is a standard?

- A standard is something considered by an authority or by general consent as a basis of comparison; it is an approved model.[16]

- A standard is the agreed level of best professional practice or description of the ideal situation.[15] Therefore, each standard has a guideline to practice. See the EAPA SA website for more details.[15]

These core technologies and standards allow practitioners to intervene holistically with employee populations in the workplace both from a proactive (marketing, training, etc) and reactive (counselling) approach.

How do EAPs assist the workplace in managing the COVID-19 and mental health challenges?

As mentioned previously, EAP is key in the fight against the pandemic of HIV. The scope of services rendered in most EAPs includes a proactive approach to employee wellness through wellness education; addressing stigma; health screening and testing as well as a reactive risk-mitigating approach of employee counselling and support. Therefore, EAPs are geared towards assisting the workplace in managing the COVID-19 pandemic using the same core technologies and principles learnt through the behaviour modification programmes of HIV programmes.

This will obviously need to be adapted to the COVID-19 context as the nature and levels of contagiousness of the virus is not like the HIV virus in how it is spread and/or transmitted. The major impact of COVID-19 has been unanimously agreed to be mental health by communities as well as the workplace. The GM: Employee Health Solutions, Nonku Pitje, of Discovery Health, a medical aid company, spoke at a seminar on mental health in June 2020 and shared the following stats:[17]

INCREASED SIGNS OF MENTAL STRESS

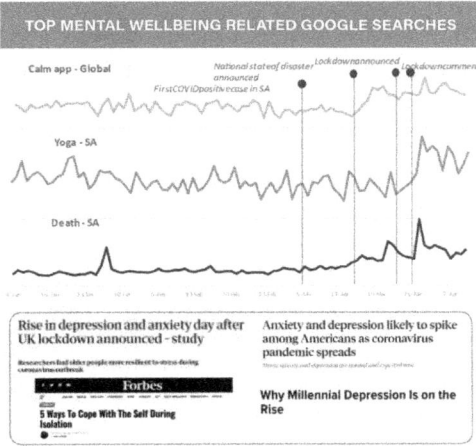

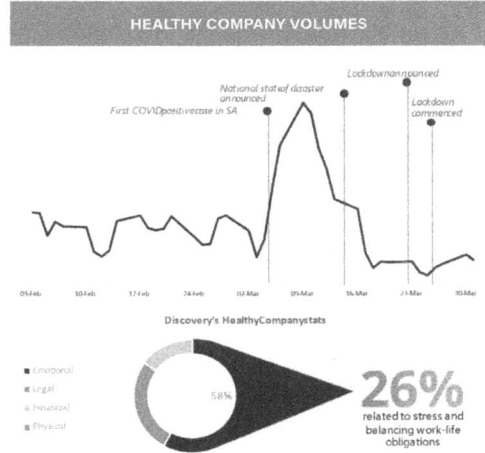

Figure 18.6: Slide on mental health stats (Discovery)[18]

The stats above were very interesting as it indicates the information accessing behaviour of google users during the initial news of COVID and lockdown. The topics trending were death, yoga and a 'calm app'. You will note a steep increase in searches relating to these topics once lockdown started. People wanted to find ways of coping with death, how to cope with lockdown, how to stay calm and even looked for tools to do it.

The second diagram indicates a sharp increase in emotional issues coming into the Discovery support line when the COVID lockdown occurred, once again indicating people's need to find better ways of coping.

COVID-19 has produced a lot of uncertainty. Daily we are being faced with questions about how best to keep ourselves and our loved ones safe, as well as how to manage changes in our routines. Information was a key driver of behaviour as per the above diagrams.

Global megatrends have caused heightened fear levels. There is an overall increase in anxiety levels. It is natural to feel overwhelmed, vulnerable, stressed, and anxious. Other additional risk factors like previous traumas or a mental health problem in the past further exacerbate these symptoms, or if you have a long-term physical health condition that makes you more vulnerable to the effects of COVID-19.

COVID-19 disrupted the EWP industry overnight just as it did with other professions. The larger, better resourced EWP providers were able to pivot quickly with some technology and Research & Development in the pipeline. However, many EWPs (especially internal EWPs) struggled with technology.

The recent pandemic has increased employer interest in the use of technology tools to provide counselling to distressed employees. Attridge[19] provides a high-level overview of the key findings in the hundreds of studies in the research literature on the purpose, use and effectiveness of mental health support provided using technology. Technology channels include the telephone, internet, and smart phone apps.

Attridge[20] explained that there are advantages and disadvantages to take note of:

Advantages of techno therapy	Disadvantages of techno therapy
<ul><li>Greater access to therapeutic support</li><li>Flexibility for the user in accessing support at anytime from anywhere with internet access</li><li>Helps offset the social stigma and related barriers to help-seeking with live counsellors</li><li>Can be as effective clinically as in-person therapy</li><li>Significantly lower cost than in-person services</li></ul>	<ul><li>Personal preference of user for live or in-person support</li><li>Early drop-out and lack of proper participation in machine-based structured programmes with multiple lessons</li><li>Counsellors need special training for effective delivery of clinical services via online or technology channels</li><li>Rigid application of iCBT approach and clinically specific content may not fit goals of user</li><li>New tech tools as challenger or collaborator role?</li></ul>

While there are other EAP service providers that have made good strides in addressing the COVID pandemic there was only one provider that shared their stats with the author for the purpose of this chapter.

ICAS Southern Africa, one of the largest EWPs, locally managed this transition seamlessly as they had been exploring technology solutions for the past few years. They have shared their COVID-19 related cases to see the trends from the start of COVID in 2019 through 2020 and the beginning of 2021 to give us an idea of the type of COVID cases that came through their platforms. This was mostly through their telephone helpline, their live chat function, and their app with various clients.

PROGRAMME UPTAKE

INDIVIDUAL

ANNUALISED INDIVIDUAL CASE UTILISATION

■ 2019 ■ 2020 ■ 2021

ANNUALISED UTILISATION SPLIT BETWEEN PSYCHOSOCIAL & COVID-19 CASES BY MONTH

- - - Psychosocial   —— COVID-19

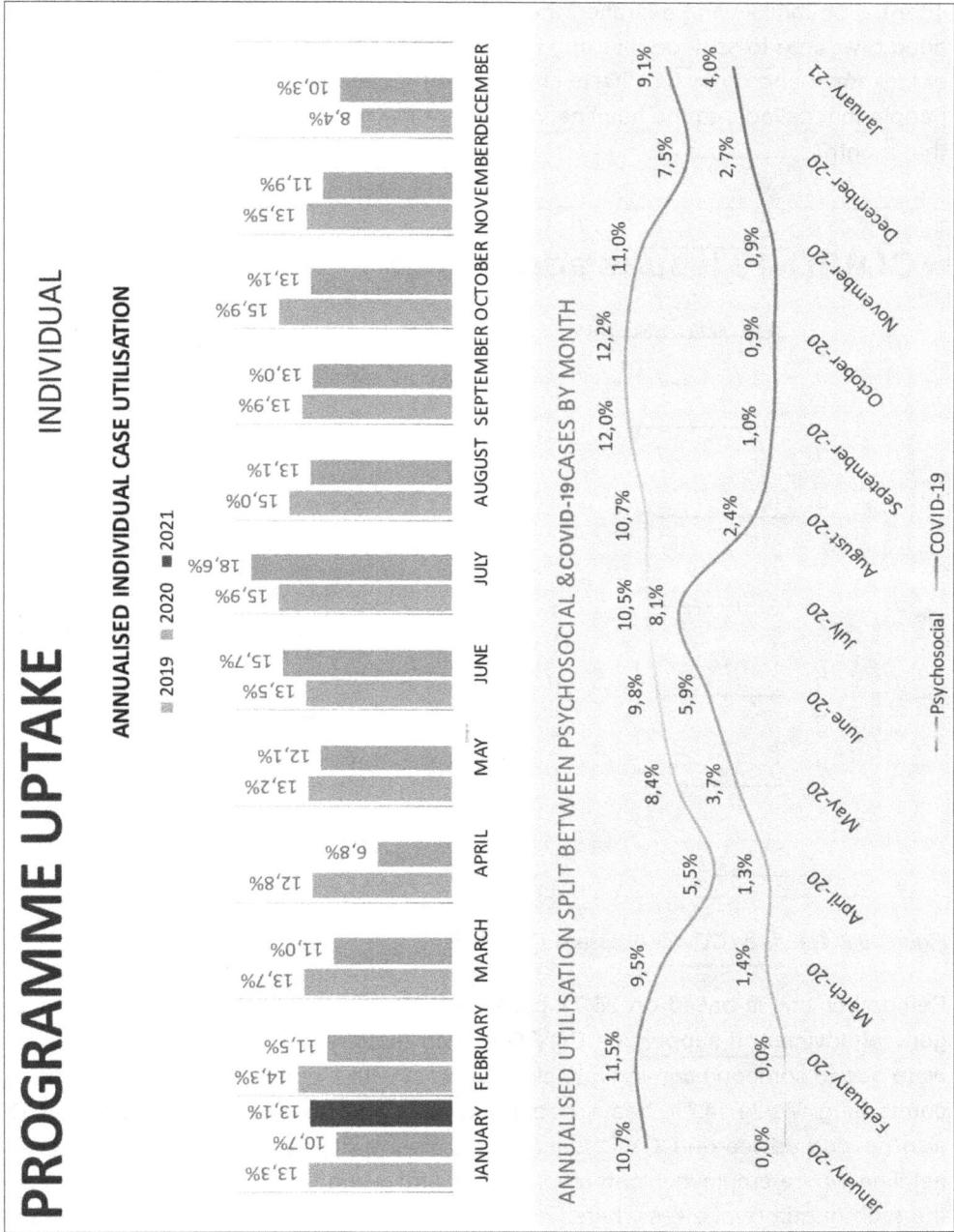

Figure 18.7: Individual Uptake of COVID-19 cases (ICAS SA)[21]

The trends show that the cases picked up at the peak of the second COVID-19 wave in South Africa. This shows the strain of employees over this lockdown period. If you compare this to the Discovery diagram earlier, you will note that people sought information initially and searched the internet. However, the above graph shows the need over time to seek counselling or professional assistance to manage the stress of lockdown and other COVID-19 stressors. At its peak it indicates 8.1% of cases or people that called into the helpline vs 10.5% of the normal psychosocial related calls that month.

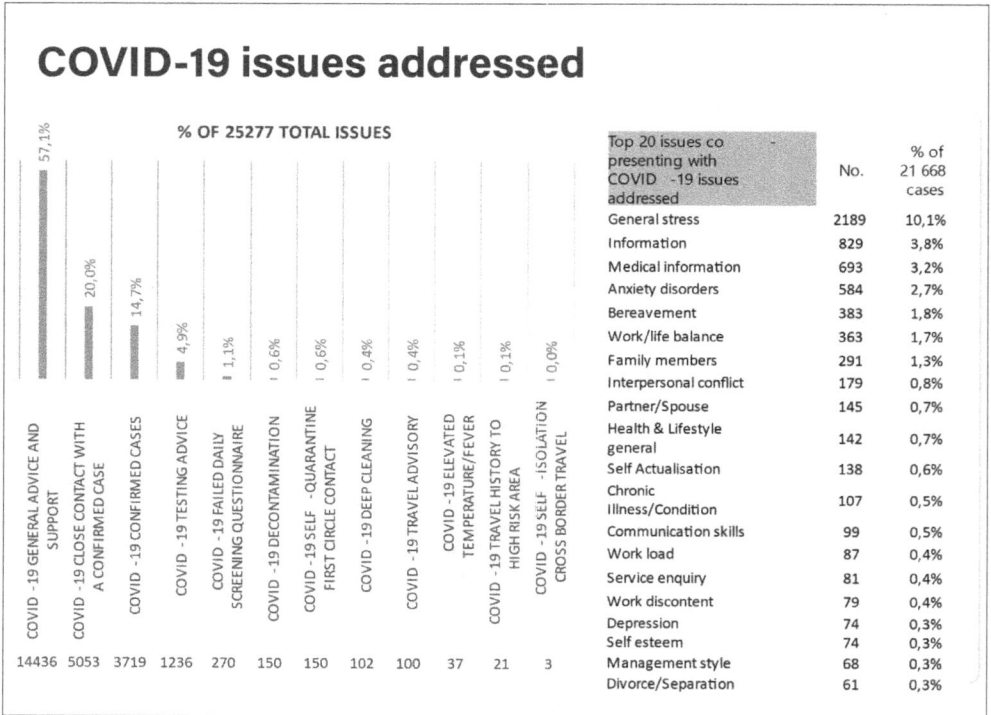

COVID-19 issues addressed

% OF 25277 TOTAL ISSUES

	57,1%	20,0%	14,7%	4,9%	1,1%	0,6%	0,6%	0,4%	0,4%	0,1%	0,1%	0,0%
	COVID -19 GENERAL ADVICE AND SUPPORT	COVID -19 CLOSE CONTACT WITH A CONFIRMED CASE	COVID -19 CONFIRMED CASES	COVID -19 TESTING ADVICE	COVID -19 FAILED DAILY SCREENING QUESTIONNAIRE	COVID -19 DECONTAMINATION	COVID -19 SELF - QUARANTINE FIRST CIRCLE CONTACT	COVID -19 DEEP CLEANING	COVID -19 TRAVEL ADVISORY	COVID -19 ELEVATED TEMPERATURE/FEVER	COVID -19 TRAVEL HISTORY TO HIGH RISK AREA	COVID -19 SELF -ISOLATION CROSS BORDER TRAVEL
	14436	5053	3719	1236	270	150	150	102	100	37	21	3

Top 20 issues co presenting with COVID -19 issues addressed	No.	% of 21 668 cases
General stress	2189	10,1%
Information	829	3,8%
Medical information	693	3,2%
Anxiety disorders	584	2,7%
Bereavement	383	1,8%
Work/life balance	363	1,7%
Family members	291	1,3%
Interpersonal conflict	179	0,8%
Partner/Spouse	145	0,7%
Health & Lifestyle general	142	0,7%
Self Actualisation	138	0,6%
Chronic Illness/Condition	107	0,5%
Communication skills	99	0,5%
Work load	87	0,4%
Service enquiry	81	0,4%
Work discontent	79	0,4%
Depression	74	0,3%
Self esteem	74	0,3%
Management style	68	0,3%
Divorce/Separation	61	0,3%

Figure 18.8: Trends on COVID-19 cases (ICAS SA)[21]

Remember this is based on 25177 cases and 57, 1% of the cases noted a need for general advice and support on COVID related matters. However, 20% of the cases were due to someone coming into close contact with a confirmed case and needing counselling. While 14,7% had a confirmed case and needed support. Lastly 4,9% also needed advice on COVID testing. This clearly illustrates the needs for a crisis helpline where employees can reach out as and when they require it. You will note the high numbers of stress, bereavement, anxiety disorders, work/life balance and interpersonal conflict being among the top trends. All of which indicate the need for supportive services.

ICAS also had a live chat function open during this time which indicated an increase of 8.3% from 2019 to 2020 according to the ICAS business intelligence team.

Trends indicate the following effects on an individual

Prolonged stress and anxiety which has also been described as a traumatic experience by many.

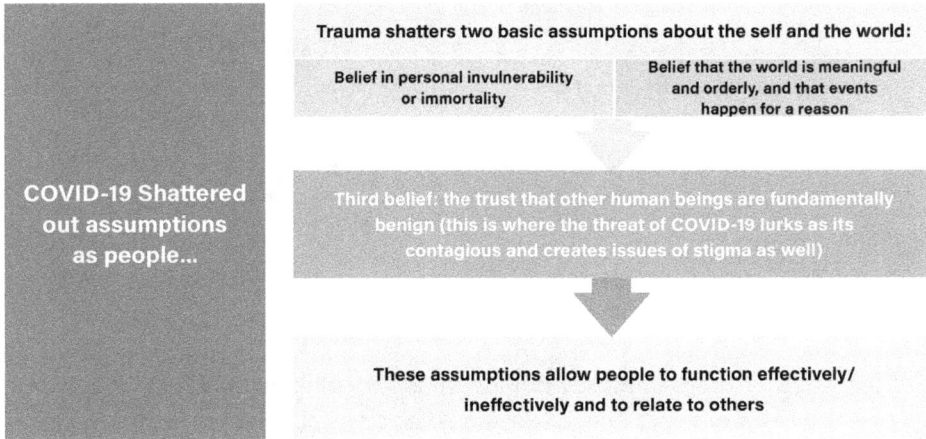

Figure 18.9: How trauma shatters our basic assumptions

The diagram indicates the struggle we face with this virus, how we must face our mortality as an individual, at the same time trying to make sense and find meaning from this unseen enemy and above all coming to terms with the fear that someone (even a loved one) can infect you. It is apparent that individuals who have always shown a high level of resilience now seem to be affected negatively over time due to the prolonged nature and impact of this pandemic.

Some people are more vulnerable to stress, especially those already struggling with a mental health problem like anxiety or depression. They needed professional assistance during this time and EWPs provided this service despite the requirement of social distancing as this service is telephonic in nature. People did not have access to their usual support systems and social isolation also had a major negative affect. People that would usually not be susceptible to depression or anxiety suddenly felt they were experiencing symptoms.

Grief also started to become an issue as the death toll started increasing over the last year. However, dealing with loss was not just loss of loved ones that was experienced it was also:

Types of Loss

Material loss: *loss of physical object or surroundings*

Relationship loss: *end of opportunities to relate*

Functional loss: *loss of muscular or neurological function*

Role loss: *oss of specific social role or identity*

Intrapsychic loss: *loss of what might have been*

Systemic loss: *disturbance of social system*

These are some of the issues the counselling part of the programmes have been addressing with employees that contact their ESP services.

However, the ESP programmes is not just made up of individual services; there are so many other components to it. ESPs should address all levels in an organisation as per the 7-cell model shared earlier:

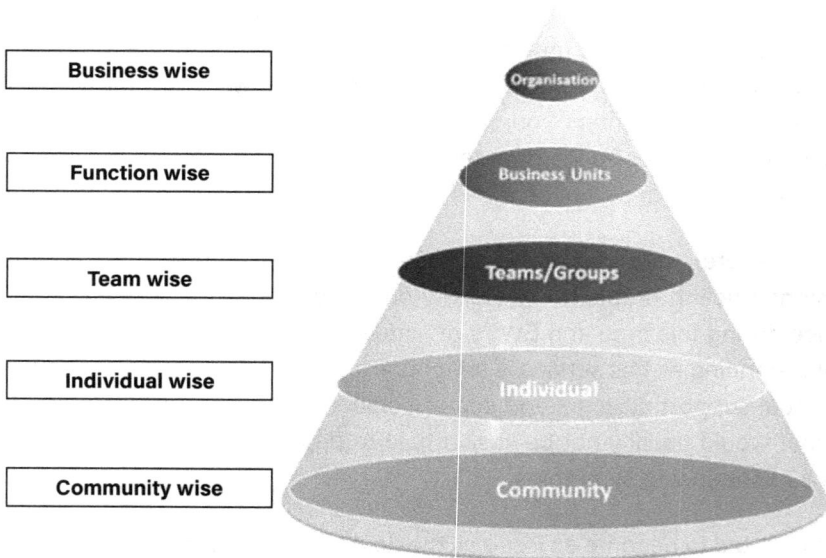

Business wise	Organisation
Function wise	Business Units
Team wise	Teams/Groups
Individual wise	Individual
Community wise	Community

Figure 18.10: Levels of influence of wellbeing interventions (HLC)[22]

At the next level of team functioning many ESPs have been intervening with teams in various ways as the face-to-face route was no longer possible. Intervening in teams and at organisational level immediately took us to the virtual space. This is when

ESPs started to get creative and use the standards that are non-clinical in nature. Marketing, training, and networking started to become a key driver to their practice.

EWPs also play an important role in creating awareness on pertinent topics such as mental health and COVID

Marketing & communicating your wellness programme as well as communicating health and wellness messages to ensure that the end user remains informed and engaged on the wellness service.

Processes, systems and tools in place will assist in improving the effectiveness of employee wellness programmes to boost participant engagement and overall programme success.

With fatigue around the traditional communication tools (e.g., posters, emailer, flyers, SMS and intranets), we all need relevant, metric-driven engagement and communication tools. So, with a combination of various communication methods with automation, reminders, and fun content, you have the foundation for an effective communications strategy.

Some options include:

1. **Personalised communications:** by curating content to employees and managers, you have a higher rate of engagement success. A technology system that tracks all data and engagement from participants in your wellness programme allows you to provide relevant content that is digital and speaks to the needs of the participant. The data engagement with video content and courses allows you to track all metrics to further curate relevant content.

2. **Push notifications:** using a data driven, video on-demand content mobile phone application with an enterprise technology back end makes it easier to keep participants accountable and energised. This also drives higher click-through rates to content and allows direct communications in platform (such as completing assessments, feedback forms, accessing services)

In SA many ESP providers will need to think of data-free solutions or employer-funded solutions due to the high cost to the employees as this will make it inaccessible to the masses.

- ESPs need to look the best possible way to reach their target audience. When addressing a blue-collar audience, the options are to send content as picture via mobile or print version which can be placed in strategic areas visible as posters onsite.

Examples of topics for talks/webinars were based on:

- Stress and anxiety of COVID
- Bereavement and trauma debriefing
- Team alignments (dealing with a new way of working and still meeting their mandate)
- Dealing with stigma
- Trauma defusing or psychological first aid
- Dealing with employees in crisis
- Being a responsive leader

Technology as an enabler

In the blink of an eye what we knew as normal changed; what was taken for granted became a luxury. We have experienced the effects of a pandemic that has changed our world forever.

In these unprecedented times we have been forced to re-evaluate what is important, how we structure our time and work-life balance. Above all it is abundantly clear that to curb the pandemic, proper education and changing behaviours will be critical in containing the outbreak. The relationship between individual and group behaviours highlighted and identified as risk.

There is no doubt that for us to change and impact the world we live in we need to find solutions that can address awareness and education and drive behaviour change. According to Alan Kohll[23] some programmes utilise common technology tools to help collect and track wellness data. An example is to make wellness work with wearables. As employees track their activity with devices like Fitbit or the Apple Watch, they can earn points for the progress they make and achieve the incentives their programmes offer. There is a clear link between managing mental health and stress with physical activity.[24] This type of measurable intervention allows companies to see ROI on the interventions they do.

Adult learning and education on the other hand can also play a pivotal role in proactively managing mental health initiatives and with technology we can enable this process. Education and effective health literacy will be necessary for individuals to make informed decisions and take actions that will impact their health status and, in turn, their mental health.

Corporates are leaning on their EWP providers to give solutions that will assist in behaviour change and to this end many of the EWP providers have adopted or championed technology solutions to comply with their requirements. The mobile phone has now become a tool for many employees. Some employers have equipped their employees with Wi-Fi, 3G access and data packages to ensure connection and ability to work from home. Baby boomers, Generation X and millennials alike were forced to get used to technology to keep productive. This created a springboard for many ESPs trying to creatively reach their target population.

The following are examples of technology platforms that were implemented to assist with driving education and awareness:

- Video chat for consults
- Zoom/MS Teams sessions for training
- Customised COVID-19 Video content
- Live webinars with topic experts
- Tracking and tracing applications
- Courses and/or short courses designed for education purposes
- Mobile lifestyle solutions

It all however comes back to the data and measurement that these platforms and tools offer to allow future decisions on how to intervene with the targeted populations following a programme/service.

ESPs and the digital age

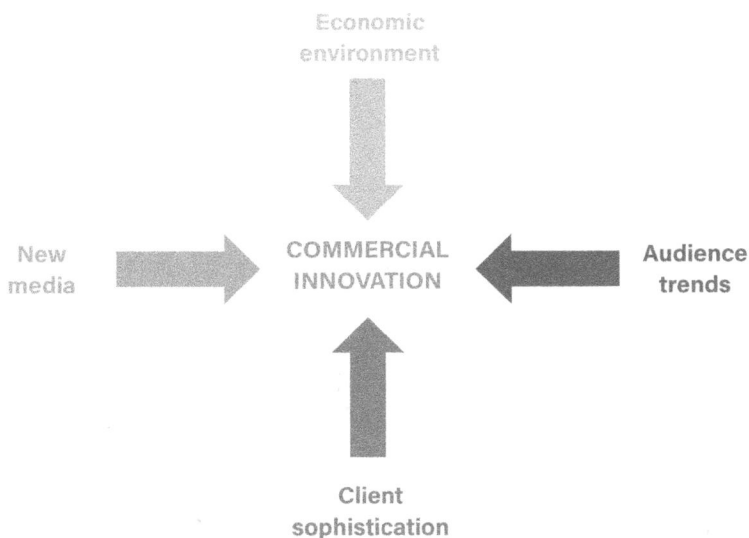

Figure 18.11: Innovation in ESPs

ESPs will need to innovate and reinvent themselves at the speed of the digital changes or they will not be relevant in the future. Also, addressing mental health issues has not been easy over the years. The stigma has clouded the good work that has been done. The digital age allows for us to address much of this as more people can access help through these digital platforms confidentially and securely. These technologies also allow the ESPs to be proactive and do much education and awareness and their reach is more effective than face-to-face campaigns.

To ensure agility within ESPs, identifying credible technology and digital providers have become critical. With the right technological partner, ESPs will be in the position to design, develop and implement solutions in an ever-changing market as soon as the need is identified. The core technologies that govern their practice must be broad and robust enough to allow for clinical integrity and technological enablement.

ESPs should look at new frameworks to drive their R&D to be responsive to the employees' ever-changing requirements. Business intelligence and data will be the cornerstone of movement and influence the marketing to reach the right risk groups within the organisations. Assessment and measurements will be a key tool going forward to target the right interventions for the right targeted audience within your population. So, in a nutshell, innovation is the wave for their future. They are the content experts, and the technology becomes a tool, thereby taking mental health interventions and broader wellbeing into a future world of work relevant to all users.

Chapter 19

The Fourth Industrial Revolution in the workplace: Career capital, mental health and wellbeing in the future of work

Frank Magwegwe

The term Fourth Industrial Revolution (4IR), which was coined by Klaus Schwab, founder and executive chairman of the World Economic Forum, has become ubiquitous nowadays. Back in 2016, he wrote: *"We are at the beginning of a revolution that is fundamentally changing the way we live, work, and relate to one another. In its scale, scope and complexity, what I consider to be the Fourth Industrial Revolution is unlike anything humankind has experienced before".*

According to history[1], there have been three industrial revolutions. The First Industrial Revolution, which emerged in the United Kingdom in the 18th century used water and steam to power and mechanise production; the second, which has been dated between 1867 and 1914 used electric power to create mass production; and the third, thought to have begun in earnest after the Second World War used electronics and information technology to automate production. The World Economic Forum offers three reasons for why 4IR is not a continuation of the Third Industrial Revolution. First, when compared with previous industrial revolutions, the speed of 4IR is exponential rather than linear. Second, 4IR is a disrupting force in nearly all industries across the globe. Finally, 4IR is predicted to transform how value is created, exchanged, and distributed in society. It is noteworthy that there is consensus that although previous industrial revolutions advanced economic development, this development came at the expense of the planet.

Although it is too early to assess the impacts of 4IR technologies, there is consensus among economic historians that technological change unleashes both benefits and challenges. The benefits include the development of new products and industries, increases in productivity and skills that lead to increased wages, and improvements in quality of life while the challenges include the disruption of some industries, the world of work (e.g., job automation, work intensification) and jobs (quality and quantity), as well as skills erosion.[2]

The societal challenges presented by 4IR are often discussed alongside the context of the 4IR-inspired changing world of work, sometimes referred to as the future of work. What does the term 'future of work' mean? According to Santana & Cobo[3], the term 'future of work' is broadly used to explain ongoing trends and changes in the workplace that can be grouped into four themes as shown in Figure 19.1 below.

Political	Economic	Social	Technological
• Industrial relations	• Wage inequality	• Satisfaction	• Gig work
• Trade unions	• Unemployment	• Burnout	• Telework
• Labour market	• Job polarisation	• Work-life conflict	• Automation
• Education policy from institutions and organisations	• Precarity	• Vulnerable workers (older workers, migrant workers, gender discrimination)	• New forms of work
		• Talent	• Crowd work
		• Career	• Innovation
		• Leader's values	• Digitalisation
		• Corporate social responsibility	• Digital transformation
		• Organisational commitment	• e-Human resources management
			• Human resources analytics
			• Virtual human resources

Figure 19.1: Classification of future of work themes, adapted from Santana & Cobo[3]

The objectives of this chapter are twofold: first, it aims to discuss some of the opportunities and challenges related to the 4IR for both employers and employees including their impact on employee mental health and wellbeing. Second, it outlines how employers and employees can respond to these challenges and opportunities. Understanding the impact of the 4IR on organisations and their employees is important because the 4IR is ushering in a future world of work that both organisations and employees must positively adapt to in order to remain competitive. Furthermore, this future world of work is expected to place more demands on employees which may negatively impact their mental health. The guiding questions for this chapter revolve around: What is the 4IR? What are the opportunities and challenges for employers and employees in the 4IR? What are the competencies (i.e., skills, knowledge, and attitude) required for the future of work that is being ushered in by 4IR technologies? What factors influence the adoption of new technologies by employees? What is the role of career capital in the future of work? What evidence-based interventions can mitigate the impact of 4IR technologies on employees' mental health and wellbeing?

The fourth industrial revolution (4IR)

The 4IR denotes fundamental changes in the creation, exchange, and distribution of economic, political, and social value and in decades ahead, will transform the nature of work, business, and society, in different ways in different parts of the world.[1] In the

4IR, the distinctions between physical, digital and biological spheres become blurred as transformative technologies unleash profound global effects on economies, organisations, people, and the world of work.[1,2] Some of these technologies include virtual and augmented reality, 3D printing, quantum computing, cyber-physical systems, drones, blockchain, autonomous vehicles, robotics, artificial intelligence, big data, Internet of Things, nanotechnology, and biotechnology.[1]

Research from a myriad of organisations including the World Economic Forum, South Africa's Presidential Commission on 4IR, large consulting firms, the Organisation for Economic Co-operation and Development, and the International Labour Organisation suggests that these new technologies present both enormous economic benefits and huge challenges. Therefore, it is important to temper the excitement at these economic benefits with caution since understanding of the various ways the 4IR may impact society is at an early stage. This is important because history has demonstrated that new technologies and their associated economic benefits can be at odds with social progress, which can lead to social disruption and discontent.[4,5] Keenly aware of this, governments across the world have responded to the opportunities and challenges of 4IR by establishing national 4IR strategies.

It is interesting to note that, despite consensus that we are still at the beginning of the 4IR, there is already some speculation about the looming Fifth Industrial Revolution (5IR). Proponents of the 5IR argue that, broadly, it is an industrial revolution about serving humanity through integrating profit, purpose, and people. However, it is worth noting that the World Economic Forum's Centre for the Fourth Industrial Revolution that has done extensive research on various topics related to the 4IR, is silent on the topic of the looming 5IR and so are the large consulting firms that are some of the leading voices on the 4IR. Also, South Africa's Presidential Commission on 4IR made no mention of the 5IR. Irrespective of whether we are already in the 5IR or it is looming, the COVID-19 pandemic has highlighted the need for organisations to put employee mental health and wellbeing on the boardroom agenda. Employee mental health and wellbeing is an important theme for the future of work.

Opportunities for employers in the 4IR

This section, through an overview of some of the technologies that characterise the 4IR, explores the opportunities employers can harness through the adoption of these technologies. The technologies explored in this section are predicted to have a profound impact on employers and employees over the next few years.[6] To manage this impact and remain competitive companies need to adjust or transform their business models by adopting some of the 4IR technologies. Therefore, there is a clear business case for the adoption of 4IR technologies to transform business operations, processes, and services in order to remain competitive.

- Artificial intelligence (AI) – complex algorithms that enable computers and machines to mimic capabilities of the human mind such as perception, learning, problem-solving, and decision-making. Machine learning (ML), a subset of AI, focuses on the development of computer programmes that when fed with data, teach themselves to learn, understand, reason, plan and act. ML can be used by insurance companies to digitally and automatically recognise and assess car damage; or by security companies to replace typed passwords with voice recognition. Some financial services companies are harnessing the 4IR by utilising AI to launch robo-financial adviser services that provide affordable financial advice to individuals in new market segments.

- Virtual Reality (VR) – the use of computer technology to create a simulated environment that shuts out the physical world. Although still on small scale, VR is being used in healthcare, for student doctors to gain access to virtual operating theatres; in the military for training bomb disposal soldiers; by oil companies in training employees to deal with dangerous scenarios on oil rigs; and for soft-skills training.[6]

- Augmented Reality (AR) – the use of computer technology to supplement reality or the environment by adding new layers of perception. The game Pokémon GO is among the best-known AR experiences. However, AR is not only limited to gaming. AR-enabled smart glasses are being used to help warehouse workers fulfil orders more accurately, and electrical workers to make repairs.[6]

- Blockchain – a distributed, tamperproof digital ledger that uses software algorithms to record and confirm transactions with reliability and anonymity. Once entered, the record of events that is shared among many parties cannot be altered. Blockchain is predicted to usher in an era of autonomous digital commerce.[6] For example, delivering better health data management that allows patients and providers to access and share their healthcare data and peer-to-peer payments technology that can serve the global unbanked population.

- Drones – unpiloted, semi-autonomous or fully autonomous aircraft that are used for various reasons such as surveillance, cinematography and delivery. For example, drones are replacing helicopters in precision agriculture, defined as farming practices that use technology such as robotics, drones, and autonomous vehicles to make farming more productive and efficient.

- Robotics – the use of machines with enhanced sensing, control and intelligence to automate, augment or assist human activities. Although robots are already being utilised in manufacturing, new opportunities include service robots to help people with vision problems, and autonomous robots that can be used in the maintenance of nuclear plants and underground mines.

- Internet of Things (IoT) – network of physical objects such as devices, vehicles, or appliances that are embedded with sensors, software, network connectivity and computing capability that enable them to collect, exchange and act on data, usually without human intervention.[6] The engine maker Rolls-Royce offers an interesting case study of harnessing IoT opportunities. To deliver optimal engine performance to their construction, mining and marine customers, Rolls-Royce, developed trackers that monitor engine utilisation and transmit data to its customer service teams through a web application.[7]

- Cloud technology and big data – cloud technology enables the delivery of computer applications and services over the internet which reduces storage and computer power requirements. 4IR companies have access to big data enabled by cloud that allows predictive relationships to form and emergence of insights for business. For example, retail and financial services companies now have extensive amounts of information on consumer spending patterns, preferences and behaviours which can be used to tailor customer value propositions.

- 3D printing – additive manufacturing techniques used to create three-dimensional objects layer-by-layer using a computer-created design method. In South Africa, the world's largest 3D metal printer is part of the Council for Scientific and Industrial Research's project to improve South Africa's market competitiveness by harnessing 4IR technologies for the manufacturing industry.

Opportunities for employees in the 4IR

In this section, the focus is on employees and the opportunities that they could realise as companies adopt 4IR technologies such as AI, robotics, IoT, and big data analytics. These opportunities are intrinsically liked to the future of work, the ongoing trends and changes in the workplace, and considered by the World Bank as one of the critical looming challenges.[8] Indeed, it is a looming challenge because the advance of 4IR technologies is changing the types of skills and competencies needed in the workplace and demanding shifts in mindset about the nature of work among individuals which in turn may negatively impact employee mental health.

Although many low-skill jobs may be lost due to the adoption of the 4IR technologies, these technologies, as discussed in the previous section, present new opportunities for companies and pave the way for new and transformed jobs, and increased productivity.[8,9] These new and transformed jobs, will, in addition to technology, problem-solving, and critical thinking skills, require soft skills such as stress tolerance, adaptability, resilience, perseverance, collaboration, and empathy.[8,9] Herein lies the opportunity for employees. The 4IR requires skilled employees to operate or work with its technologies such as AI, IoT, or drones. Thus, in addition to adopting 4IR technologies, companies will need to invest in continuous reskilling and upskilling of their employees to meet the job demands of the changing nature of work. In summary, companies striving to remain competitive in the global market will adopt technologies of the 4IR. Thus, employees will primarily benefit from human capital investments, a no-regrets strategy that equips employees with the skills and competencies required in the future of work.[8] Investing in human capital not only helps employees to retain their current jobs but generates more opportunities for them to find better jobs. Also, employees with high levels of human capital have higher levels of wellbeing.[10]

Challenges for employers and employees in the 4IR

The previous sections focused on the opportunities for both employers and employees in the 4IR. However, these opportunities come with their challenges. One key challenge is the fear that 4IR technologies will lead to significant job losses. This threat was identified by both the National Planning Commission[11] and the Presidential Commission on 4IR.[12] The Presidential Commission on 4IR recommended that South Africa should prioritise the development of human capital to ensure that the 4IR contributes to the "economic and social life of the nation".[12]

Concern that new technologies can cause unemployment is not new. In fact, as far back as 1937, John Maynard Keynes postulated that technological change causes loss of jobs in his technological unemployment theory.[13] To understand what the impact of the 4IR on unemployment will be, one needs to first understand that new technologies can affect employment through displacement and productivity effects. Whereas the displacement effect refers to new technologies directly displacing workers from tasks they were previously performing, the productivity effect refers to the expansion of the demand for labour as a result of new technologies. Despite the myriad academic perspectives on the potential impact of 4IR technologies on employment, there is still no consensus on which of the two labour market effects – displacement or productivity – will dominate in the 4IR.[14] However, based on past industrial revolutions, while in the short-run the displacement effect may dominate, in the long-run, the productivity effect can dominate, leading to new technologies having a positive impact on employment.[14] It is noteworthy that both the short- and long-run outcomes of the adoption of new technologies impact employee mental health through job loss concerns among employees in lower-skill jobs that get automated, and pressure to upskill faster among employees in higher-skill jobs that have increased reliance on new technologies that complement human skills.

Another key challenge to harnessing the opportunities of the 4IR in the workplace is lack of or limited supporting infrastructure for businesses.[11,12] Such infrastructure includes broadband fibre (nationally and internationally, on land and in seas), data centres, wireless technology with emphasis on 5G, computing and storage facilities, and cybersecurity.[12] Unless business has access to high-quality infrastructure to support the adoption of 4IR technologies, South Africa will fail to utilize the 4IR as an opportunity to achieve its Vision2030.[12] Because the challenge of infrastructure to support the adoption of 4IR technologies requires interventions by the government, the recommendations on infrastructure investments by the Presidential Commission on 4IR and the National Planning Committee are very encouraging.

In addition to the fear of job losses and the need for adequate infrastructure to adopt 4IR technologies, businesses need workers (technicians, data scientists, programmers, etc.) with the appropriate skills to support the development, implementation and use of the technologies. According to the National Planning Commission, this is a huge challenge for South Africa because its labour and skills supply was already inadequate for the digital demands of the Third Industrial Revolution. This mismatch was attributed to an oversupply of graduates in humanities and an undersupply of science, technology, engineering, and mathematics (STEM) graduates that resulted in a huge shortage of scientists, engineers, data scientists and specialised software developers and coders.[11] A short-term solution to this skills challenge involves on-the-job reskilling and upskilling to develop an adaptive workforce while a medium-term solution involves developing the school curriculum such that it encourages the take-up of STEM courses, and a long-term solution requires the restructuring of South Africa's human development ecosystem[11,12] that consists of early child development, primary, secondary, and tertiary education, and sector-specific education training. It is noteworthy that on-the-job reskilling and upskilling to develop an adaptive workforce often introduces job stress that requires support for employees through resilience training that equips them with healthy coping strategies. In the absence of such training, employees are often overwhelmed by reskilling and upskilling initiatives which in turn negatively impact their mental health.

Another challenge of the 4IR is that its opportunities are likely to be harnessed differentially across businesses with large businesses investing more in 4IR technologies compared to small, medium, and micro enterprises (SMMEs). Such a development would result in SMMEs falling behind and losing market share which in turn would lead to a market dominated by few very large companies, raising competition concerns. The Presidential Commission on 4IR identified this challenge and recommended that government should incentivise SMMEs to adopt the technologies of the 4IR. According to the National Development Plan, a vibrant SMME sector is important for advancing inclusive growth and development in South Africa.

Employee adaption to 4IR technologies

The COVID-19 pandemic accelerated digitalisation while providing deep insights into the essential role of resilience and adaptability in employees' ability to positively adapt to extensive job and technological disruption.[15] Digitalisation is defined by Gartner's online technology dictionary as the *"use of digital technologies to change a business model and provide new revenue and value-producing opportunities; it is the process of moving to a digital business."* Defined this way, digitalisation can provide useful insights into the possible impact of the adoption of 4IR technologies on employees. Recent studies of digitalisation have identified four factors that influence how employees adapt to the adoption of new technologies: 1) technology acceptance and adoption, 2) perceptions and attitudes toward technological change, 3) skills and training, and 4) workplace adaptability.[15]

- Technology acceptance and adoption – an important factor for technology acceptance and adoption is whether the use of the new technology is voluntary or mandatory. The nature of 4IR technologies suggests that they will be mandatory. In such cases, perceived usefulness and ease-of-use of the technology among employees is important, suggesting the need for employers to invest time in explaining to employees the features of new technology and how these fit in the broader organisational strategy.

- Perceptions and attitudes towards technological change – in general, mere awareness of the 4IR technologies such as AI and robotics, was related to perceptions of job losses, cynicism, depression, reduced career satisfaction and organisational commitment, and increased intentions to leave the organisation among employees.[15] This emphasises the need for organisations to target employee perceptions and attitudes towards technological change as part of their new technology change management strategy.

- Skills and training – willingness to learn new skills, skill level, opportunities for both formal and informal, self-directed, and continuous workplace learning impact how employees adapt to new technologies. This suggests that organisations should target these various elements of skills and training as part of their new technology change management strategy.

- Workplace adaptability – adaptability at work, broadly defined as the ability to *"make cognitive, affective, motivational, and behavioural adaptations when tasks or work demands change"* is important for employees' positive adaptation to new technologies.[15] Workplace adaptability is related to resilience, defined by the American Psychological Association's online dictionary as *"the process and outcome of successfully adapting to difficult or challenging life experiences, especially through mental, emotional, and behavioural flexibility and adjustment to external and internal demands".* Therefore, resilience, as discussed in Chapter 15, a skill that can be developed,[15] is an important psychological resource for an employee's positive adaption to technological change. Finally, confidence to deal with work challenges, establishing work-life balance, and mindset towards current job and professional development helps employees with positive adaption to technological change.[15]

Career capital and the future of work in the 4IR

According to career researchers, one consequence of globalisation, digitalisation, and broad societal and economic shifts is that companies no longer offer individuals jobs and careers for life.[16] Consequently, the responsibility for career management has shifted from the organisation to the employee. Individuals who positively adapt to this changing nature of work experience better career outcomes. This trend will likely be exacerbated over the coming decades by the adoption of 4IR technologies and the changing nature of work. This places pressure on individuals to keep up with a fast-paced and changing work environment and to remain focused on upskilling. This pressure manifests as job stress in the workplace as employers strive to adopt new technologies to keep up with an ever-changing business environment and employees must upskill to enable them to work with the new technologies. As emphasised in Part 1 of this book, with increased exposure to stress, particularly from the workplace, individuals are finding it harder to address their mental health needs.

4IR technologies and the changing nature of work have shifted the types of skills and competencies desired by employers. What skills and competencies are needed to flourish in the future of work? In addition to specialised technical skills in 4IR technologies such as AI, IoT, robotics, and software development, employers are putting growing emphasis on soft skills such as learning agility (i.e., willingness and ability to learn), interpersonal skills, complex problem-solving, and self-management skills such as willingness to be flexible, adaptability, stress tolerance, and resilience.[15,17] A recent exhaustive literature review identified four broad competencies for 4IR that, in combination with deep functional expertise, *"promise to deliver excellence in future jobs, including the ones that might not exist yet".*[18] These four competencies are: human literacy, digital fluency, hyper-learning, systems and design thinking. See Figure 19.2 below. Human literacy is about developing the knowledge and skills to understand oneself and others, and the ability to meaningfully connect with others.[18]

Human literacy	Digital fluency
• Empathy • Communication • Collaboration • Emotional intelligence • Networking & influencing • Cultural agility • Ethics • Confidence	• Data fluency • Technology fluency • Coding • Digital storytelling • Critical consumption of information
Hyper-learning	**Systems & design thinking**
• Fast, continuous learning • Learning, unlearning, and re-learning • Reflecting on learning • Deliberate practice	• Critical thinking and problem-solving • Creativity/ innovation/imagination • Thinking holistically • Agile frameworks • Change management • Entrepreneurship

Figure 19.2: 4IR competencies. Adapted from Jones et.al.[18, p. 6]

Reskilling or upskilling to acquire the 4IR competencies (Figure 19.2) can be quite daunting and stressful. The concept of career capital provides a useful framework for how individuals can harness 4IR competencies to develop long-term employability and generate career success in the future of work. Career capital refers to the individual resources and relationships that have a positive influence on career-related outcomes and consists of three specific career competencies or "ways of knowing" that are essential for career growth: knowing-how, knowing-whom, and knowing-why.[19]

Knowing-how competencies represent the cumulative skills, capabilities, and knowledge that individuals have developed and utilise at work while knowing-whom competencies represent the career-related contacts and social networks that contribute to career success and knowing-why competencies help individuals to make sense of the changing world of work and provide motivation for personal career management.[19] These three ways of knowing complement each other[19] as shown in Figure 19.3. Building career capital helps to mitigate the stresses and lack of future resources in coping in the fast-paced environment and future world of work. This is key in enhancing individual mental health and wellbeing.

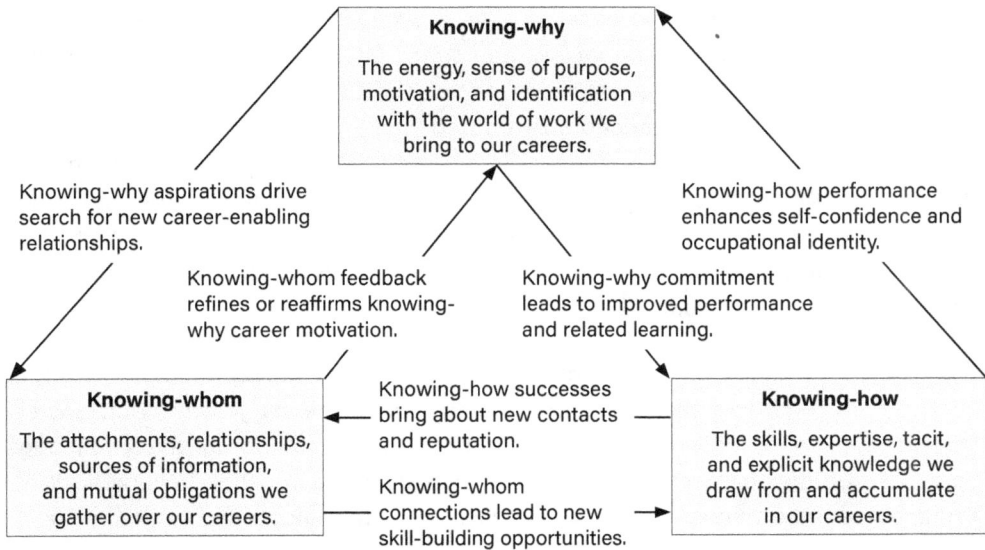

Knowing-why

The energy, sense of purpose, motivation, and identification with the world of work we bring to our careers.

Knowing-why aspirations drive search for new career-enabling relationships.

Knowing-how performance enhances self-confidence and occupational identity.

Knowing-whom feedback refines or reaffirms knowing-why career motivation.

Knowing-why commitment leads to improved performance and related learning.

Knowing-whom

The attachments, relationships, sources of information, and mutual obligations we gather over our careers.

Knowing-how successes bring about new contacts and reputation.

Knowing-whom connections lead to new skill-building opportunities.

Knowing-how

The skills, expertise, tacit, and explicit knowledge we draw from and accumulate in our careers.

Figure 19.3. Three ways of knowing and the accumulation of career capital. Adapted from Inkson & Arthur[19, p. 52]

Mental health and wellbeing, and the future of work in the 4IR

The future of work in the 4IR will likely be a future that includes high levels of employee stress and anxiety. Why? Because even before the COVID-19 pandemic, research was pointing to workers experiencing high levels of stress and anxiety. For example, the World Health Organisation identified stress as the epidemic of the 21st Century with the workplace being the principal source.[20] Also, the 4IR has been referred to as the "emerging age of anxiety" because of the anxiety about job losses and digitalisation.[21] Research has found that adoption of new technologies in the workplace can lead to technostress, defined as stress experienced by an individual as a result of the demands from the new technologies exceeding the individual's available coping resources.[15] Elevated levels of technostress, other work-related stress, and work-related anxiety have a negative impact on employees' mental health and wellbeing which in turn have adverse effects on employee performance and engagement. To better understand why work-related stress and anxiety negatively impact employees' mental health, one must define mental health as well as appreciate the role of work in adult lives.

The American Psychological Association's online dictionary defines mental health as *"a state of mind characterized by emotional wellbeing, good behavioural adjustment, relative freedom from anxiety and disabling symptoms, and a capacity to establish constructive relationships and cope with the ordinary demands and stresses of life"* and wellbeing as *"a state of happiness and contentment, with low levels of distress, overall good physical and mental health and outlook, or good quality of life".* These definitions, together with concepts discussed earlier in the book, suggest a link between mental health and wellbeing. Employment occupies central place in adult lives and shapes individuals' identities.[22] That employment and mental health are integrally linked is highlighted by research that found that satisfying employment is linked to good mental health, whereas underemployment and unemployment are linked to poor mental health.[22]

Extant research on the opportunities and challenges presented by the 4IR is unequivocal regarding the need for proactive response by government, society, organisations and individuals to ensure positive adaptation to the challenges. Since part of this chapter's focus is on the individual, the question becomes: "What evidence-based approaches can individuals adopt to mitigate the negative effects of the 4IR challenges on their mental health and wellbeing?" Positive psychology research suggests that positive psychology interventions (PPIs) may mitigate the disruptive impact of the adoption of 4IR technologies in the workplace on employees. PPIs are intentional activities such as expressing gratitude, practising kindness, or pursuing hope and meaning that are designed to improve wellbeing by emulating the behaviours of people with high levels of wellbeing.[23]

Researchers have investigated a variety of PPIs by prompting people to deliberately practise: expressing gratitude or appreciation, counting blessings, performing kind acts, cultivating optimism, enhancing close relationships, cultivating strengths, visualising ideal future selves, and meditating on positive feelings toward the self and others. Research on PPIs has shown that they work.[23] A reasonable question that follows is, "How do PPIs work?" Prompting people to deliberately practise PPIs increases their positive emotions, positive thoughts, positive behaviours, and satisfaction with basic psychological needs, which, in turn, increases their wellbeing.[24] One of the strengths of PPIs is that they are short, self-administered, and cost-effective.

Conclusion

The research findings presented in this chapter indicate that although the 4IR presents opportunities to employers and employees, there is also a growing realisation of its challenges. The COVID-19 pandemic accelerated digitalisation while providing deep insights into the challenges associated with extensive job and technological disruption as well as the need for both employers and employees to positively adapt to such challenges. The assertion of this chapter is this: given the centrality of employment to adult lives, the changing nature of work, the new skills and competencies needed, and the fear of job losses, challenges of the 4IR must be anticipated and prepared for in advance so that employees can adapt positively to these challenges. This is important for employee mental health and wellbeing. Even before the COVID-19 pandemic, across the world, employee mental health had been deteriorating, putting increased concerns on employee wellbeing and performance. The 4IR presents huge additional threats to global employee mental health due to work-related stress and anxiety, pressure to reskill and upskill, and fear of job losses. The concept of career capital provides a useful framework for employees to use as they continuously reskill and upskill to meet the ever-increasing skills requirements of the future of work in the 4IR. This suggests that society must rethink the concept of work–life balance, perhaps as work–life–learn integration. Finally, PPIs provide employees and employers with evidence-based approaches to increase the wellbeing of employees, which, in turn, would help them to positively adapt to the challenges of the 4IR.

Resources available for support

Your dedicated Employee Wellness Programme toll-free number

PsychMatters Centre

0114503576 /0629758442

www.psychmatters.co.za | info@psychmatters.co.za

Suicide Crisis Line

0800 567 567 SADAG Mental Health Line 011 234 4837

Akeso Psychiatric Response Unit 24 Hour

0861 435 787

POWA

076 694 5911 | 0115916803 | info@powa.co.za

Tears Foundation

0105905920

Cipla 24hr Mental Health Helpline

0800 456 789

References

Chapter 1 (Bibliography)

Allison, S. (2014). *The Responsive Organization: Coping with new technology and disruption. Forbes*. Retrieved from: https://www.forbes.com/sites/scottallison/2014/02/10/the-responsive-organization-how-to-cope-with-technology-and-disruption/?sh=5f33045c3cdd

Bever, L. (2018). *Teens Are Daring Each Other to Eat Tide Pods. We don't need to tell you it's a bad idea. Health. The Washington Post*. Retrieved from: https://www.washingtonpost.com/news/to-your-health/wp/2018/01/13/teens-are-daring-each-other-to-eat-tide-pods-we-dont-need-to-tell-you-thats-a-bad-idea/

Bolan, P. (2012). *Sinking of the Titanic. National Geographic Resource Library*. Retrieved from: https://www.nationalgeographic.org/media/sinking-of-the-titanic/

Bridges, W. (1991). *Managing transitions: Making the most of change*. Massachusetts: Addison-Wesley.

Champy, J. & Hammer, M. (1993). *Reengineering the Corporation: A Manifesto for Business Revolution*. New York: Harper Collins.

Elliot, S. (2012). A Product To Add Sparkle and Pop To Laundry Day. *The New York Times*. Retrieved from: https://www.nytimes.com/2012/02/15/business/media/procter-gamble-introduces-one-step-laundry-product.html

Ewenstein, B., Smith, W., & Sologar, A. (2015). Changing Change Management. *McKinsey*. Retrieved from: https://www.mckinsey.com/featured-insights/leadership/changing-change-management

Glassman, A. & Temin, M. (2016). *Millions Saved: New Cases of Proven Success in Global Health*. Washington, DC: Center for Global Development.

Li, C. (2019). *The Disruption Mindset: Why some organizations transform while others fail*. Washington: Idea Press Publishing.

McCarthy, C. (2018). *Why Teenagers Eat Tide Pods. Children's Health. Harvard Health Publishing*. Retrieved from: https://www.health.harvard.edu/blog/why-teenagers-eat-tide-pods-2018013013241

Meth, J. (2019). *The Tragic Side of Tide Pods*. Retrieved from: https://fortune.com/longform/tide-pod-poisoning-injuries-epidemic/

National Geographic. (2019). *How the Titanic was lost and found.* (2019). *National Geographic.* Retrieved from: https://www.nationalgeographic.com/culture/article/titanic-lost-found

Savage, M. (2015). Five Safety Lessons Learned from the Sinking of the Titanic. *EHSToday*. Retrieved from: https://www.ehstoday.com/safety/article/21916859/five-safety-lessons-learned-from-the-sinking-of-the-titanic

Simpson, J.A., Weiner, E S.C., & Oxford University Press. (1989*). The Oxford English Dictionary*. Oxford: Clarendon Press.

Tasler, N. (2017). Stop Using the Excuse "Organizational Change Is Hard". Change Management. *Harvard Business Review*. Retrieved from: https://hbr.org/2017/07/stop-using-the-excuse-organizational-change-is-hard

The Walt Disney Company. (2021). *The Walt Disney Company Reports: Second Quarter and Six Months Earnings for Fiscal 2021*. Retrieved from: https://thewaltdisneycompany.com/app/uploads/2021/05/q2-fy21-earnings.pdf

Thomas, O. (2012). Why Apple Cannibalized The iPod. *Business Insider*. Retrieved from: https://www.businessinsider.com/apple-ipod-cannibalization-2012-10?IR=T

Tikannen, A. (2021). Timeline of the *Titanic*'s Final Hours. *Britannica*. https://www.britannica.com/story/timeline-of-the-titanics-final-hours

Vateesatokit, P., Hughes, B. & Ritthphakdee, B. (2000). Thailand: winning battles, but the war's far from over. *Tobacco Control*, 9(1): 122-127. Retrieved from: https://tobaccocontrol.bmj.com/content/9/2/122

What's on Disney Plus. (2021). *Disney to Close 100 TV Channels in 2021*. Retrieved from: https://whatsondisneyplus.com/disney-to-close-100-tv-channels-in-2021/

Chapter 2

1. Balfour, T.G., Govender, V.G., Baloyi, K. (2016). *The Story of HIV, AIDS and TB in the Mining Industry in Southern Africa.* In B. Ngcaweni. (2016). *Sizonqoba! Outliving AIDS in Southern Africa*. Pretoria: Africa Institute of South Africa. p. 302 – 326.

2. United Nations. (2015). *Sustainable Development Goals* 2015. Department of Economic and Social Affairs. Available from: https://sustainabledevelopment.un.org/content/documents/1758GSDR%202015%20Advance%20Unedited%20Version.pdf

3. National Institute for Drug Abuse. (2020). *Do people with mental illness and substance use disorders use tobacco more often?* Available from: https://www.drugabuse.gov/publications/research-reports/tobacco-nicotine-e-cigarettes/do-people-mental-illness-substance-use-disorders-use-tobacco-more-often [cited 10 March 2021].

4. World Health Organization. (2021). *Noncommunicable diseases*. Available from: https://www.who.int/health-topics/noncommunicable-diseases#tab=tab_1

5. Goetzel, R.Z., Roemer, E.C., Holingue, C., Fallin, M.D., McCleary, K., Eaton, W., Agnew, J., Azocar, F., Ballard, D., Bartlett, J., Braga, M., Conway, H., Crighton, K.A., Frank, R., Jinnett, K., Keller-Greene, D., Rauch, S., Safeer, R., Saporito, D., Schill, A., Shern, D., Strecher, V., Wald, P., Wang, P. & Mattingly, C.R. (2018). Mental Health in the Workplace: A Call to Action Proceedings From the Mental Health in the Workplace–Public Health Summit. *Journal of Occupational and Environmental Medicine, 60*(4): p. 322-330.

6. Patel, V., Saxena, S. & Lund, C.E.A. (2018). The Lancet Commission on global mental health and sustainable development. *Lancet, 392*(10157): p. 1553-1598.

7. Centers for Disease Control and Prevention. (2020). *Depression.* Available from: https://www.cdc.gov/workplacehealthpromotion/health-strategies/depression/.

8. Burton, J. (2010). *WHO Healthy Framework and Model: background, supporting literature and practices.* Geneva, Switzerland: World Health Organization.

9. World Health Organization. (2019). *Burnout an occupational phenomemon*. Available from: https://www.who.int/news/item/28-05-2019-burn-out-an-occupational-phenomenon-international-classification-of-diseases.

10. World Health Organization. (2005). *Mental health policies and programmes in the workplace*. Available: https://apps.who.int/iris/handle/10665/205530

11. Ronald Loeppke, R., Taitel, M., Haufle, V., Parry, T., Kessler, R.C. & Jinnett,K. (2009). Health and productivity as a business strategy: a multiemployer study. *J Occup Environ Med, 51*(4): p. 411-28.

12. Govender, V.G. (2020). *Webinar: COVID-19 and occupational stress.* Johannesburg Department of Family Medicine. 17 April 2020; Available from: https://youtu.be/IXzYW-A9fF4.

13. Putnam, K. & McKibbin, L. (2004). Managing workplace depression: an untapped opportunity for occupational health professionals. *Aaohn j, 52*(3): p. 122-9; quiz 130-1.

14. National Institute for Occupational Safety and Health. (2021). *Hierarchy of Controls Applied to NIOSH Total Worker Health®*. Available from: https://www.cdc.gov/niosh/twh/guidelines.html.

15. International Standards Organisation. (2021). *SO/FDIS 45003. Occupational health and safety management – Psychological health and safety at work – Guidelines for managing psychosocial risks*. Available from: https://www.iso.org/obp/ui/#iso:std:iso:45001:ed-1:v1:en

16. United Nations. (2020). *Policy Brief: COVID-19 and the Need for Action on Mental Health*. Available from: https://unsdg.un.org/sites/default/files/2020-05/UN-Policy-Brief-COVID-19-and-mental-health.pdf

17. World Health Organization. (2003). *Planning and budgeting to deliver mental health services*. Geneva: Who.

18. The National Department of Health. (2014). *The National Mental Health Policy Framework and Strategic Plan 2013-2020*. 2014: South Africa.

19. Govender, V.G. *Stress in nurses working with HIV/AIDS patients*. 1999, University of Witwatersrand: Johannesburg, South Africa.

20. Wade, K. and E.P. Simon, Survival bonding: a response to stress and work with AIDS. *Soc Work Health Care*, 1993. 19(1): p. 77-89.

21. Smit, S. (2020). *COVID-19 Health Workers accused of 'carelessness'*. M.a. Guardian, Editor.

22. Harvard Health Publishing. (2010). *Mental health problems in the workplace*. Available from: https://www.health.harvard.edu/newsletter_article/mental-health-problems-in-the-workplace.

Chapter 3

1. World Health Organisation. (2001). *Mental disorders affect one in four people*. Retrieved from: http://www.who.int/whr/2001/media_centre/press_release/en/

2. Lund, C. (2015). *Mental health under-budgeting undermining SA's economy*. Retrieved from: http://www.scielo.org.za/scielo.php?script=sci_arttext&pid=S0256-95742015000100005

3. World Health Organisation. (2007). *WHO-AIMS Report on Mental Health System in South Africa*. Retrieved from: https://www.who.int/mental_health/evidence/south_africa_who_aims_report.pdf

4. Lund, C. (2015). *Mental health under-budgeting undermining SA's economy*. Retrieved from: http://www.scielo.org.za/scielo.php?script=sci_arttext&pid=S0256-95742015000100005

5. Mall, S., Lund, C., Vilagut, G., Alonzo, J., Williams, D.R., Stein, D.J. (2014). Days out of role due to mental and physical illness in the South African stress and health study. *Social Psychiatry and Psychiatric Epidemiology, 50*(3): 461-8.

6. Watson, R. (2017). *Megatrends and Technologies 2017-2050*. Retrieved from: https://www.nowandnext.com/PDF/Mega%20Trends%20and%20Technologies%202017-2050%20(Web).png

7. ICAS data. (2019). Manifestation of mental health disorders in the workplace. Available from https://www.icas.co.za

8. Sawaf, A., Gabrielle, R. (2014). *Sacred Commerce: A Blueprint for a New Humanity (2nd Edition)*. Ojai, CA: EQ Enterprises. p. 24-28.

9. Tromp, B. (2015). *Everyone wins with healthy fourth bottom line*. Retrieved from: https://www.iol.co.za/business-report/opinion/everyone-wins-with-healthy-fourth-bottom-line-1835405

10. Wellable. (2021). (2021). *Employee Wellness Industry Trends Report.* Retrieved from: https://resources.wellable.co/2021-employee-wellness-industry-trends-report#:~:text=Rising%20Star,wellness%20passport%20(63%25)%20programs.
11. Ibid.
12. Smith, D.C., Leinberger, C., Katsikakis, D., Rodriguez, M., Rockey, R. & Bitner, D. (2021). *Future Workplace* – 11 March 2021 Report. Cushman & Wakefiled. Retrieved from: https://www.cushmanwakefield.com/en/insights/covid-19/the-future-of-workplace

Chapter 4

1. Prideaux, E. (2021). *How to heal the 'mass trauma' of COVID-19.* Retrieved from: https://www.bbc.com/future/article/20210203-after-the-covid-19-pandemic-how-will-we-heal
2. Yong, E. (2021). *What Happens When Americans Can Finally Exhale. The pandemic's mental wounds are still wide open.* Retrieved from: https://www.theatlantic.com/health/archive/2021/05/pandemic-trauma-summer/618934/
3. Mari, J., & Oquendo, M.A. (2020). Mental health consequences of COVID-19: the next global pandemic. *Trends in Psychiatry and Psychotherapy, 42*(9).
4. Elizarrarás-Rivas, J., Vargas-Mendoza, J.E., Mayoral-García, M., Matadamas-Zarate, C., Elizarrarás-Cruz, A., Taylor, M., et al. Psychological response of family members of patients hospitalised for influenza A/H1N1 in Oaxaca, Mexico. *BMC Psychiatry, 10*(1), 104.
5. Brooks, S.K., Webster, R.K., Smith, L.E., Woodland, L., Wessely, S., Greenberg, N., & Rubin, G.J. (2020). The psychological impact of quarantine and how to reduce it: rapid review of the evidence. *Lancet, 395*(10227): 912-920.
6. Terhakopian, A., & Benedek, D.M. (2007). Hospital disaster preparedness: mental and behavioral health interventions for infectious disease outbreaks and bioterrorism incidents. *Am J Disaster Med, 2*(1): 43–50
7. Mari, J., & Oquendo, M.A. (2020). Mental health consequences of COVID-19: the next global pandemic. *Trends in Psychiatry and Psychotherapy, 42*(9).
8. Howard, J., & Kane, A. (2020). *CDC study sheds new light on mental health crisis linked to coronavirus pandemic. CNN.* Retrieved from: https://edition.cnn.com/2020/08/13/health/mental-health-coronavirus-pandemic-cdc-study-wellness/index.html
9. Mari, J., & Oquendo, M.A. (2020). Mental health consequences of COVID-19: the next global pandemic. *Trends in Psychiatry and Psychotherapy, 42*(9).
10. Forte, G., Favieri, F., Tambelli, R., Casagrande, M. (2020). COVID-19 Pandemic in the Italian Population: Validation of a Post-Traumatic Stress Disorder Questionnaire and Prevalence of PTSD Symptomatology. Int J Environ Res Public Health. 2020, *17*(11): 4151.
11. Hawryluck, L, Gold, WL, Robinson, S, Pogorski, S, Galea, S, Styra R. (2004). SARS controland psychological effects of quarantine. Toronto, Canada. *Emerg Infect Dis.* 2004,10: 1206-12.
12. Howard, J., & Kane, A. (2020). CDC study sheds new light on mental health crisis linked to coronavirus pandemic. CNN. Retrieved from: https://edition.cnn.com/2020/08/13/health/mental-health-coronavirus-pandemic-cdc-study-wellness/index.html
13. Reger, M.A., Stanley, I.H.,& Joiner, T.E. (2020). Suicide mortality and coronavirus disease 2019: A perfect storm? *JAMA Psychiatry, 77*(11). doi: 10.1001/jamapsychiatry.2020.1060.
14. Prideaux, E. (2021). *How to heal the 'mass trauma' of COVID-19.* Retrieved from: https://www.bbc.com/future/article/20210203-after-the-covid-19-pandemic-how-will-we-heal
15. Trautmann S, Rehm J, & Wittchen H-U. (2016). The economic costs of mental disorders. Do our societies react appropriately to the burden of mental disorders? *EMBO Rep, 17*(9): 1245-9.

16. Lai, J., Ma, S., Wang, Y., Cai, Z., Hu, J., Wei, N., et al. (2020). Factors associated with mental health outcomes among health care workers exposed to coronavirus disease 2019. *Jama Network*, 3(3): e203976. Retrieved from: https://jamanetwork.com/journals/jamanetworkopen/fullarticle/2763229

17. Berinato, S. (2020). That Discomfort You're Feeling Is Grief. *Harvard Business Review*. Retrieved from: https://hbr.org/2020/03/that-discomfort-youre-feeling-is-grief

18. Ibid.

19. Holmes, M.R., Rentrope, C.R., Korsch-Williams, A. *et al.* Impact of COVID-19 Pandemic on Post-traumatic Stress, Grief, Burnout, and Secondary Trauma of Social Workers in the United States. *Clin Soc Work J* (2021). https://doi.org/10.1007/s10615-021-00795-y

20. Hirschberger, G. (2018). Collective trauma and the social construction of meaning. *Frontiers in Psychology, 9*, 1441. https://doi.org/10.3389/fpsyg.2018.01441.

21. Prideaux, E. (2021). *How to heal the 'mass trauma' of COVID-19*. Retrieved from: https://www.bbc.com/future/article/20210203-after-the-covid-19-pandemic-how-will-we-heal

22. Ibid.

23. Greenberg, N., & Rafferty, L. (2021). Post-traumatic stress disorder in the aftermath of COVID-19 pandemic. *World Psychiatry, 1*(1): 53-54. https://doi.org/10.1002/wps.20838

24. Lund, C. (2015). *Mental health under-budgeting undermining SA's economy*. Retrieved from: http://www.scielo.org.za/scielo.php?script=sci_arttext&pid=S0256-95742015000100005

25. Yuan, K., Gong, YM., Liu, L. et al. (2021). Prevalence of posttraumatic stress disorder after infectious disease pandemics in the twenty-first century, including COVID-19: a meta-analysis and systematic review. *Mol Psychiatry*. Retrieved from: https://www.nature.com/articles/s41380-021-01036-x

26. Bo, H., Li, W., Yang, Y., Wang, Y, Zhang, Q., Cheung, T., W, X., & Xiang, Y. (2020). Posttraumatic stress symptoms and attitude toward crisis mental health services among clinically stable patients with COVID-19 in China. Psychol Med, *51*(6): 1-2.

27. Davydow, D.S., Gifford, J.M., Desai, S.V., Needham, D.M., & Bienenu, O.J. (2008). Posttraumatic stress disorder in general intensive care unit survivors: a systematic review. *Gen Hosp Psychiatry, 30*(5): 421-34.

28. Yuan, K., Gong, YM., Liu, L. et al. (2021). Prevalence of posttraumatic stress disorder after infectious disease pandemics in the twenty-first century, including COVID-19: a meta-analysis and systematic review. *Mol Psychiatry*. Retrieved from: https://www.nature.com/articles/s41380-021-01036-x

29. Alderton, M. (n.d.). *PTSD & Brain Fog*. Retrieved from: https://traumapractice.co.uk/ptsd-brain-fog/

30. Williamson, V., Stevelink, S.A.M., & Greenberg, N. (2018). Occupational moral injury and mental health: Systematic Review and Meta-analysis. *Br J Psychiatry, 212*(6): 339-46.

31. Greenberg, N., & Rafferty, L. (2021). Post-traumatic stress disorder in the aftermath of COVID-19 pandemic. *World Psychiatry, 1*(1): 53-54. https://doi.org/10.1002/wps.20838

32. Prideaux, E. (2021*). How to heal the 'mass trauma' of COVID-19*. Retrieved from: https://www.bbc.com/future/article/20210203-after-the-covid-19-pandemic-how-will-we-heal

33. Miller, B.J., & Berger, S. (2019). *A Beginner's Guide to the End: How to Live Life to the Full and Die a Good Death.* London, UK: Quercus Publishing.

34. Yong, E. (2021). *What Happens When Americans Can Finally Exhale. The pandemic's mental wounds are still wide open*. Retrieved from: https://www.theatlantic.com/health/archive/2021/05/pandemic-trauma-summer/618934/

35. Thomas, N., & Romano, S. (2020). *A 'second wave' of mental health devastation due to COVID-19 is imminent, experts say*. Retrieved from: https://www.wxii12.com/article/second-wave-of-mental-health-devastation-due-to-covid-19-is-imminent-experts-say/34363974#

36. Prideaux, E. (2021). *How to heal the 'mass trauma' of COVID-19*. Retrieved from: https://www.bbc.com/future/article/20210203-after-the-covid-19-pandemic-how-will-we-heal

37. Yuan, K., Gong, YM., Liu, L. et al. (2021). Prevalence of posttraumatic stress disorder after infectious disease pandemics in the twenty-first century, including COVID-19: a meta-analysis and systematic review. *Mol Psychiatry*. Retrieved from: https://www.nature.com/articles/s41380-021-01036-x

38. Tucker, P. & Czapla, C.S. (2021). Post-COVID Stress Disorder: Another Emerging Consequence of the Global Pandemic. *Psychiatric Times*, *38*(1). Retrieved from: https://www.psychiatrictimes.com/view/post-covid-stress-disorder-emerging-consequence-global-pandemic

39. Ibid.

40. Czeisler, M.É., Lane, R.I., Petrosky, E., et al. (2020). Mental Health, Substance Use, and Suicidal Ideation During the COVID-19 Pandemic. *Centers for Disease Control and Prevention, 69*(32): 1049–1057.

41. Prideaux, E. (2021). *How to heal the 'mass trauma' of COVID-19*. Retrieved from: https://www.bbc.com/future/article/20210203-after-the-covid-19-pandemic-how-will-we-heal

42. Wellable. (2021). 2021 *Employee Wellness Industry Trends Report*. Retrieved from: https://resources.wellable.co/2021-employee-wellness-industry-trends-report#:~:text=Rising%20Star,wellness%20passport%20(63%25)%20programs.

Chapter 5

1. Berne, E. (1964). *Games People Play*. London, UK: Penguin Random House.
2. Stone, D., Patten, B. & Heen, S. (1999). *Difficult Conversations: How to Discuss What Matters Most*. New York, Portfolio Penguin.

Chapter 6

1. Houston, E. (2020). *The importance of positive relationships in the workplace*. Available from: https://positivepsychology.com/positive-relationships-workplace/

2. Priesemuth, M. (2020). Time's up for toxic workplaces. *Harvard Business Review*. Available from: https://hbr.org/2020/06/times-up-for-toxic-workplaces

3. Huff, C. (2021). Employers are increasing support for mental health. *APA Monitor, 52*(1), 84. Available fom: https://www.apa.org/monitor/2021/01/trends-employers-support

4. Slattery, A., & McCrary-Ruiz-Esparza, E. (2019). 13 Signs of a toxic workplace and when it becomes illegal. *In Her Sight*. Available from: https://www.inhersight.com/blog/insight-commentary/toxic-work-environment

5. Bennett, R.J., Marasi,S., & Locklear, L. (2018). *Workplace Deviance*. In *Oxford Research Encyclopedia of Business and Management*, 1-27. Available from: https://www.researchgate.net/profile/Shelly_Marasi/publication/323626584_Workplace_Deviance/links/5b2c09780f7e9b0df5ba4d58/Workplace-Deviance.pdf

6. Priesemuth, M. (2020). Time's up for toxic workplaces. *Harvard Business Review*. https://hbr.org/2020/06/times-up-for-toxic-workplaces.

7. Akhtar, R. (2021). *Feedback is a force for change*. Deeper Signals. Available from: https://www.deepersignals.com/blog/feedback-is-a-force-for-change

8. Hogan, R. (2007). *Personality and the fate of organizations.* Mahwah, NJ: Lawrence Erlbaum Associates.

9. Chamorro-Premuzic, T. (2020). *The self-awareness fix for leadership development problems.* Deeper Signals. Available from: https://www.deepersignals.com/blog/the-self-awareness-fix-for-leadership-development-problems

10. Porath, C. L., & Gerbasi, A. (2015). Does civility pay? *Organizational Dynamics, 44*(4), 281–286. Available from: https://doi.org/10.1016/j.orgdyn.2015.09.005

11. Porath, C. L. (2015). The costs of bad behavior: And what leaders and organizations can do to manage it [Editorial]. *Organizational Dynamics, 44*(4), 254–257.

12. Williamson, M.K., & Perumal, K. (2021). Exploring the consequences of person–environment misfit in the workplace: A qualitative study. *SA Journal of Industrial Psychology/SA Tydskrif vir Bedryfsielkunde, 47*(0), a1798. https://doi.org/10.4102/sajip.v47i0.1798

13. Pendell, R. (2020, December 11). 7 Gallup workplace insights: What we learned in 2020. *Gallup.* https://www.gallup.com/workplace/327518/gallup-workplace-insights-learned-2020.aspx

14. Baccarella, S. V., Wagner, T. F., Kietzman, J. H., & McCarthy, I. P. (2018, August). Social Media? It's serious! Understanding the dark side of social media. *European Management Journal, 36*(4), 431-438. https://doi.org/10.1016/j.emj.2018.07.002

15. Nyilasy, G. (2019). Fake news: When the dark side of persuasion takes over. *International Journal of Advertising, 38*(2), 336-342, DOI: 10.1080/02650487.2019.1586210

16. Swanson, C. (2019, August 22). Are you enabling a toxic culture without realizing it? *Harvard Business Review.* https://hbr.org/2019/08/are-you-enabling-a-toxic-culture-without-realizing-it

17. Lovelace, J. B. (2013, April 11-13). *Destructive leadership: A holistic view for minimizing its toxic influence.* Society for Industrial and Organizational Psychology (SIOP) Annual Conference, Houston, Texas.

18. Curnow-Chavez, A. (2018, April 10). 4 Ways to deal with a toxic co-worker. *Harvard Business Review.* https://hbr.org/2018/04/4-ways-to-deal-with-a-toxic-coworker

19. McKee, A. (2019, April 29). Keep your company's toxic culture from infecting your team. *Harvard Business Review.* https://hbr.org/2019/04/keep-your-companys-toxic-culture-from-infecting-your-team

20. Tararukhina, O. (2020). Workplace relationships as a symptom of organizational culture and a lever for culture transformation. In C. Pracana, & M. Wang (Eds.), *Psychological Applications and Trends* (399- 403). InScience Press.

21. VandenBos, G.R. (2007). *APA Dictionary of Psychology.* Washington, DC: American Psychological Association.

22. Hogan, R. (2013, April 11-13). *How to define destructive leadership.* Society for Industrial and Organizational Psychology (SIOP) Annual Conference, Houston, Texas.

23. Hogan, J., Hogan, R., & Kaiser, R. B. (2011). Management derailment. In S. Zedeck (Ed.), *APA handbooks in psychology®. APA handbook of industrial and organizational psychology, Vol. 3. Maintaining, expanding, and contracting the organization* (p. 555–575). American Psychological Association. https://doi.org/10.1037/12171-015

24. Kaiser, R. B., LeBreton, J. M., & Hogan, J. (2015). The dark side of personality and extreme leader behavior. *Applied Psychology: An International Review, 64*(1), 55-92.

25. Nei, K. S., Foster, J. L., Ness, A. M., & Nei, D. S. (2018, March). Rule breakers and attention seekers: Personality predictors of integrity and accountability in leaders. *International Journal of Selection and Assessment, 26*(1), 17-26.

26. Padilla, A., Hogan, R., & Kaiser, R. B. (2007). The toxic triangle: Destructive leaders, susceptible followers, and conducive environments. *The Leadership Quarterly, 18,* 176-194. https://doi.org/10.1016/j.leaqua.2007.03.001

27. Harms, P. D., Spain, S. M., & Hannah, S. T. (2011). Leadership development and the dark side of personality. *The Leadership Quarterly, 22,* 495-509. https://doi.org/10.1016/j.leaqua.2011.04.007

28. Landay, K., Harms, P. D., & Credé, M. (2019). Shall we serve the dark lords? A meta-analytic review of psychopathy and leadership. *Journal of Applied Psychology, 104*(1), 183-196.

29. Hare, R. D. (1993). *Without conscience – The disturbing worlds of the psychopaths among us.* The Guildford Press.

30. Ajaikumar, N. (2020, October 18). The role of self-awareness in managing our extreme tendencies. *Deeper Signals.* https://www.deepersignals.com/blog/the-role-of-self-awareness-in-managing-our-extreme-tendencies

31. Bar-On, R. (2000). Emotional and social intelligence: Insights from the Emotional Quotient Inventory. In R. Bar-On & J. D. A. Parker (Eds.), *The handbook of emotional intelligence: Theory, development, assessment, and application at home, school, and in the workplace* (p. 363–388). Jossey-Bass.

32. Middleton, J., Buboltz, W. C., & Sopon, B. (2015, September). The relationship between psychological reactance and emotional intelligence. *The Social Science Journal, 52*(2), 542-549. https://doi.org/10.1016/j.soscij.2015.08.002

33. Staglin, G. K. (2020, December 4). 5 things we learned about mental health in the workplace in 2020. *World Economic Forum.* https://www.weforum.org/agenda/2020/12/5-things-we-learned-about-mental-health-in-the-workplace-in-2020/

34. Fuhrmeister, K., & Ferrell, B. (2021). *The added value of dark personality for selection.* JVR Psychometrics.

35. Van Nieuwerburgh, C. (2020, November 4). 6 Evidenced-based ways to look after your mental health during a second lockdown. *World Economic Forum.* https://www.weforum.org/agenda/2020/11/covid19-lockdown-wellness-mental-health-psychological

36. MacDonald, A. (2020). Nine leadership lessons 2020 gave us. *MIT Sloan Management Review.* https://sloanreview.mit.edu/article/nine-leadership-lessons-2020-gave-us/

37. Sanchez-Burks, J., Bradley, C., & Greer, L. (2020, December 16). How leaders can optimize teams' emotional landscapes. *MIT Sloan Management Review.* https://sloanreview.mit.edu/article/how-leaders-can-optimize-teams-emotional-landscapes/?og=Home+Tiled

38. Charan, R., Drotter, S., & Noel, J. (2011). *The leadership pipeline: How to build the leadership powered company.* Jossey-Bass.

39. Petrie, K., Joyce, S., Tan, L., Henderson, M., Johnson, A., Nguyen, H., Modini, M., Growth, M., Glozier, N., & Harvey, S. B. (2018). A framework to create more mentally healthy workplaces: A viewpoint. *Australian & New Zealand Journal of Psychiatry, 52*(1), 15-23. https://doi.org/10.1177/0004867417726174

Chapter 7

1. Morse, G., Salyers, M.P., Rollins, A.L., Monroe-DeVita, M. & Pfahler, C. (2012). Burnout in Mental Health Services: A Review of the Problem and Its Remediation. *Administration and Policy in Mental Health and Mental Health Services Research, 39*: 341–352. Available from: https://doi.org/10.1007/s10488-011-0352-1.

2. Rowe, D.S. (2012). *The stress burden: strategies for management.* Nevada RNformation, *21*(12): 12.
3. Aumayr-Pintar, C., Cerf, C., & Parent-Thirion, A. (2018). *Burnout in the workplace: A review of data and policy responses in the EU.* Eurofound. Available from: https://www. eurofound.europa.eu/sites/default/files/ef_publication/field_ef_document/ef18047en. pdf
4. World Health Orgnisation (WHO). (2019). *Burn-out an "occupational phenomenon":* International Classification of Diseases. Department News. Available from: https:// www.who.int/news/item/28-05-2019-burnout-an-occupational-phenomenon-international-classification-of-diseases
5. Taris T.W. (2006). Is there a relationship between burnout and objective performance? A critical review of 16 studies. *Work & Stress, 20*(4):316 – 334.
6. Corrigan P.W. (1990). Consumer satisfaction with institutional and community care. *Community Mental Health Journal, 26*(2):151–165.
7. Morse, G., Salyers, M.P., Rollins, A.L., Monroe-DeVita, M., & Pfahler, C. (2012). Burnout in Mental Services: A Review of the Problem and its Remediation. *Adm Policy Ment Health, 39*(5): 341–352.
8. International Labour Organisation. (2016). *Workplace Stress: a collective challenge.* Available from: https://www.ilo.org/wcmsp5/groups/public/---ed_protect/---protrav/---safework/documents/publication/wcms_466547.pdf
9. Stalker C, Harvey C. Partnerships for Children and Families Project. Wilfrid Laurier University; 2002. *Professional burnout: A review of theory, research, and prevention.* [Google Scholar]
10. Ahola K., Honkonen T., Isometsä E., Kalimo R., Nykyri E., Aromaa A., & Lönnqvist J. (2005). The relationship between job-related burnout and depressive disorders – results from the Finnish Health 2000 Study. *Journal of Affective Disorders, 88*(1):55–62.
11. Sora, B., De Cuyper, N., Caballer, A., Peiró, J.M., & De Witte, H. (2013). Outcomes of Job Insecurity Climate: The Role of Climate Strength. *Applied Psychology: An International Review.* 62(3), 382-405.
12. Peterson, U., Demerouti, E., Bergström, G., Samuelsson, M., Åsberg,. M., Nygren, Å. (2008). Burnout and physical and mental health among Swedish healthcare workers. *Journal of Advanced Nursing, 62*(1): 84–95.
13. Khasne, R.W., Dhakulkar, B.S., Mahajan H.C., & Kulkarni, A.P. (2020). Burnout among Healthcare Workers during COVID-19 Pandemic in India: Results of a Questionnaire-based Survey. *Appl. Psychol.*
14. Trumello C., Bramanti M., & Ballarotto G., et.al. (2020). Psychological Adjustment of Healthcare Workers in Italy during the COVID-19 Pandemic: Differences in Stress, Anxiety, Depression, Burnout, Secondary Trauma, and Compassion Satisfaction between Frontline and Non-Frontline Professionals. *Int J Environ Res Public Health, 17*(22): 8358.
15. Statistics South Africa. (2020). *Quarterly Labour Force Survey Quarter 2.* Available from: http://www.statssa.gov.za/publications/P0211/P02112ndQuarter2020.pdf
16. Listen Notes. (2019). *Nathan Rogerson – Millennial Burn Out.* Available from: https:// www.listennotes.com/podcasts/management-tips/nathan-rogerson-millennial-Ob8Y2fVcha6/.
17. Peeters, M.C.W., Montgomery, A.J., Bakker, A.B., & Schaufeli, W.B. (2005). Balancing Work and Home: How Job and Home Demands Are Related to Burnout. International Journal of Stress Management, 12(1): 43–61. https://doi.org/10.1037/1072-5245.12.1.43

18. Karkoulian, S., Srour, J., & Sinan, T.A. (2016). Gender perspective on work-life balance, perceived stress, and locus of control. *Journal of Business Research. 69*(11), 4918-4923.
19. Giattino, C., Ortiz-Ospina, E., Roser, M. (2020). *Working Hours. Our World in Data*. Available from: https://ourworldindata.org/working-hours#annual-working-hours-since-1950
20. International Labour Organization (ILO). (2020). *The Leading source of labour statistics*. Available from: https://www.ilo.org/ilostat/faces/oracle/webcenter/portalapp/pagehierarchy/Page27.jspx
21. Deloitte. (2018). *Workplace Burnout Survey: Burnout without borders*. Available from: https://www2.deloitte.com/us/en/pages/about-deloitte/articles/burnout-survey.html
22. Samra, J., Gilbert, M., Shain M., Bilsker, D., & Simon. Fraser University. (2020). *Guarding Minds at Work*. Available from: https://www.guardingmindsatwork.ca/
23. Brandstätter, V., Job, V. & Schulze, B. (2016). Motivational Incongruence and Wellbeing at the Workplace: Person-Job Fit, Job Burnout, and Physical Symptoms. *Frontiers In Psychology*. Available from: https://www.frontiersin.org/articles/10.3389/fpsyg.2016.01153/full
24. Maslach, C. & Leiter, M.P. (2016). Understanding the burnout experience: recent research and its implications for psychiatry. *World Psychiatry. 15*(2): 103-11.
25. Schwabe, W. (2015). 5 Stages of Burnout. Available from: http://www.vitango-stress.com/burnout-syndrome/5-stages-of-burnout/
26. Brown, L.W., & Quick, J.C. (2013). Environmental Influences on Individual Burnout and a Preventive Approach for Organizations. *Journal of Applied Biobehavioral Research, 18*(2): 104–121.
27. Lipton, B.H. (2015). *The Biology of Belief*. Carlsbad, California: Hay House.
28. Sia, P.D. & Licata, I. (2016). Nano-Modelling and Computation in Bio and Brain Dynamics. *Bioengineering, 3*(11).
29. Demartini, J.F. (2013). *The Values Factor: The Secret to Creating an Inspired and Fulfilling Life*. New York: Penguin.
30. Holford, P. & Cass, H. (2003). *Natural Highs chill*. London: Judy Piatkus Ltd.
31. Sharon-David, H. & Tenenbaum, G. (2017). The Effectiveness of Exercise Interventions on Coping with Stress: Research Synthesis. *Studies in Sport Humanities, 22* :19-29, DOI: 10.5604/01.3001.0012.6520
32. Weinstein, N., Brown, K.W. & Ryan, R.M. (2009). A multi-method examination of the effects of mindfulness on stress attribution, coping, and emotional wellbeing. *Journal of Research in Personality, 43*(3) 374-385, https://doi.org/10.1016/j.jrp.2008.12.008.

Chapter 8

1. Harnois, G. & Gabriel, P. (2000). *International Labour Organisation, Mental health and work: Impact issues and good practices*. Available from: https://www.who.int/mental_health/media/en/712.pdf
2. World Health Organization. (2009a). *Disease and injury regional estimates for 2004*. Geneva, Switzerland: WHO.
3. Chopra, P. (2009). Mental health and the workplace: issues for developing countries. *International Journal of Mental Health Systems, 3*(1): 4. https://doi.org/10.1186/1752-4458-3-4
4. Wang, P.S., Simon, G., & Kessler, R.C. (2003). The economic burden of depression and the cost-effectiveness of treatment. *International Journal of Methods in Psychiatric Research, 12*(1): 22-33.

5.   Murray, C.J.L., & Lopez, A.D. (1996). The global burden of disease: a comprehensive assessment of mortality and disability from disease, injuries, and risk factors in 1990 and projected to 2020. Cambridge: Harvard School of Public Health.

6.   American Psychiatric Association. (2013). *Diagnostic and Statistical Manual of Mental Disorders (DSM-5®), Fifth Edition*. Washington, DC: American Psychiatric Association.

7.   National Institute of Mental Health. (2018). *Anxiety Disorders*. Available from: https://www.nimh.nih.gov/health/topics/anxiety-disorders/index.shtml

8.   Funk, M., Drew, N., & Knapp, M. (2012). Mental health, poverty and development. *Journal of public mental health, 11*(4): 166-185.

9.   Ormel, J., Petukhova, M., Chatterji, S., et al., (2008). Disability and treatment of specific mental and physical disorders across the world. *British Journal of Psychiatry, 192*(5): 368-75.

10.   Chamberlain, C. J. G., Johnson, G., & Theobald, J., (2007). *Homelessness in Melbourne: Confronting the Challenge*. Melbourne: RMIT University Press, Melbourne.

11.   Ssebunnya, J., Kigozi, F., Lund, C., & Kizza, D. (2009). Stakeholder perceptions of mental health stigma and poverty in Uganda. *BMC International Health and Human Rights, 9*(1): 5.

12.   Sanderson K., & Andrews, G. Common mental disorders in the workforce: recent findings from descriptive and social epidemiology. *Canadian Journal of Psychiatry, 51*(2): 63-75.

13.   Munn-Giddings, C., Hart, C., & Ramon, S. (2005). A participatory approach to the promotion of wellbeing in the workplace: Lessons from empirical research. *International Review of Psychiatry, 17*(5): 409-417.

14.   Chopra, P. (2009). Mental health and the workplace: issues for developing countries. *International Journal of Mental Health Systems, 3*(1): 4. https://doi.org/10.1186/1752-4458-3-4.

15.   World Economic Forum. (2020). *5 things we learned about mental health in the workplace in 2020*. Retrieved from: https://www.weforum.org/agenda/2020/12/5-things-we-learned-about-mental-health-in-the-workplace-in-2020/

16.   Konco, T. (2021). SADAG predicts increase in suicides for South African youth. Available from: https://www.iol.co.za/weekend-argus/news/sadag-predicts-increase-in-suicides-for-south-african-youth-15398e10-5ce7-4dfe-8a63-e36288747096

17.   World Health Organization. (2021). Suicide. Available from: https://www.who.int/news-room/fact-sheets/detail/suicide

18.   U.S. Department of Health & Human Services (HHS). (n.d.). Does depression increase the risk for suicide? Available from: https://www.hhs.gov/answers/mental-health-and-substance-abuse/does-depression-increase-risk-of-suicide/index.html

19.   Schermuly, C.C., & Meyer, B. (2009). Good relationships at work: The effects of Leader–Member Exchange and Team–Member Exchange on psychological empowerment, emotional exhaustion, and depression. *Journal of Organisational Behaviour, 37*(5): 673-691.

Chapter 9

1.   Eyal, N., & Hoover, R. (2014). *Hooked: how to build habit-forming products*. London: Penguin Books.

2.   Tankovska, H. (2021). *Number-of-worldwide-social-network-users*. Retrieved from: https://www.statista.com/statistics/278414/number-of-worldwide-social-network-users [Accessed 22 February 2021].

3. Mackay, J. (2019). *Screen time stats 2019: Here's how much you use your phone during the workday*. Retrieved from: https://blog.rescuetime.com/screen-time-stats-2018/ [Accessed 22 February 2021].

4. Killingsworth, M.A. & Gilbert. D.T. (2010). A wandering mind is an unhappy mind. *Science, 330*(6006): 932.

5. Snibbe, K. (2010). *Wandering mind not a happy mind*. Retrieved from: .https://news. harvard.edu/gazette/story/2010/11/wandering-mind-not-a-happy-mind/ [Accessed 16 February 2021].

6. Griffey, H. (2018). *The lost art of concentration: being distracted in a digital world*. Retrieved from: https://www.theguardian.com/lifeandstyle/2018/oct/14/the-lost-art-of-concentration-being-distracted-in-a-digital-world [Accessed 22 February 2021].

7. Goleman, D. (2013). *Focus: the hidden driver of excellence. 1st edition*. New York: Harper.

8. Simon, E.B. & Walker, M.P. (2018). Under slept and overanxious: the neural correlates of sleep-loss induced anxiety in the human brain. Lecture presented at: Neuroscience 2018; November 4, 2018; Berkeley, CA.

9. Walker, M. (2018). *Why We Sleep: Unlocking the Power of Sleep and Dreams*. London: Penguin Books.

10. Gazzaley, A. & Rosen, L. D. (2016). *The distracted mind: ancient brains in a high-tech world*. Cambridge, MA: MIT Press.

11. Healthista Expert. (2018). *6 reasons social media is making you unhappy (and what to do instead)*. Retrieved from: https://www.healthista.com/reasons-social-media-making-you-unhappy/ [Accessed 11 February 2021].

12. Harvard Health Letter. (2017). *Can relationships boost longevity and wellbeing?* Retrieved from: https://www.health.harvard.edu/mental-health/can-relationships-boost-longevity-and-wellbeing [Accessed 10 February 2021].

13. Weinschenk, S. (2012). *The true cost of multitasking*. https://www.psychologytoday. com/us/blog/brain-wise/201209/the-true-cost-multi-tasking [Accessed 9 February 2021].

14. Brewer, J., & Kabat-Zinn, J. (2017). *The craving mind: from cigarettes to smartphones to love – why we get hooked and how we can break bad habits*. Ashland: Blackstone Audio.

15. Csikszentmihalyi, M. (1990). *Flow: the psychology of optimal experience*. New York: Harper & Row.

16. Eyal, N, (2019). *Indistractable, how to control your attention and choose your life*. Dallas, TX: BenBella Books.

17. DeMartini, J. (2021). *Focus on Your High Priority Actions: It's Your Life!* Retrieved from: https://drdemartini.com/high-priority-actions-life/ [Accessed 15 February 2021].

18. Harris, R. (2008). *The Happiness Trap how to stop struggling and start living*. Boulder: Trumpeter.

19. Maté, G. (2008). *In the realm of hungry ghosts: close encounters with addiction*. Toronto: Knopf Canada.

20. DeNoon, D.J. (2009). *7 Rules for Eating*. Retrieved from: https://www.webmd.com/food-recipes/news/20090323/7-rules-for-eating [Accessed 16 February 2021].

21. Ratey, J.J., & Hagerman, E. (2008). *Spark: the revolutionary new science of exercise and the brain*. New York: Little, Brown.

22. American Heart Association. (2018). *American Heart Association Recommendations for Physical Activity in Adults and Kids*. Retrieved from: https://www.heart.org/en/healthy-living/fitness/fitness-basics/aha-recs-for-physical-activity-in-adults [Accessed 18 February 2021].

23. Hickey, G. (2021). *The Effects of Exercise on the Brain with Dr John Ratey*. Retrieved from: https://www.kinesophy.com/the-effects-of-exercise-on-the-brain-with-dr-john-ratey/ [Accessed 20 February 2021].

24. Mintzer, A. (2020). *Paying Attention: The Attention Economy*. Retrieved from: https://econreview.berkeley.edu/paying-attention-the-attention-economy/ [Accessed 20 February 2021].

25. Bono, T. (2018). When Likes Aren't Enough: Using the Science of Happiness to Find Meaning and Connection in a Modern World. London: Orion Publishing Co.

Chapter 10

1. GBD 2017 Collaborators. (2019). Health effects of dietary risks in 195 countries, 1990–2017: a systematic analysis for the Global Burden of Disease Study 2017. *The Lancet, 393*(10184), pp. 1958-1972.

2. Firth, J., Marx, W., Dash, S., Carney, R., Teasdale, S.B., Solmi, M., Stubbs, B., Schuch, F.B., Carvalho, A.F., Jacka, F., & Sarris, J. (2019). The Effects of Dietary Improvement on Symptoms of Depression and Anxiety: A Meta-Analysis of Randomized Controlled Trials. *Psychosomatic Medicine, 81*(3), pp. 265-280.

3. Lopresti, A.L., Hood, S.D. & Drummond, P.D. (2013). A review of lifestyle factors that contribute to important pathways associated with major depression: Diet, sleep and exercise. *Journal of Affective Disorders, 148*(1), pp. 12-27.

4. Escott-Stump, S. (2012). *Nutrition and Diagnosis-Related Care,* Baltimore: Lippincott Williams & Wilkins, a Wolters Kluwer Business.

5. Alenko, A., Markos, Y., Fikru, C., Tadesse, E., & Gedefaw, L. (2020). Association of serum cortisol level with severity of depression and improvement in newly diagnosed patients with major depressive disorder in Jimma medical center, Southwest Ethiopia. *PLoS ONE, 15*(10): e0240668.

6. Mahan, K.L., Escott-Stump, S. & Raymond, J.L. (2012). *Krause's Food & the Nutrition Care Process.* 13th ed. Missouri: Elsevier Saunders.

7. Jacka, F. (2019). *Brain Changer.* London: Yellow Kite.

8. Ventriglio, A., Sancassiani, F., Contu, M.P., Latorre, M., Di Slavatore, M., Fornaro, M. & Bhugra, D. (2020). Mediterranean Diet and its Benefits on Health and Mental Health: A Literature Review. *Clinical Practice & Epidemiology in Mental Health, 16*(Supplement-1), pp. 156-164.

9. Ministry of Health and Wellfare, S.S.H.C. (1999). Dietary Guidelines for Adults in Greece. *Archives of Hellenic Medicine, 16*(5), pp. 516-524.

10. Bach-Faig, A., Berry, E.M., Lairon, D., Reguant, J., Trichopoulou, A., Dernini, S., Medina, F.X., Battino, M., Belahsen, R., Miranda, G., Serra-Majem, L. & Mediterranean Diet Foundation Expert Group. (2011). Mediterranean diet pyramid today.. *Public Health and Nutrition, 14*(12A), pp. 2274-2284.

11. Oldways. (n.d.). *Mediterranean Diet Pyramid.* Retrieved from: http://oldwayspt.org/resources/heritage-pyramids/mediterranean-pyramid/overview [Accessed February 2020].

12. Steyn, N.P., Parker, W, Lambert E.V., Mchiza, Z. (2009). Nutrition interventions in the workplace: Evidence of best practice. *South African Journal of Clinical Nutrition, 22*(3), pp. 111-117.

13. Woolf, S.H., Purnell, J.Q. (2016). The good life: working together to promote opportunity and improve population health and wellbeing. *Journal of the American Medical Association, 315*(16), pp. 1706-1708.

14. Medibank Private. (2005). *The Health of Australia's Workforce*. Retrieved from: http://www.trenchhealth.com.au/articles/MEDI_Workplace_Web_Sp.pdf [Accessed February 2020].

15. Oakman, J., Kinsman, N., Stuckey, R., Graham, M., & Weale, V. (2020). A rapid review of mental and physical health effects of working at home: how do we optimise health?. *BioMed Central Public Health*, *20*(1), pp. 1825.

16. Restrepo, B.J., & Zeballos, E. (2020). The effect of working from home on major time allocations with a focus on food-related activities. *Review of Economics of the Household*, *18*(4), pp. 1165-1187.

17. Monsivais, P., Aggarwal, A., & Drewnowski, A. (2014). Time Spent on Home Food Preparation and Indicators of Healthy Eating. *American Journal of Preventive Medicine*, *47*(6), pp. 796–802.

18. Wolfson, J.A., & Bleich, S.N. (2015). Is cooking at home associated with better diet quality or weight- loss intention? *Public Health Nutrition*, *18*(8), 1397–1406.

19. Ng, Q.X., Koh, S.S.H., Chan, H.W., & Ho, C.Y.X. (2017). Clinical Use of Curcumin in Depression: A Meta-Analysis. *Journal of the American Medical Directors Association*, *18*(6), pp. 503-508.

20. Capuco, A., Urits, I., Hasoon, J., Chun, R., Gerald, B., Wang, J.K., Kassem, H., Ngo, A.L., Abd-Elsayed, A., Simopolous, T., Kaye, A.D., & Viswanath, O. (2020). Current perspectives on gut microbiome and depression. *Advanced Therapeutics*, *37*(4), pp. 1328-1346.

Chapter 11

1   World Health Organization. (2004). *Promoting Mental Health: Concepts, Emerging Evidence, Practice*. Retrieved from: https://www.who.int/mental_health/evidence/en/promoting_mhh.pdf

2   Mental Health Foundation. (2021). *Mental and physical health*. Retrieved from: https://www.mentalhealth.org.uk/a-to-z/

3   Salari, N., Hosseinian-Far, A., Jalali, R., Vaisi-Raygani, A., Rasoulpoor, S., Mohammadi, M., Rasoulpoor, S., & Khaledi-Paveh, B. (2020). Prevalence of stress, anxiety, depression among the general population during the COVID-19 pandemic: a systematic review and meta-analysis. *Globalization and Health*, *16*(1): 57. Retrieved from: https://globalizationandhealth.biomedcentral.com/articles/10.1186/s12992-020-00589-w

4   Makhashvili, N., Jana Darejan Javakhishvili, Lela Sturua, Ketevan Pilauri, Daniela C. Fuhr and Bayard Roberts. (2020). The influence of concern about COVID-19 on mental health in the Republic of Georgia: A cross-sectional study. *Globalization and Health*, *16*:(1): 111. Retrieved from: https://globalizationandhealth.biomedcentral.com/articles/10.1186/s12992-020-00641-9

5   Galderisi, S., Heinz, A., Kastrup, M., Beezhold, J., & Sartorius, N. (2015). Toward a new definition of mental health. *World Psychiatry*, *14*(2): 231–233.

6   World Health Organization (WHO). (1986). A Discussion Document on the Concept and Principles of Health Promotion. Health Promotion. *PubMed*, *1*(1):73–78.

7   Ohrnberger, J., Ficherab, E., & Suttona, M. (2017). The relationship between physical and mental health: A mediation analysis. *Social Science & Medicine*, *195*(1): 42-49.

8   Wayne. J., Katon, M.D. (2011). Epidemiology and treatment of depression in patients with chronic medical illness. *Dialogues Clin Neurosci*, *13*(1): 7–23.

9   University of Sydney. (2015). *Keep calm, anger can trigger a heart attack!* Retrieved from: https://www.sciencedaily.com/releases/2015/02/150224083819.htm

10   Batty, G.D., Russ, T.C., MacBeath, M., & Stamatakis, E., & Kivimäk, M. (2017). Psychological distress in relation to site specific cancer mortality: pooling of unpublished data from 16 prospective cohort studies. Retrieved from: https://www.bmj.com/content/356/bmj.j108

11   Correll, C.U., Solmi, M., Veronese, N., Bortolato, B., et al. (2017). Prevalence, incidence and mortality from cardiovascular disease in patients with pooled and specific severe mental illness: a large-scale meta-analysis of 3,211,768 patients and 113,383,368 controls. *World Psychiatry, 16*(2): 163-180.

12   Harvard T.H. Chan School of Public Health. (2012). *Positive feelings may help protect cardiovascular health.* Retrieved from: https://www.hsph.harvard.edu/news/press-releases/positive-emotions-cardiovascular-health/

13   Economic and Social Research Council (ESRC). (2012). *A healthy teenager is a happy teenager.* ScienceDaily. Retrieved from: https://www.sciencedaily.com/releases/2012/03/120302082911.htm

14   Rosiek, A., Frąckowiak Maciejewska, N., Leksowski, K., Rosiek-Kryszewska, A., & Leksowski, T. (2015). Effect of Television on Obesity and Excess of Weight and Consequences of Health. *Int J Environ Res Public Health, 12*(8): 9408–9426.

14   Rosado, J.I. (n.d.). *The relationship between mental health & physical health.* Retrieved from: https://www.migrantclinician.org/files/staff/MCNFSU%20-%20%20Physical%20and%20Mental%20Health%20%28Converted%20PPT%20Slides%29.pdf

16   Mental Health Foundation. (2016). *Physical health and mental health.* Retrieved from: https://www.mentalhealth.org.uk/a-to-z/p/physical-health-and-mental-health

17   Haupt, A. (2012). *Can Your Mental Health Affect Your Longevity?* Retrieved from: https://health.usnews.com/health-news/articles/2012/04/27/can-your-mental-health-affect-your-longevity

18   Harvard T.H. Chan School of Public Health. (2012). *Positive feelings may help protect cardiovascular health.* Retrieved from: https://www.hsph.harvard.edu/news/press-releases/positive-emotions-cardiovascular-health/

Chapter 12

1.   Interface Employee Financial Solutions. (2021). *Improve Your Employee's Financial Lives.* Retrieved from: https://www.interfaceinc.co.za/

2.   Kagan, J. (2021). *Financial Health.* Retrieved from: https://www.investopedia.com/terms/f/financial-health.asp

3.   CABA.org. (2021). *What is Financial Wellbeing?* Retrieved from: https://www.caba.org.uk/help-and-guides/information/what-financial-wellbeing#:~:text=Share,allow%20you%20to%20enjoy%20life

4.   Nanziri, L.E., & Olckers, M. (2019). *Financial literacy in South Africa.* Retrieved from: http://www.nids.uct.ac.za/images/papers/2019_09_NIDSW5.pdf

5.   Cruze R. (2021). *How to Deal with Financial Stress.* Retrieved from: https://www.ramseysolutions.com/budgeting/how-to-deal-with-financial-stress#:~:text=What%20Is%20Financial%20Stress%3F,exactly%20what%20that%20feels%20like

6.   Interface Employee Financial Solutions. (2021). *Financial Wellness Programs.* Retrieved from: https://www.interfaceinc.co.za/financial-wellness-programs/

7.   Better Health Channel. (2014). *Self esteem.* Retrieved from: https://www.betterhealth.vic.gov.au/health/healthyliving/self-esteem

8. The South African Depression & Anxiety Group. (2021). *There is hope.* Retrieved from: https://www.sadag.org/index.php?option=com_content&view=article&id=314:the-high-emotional-cost-of-south-africa-s-financial-crisis&catid=64&Itemid=132
9. Ibid.
10. Human Science Research Council (HSRC). (2020). *Living through global trauma: Mental-health implications of COVID-19 from a developing country perspective.* Retrieved from: http://www.hsrc.ac.za/en/news/general/mental-health-covid-19
11. Preller, B. (2012). *The Top 10 Reasons for Divorce in South Africa.* Retrieved from: https://www.news24.com/news24/xArchive/Voices/the-top-10-reasons-for-divorce-in-south-africa-20180719
12. Interface Employee Financial Solutions. (2021). *Improve Your Employees' Financial Lives.* Retrieved from: https://www.interfaceinc.co.za/
13. Help Guide. (2021). *Coping with Financial Stress.* Retrieved from: https://www.helpguide.org/articles/stress/coping-with-financial-stress.htm
14. Old Mutual. (2020). *The History of the Old Mutual Savings & Investment Monitor (OMSIM).* Retrieved from: https://www.oldmutual.co.za/savingsmonitor
15. Dlamini, S. (2020). *85% of South Africans in need of financial help, 55% has no access to credit.* Retrieved from: https://www.iol.co.za/business-report/economy/85-of-south-africans-in-need-of-financial-help-55-has-no-access-to-credit-ed0a6314-7f4e-4fd0-86de-7f50f8e4b42c
16. Old Mutual. (2020). *The History of the Old Mutual Savings & Investment Monitor (OMSIM).* Retrieved from: https://www.oldmutual.co.za/savingsmonitor
17. Interface Employee Financial Solutions. (2021). Financial Wellness Programs. Retrieved from: https://www.interfaceinc.co.za/financial-wellness-programs/
18. Old Mutual. (2020). *The History of the Old Mutual Savings & Investment Monitor (OMSIM).* Retrieved from: https://www.oldmutual.co.za/savingsmonitor
19. Mathe, T. (2020). *SA has a retirement savings crisis.* Retrieved from: https://mg.co.za/business/2020-11-01-sa-has-a-retirement-savings-crisis/
20. Le Roux, K. (2019). *Young(ish) South Africans tell stories of the mixed emotions they feel when supporting family members, and tips from an advisor.* Retrieved from: http://www.702.co.za/articles/307442/black-tax-working-hard-earning-well-but-struggling-financially
21. Interface Employee Financial Solutions. (2021). *Improve your Employees' Financial Lives.* Retrieved from: https://www.interfaceinc.co.za/
22. Stats SA. (2021). *More people participate in the South African labour market in the 4th quarter of 2020.* Retrieved from: http://www.statssa.gov.za/?p=14031
23. Klontz, B. (2021). Dr Brad Klontz: Leading expert in financial psychology. Retrieved from: https://www.bradklontz.com/
24. Mehta, R. (2019). *Do you have the symptoms of these money disorders?* Retrieved from: https://economictimes.indiatimes.com/wealth/plan/do-you-have-the-symptoms-of-these-money-disorders/articleshow/69383969.cms?utm_source=contentofinterest&utm_medium=text&utm_campaign=cppst
25. Holkar, M. (n.d.). Seeing through the fog. Retrieved from: https://www.moneyandmentalhealth.org/seeing-through-the-fog-blog/
26. Money and Mental Health Policy Institute. (2021). *The Facts: What you need to know.* Retrieved from: https://www.moneyandmentalhealth.org/money-and-mental-health-facts/#:~:text=Half%20(46%25)%20of%20people,their%20mental%20health%20problems%20worse

27. American Psychological Association. (2015). *American Psychological Association Survey Shows Money Stress Weighing on Americans' Health Nationwide*. Retrieved from: https://www.apa.org/news/press/releases/2015/02/money-stress?utm_content=buffer187d9&utm_medium=social&utm_source=facebook.com&utm_campaign=buffer

28. South African Government News Agency. (2020). *Regulator releases credit extension report*. Retrieved from: https://www.sanews.gov.za/south-africa/regulator-releases-credit-extension-reports

29. Insurance (2017). *Sanlam benchmark survey finds that financial stress is pervasive amongst South Africa's middle class*. Retrieved from: https://www.sanlam.co.za/corporate/retirement/benchmarksurvey/mediacentre/Documents/00123_BM%20survey%20finds%20financial%20stress%20pervasive%20amongst%20SA%20middle%20class.pdf

30. Interface Employee Financial Solutions. (2021). *Financial Wellness Programs*. Retrieved from: https://www.interfaceinc.co.za/financial-wellness-programs/

31. The South African Depression & Anxiety Group. (2021). *There is hope*. Retrieved from: https://www.sadag.org/index.php?option=com_content&view=article&id=314:the-high-emotional-cost-of-south-africa-s-financial-crisis&catid=64&Itemid=132

32. Ibid.

33. Kahla, C. (2019). *Young professionals in South Africa are experiencing increased financial stress, new study shows*. Retrieved from: https://www.thesouthafrican.com/news/young-professionals-increased-financial-stress-south-africa/

34. Pierce, K. (2009). *The Impact of Absenteeism in the Public Service in the Context of GEMS*. Retrieved from: https://www.pggmeds.co.za/Files/(1152009105647%20AM)%20Symposium%20-%20Absenteeism%2026%20October%202009.pdf

Additional Reading (Chapter 12)

American Psychological Association. (2014). *Stress in America: Paying with our health*. Retrieved from: https://www.apa.org/news/press/releases/stress/2014/stress-report.pdf

Kraft, A.D., Quimbo, S.A., Solon, O., Shimkhada, R., Florentino, J., & Peabody, J.W. (2009). The health and cost impact of care delay and the experimental impact of insurance on reducing delays. *J Pediatr, 155*(2):281-285. doi:10.1016/j.jpeds.2009.02.035

Richardson, T., Elliott, P., & Roberts, R. (2013). The relationship between personal unsecured debt and mental and physical health: a systematic review and meta-analysis. *Clin Psychol Rev, 33*(8): 1148-1162. doi:10.1016/j.cpr.2013.08.009

Saad, L. (2018). *Delaying care a healthcare strategy for three in 10 Americans*. Retrieved from: https://news.gallup.com/poll/245486/delaying-care-healthcare-strategy-three-americans.aspx

Tran A.G.T.T., Mintert .JS., Llamas J.D., & Lam C.K. (2018). At what costs? Student loan debt, debt stress, and racially/ethnically diverse college students' perceived health. *Culture Divers Ethnic Minor Psychol, 24*(4):459-469. doi:10.1037/cdp0000207

Warth, J., Puth, M-T., Tillmann, J., et al. (2019). Over-indebtedness and its association with sleep and sleep medication use. *BMC Public Health, 19*(1): 957. doi:10.1186/s12889-019-7231-1

Chapter 13

1. World Health Organization (WHO). (2021). *Mental Health.* Retrieved from: https://www. who.int/health-topics/mental-health (Accessed 4 February 2021).
2. Matthews, C. (2020). *Putting a number on mental health costs.* Retrieved from: https:// www.wits.ac.za/news/latest-news/research-news/2020/2020-09/putting-a-number-on-mental-health-costs.html (Accessed 6 February 2021).
3. Chartered Institute of Personnel and Development (CIPD). (2020). *Health and Wellbeing at Work Survey Report.* Retrieved from: https://www.cipd.co.uk/Images/health-and-wellbeing-2020-report_tcm18-73967.pdf.
4. Harvard Health Publishing. (2021). *The gut-brain connection.* Retrieved from: https:// www.health.harvard.edu/diseases-and-conditions/the-gut-brain-connection (Accessed 8 February 2021).
5. Northouse, P.G. (2016). *Leadership Theory and Practice*, 7th edition. Thousand Oaks: Sage Publication, pp. 173-176.

Chapter 14

1. World Health Organization (WHO). (2013). *Investing in Mental Health: Evidence for Action.* Geneva: Switzerland. Retrieved from: https://apps.who.int/iris/bitstream/ handle/10665/87232/9789241564618_eng.pdf?sequence=1
2. Adolphs, R. (2009). The Social Brain: Neural Basis of Social Knowledge. *Annual Review of Psychology, 60*(1): 693–716. https://doi.org/10.1146/annurev.psych.60.110707.163514.
3. Barrett, L. F., Adolphs, R., Marsella, S., Martinez, A. M., & Pollak, S. D. (2019). Emotional expressions reconsidered: challenges to inferring emotion from human facial movements. *Psychological Science in the Public Interest, 20*(1), 1–68.
4. Fiske, S.T., & Taylor, S.E. (2013). *Social cognition: From brains to culture.* London: Sage.
5. Garland, E.L., Farb, N.A., Goldin, P.R., & Fredrickson, B.L. (2015). The Mindfulness-to-Meaning Theory: Extensions, Applications, and Challenges at the Attention–Appraisal–Emotion Interface. *Psychological Inquiry, 26*(4), 377–387. https://doi.org/10.1080/1047840X.2015.1092493
6. Gross, J.J. (2007). *Handbook of emotion regulation.* (J. J. Gross, Ed.). New York: Guilford publications.
7. Lieberman, M. D. (2007). Social Cognitive Neuroscience: A Review of Core Processes. *Annual Review of Psychology, 58*(1), 259–289. https://doi.org/10.1146/annurev. psych.58.110405.085654
8. Louw, A., Zimney, K., Puentedura, E.J., & Diener, I. (2016). The efficacy of pain neuroscience education on musculoskeletal pain: a systematic review of the literature. *Physiotherapy Theory and Practice, 32*(5), 332–355.
9. Tabibnia, G., & Radecki, D. (2018). Resilience training that can change the brain. *Consulting Psychology Journal: Practice and Research, 70*(1), 59.
10. Osório, C., Probert, T., Jones, E., Young, A.H., & Robbins, I. (2017). Adapting to stress: understanding the neurobiology of resilience. *Behavioral Medicine, 43*(4), 307–322.
11. Ibid.
12. American Psychological Association. (2020). *APA Dictionary of Psychology.* Retrieved from: https://dictionary.apa.org/pdf
13. Seligman, M.E.P. (2012). *Flourish: A visionary new understanding of happiness and wellbeing.* New York, NY: Simon and Schuster.

14. Rautenbach, C., & Rothmann, S. (2017). Psychometric validation of the Flourishing-at-Work Scale–Short Form (FWS-SF): Results and implications of a South African study. *Journal of Psychology in Africa, 27*(4), 303–309.

15. Keyes, C.L.M. (2013). Promoting and protecting positive mental health: Early and often throughout the lifespan. In C.L.M. Keyes (Ed.), Mental wellbeing: International contributions to the study of positive mental health (p. 3–28). Springer Science + Business Media.

16. Keyes, C.L.M., & Annas, J. (2009). Feeling good and functioning well: Distinctive concepts in ancient philosophy and contemporary science. *The Journal of Positive Psychology, 4*(3), 197–201.

17. Robertson, I. T., Cooper, C. L., Sarkar, M., & Curran, T. (2015). Resilience training in the workplace from 2003 to 2014: A systematic review. *Journal of Occupational and Organizational Psychology, 88*(3), 533–562.

18. American Psychological Association. (2020). *Building your resilience*. Retrieved from: https://www.apa.org/topics/resilience

19. Kandel, E.R., Schwartz, J.M., & Jessell, T.M. (2013). *Principles of Neural Science. McGraw-Hill editon* (5th ed.). New York: McGraw-Hill. https://doi.org/10.1036/0838577016

20. Van der Walt, E. (2017). The *Neurozone Model of Brain Performance*. Retrieved from: https://neurozone.com/#our-products.

21. Ward, J. (2016). *The student's guide to social neuroscience*. London: Psychology Press.

22. Cesario, J., Johnson, D.J., & Eisthen, H.L. (2020). Your Brain Is Not an Onion With a Tiny Reptile Inside. *Current Directions in Psychological Science, 29*(3), 255–260. https://doi.org/10.1177/0963721420917687

23. Barrett, L.F., Adolphs, R., Marsella, S., Martinez, A.M., & Pollak, S.D. (2019). Emotional expressions reconsidered: challenges to inferring emotion from human facial movements. *Psychological Science in the Public Interest, 20*(1), 1–68.

24. Russell, J. A., & Barrett, L. F. (1999). Core affect, prototypical emotional episodes, and other things called emotion: dissecting the elephant. *Journal of Personality and Social Psychology, 76*(5), 805.

25. Barrett, L.F., Adolphs, R., Marsella, S., Martinez, A.M., & Pollak, S.D. (2019). Emotional expressions reconsidered: challenges to inferring emotion from human facial movements. *Psychological Science in the Public Interest, 20*(1), 1–68.

26. Diener, E., & Seligman, M.E.P. (2018). Beyond money: Progress on an economy of wellbeing. *Perspectives on Psychological Science, 13*(2), 171–175.

27. Nosakhare, E., & Picard, R. (2020). Toward assessing and recommending combinations of behaviors for improving health and wellbeing. *ACM Transactions on Computing for Healthcare, 1*(1), 1–29.

28. Schwartz, J. M., Stapp, H. P., & Beauregard, M. (2005). Quantum physics in neuroscience and psychology: a neurophysical model of mind-brain interaction. *Philosophical Transactions of the Royal Society B: Biological Sciences, 360*(1458), 1309–1327.

29. McEwen, B.S. (2006). Protective and damaging effects of stress mediators: central role of the brain. *Dialogues in Clinical Neuroscience, 8*(4), 367.

30. De Couck, M., Caers, R., Musch, L., Fliegauf, J., Giangreco, A., & Gidron, Y. (2019). How breathing can help you make better decisions: Two studies on the effects of breathing patterns on heart rate variability and decision-making in business cases. *International Journal of Psychophysiology, 139*(2019): 1-9.

31. Kahneman, D. (2011). Thinking, Fast and Slow. New York, NY: Macmillan.

32. Farb, N.A.S., Segal, Z.V, & Anderson, A.K. (2013). Mindfulness meditation training alters cortical representations of interoceptive attention. *Social Cognitive and Affective Neuroscience, 8*(1), 15–26.

33. Jha, A.P., Morrison, A.B., Parker, S.C., & Stanley, E.A. (2017). Practice is protective: Mindfulness training promotes cognitive resilience in high-stress cohorts. *Mindfulness, 8*(1), 46–58.
34. Farb, N.A.S., Segal, Z.V, Mayberg, H., Bean, J., Mckeon, D., Fatima, Z., & Anderson, A.K. (2007). Attending to the present: Mindfulness meditation reveals distinct neural modes of self-reference. *Social Cognitive and Affective Neuroscience, 2*(4), 313–322. https://doi.org/10.1093/scan/nsm030
35. Ibid.
36. Barrett, L.F., Gross, J., Christensen, T.C., & Benvenuto, M. (2001). Knowing what you're feeling and knowing what to do about it: Mapping the relation between emotion differentiation and emotion regulation. *Cognition & Emotion, 15*(6), 713–724.
37. Barrett, L.F. (2006). Solving the emotion paradox: Categorization and the experience of emotion. *Personality and Social Psychology Review, 10*(1), 20–46.
38. Lane, R.D., & Garfield, D.A.S. (2005). Becoming aware of feelings: Integration of cognitive-developmental, neuroscientific, and psychoanalytic perspectives. *Neuropsychoanalysis, 7*(1), 5–30.
39. Lindquist, K. A., & Barrett, L. F. (2008). Constructing emotion: The experience of fear as a conceptual act. *Psychological Science, 19*(9), 898–903.
40. Barrett, L.F., Gross, J., Christensen, T.C., & Benvenuto, M. (2001). Knowing what you're feeling and knowing what to do about it: Mapping the relation between emotion differentiation and emotion regulation. *Cognition & Emotion, 15*(6), 713–724.
41. Demiralp, E., Thompson, R.J., Mata, J., Jaeggi, S.M., Buschkuehl, M., Barrett, L.F., & Deldin, P.J. (2012). Feeling blue or turquoise? Emotional differentiation in major depressive disorder. *Psychological Science, 23*(11), 1410–1416.
42. Boden, M.T., Thompson, R.J., Dizén, M., Berenbaum, H., & Baker, J.P. (2013). Are emotional clarity and emotion differentiation related? *Cognition & Emotion, 27*(6), 961–978.
43. Kashdan, T.B., Barrett, L.F., & McKnight, P.E. (2015). Unpacking emotion differentiation: Transforming unpleasant experience by perceiving distinctions in negativity. *Current Directions in Psychological Science, 24*(1), 10–16.
44. Ibid.
45. O'Toole, M.S., Jensen, M.B., Fentz, H.N., Zachariae, R., & Hougaard, E. (2014). Emotion differentiation and emotion regulation in high and low socially anxious individuals: An experience-sampling study. *Cognitive Therapy and Research, 38*(4), 428–438.
46. Garber, J., Frankel, S.A., & Herrington, C.G. (2016). Developmental demands of cognitive behavioral therapy for depression in children and adolescents: Cognitive, social, and emotional processes. *Annual Review of Clinical Psychology, 12*, 181–216.
47. Barrett, L.F. (2018). *Try these two smart techniques to help you master your emotions.* Retrieved from: https://ideas.ted.com/try-these-two-smart-techniques-to-help-you-master-your-emotions/
48. Barrett, L. F., Wilson-Mendenhall, C. D., & Barsalou, L. W. (2014). *A psychological construction account of emotion regulation and dysregulation: The role of situated conceptualizations.* In J.J. Gross (Ed.), *Handbook of emotion regulation* (pp. 447–465). New York, NY: The Guilford Press.
49. Barrett, L. F., Tugade, M. M., & Engle, R. W. (2004). Individual differences in working memory capacity and dual-process theories of the mind. *Psychological Bulletin, 130*(4), 553.
50. Hayes, S. (1999). Wilson. *Acceptance and Commitment Therapy: An Experimental Approach to Behaviour of Change.* New York: Guilford Press.
51. Kross, E., & Ayduk, O. (2011). Making meaning out of negative experiences by self-distancing. *Current Directions in Psychological Science, 20*(3), 187–191.

52. Gross, J.J., & Feldman Barrett, L. (2011). Emotion generation and emotion regulation: One or two depends on your point of view. *Emotion Review, 3*(1), 8–16.

53. Garnefski, N., & Kraaij, V. (2006). Cognitive emotion regulation questionnaire – development of a short 18-item version (CERQ-short). *Personality and Individual Differences, 41*(6), 1045–1053.

54. Stockdale, Laura A, Robert G Morrison, and Rebecca L Silton. 2020. The Influence of Stimulus Valence on Perceptual Processing of Facial Expressions and Subsequent Response Inhibition. *Psychophysiology 57*(2): e13467.

55. Fredrickson, Barbara L. (1998). What Good Are Positive Emotions? *Review of general psychology 2*(3): 300–319.

56. Lieberman, M.D., & Eisenberger, N.I. (2008). The pains and pleasures of social life: A social cognitive neuroscience approach. *IN PRESS, Neuroleadership*, 1–38.

57. Ibid.

58. McKnight, P.E., & Kashdan, T.B. (2009). Purpose in life as a system that creates and sustains health and wellbeing: An integrative, testable theory. *Review of General Psychology, 13*(3), 242–251.

59. Ryan, R.M., & Deci, E.L. (2000). Intrinsic and extrinsic motivations: Classic definitions and new directions. *Contemporary Educational Psychology, 25*(1), 54–67.

60. Peters, J., & Büchel, C. (2010). Episodic future thinking reduces reward delay discounting through an enhancement of prefrontal-mediotemporal interactions. *Neuron, 66*(1), 138–148.

61. Schacter, D.L., Benoit, R.G., & Szpunar, K.K. (2017). Episodic future thinking: Mechanisms and functions. *Current Opinion in Behavioral Sciences, 17*, 41–50.

62. Vainio, M.M., & Daukantaitė, D. (2016). Grit and different aspects of wellbeing: Direct and indirect relationships via sense of coherence and authenticity. *Journal of Happiness Studies, 17*(5), 2119–2147.

63. Duckworth, A.L., Peterson, C., Matthews, M.D., & Kelly, D.R. (2007). Grit: perseverance and passion for long-term goals. *Journal of Personality and Social Psychology, 92*(6), 1087.

64. Brockington, Guilherme et al. 2021. "Storytelling Increases Oxytocin and Positive Emotions and Decreases Cortisol and Pain in Hospitalized Children." *Proceedings of the National Academy of Sciences 118*(22).

65. Holt-Lunstad, J., Smith, T.B., Baker, M., Harris, T., & Stephenson, D. (2015). Loneliness and social isolation as risk factors for mortality: a meta-analytic review. *Perspectives on Psychological Science, 10*(2), 227–237.

66. Shield, B.C.B. (2018). *Major depression: The impact on overall health*. Retrieved from: https://www. bcbs. com/the-health-of-america/reports

67. Xu, G., Strathearn, L., Liu, B., Yang, B., & Bao, W. (2018). Twenty-year trends in diagnosed attention-deficit/hyperactivity disorder among US children and adolescents, 1997-2016. *JAMA Network Open, 1*(4), e181471–e181471.

68. American Psychological Association. (2012). *APA Dictionary of Psychology*. Retrieved from: https://dictionary.apa.org/

Chapter 15

1. Patel, V., & Goodman, A. (2007). Researching protective and promotive factors in mental health. *International Journal of Epidemiology, 36*(4), 703-707.

2. Rossi, A. (1962). Some pre-World War II antecedents of community mental health theory and practice. *Mental Hygiene, 46*(1), 78–98.

3. Hoopes, L. (2017). *Prosilience. Building your resilience for a turbulent world.* Atlanta: Dara Press.
4. Baum, F., Narayan, R., Sanders, D., Patel, V., Quizhpe, A. (2009). Social vaccines to resist and change unhealthy social and economic structures: a useful metaphor for health promotion. Health Promotion International, 24(4): 428-433, https://doi.org/10.1093/heapro/dap026
5. Ibid.
6. John, T.J., & Tharyan, P. (2020*). A shot of hope with a game changing vaccine.* Retrieved from: https://www.thehindu.com/opinion/lead/a-shot-of-hope-with-a-game-changing-vaccine/article31383184.ece
7. American Psychological Association (2012). *Building your resilience.* Retrieved from: https://www.apa.org/topics/resilience
8. Newman, K. (2016). *Five Science-Backed Strategies to Build Resilience. When the road gets rocky, what do you do?* Retrieved from: https://greatergood.berkeley.edu/article/item/five_science_backed_strategies_to_build_resilience
9. Ferris, K. (2020). *Resilience – Psychological Safety.* Retrieved from: https://www.thedigitaltransformationpeople.com/channels/people-and-change/resilience-psychological-safety/
10. Levy, J. (2021). *They're the Resilient Generation, Not the COVID Generation.* Retrieved from: https://www.the74million.org/article/resilience-amid-pandemic-sel-panel/
11. Yancey-Bragg, N. (2020). *Coronavirus will define the next generation: What experts are predicting about 'Generation C'.* Retrieved from: https://www.usatoday.com/story/news/nation/2020/05/01/gen-c-coronavirus-covid-19-may-define-next-generation/3046809001/
12. Solis, B. (2018). *Defying demogaphics: Generation-C, Today's hyperconnected consumer 'generation'.* Retrieved form: https://www.briansolis.com/2018/01/defying-demographics-generation-c-todays-hyperconnected-consumer-generation/
13. Infomentum. (2014). *Generating success with Generation C.* Retrieved from: https://cdn2.hubspot.net/hubfs/2612720/Gen%20C/Infomentum%20Generating%20Success%20with%20Generation%20C%20Report.pdf?__hstc=192468469.bddea28c-681c0b92d36d3f0f04f1d46c.1622913707797.1622913707797.1622913707797.1&__hssc=192468469.1.1622913707798&__hsfp=503706157&hsCtaTracking=cb59533b-f6a2-40d9-8a43-f976cb1f0769%7C90172407-4370-4541-ac9d-ceb88e7d9982
14. Grossman, R. (2021). *How to create psychological safety and resilience in the workplace.* Retrieved from: https://www.blackdiamondleadership.com/psychological-safety-and-resilience/
15. Edmondson, A. (1999). Psychological safety and learning behaviour in work teams. *Administrative Science Quarterly 44(2):* 350-383.
16. Grossman, R. (2021). *How to create psychological safety and resilience in the workplace.* Retrieved from: https://www.blackdiamondleadership.com/psychological-safety-and-resilience/
17. Makarius, E.E., Larson, B.Z., & Vroman, S.R. (2021). What Is Your Organization's Long-Term Remote Work Strategy? *Harvard Business Review.* Retrieved from: https://hbr.org/2021/03/what-is-your-organizations-long-term-remote-work-strategy?utm_medium=email&utm_source=newsletter_daily&utm_campaign=mtod_notactsubs
18. Grossman, R. (2021). *How to create psychological safety and resilience in the workplace.* Retrieved from: https://www.blackdiamondleadership.com/psychological-safety-and-resilience/

19. Ferris, K. (2020). *Resilience – Psychological Safety*. Retrieved from: https://www.thedigitaltransformationpeople.com/channels/people-and-change/resilience-psychological-safety/

20. Fahrbach, C., Weidling, A., & Behrens, D. (2020). *Performance Through Care – Why Psychological Safety and Resilience Are Key to Navigating the Crisis*. Retrieved from: https://www.egonzehnder.com/what-we-do/leadership-solutions/insights/performance-through-care-why-psychological-safety-and-resilience-are-key-to-navigating-the-crisis

21. Makarius, E.E., Larson, B.Z., & Vroman, S.R. (2021). What Is Your Organization's Long-Term Remote Work Strategy? *Harvard Business Review*. Retrieved from: https://hbr.org/2021/03/what-is-your-organizations-long-term-remote-work-strategy?utm_medium=email&utm_source=newsletter_daily&utm_campaign=mtod_notactsubs

22. Fahrbach, C., Weidling, A., & Behrens, D. (2020). *Performance Through Care – Why Psychological Safety and Resilience Are Key to Navigating the Crisis*. Retrieved from: https://www.egonzehnder.com/what-we-do/leadership-solutions/insights/performance-through-care-why-psychological-safety-and-resilience-are-key-to-navigating-the-crisis

23. Ibid.

24. Ibid.

25. Ibid.

26. Hoopes, L. (2017). *Prosilience. Building your resilience for a turbulent world*. Atlanta: Dara Press.

27. Thagard, P. (2013). *Better Than Resilient – Prosilient*. Retrieved from: https://www.psychologytoday.com/za/blog/hot-thought/201308/better-resilient-prosilient

28. Seery, M.D., Holman, E.A. & Silver, R.C. (2010). Whatever does not kill us: cumulative lifetime adversity, vulnerability, and resilience. *J Pers Soc Psychol*, 99(6): 1025-41.

29. Hoopes, L. (2017). *Prosilience. Building your resilience for a turbulent world*. Atlanta: Dara Press.

30. American Psychological Association. (2012). *APA Dictionary of Psychology*. Retrieved from: https://dictionary.apa.org/

31. Hoopes, L. (2017). *Prosilience. Building your resilience for a turbulent world*. Atlanta: Dara Press.

Chapter 16

1. Gethin, R. (2011). On some definitions of mindfulness. *Contemporary Buddhism, 12*(1): 263-279.

2. Johnson, K.R., Park, S., & Chaudri, S. (2020). Mindfulness training in the workplace: exploring its scopes and outcomes. *European Journal of Training and Development, 44*(4/5): 341-354.

3. Mahon, M.A., Mee, L., Brett, D. & Bowling, M. (2017). Nurses perceived stress and compassion following a mindfulness meditation and self compassion training. *Journal of Research in Nursing, 22*(8): 572-594.

4. Rupprecht, S. & Walach, H. (2016). *Mindfulness at work: how mindfulness training may change the way we work*. In Wiencke, M., Cacace, M & Fischer, S. (Eds). *Health at Work*. Springer: Cham.

5. Van Gordon, W., Shonin, E., Sumach, A., Sundin E. & Griffiths, M.D. (2013). Meditation awareness training (MAT) for psychological wellbeing in a sub-clinical sample of university students: a controlled pilot study. *Mindfulness, 5*(4): 381-391.

6. Bostock, A., Crosswalk, A.D., Prather, A.A. & Steptoe, A. (2009). Mindfulness on-the-go: effects of a mindfulness meditation app on work stress and wellbeing. *Journal of Occupational Health Psychology, 24*(1): 127-138.
7. Payutto, P.A (2002). *Samadhi in Buddhism.* 2nd ed. Bangkok: Buddha Dhamma Foundation.
8. Petchsawang, P. & McLean, G.N. (2017). Workplace Spirituality, Mindfulness Meditation, and Work Engagement. *Journal of Management, Spirituality & Religion,* 14(3): 216-244.
9. Saks, A.M. (2006). Antecedents and consequences of employee engagement. *Journal of Managerial Psychology,* 21(7): 600-619.
10. Glomb, T.M., Duffy, M.K., Bono, J.E. & Yang, T. (2011). Mindfulness at work. *Research in Personnel and Human Resources Management, 30(1):* 115-157.

Chapter 17

1. Kropp, B. (2021). *9 work trends that hr leaders can't ignore in 2021.* Retrieved from: https://www.gartner.com/smarterwithgartner/9-work-trends-that-hr-leaders-cant-ignore-in-2021/
2. Hayes, S.C., Strosahl, K.D., Bunting, K., Twohig, M., & Wilson, K.G. (2004). What is acceptance and commitment therapy?, in *A practical guide to acceptance and commitment therapy,* edited by SC. Hayes (Ed.). New York, NY: Springer, pp. 31-58.
3. Roberts, B.W. & Robbins, R.W. (2000). Broad dispositions, broad aspirations: the intersection of personality traits and major life goals. *Personality and Social Psychology Bulletin,* 26, pp. 1284-1296. doi: 10.1177/0146167200262009
4. Locke, E.A., & Latham, G.P. (2013). Goal setting theory, 1990, in *New developments in goal setting and task performance,* edited by EA. Locke & GP. Latham, New York, NY: Routledge, pp. 3-15.
5. Stoll, G., Einarsdóttir, S., Song, Q.C., Ondish, P., Sun, J.J., & Rounds, J., (2020). The roles of personality traits and vocational interests in explaining what people want out of life. *Journal of Research in Personality,* 86, pp. 1-19. doi: 10.1016/j.jrp.2020.103939
6. Oettingen, G., Wittchen, M., & Gollwitzer, P.M. (2013). Regulating goal pursuit through mental contrasting with implementation intentions, in *New developments in goal setting and task performance,* edited by EA. Locke & GP. Latham, New York, NY: Routledge, pp. 523-548.
7. Gollwitzer, P.M., & Sheeran, P. (2006). Implementation intentions and goal achievement: A meta-analysis of effects and processes. *Advances in Experimental Social Psychology,* 38(1): pp. 69-119. doi: 10.1016/S0065-2601(06)38002-1
8. Kashdan, T.B., & Rottenberg, J. (2010). Psychological flexibility as a fundamental aspect of health. *Clinical Psychology Review,* 30, pp. 865-878. doi: 10.1016/j.cpr.2010.03.001
9. Hayes, S.C., Strosahl, K.D., & Wilson, K.G. (2012). *Acceptance and commitment therapy: The process and practice of mindful change.* New York, NY: Guilford Press.
10. Van Lill, X., Roodt, G. & De Bruin, G.P. (2020). The relationship between managers' goal-setting styles and subordinates' goal commitment. *South African Journal of Economic and Management Sciences, 23*(1), pp. 1-11. doi: 10.4102/sajems.v23i1.3601
11. Latham, G.P., & Locke, E.A. (2006). Enhancing the benefits and overcoming the pitfalls of goal setting. *Organizational Dynamics,* 35(4), pp. 332-340. doi: 10.1016/j.orgdyn.2006.08.008
12. Pulakos, E.D., Arad, S., Donovan, M.A., & Plamondon, K.E. (2000). Adaptability in the workplace: Development of a taxonomy of adaptive performance. *Journal of Applied Psychology,* 85, pp. 612–624. doi: 10.1037/0021-9010.85.4.612

Chapter 18

1. Kholl A. (2016). *8 Things You Need to Know About Employee Wellness Programs*. Forbes Magazine. Retrieved from: https://www.forbes.com/sites/alankohll/2016/04/21/8-things-you-need-to-know-about-employee-wellness-programs/?sh=6513a9b240a3

2. Healthy Living Consulting (HLC). (2019). Leader in Corporate Wellbeing. Retrieved from: www.hlconsulting.co.za

3. Gilbert, T. (2014). *Gilbert's Behavior Engineering Model (BEM)*. Retrieved from: http://hpt2014.weebly.com/gilberts-bem.html

4. Meyer, P.J. (1960). *The Complete Guide to The Wheel of Life (for Coaches)*. Retrieved from: https://www.thecoachingtoolscompany.com/wheel-of-life-complete-guide-everything-you-need-to-know/

5. Van Tiem, D., Moseley, J.L., & Dessinger, J.C. (2004). Fundamentals of performance technology: A guide to improving people, process, and performance (2nd ed.). Silver Spring, MD: *International Society for Performance Improvement, 44*(1): 41-42.

6. Gilbert T (1996.) *Human Competence: Engineering Human Perrmance*. Pennsylvania: Wiley Publishers.

7. Davies, A. (2006). *EAP business case*. Internal ICAS document.

8. Ronnie, L. (2018). *Tackling mental health in the workplace*. Retrieved from: https://www.news.uct.ac.za/article/-2018-05-17-tackling-mental-health-in-the-workplace

9. Klep, R. (n.d.). *Learning from Practice: How we calculated the added value of an employee wellness intervention.* Retrieved from: https://www.aihr.com/blog/added-value-employee-wellness-intervention/?_ga=2.240431171.1196524938.1623751502-1560622974.1623751502

10. AIHR Digital. (2020). *Absenteeism in the Workplace: A Full Guide*. Retrieved from: https://www.digitalhrtech.com/absenteeism/

11. Rucker, M.R. (2017). Workplace wellness strategies for small businesses. *International Journal of Workplace Health Management, 10*(1): pp. 55-68. https://doi.org/10.1108/IJWHM-07-2016-0054

12. Torre, T. (2017). Healthcare financial management: the missing piece of the employee wellness puzzle. *Strategic HR Review, 16*(1): pp. 13-16. https://doi.org/10.1108/SHR-11-2016-0103

13. Terblanche L.S. (2018). *Creating a legacy in EAP Business: The Southern African Approach towards Employee Assistance*. Pretoria: St Paul and John Publishers.

14. Department of Public Service and Administration (DPSA). (2011). *Policy and Procedure on Occupational Health Safety (Pillar 3 SHERQ)*. Retrieved from: http://policyresearch.limpopo.gov.za/bitstream/handle/123456789/728/Occupational%20Health%20and%20Safety%20Policy.pdf?sequence=1

15. Employee Assistance Professionals Association of South Africa (EAPASA). (2015). *Standards for Employee Assistance Programmes in South Africa*. Retrieved from: https://www.eapasa.co.za/wp-content/uploads/2019/07/EAPA-SA-Standards-4th-edition-2015.pdf

16. Dictionary.com. (n.d.). Standard. Retrieved from: https://www.dictionary.com/browse/standard4

17. Pitje, N. (2020). *Mental Health in the Workplace During Coronavirus: 10 Key Points from the Research on Techno-Therapy. Online Seminar: Workplace Mental Health in the Workplace During COVID-19*. Knowledge Resources, South Africa.

18. Pitje, N. (2020). Mental Health in the Workplace During Coronavirus: 10 Key Points from the Research on Techno-Therapy. Online Seminar: *The Impact of the coronavirus pandemic on employees' mental health and wellbeing: Stats and analysis.* Knowledge Resources, South Africa.

19. Attridge, M. (2020). *Mental Health in the Workplace During Coronavirus: 10 Key Points from the Research on Techno-Therapy. Online Seminar: Workplace Mental Health in the Workplace During COVID-19.* Knowledge Resources, South Africa. Retrieved from: https://archive.hshsl.umaryland.edu/handle/10713/13162

20. Attridge, M. (2003). Internet and Telephonic Delivery of Employee Assistance Services: A Position Paper from the EAPA Professional Practices Committee. EAPA International.

21. ICAS SA. (2021). *COVID 10 Trend and Statistics.* Business Intelligence ICAS. ICAS Database.

22. Healthy Living Consulting (HLC). (2019). *Leader in Corporate Wellbeing.* Retrieved from: www.hlconsulting.co.za.

23. Kholl A. (2016). *8 Things You Need to Know About Employee Wellness Programs.* Forbes Magazine. Retrieved from: https://www.forbes.com/sites/alankohll/2016/04/21/8-things-you-need-to-know-about-employee-wellness-programs/?sh=6513a9b240a3

24. Mayo Clinic. (2020). *Exercise and stress: Get moving to manage stress.* Retrieved from: https://www.mayoclinic.org/healthy-lifestyle/stress-management/in-depth/exercise-and-stress/art-20044469

Chapter 19

1. Schwab, K. (2016). *The Fourth Industrial Revolution.* Geneva: World Economic Forum.

2. Burgess, J. & Connell, J. (2020). New technology and work: Exploring the challenges. *The Economic and Labour Relations Review, 31*(3): pp.310-323.

3. Santana, M. & Cobo, M.J. (2020). What is the future of work? A science mapping analysis. *European Management Journal, 38*(6), pp.846-862.

4. Polanyi, K. (2001). *The Great Transformation: the political and economic origins of our time,* 2nd ed., Boston: Beacon Press.

5. Rodrik, D., 2011, *The globalization paradox: why global markets, states, and democracy can't coexist.* Oxford University Press.

6. PwC. (n. d.). *The essential eight: Your guide to the emerging technologies revolutionising business now.* Retrieved from: https://www.pwc.com/gx/en/issues/technology/essential-eight-technologies.html#cta-1 (Accessed on 29 April 2021).

7. Rolls-Royce. (n. d.). *Powering better performance and customer experience with the Internet of Engines.* Retrieved from: https://www.rolls-royce.com/country-sites/sea/discover/2019/delivering-better-engine-performance-with-iot.aspx (Accessed on 29 April 2021).

8. World Bank. (2018). World development report 2019: The changing nature of work.

9. World Economic Forum (WHO). (2020). The Future of Jobs Report 2020. *World Economic Forum.* Geneva, Switzerland.

10. Costanza, R., Fisher, B., Ali, S., Beer, C., Bond, L., Boumans, R., Danigelis, N.L., Dickinson, J., Elliott, C., Farley, J. & Gayer, D.E. (2007). Quality of life: An approach integrating opportunities, human needs, and subjective wellbeing. *Ecological economics, 61*(2-3), pp. 267-276.

11. National Planning Commission. (2020). *Digital Futures: South Africa's digital readiness for the fourth industrial revolution.* Retrieved from: https://www.nationalplanningcommission.org.za/assets/Documents/DIGITAL%20FUTURES%20-%20SOUTH%20AFRICA'S%20READINESS%20FOR%20THE%20FOURTH%20INDUSTRIAL%20REVOLUTION.pdf (Accessed on 29 April 2021).

12. Presidential Commission on the Fourth Industrial Revolution. (2020). *Report Recommendations and Way Forward*. Retrieved from: https://www.gov.za/sites/default/files/gcis_document/202010/43834gen591.pdf (Accessed on 29 April 2021).

13. Keynes, J. M. (1937). The General Theory of Employment. *Quarterly Journal of Economics, 51*(2): 209–23.

14. Petropoulos, G. (2018). The impact of artificial intelligence on employment. *In Work in a digital age*. Rowman & Littlefield. Retrieved from: https://bruegel.org/2018/07/the-impact-of-artificial-intelligence-on-employment/ (Accessed on 29 April 2021).

15. Trenerry, B., Chng, S., Wang, Y., Suhaila, Z.S., Lim, S.S., Lu, H.Y. & Oh, P.H., (2021). Preparing Workplaces for Digital Transformation: An Integrative Review and Framework of Multi-Level Factors. *Frontiers in Psychology, 12*(620766): p. 1-24.

16. Wiernik, B.M. & Kostal, J.W. (2019). Protean and boundaryless career orientations: A critical review and meta-analysis. *Journal of Counseling Psychology, 66*(3), p.280-307.

17. World Economic Forum. (2020). The Future of Jobs Report 2020. *World Economic Forum*. Geneva, Switzerland.

18. Jones, B., Pilot, A., van Eijl, P. & Lappia, J. (2020). The W-shaped model of professional competencies for the Fourth Industrial Revolution and its relevance to honors programs. *Journal of the European Honors Council, 4*(1), pp.1-16.

19. Inkson, K. & Arthur, M.B. (2001). How to be a successful career capitalist. *Organizational Dynamics, 30*(1): pp. 48–62.

20. Attridge, M. (2020, June). *Mental health in the workplace during Coronavirus: 10 key points from the research on techno-therapy*. Online Seminar: Workplace Mental Health in the Workplace During COVID-19. Knowledge Resources, South Africa. Slides available at EAP Digital Archive: http://hdl.handle.net/10713/13162 Video available at: https://lnkd.in/eMKU2aR

21. Broad, J.D. & Luthans, F. (2020). Positive resources for psychiatry in the fourth industrial revolution: building patient and family focused psychological capital (PsyCap). *International Review of Psychiatry, 32*(7-8): pp. 542-554.

22. Mayer, C.H. (2020). Key concepts for managing organizations and employees turning towards the Fourth Industrial Revolution. *International Review of Psychiatry, 32*(7-8): pp. 673-684.

23. Fouad, N.A. & Bynner, J., 2008. Work transitions. *American Psychologist, 63*(4), pp. 241-251.

24. Lyubomirsky, S. & Layous, K. (2013). How do simple positive activities increase wellbeing? *Current directions in psychological science, 22*(1): pp.57-62.

Index

U

V

W

www.ingramcontent.com/pod-product-compliance
Lightning Source LLC
Chambersburg PA
CBHW080605270326
41928CB00016B/2930